Self and Subjectivity

BLACKWELL READINGS IN CONTINENTAL PHILOSOPHY

Series Editor: Simon Critchley, University of Essex

Each volume in this superb new series provides a detailed introduction to and overview of a central philosophical topic in the Continental tradition. In contrast to the author-based model that has hitherto dominated the reception of the Continental philosophical tradition in the English-speaking world, this series presents the central issues of that tradition, topics that should be of interest to anyone concerned with philosophy. Cutting across the stagnant ideological boundaries that mark the analytic/Continental divide, the series will initiate discussions that reflect the growing dissatisfaction with the organization of the English-speaking philosophical world. Edited by a distinguished international forum of philosophers, each volume provides a critical overview of a distinct topic in Continental philosophy through a mix of both classic and newly commissioned essays from both philosophical traditions.

Self and Subjectivity

Edited with commentary by
Kim Atkins

Blackwell
Publishing

Editorial material and organization © 2005 by Blackwell Publishing Ltd

BLACKWELL PUBLISHING
350 Main Street, Malden, MA 02148-5020, USA
108 Cowley Road, Oxford OX4 1JF, UK
550 Swanston Street, Carlton, Victoria 3053, Australia

First published 2005 by Blackwell Publishing Ltd

Library of Congress Cataloging-in-Publication Data

Self and subjectivity / edited by Kim Atkins.
    p.   cm. – (Blackwell readings in Continental philosophy; 8)
Includes bibliographical references and index.
ISBN 1-4051-1205-0 (hardcover : alk. paper) – ISBN 1-4051-1204-2 (pbk. :
alk. paper)   1. Self (Philosophy)   2. Subjectivity.   3. Self (Philosophy) –
History.   4. Subjectivity – History.   I. Atkins, Kim.   II. Series.

BD438.5.S43 2005
126 – dc22
                                                                2004016179

A catalogue record for this title is available from the British Library.

Set in 10.5 on 12.5 pt Bembo
by SNP Best-set Typesetter Ltd, Hong Kong

For further information on
Blackwell Publishing, visit our website:
www.blackwellpublishing.com

For my mother, Penny

CONTENTS

ACKNOWLEDGMENTS

I would like to thank those generous friends and colleagues who helped in various ways to realize this book. They are, in alphabetical order: Barbara Baird, Jay Bernstein, Simon Critchley, Jean-Philippe Deranty, Fiona Hughes, Catriona Mackenzie, Nigel McKinlay, Peter Menzies, Linn Miller, Moira Nicholls, Jack Reynolds, Leila Toiviainen, and John Sutton. Thanks are also due to Jeff Dean and Nirit Simon at Blackwell Publishing.

The editor and publisher gratefully acknowledge the permission granted to reproduce the copyright material in this book:

1 René Descartes: "Meditation II" in "Meditations on First Philosophy," from *The Essential Descartes*, edited by Margaret D. Wilson, translated by E. S. Haldane and G. T. R. Ross (New York: New American Library/Meridian, 1983), pp. 170–9.

2 John Locke: "Of Identity and Diversity," from *An Essay Concerning Human Understanding*, abridged and edited by Raymond Wilburn (London: J. M. Dent & Sons, 1947), pp. 162–74.

3 David Hume: "Of Personal Identity," from *A Treatise of Human Nature: Being an Attempt to Introduce the Experimental Method of Reasoning into Moral Subjects*, edited with an introduction by D. G. C. Macnabb (Glasgow: Fontana/Collins, 1970), pp. 300–12. Reprinted by permission of HarperCollins Publishers Ltd.

4 Immanuel Kant: "Paralogisms of Pure Reason (A)" (first, second, and third paralogisms), from *Critique of Pure Reason*, translated by Norman Kemp Smith (Basingstoke and London: Macmillan, 1990), pp. 333–44. Reprinted by permission of Palgrave Macmillan.

5 G. W. F. Hegel: "Self-consciousness," from *Phenomenology of Spirit*, translated by A. V. Miller with analysis and foreword by J. N. Findlay (Oxford: Clarendon Press, 1977), pp. 110–19. Reprinted by permission of Oxford University Press.

6 Friedrich Nietzsche: excerpts from *The Birth of Tragedy and The Genealogy of Morals*, translated by Francis Golffing (Garden City, NY: Doubleday Anchor, 1956), pp.

170–3, 177–80, 189–95, 217–21. Used by permission of Doubleday, a division of
Random House, Inc.

7   Jean-Paul Sartre: "The Look," from *Being and Nothingness*, translated and introduced by Hazel E. Barnes (New York: Washington Square Press, 1966), pp. 340–51
(part 3, ch. 1, section IV). Reproduced by permission of The Philosophical Library,
New York.

8   Maurice Merleau-Ponty: excerpt from "The Spatiality of One's Own Body and
Motility," in *Phenomenology of Perception*, translated by Colin Smith (London:
Routledge, 1992), pp. 98–106.

9   Martin Heidegger: "Exposition of the Task of a Preparatory Analysis of Dasein,"
from *Being and Time*, translated by John Macquarrie and Edward Robinson
(Oxford: Blackwell, 1962), pp. 67–77.

10 P. F. Strawson: "Persons," from *Individuals* (London: Methuen, 1964), pp. 101–12.

11 Harry Frankfurt: "Freedom of the Will and the Concept of a Person," in *The Journal
of Philosophy*, 68:1 (1971), pp. 5–16. Reproduced by permission of *The Journal of
Philosophy* and the author.

12 Sydney Shoemaker: "Personal Identity: A Materialist's Account," from Sydney
Shoemaker and Richard Swinburne, *Personal Identity* (Oxford: Blackwell, 1984),
pp. 89–97. Reprinted by permission of Blackwell Publishing.

13 Bernard Williams: "Bodily Continuity and Personal Identity," from *Problems of the
Self: Philosophical Papers, 1956–1972* (Cambridge, UK: Cambridge University Press,
1973), pp. 19–25. Reprinted by permission of Mrs P. Williams.

14 Derek Parfit: "What We Believe Ourselves To Be," from *Reasons and Persons*
(Oxford: Clarendon Press, 1984), pp. 199–213. Reprinted by permission of Oxford
University Press.

15 Sigmund Freud: "The Ego and the Id," from *On Metapsychology: The Theory of Psychoanalysis* (London: Penguin, 1991), pp. 357–66. © by The Institute of Psychoanalysis and The Hogarth Press; reprinted by permission of the Random House
Group Ltd. from *The Standard Edition of the Complete Psychological Works of Sigmund
Freud*, translated and edited by James Strachey.

16 Michel Foucault: "About the Beginnings of the Hermeneutics of the Self: Two
Lectures at Dartmouth," with an introductory note by Mark Blasius, from *Political Theory*, 21 (1993), pp. 200–4, 210–15, 223–7 (notes). Reprinted by permission
of Sage Publications.

17 Paul Ricoeur: "Personal Identity and Narrative Identity," from *Oneself As Another*,
translated by Kathleen Blamey (Chicago and London: University of Chicago Press,
1992), pp. 115–18, 129–39. Reprinted by permission of The University of Chicago
Press and Paul Ricoeur.

18 Simone de Beauvoir: "Introduction," from *The Second Sex*, translated and edited
by H. M. Parshley (New York: Alfred A. Knopf, 1953), pp. 13–25 from the 1988

Picador reprint published by Pan Books. © 1952 and renewed 1980 by Alfred A. Knopf, a division of Random House, Inc. Used by permission of Alfred A. Knopf, a division of Random House, Inc. and the Random House Group Limited.

19   Judith Butler: excerpt from *Gender Trouble: Feminism and the Subversion of Identity* (New York: Routledge, 1990), pp. 16–25. © 1990 by Judith Butler. Reproduced by permission of Routledge and Taylor & Francis Books, Inc.

20   Luce Irigaray: "Any Theory of the 'Subject' Has Always Been Appropriated by the 'Masculine,'" from *Speculum of the Other Woman*, translated by Gillian C. Gill (Ithaca, NY: Cornell University Press, 1985), pp. 133–6, 139–46. Translation © 1985 by Cornell University Press. Used by permission of the publisher, Cornell University Press.

21   Catriona Mackenzie: "Imagining Oneself Otherwise," from Catriona Mackenzie and Natalie Stoljar (eds.), *Relational Autonomy: Feminist Perspectives on Autonomy, Agency and the Social Self* (New York and Oxford: Oxford University Press, 2000), pp. 133–4, 146–50 (notes). © 2000 by Oxford University Press, Inc. Used by permission of Oxford University Press, Inc.

Every effort has been made to trace copyright holders and to obtain their permission for the use of copyright material. The publisher apologizes for any errors or omissions in the above list and would be grateful if notified of any corrections that should be incorporated in future reprints or editions of this book.

INTRODUCTION

Human beings, perhaps alone among the creatures of the world, have the capacity to reflect upon and evaluate their thoughts, feelings, and actions. This capacity – for self-reflective activity, or, broadly speaking, subjectivity – is the essence of philosophy. This collection of essays attempts to trace a trajectory of philosophical attitudes and ideas about subjectivity from Descartes's account of self-consciousness in the *Meditations* to the most recent Anglo–American and European work in personal identity and autonomy. Despite the various challenges to the "philosophy of the subject" posed by reductionist neuroscience and postmodern critique, the essays in this collection attest to the continued relevance of concepts of self and subjectivity.

The selections in this book are intended to be representative, not exhaustive, of the broad range of views on the topic. It is divided into parts in order to convey a sense of the historical development of ideas as well as the diversity of views within different intellectual movements. These divisions are inevitably arbitrary and will, to some degree, understate or overemphasize the connections between the philosophers' ideas. However, I hope that the structure will assist readers in orienting themselves to the particular concerns and questions that drive the different approaches presented here.

It is commonplace and quite acceptable to speak of "the self." However, this expression is more appropriately understood as a colloquial umbrella term that encompasses a range of concepts that relate to self-reflective activity, for example, "consciousness," "ego," "soul," "subject," "person," or "moral agent." It is interesting to note in the philosophical literature how few authors and translators refer to "the self," including Descartes, who quite consistently writes of the *cogito* or "I" rather than "the self." This has not prevented philosophers from arguing, with some justification, against the notion of an entity "the self." For these reasons, the reader is cautioned against the assumption of such a concept in the accounts of subjectivity and personal identity that follow, and is advised to take a critical attitude toward the use of the, sometimes loose, network of terms that comprises the idea of "the self."

A common theme in the accounts of subjectivity in this collection is the idea that the reflective activity constitutive of philosophy must be grounded in one way or another, for example, in God, spirit, nature, society, the body, the brain, or some combination of these. The different conceptions of the grounds of self-reflection accord-ingly emphasize different aspects and give rise to different kinds of questions. For example, Descartes regarded subjectivity as the direct expression of God, and conse-quently his is a philosophy oriented to questions about the truth of perception, man-ifested in his expansive studies of natural philosophy. Beauvoir, by contrast, regarded subjectivity as the expression of the human body enmeshed in a social matrix, and so her philosophy is oriented to questions about the ontology of interpersonal relations (intersubjectivity) and the interrelation of biology and politics.

Our contemporary ideas concerning self and subjectivity stem from Descartes's prob-lematic description of the human situation in terms of both natural philosophy and rationalism. His description attempted to unite the metaphysical and logical tensions that eventually came to characterize two distinct philosophical schools – the analytical and the Continental – and which tend to pit moral philosophy against the different reductive philosophies within each school. Descartes's characterization of the human subject in terms of the mutual exclusivity of matter (*res extensa*) and thought (*res cogi-tans*) was expressive of his twin commitments: science and religion. Consequently, the history of the philosophy of subjectivity is also the history of the negotiation of these twin concerns (with their metaphysical, political, emotional, and conceptual dimen-sions) in the attempt to explicate the aspects of human experience that underpin those belief systems. For example, Locke puts science (in the form of empiricism) to the service of God via an account of personal identity shaped around moral responsibility. Hume, taking up Locke's empiricism, tries to dispense with God once and for all, only to fall prey to skepticism, and in doing so, provides the opportunity for Kant to play the ball straight back into God's court through his idea of the noumenal self. However, in the process, Kant also opens up a diversionary route for the empiricist through his account of the apperceptive "I" as part of the purely logical structure of the understanding.

Kant's critique of Descartes's conception of the "I" as soul gave rise to two antago-nistic philosophical pathways. On the one hand, a line of thought that emphasized the linguistic form of the objective conditions of the understanding led eventually to ana-lytical philosophy of language and philosophy of mind. On the other hand, a line of thought that emphasized the subjective nature of understanding led to phenomenol-ogy. Accordingly, each path tended to take a different metaphysical view of the self and world. Analytical philosophy is in general materialist and empiricist. Some materialists take an openly reductionist and eliminativist approach, and some actively resist that approach. This division distinguishes those who argue that terms such as "self" or "sub-jective" can be entirely replaced by objective and impersonal concepts (for example, Parfit), from those who argue that concepts of body, brain, psychological states, and so forth are derivative of a holistic conception of a person (for example, Strawson and Shoemaker).

Continental philosophy has tended to encompass a broader range of metaphysical outlooks, from the theologically informed views of Hegel, Heidegger, and Ricoeur, to the emphatically atheistic, Romantically influenced accounts of Nietzsche, Freud, and Foucault. Others, like Beauvoir and Merleau-Ponty, are broadly materialist, but perhaps more accurately described as metaphysically neutral. The style of materialism that differentiates the Continental from the analytical approach (for example, Merleau-Ponty from Shoemaker or Strawson), turns on the role of the body. Analytical materialists tend to regard the body as a rather complex physical object that, for reasons not yet fully understood, manifests subjective states.

Philosophers in the phenomenological tradition such as Merleau-Ponty, Beauvoir, and Butler, highlight the active powers of embodiment in structuring perception and consciousness, thereby undermining the possibility of a strictly empirical account of either self or world. The insights and implications of this view have only recently infiltrated analytical philosophy, but promise a productive encounter.[1] In a different way, Nietzsche, Freud, and Foucault give a key role to the body in determining subjectivity. They regard the living body as a constellation of powerful and often conflictual urges and impulses that give rise to different forms of subjectivity according to the organism's internal organization and the "disciplinary" effects of socially regulated practices and norms.

The idea that the body has a dynamic and vital role in structuring our subjectivities, our perceptions, and our understanding, has been a central theme of feminist philosophy. Beauvoir, for example, argued that women's subjectivity and social oppression was partly an effect of their embodiment: the burden of women's biological role in the reproduction of the species gave men a practical advantage by affording them the opportunity and the power to determine that the organization of society would further their interests. Irigaray takes up the issue of maternity in a very different way, using psychoanalytic theory to argue that subjectivity crucially depends upon the maternal relation: ego development and language acquisition are premised upon a bodily unity achieved through the child's infantile experiences of its own body in relation to its maternal carer. However, she argues, psychoanalysis and philosophy has systematically obscured the maternal debt and, as a result, denies the possibility of a female subjectivity. Butler argues that the acquisition of language is itself a gendered process: a process premised upon a "compulsory heterosexuality," giving what is essentially political – the construction of gender-identity – all the appearance of nature.

Whether one is oriented to philosophy by way of conceptual analysis or a descriptive philosophy, or both, one cannot avoid a direct confrontation with the question of subjectivity within moral philosophy. Typically this concerns questions of moral responsibility and autonomy, represented in this collection by Frankfurt and Mackenzie. Frankfurt connects autonomy directly to the capacity for self-reflection by describing moral agency in terms of critical reflection upon one's desires and actions (which he calls second-order volitions). Mackenzie draws out the connection between critical reflection, imagination, and autonomy to argue that the capacity for autonomy and agency is an acquired competency that can be systematically disabled by the cognitive and emotional effects of culturally available images and representations. One of the most recent accounts of self and subjectivity that attempts to provide a multileveled model premised upon the ethical nature of the human situation is Ricoeur's account of narrative identity. This model refuses reductionism while accommodating the sciences, and attempts to construct an exchange between biology, history, and ethics through the medium of literary and philosophical resources.

This collection offers a diverse range of historical and philosophical sources that, I hope, will provide useful for understanding current as well as past controversies pertaining to those most troublesome of creatures: persons, subjects, and selves.

Note

1   See J. L. Bermúdez, A. Marcel, and N. Eilan (eds), *The Body and the Self* (Cambridge, MA and London: Bradford/MIT Press, 1998).

PART I

EARLY MODERN PHILOSOPHY

1

COMMENTARY ON DESCARTES

René Descartes was born in France in 1596 and died in 1650. He lived during a significant period in the transition from the medieval to the modern age: an age that saw the rise of what became the scientific method. His contemporaries were Galileo, Kepler, and Francis Bacon, and Descartes himself was an accomplished natural philosopher, writing studies of optics, mechanics, physiology, and meteorology. He is perhaps best known as the father of substance dualism, the idea that mind and body are composed of metaphysically distinct substances – a view that continues to resonate within contemporary philosophy.

Descartes has been attributed with the inception of the philosophy of the subject, but he was not the first to give a philosophical role to the "self." Centuries earlier Augustine had drawn attention to the importance of the "*interiore homine*" or the "inner man,"[1] but it was certainly Descartes who moved subjectivity to center stage in philosophy, grounding in the first person perspective of the self-conscious "I" the traditional philosophical values of truth and certainty, and setting the terms of reference for the next 400-odd years of philosophy and cognitive science. Descartes is both fascinating and deservedly famous for the ways in which he attempts, unsuccessfully, to delineate the mental from the physical in the context of the human body, but also for the numerous ambiguities he continually uncovers in that domain. These are wonderful sources for later French philosophers of the body, notably Gabriel Marcel and Maurice Merleau-Ponty. Despite Descartes's efforts, his account is torn between what experience tells us and what reason demands – a tension that continues to characterize contemporary approaches to subjectivity and personal identity.

Descartes arrives at his views through a philosophical endeavor that was informed by a number of concerns. One was to show the limits of skepticism by establishing a system of philosophy in which indubitable first principles could be demonstrated. Another was a reaction to the oppressive dogma of scholasticism with its disdain for either critique or innovation, which Descartes found antithetical to genuine philosophy. However, central to Descartes's work was the aim of grounding natural philosophy in principles of mechanics. Finally, Descartes is reputed to have had a series of evocative dreams that inspired him to set out on his lifelong mission to develop a new system of philosophy.[2]

Descartes employs a method of doubt in order to establish one single indubitable fact from which all other truths could be determined, and which would thus provide the first principles of philosophy. This fact is the existence of the "I," the immaterial thinking thing that is the subject of consciousness. Descartes's famous conclusion – *cogito ergo sum*, I think therefore I am[3] – installs subjectivity as a fully fledged concept in the heart of his philosophical system, and sets the scene for later idealism and phenomenology.

Descartes's method in establishing the indubitability of the "I" is to call into question every single one of his beliefs, including the apparently self-evident truths of arithmetic and geometry.[4] In *Meditation II*, Descartes sets forth a series of doubts and responses through which he unfolds the necessity and nature of the "I," employing the thought experiment of the evil genius. He argues that even if I can call into doubt everything I perceive or believe, including my very existence, I *cannot* doubt that I am doubting. Since doubt is a form of thought, in each instance that I doubt I thereby confirm that I am thinking; hence Descartes's goad to the evil genius to "let him deceive me as much as he will." Any amount of doubt simply reiterates the truth that I, as a thinking thing, exist. Significantly, the truth of this exercise can be demonstrated by anyone who cares to try it out. Descartes was critical of the authoritarian dogmatism of scholasticism and sought to present philosophy as a task that each person must undertake for himself or herself. Descartes was convinced that reason could prove itself independent of the biases of institutionalized learning.[5] For Descartes, it is in one's reason, not one's learning, that the principles of philosophy are to be found.

In *Meditation II*, Descartes describes the *cogito* from two different perspectives. The first is a negative characterization of the *cogito* as nonbodily, and the second is a positive characterization of it as a "thinking thing." The first is expressed in Descartes's argument from doubt: I can doubt that my body exists, but I cannot doubt that I exist as a thinking thing; therefore, I can safely conclude that I exist as such a being, and, with equal assurance, conclude that I cannot be a bodily being. By a process of elimination, Descartes concludes that it is thinking alone that "cannot be separated from me." This point is restated in *Meditation VI* where he states that my "clear and distinct perception" (which, for Descartes, has a specific technical meaning)[6] of myself as existing without my body is proof of my nonbodily existence.[7]

Having apparently proven that the "I" is nonphysical being, Descartes then introduces the second description by asking about the nature of this being. His answer is immediate and consists in a description of consciousness in terms of modes of thought: "But what then am I? A thing which thinks. What is a thing which thinks? It is a thing which doubts, understands, affirms, denies, wills, refuses, which also imagines and feels."[8]

Descartes gives a further defense of this positive characterization in *Meditation VI*, where he presents the argument from the indivisibility of consciousness. He states that it is impossible to distinguish any parts in the mind; the "I" – the *cogito* – cannot be broken down into any components, as can the body, therefore the "I" is not bodily. This is supported by the argument from clear and distinct perceptions: if "I" had parts, those parts would be clearly and distinctly perceived by me; God has guaranteed that much.

There are a number of objections to these arguments. With respect to the claim that we have an immediate and intuitive grasp of the nature of the mind, it is quite conceivable that there are many properties of mind and body of which we are unaware. We have no direct awareness of the many physiological processes of the brain involved in cognition, such as the type and level of neurotransmitters needed for conscious awareness. Although science has been able to demonstrate the role of neurotransmitters in causing explicit consciousness, one is nevertheless unaware of those chemical processes themselves as they occur. Furthermore, as this example from neuroscience shows, there are many properties that the body shares with the mind. Descartes concedes that his concept of mind may not be adequate, but nevertheless maintains that it is "complete."[9] It is complete because, on his view, his being explicitly aware of his conscious thoughts is sufficient for him to exist with that attribute alone, that is, as a purely thinking thing. Because Descartes takes "thinking" to be the totality of what one is explicitly conscious of thinking, any thinking will always necessarily imply, and in that sense "prove," the existence of the "I" whose thoughts they are (as Kant would also famously argue, but with a rather different conclusion). While Descartes may well still insist that the argument from doubt shows that we can each know ourselves as thinking beings, it does not shed any light on the substantive question of *Meditation II*, which is the question of "what I am, I who am certain that I am."[10]

Descartes's view of the simple and indivisible unity of thought is also questionable. It is frequently observed that people have conflicting beliefs or goals, as well as ambivalent feelings and attitudes; for example, we talk about feeling "torn" between alternatives. Furthermore, even if the mind is unified, that unity may be predicated upon a divisible material system, such as the brain or the coordination of other bodily activities (something that Nietzsche makes much of). However, the most damning criticisms will come, initially, from Locke and Hume, then more comprehensively from Kant, as these philosophers argue for the impossibility of knowledge of the "I" as immaterial substance.

There are two basic problems of mind–body dualism known as the problem of interaction and the "mental or physical dilemma." The interaction problem concerns the difficulty of establishing how the *cogito* – an immaterial, nonphysical being – is able to affect the physical body. This is an irresolvable problem because Descartes defines mind and body by mutually exclusive attributes. For the *cogito* to play a role in human action (as it must from the point of view of morality), it would have to have physical properties; for example, the *cogito* would have to have a spatiotemporal location because it has to be where my body is.

The problem of interaction also arises from the mutual exclusivity of mind and body. There are some attributes that do not easily fall into either category, for example, vision and hearing. As Descartes knew, vision requires physical processes: my eyes must be open, there must be light, and the parts of my eyes must move to accommodate the object of vision. At the same time, I seem to experience vision as a nonphysical phenomenon: the objects of my vision are grasped immediately and from a distance, as if by nonphysical contact. Descartes's explanation is simply to call these "confused" modes of thought. His defense of dualism goes so far as to argue that bodily damage does not affect the mind.[11] This is an odd comment from Descartes because as a scientist he would have had ample evidence that bodily damage, in particular head injuries, does affect the mind.

Conceived as nonmaterial, the *cogito* cannot be fundamentally involved *in* the world; it must always be an outsider, content to observe and never to participate. The latter is precisely the fate of the Cartesian subject. Once evicted, nothing will repatriate the metaphysical subject to the world, and the rest of the history of the philosophy of the subject is the history of the attempt to resolve the unbearable tensions of a subject in exile, either through the reintegration of self and world or through the dissolution of the very concept of self.

Notes

1   See, for example, Charles Taylor, *Sources of the Self* (Cambridge, UK: Cambridge University Press, 1989), p. 129.
2   John Cottingham, *Descartes*, 10th edn (Oxford and Malden, MA: Blackwell, 1998), pp. 9–10.
3   This particular expression is found in the *Discourse on Method*, not in the *Meditations*.
4   Mathematical truths could be false, Descartes reasons, simply because it is conceivable that God, being omnipotent, could cause him to err each time he makes a calculation. René Descartes: "Meditation I" in "Meditations on First Philosophy," reprinted in *The Essential Descartes*, ed. Margaret D. Wilson (New York: Meridian, 1969), p. 168.
5   Hiram Caton, *The Origins of Subjectivity* (New Haven, CT and London: Yale University Press, 1973), p. 30.
6   Note that for Descartes a perception is not clear and distinct simply because I regard it as obvious, but rather because it is a perception of something simple in structure which is accessible to "the attentive mind." See Cottingham (1998), pp. 25–6.
7   Wilson (ed., 1969), p. 213.
8   Ibid, p. 174.
9   Cottingham (1998), p. 114.
10   Cottingham (1998, p. 113) notes that in comments on Meditation II, published in 1647, Descartes does concede that his argument from doubt has not proven that the mind is exclusive of anything bodily.
11   Wilson (ed., 1969), p. 220: "although the whole mind seems to be united to the whole body, yet if a foot or an arm or some other part, is separated from my body, I am aware that nothing has been taken away from my mind."

Main Texts by Descartes

Charles Adam and Paul Tannery (eds.), *Oeuvres de Descartes*, 11 vols (Paris: Librairie Philosophique J. Vrin, 1983).
Stephen H. Voss (trans.), *The Passions of the Soul* (Indianapolis: Hackett Publishing Company, 1989).
John Cottingham, Robert Stoothoff, and Dugald Murdoch (trans.), *The Philosophical Writings of Descartes*, 3 vols (Cambridge, UK: Cambridge University Press, 1988).
V. R. Miller and R. P. Miller (trans.), *Principles of Philosophy*, trans. (Dordrecht: D. Reidel, 1983).

Further Reading

Ariew, Roger, John Cottingham, and Tom Sorell (eds.), *Descartes' Meditations: Background Source Materials* (Cambridge, UK: Cambridge University Press, 1998).

Cottingham, John (ed.), *The Cambridge Companion to Descartes* (Cambridge, UK: Cambridge University Press, 1992).

Gaukroger, Stephen, *Descartes: An Intellectual Biography* (Oxford: Clarendon Press, 1995).

Kenny, Anthony, *Descartes: A Study of His Philosophy* (Bristol, UK: Thoemmes Press, 1968).

Oksenberg Rorty, Amelie (ed.), *Essays on Descartes' Meditations* (Berkeley: University of California Press, 1986).

Sorell, Tom, *Descartes* (Oxford: Oxford University Press, 1987).

"MEDITATION II"

René Descartes

Of the Nature of the Human Mind; and that it is More Easily Known than the Body.

The Meditation of yesterday filled my mind with so many doubts that it is no longer in my power to forget them. And yet I do not see in what manner I can resolve them; and, just as if I had all of a sudden fallen into very deep water, I am so disconcerted that I can neither make certain of setting my feet on the bottom, nor can I swim and so support myself on the surface. I shall nevertheless make an effort and follow anew the same path as that on which I yesterday entered, i.e. I shall proceed by setting aside all that in which the least doubt could be supposed to exist, just as if I had discovered that it was absolutely false; and I shall ever follow in this road until I have met with something which is certain, or at least, if I can do nothing else, until I have learned for certain that there is nothing in the world that is certain. Archimedes, in order that he might draw the terrestrial globe out of its place, and transport it elsewhere, demanded only that one point should be fixed and immoveable; in the same way I shall have the right to conceive high hopes if I am happy enough to discover one thing only which is certain and indubitable.

I suppose, then, that all the things that I see are false; I persuade myself that nothing has ever existed of all that my fallacious memory represents to me. I consider that I possess no senses; I imagine that body, figure, extension, movement and place are but the fictions of my mind. What, then, can be esteemed as true? Perhaps nothing at all, unless that there is nothing in the world that is certain.

But how can I know there is not something different from those things that I have just considered, of which one cannot have the slightest doubt? Is there not some God, or some other being by whatever name we call it, who puts these reflections into my mind? That is not necessary, for is it not possible that I am capable of producing them

From "Meditations on First Philosophy" from *The Essential Descartes*, edited by Margaret D. Wilson, translated by E. S. Haldane and G. T. R. Ross (New York: New American Library/Meridian, 1983), pp. 170–9.

myself? I myself, am I not at least something? But I have already denied that I had senses and body. Yet I hesitate, for what follows from that? Am I so dependent on body and senses that I cannot exist without these? But I was persuaded that there was nothing in all the world, that there was no heaven, no earth, that there were no minds, nor any bodies: was I not then likewise persuaded that I did not exist? Not at all; of a surety I myself did exist since I persuaded myself of something [or merely because I thought of something]. But there is some deceiver or other, very powerful and very cunning, who ever employs his ingenuity in deceiving me. Then without doubt I exist also if he deceives me, and let him deceive me as much as he will, he can never cause me to be nothing so long as I think that I am something. So that after having reflected well and carefully examined all things, we must come to the definite conclusion that this proposition: I am, I exist, is necessarily true each time that I pronounce it, or that I mentally conceive it.

But I do not yet know clearly enough what I am, I who am certain that I am; and hence I must be careful to see that I do not imprudently take some other object in place of myself, and thus that I do not go astray in respect of this knowledge that I hold to be the most certain and most evident of all that I have formerly learned. That is why I shall now consider anew what I believed myself to be before I embarked upon these last reflections; and of my former opinions I shall withdraw all that might even in a small degree be invalidated by the reasons which I have just brought forward, in order that there may be nothing at all left beyond what is absolutely certain and indubitable.

What then did I formerly believe myself to be? Undoubtedly I believed myself to be a man. But what is a man? Shall I say a reasonable animal? Certainly not; for then I should have to inquire what an animal is, and what is reasonable; and thus from a single question I should insensibly fall into an infinitude of others more difficult; and I should not wish to waste the little time and leisure remaining to me in trying to unravel subtleties like these. But I shall rather stop here to consider the thoughts which of themselves spring up in my mind, and which were not inspired by anything beyond my own nature alone when I applied myself to the consideration of my being. In the first place, then, I considered myself as having a face, hands, arms, and all that system of members composed of bones and flesh as seen in a corpse which I designated by the name of body. In addition to this I considered that I was nourished, that I walked, that I felt, and that I thought, and I referred all these actions to the soul: but I did not stop to consider what the soul was, or if I did stop, I imagined that it was something extremely rare and subtle like a wind, a flame, or an ether, which was spread throughout my grosser parts. As to body I had no manner of doubt about its nature, but thought I had a very clear knowledge of it; and if I had desired to explain it according to the notions that I had then formed of it, I should have described it thus: By the body I understand all that which can be defined by a certain figure: something which can be confined in a certain place, and which can fill a given space in such a way that every other body will be excluded from it; which can be perceived either by touch, or by sight, or by hearing, or by taste, or by smell: which can be moved in many ways not, in truth, by itself, but by something which is foreign to it, by which it is touched [and from which it receives impressions]: for to have the power of self-movement, as also of feeling or of thinking, I did not consider to appertain to the nature of body: on the contrary, I was rather astonished to find that faculties similar to them existed in some bodies.

But what am I, now that I suppose that there is a certain genius which is extremely powerful, and, if I may say so, malicious, who employs all his powers in deceiving me? Can I affirm that I possess the least of all those things which I have just said pertain to the nature of body? I pause to consider, I revolve all these things in my mind, and I find none of which I can say that it pertains to me. It would be tedious to stop to enumerate them. Let us pass to the attributes of soul and see if there is any one which is in me? What of nutrition or walking [the first mentioned]? But if it is so that I have no body it is also true that I can neither walk nor take nourishment. Another attribute is sensation. But one cannot feel without body, and besides I have thought I perceived many things during sleep that I recognized in my waking moments as not having been experienced at all. What of thinking? I find here that thought is an attribute that belongs to me; it alone cannot be separated from me. I am, I exist, that is certain. But how often? Just when I think; for it might possibly be the case if I ceased entirely to think, that I should likewise cease altogether to exist. I do not now admit anything which is not necessarily true: to speak accurately I am not more than a thing which thinks, that is to say a mind or a soul, or an understanding, or a reason, which are terms whose significance was formerly unknown to me. I am, however, a real thing and really exist; but what thing? I have answered: a thing which thinks.

And what more? I shall exercise my imagination [in order to see if I am not something more]. I am not a collection of members which we call the human body: I am not a subtle air distributed through these members, I am not a wind, a fire, a vapour, a breath, nor anything at all which I can imagine or conceive; because I have assumed that all these were nothing. Without changing that supposition I find that I only leave myself certain of the fact that I am somewhat. But perhaps it is true that these same things which I supposed were non-existent because they are unknown to me, are really not different from the self which I know. I am not sure about this, I shall not dispute about it now; I can only give judgment on things that are known to me. I know that I exist, and I inquire what I am, I whom I know to exist. But it is very certain that the knowledge of my existence taken in its precise significance does not depend on things whose existence is not yet known to me; consequently it does not depend on those which I can feign in imagination. And indeed the very term *feign* in imagination[1] proves to me my error, for I really do this if I image myself a something, since to imagine is nothing else than to contemplate the figure or image of a corporeal thing. But I already know for certain that I am, and that it may be that all these images, and, speaking generally, all things that relate to the nature of body are nothing but dreams [and chimeras]. For this reason I see clearly that I have as little reason to say, 'I shall stimulate my imagination in order to know more distinctly what I am,' than if I were to say, 'I am now awake, and I perceive somewhat that is real and true: but because I do not yet perceive it distinctly enough, I shall go to sleep of express purpose, so that my dreams may represent the perception with greatest truth and evidence.' And, thus, I know for certain that nothing of all that I can understand by means of my imagination belongs to this knowledge which I have of myself, and that it is necessary to recall the mind from this mode of thought with the utmost diligence in order that it may be able to know its own nature with perfect distinctness.

But what then am I? A thing which thinks. What is a thing which thinks? It is a thing which doubts, understands [conceives], affirms, denies, wills, refuses, which also imagines and feels.

Certainly it is no small matter if all these things pertain to my nature. But why should they not so pertain? Am I not that being who now doubts nearly everything, who nevertheless understands certain things, who affirms that one only is true, who denies all the others, who desires to know more, is averse from being deceived, who imagines many things, sometimes indeed despite his will, and who perceives many likewise, as by the intervention of the bodily organs? Is there nothing in all this which is as true as it is certain that I exist, even though I should always sleep and though he who has given me being employed all his ingenuity in deceiving me? Is there likewise any one of these attributes which can be distinguished from my thought, or which might be said to be separated from myself? For it is so evident of itself that it is I who doubts, who understands, and who desires, that there is no reason here to add anything to explain it. And I have certainly the power of imagining likewise; for although it may happen (as I formerly supposed) that none of the things which I imagine are true, nevertheless this power of imagining does not cease to be really in use, and it forms part of my thought. Finally, I am the same who feels, that is to say, who perceives certain things, as by the organs of sense, since in truth I see light, I hear noise, I feel heat. But it will be said that these phenomena are false and that I am dreaming. Let it be so; still it is at least quite certain that it seems to me that I see light, that I hear noise and that I feel heat. That cannot be false; properly speaking it is what is in me called feeling;[2] and used in this precise sense that is no other thing than thinking.

From this time I begin to know what I am with a little more clearness and distinctness than before; but nevertheless it still seems to me, and I cannot prevent myself from thinking, that corporeal things, whose images are framed by thought, which are tested by the senses, are much more distinctly known than that obscure part of me which does not come under the imagination. Although really it is very strange to say that I know and understand more distinctly these things whose existence seems to me dubious, which are unknown to me, and which do not belong to me, than others of the truth of which I am convinced, which are known to me and which pertain to my real nature, in a word, than myself. But I see clearly how the case stands: my mind loves to wander, and cannot yet suffer itself to be retained within the just limits of truth. Very good, let us once more give it the freest rein, so that, when afterwards we seize the proper occasion for pulling up, it may the more easily be regulated and controlled.

Let us begin by considering the commonest matters, those which we believe to be the most distinctly comprehended, to wit, the bodies which we touch and see; not indeed bodies in general, for these general ideas are usually a little more confused, but let us consider one body in particular. Let us take, for example, this piece of wax: it has been taken quite freshly from the hive, and it has not yet lost the sweetness of the honey which it contains; it still retains somewhat of the odour of the flowers from which it has been culled; its colour, its figure, its size are apparent; it is hard, cold, easily handled, and if you strike it with the finger, it will emit a sound. Finally all the things which are requisite to cause us distinctly to recognise a body, are met with in it. But notice that while I speak and approach the fire what remained of the taste is exhaled, the smell evaporates, the colour alters, the figure is destroyed, the size increases, it becomes liquid, it heats, scarely can one handle it, and when one strikes it, no sound is emitted. Does the same wax remain after this change? We must confess that it remains; none would judge otherwise. What then did I know so distinctly in this piece of wax? It could certainly be nothing of all that the senses brought to my notice, since all these things which fall under taste, smell, sight, touch, and hearing, are found to be changed, and yet the same wax remains.

Perhaps it was what I now think, viz. that this wax was not that sweetness of honey, nor that agreeable scent of flowers, nor that particular whiteness, nor that figure, nor that sound, but simply a body which a little while before appeared to me as perceptible under these forms, and which is now perceptible under others. But what, precisely, is it that I imagine when I form such conceptions? Let us attentively consider this, and, abstracting from all that does not belong to the wax, let us see what remains. Certainly nothing remains excepting a certain extended thing which is flexible and movable. But what is the meaning of flexible and movable? Is it not that I imagine that this piece of wax being round is capable of becoming square and of passing from a square to a triangular figure? No, certainly it is not that, since I imagine it admits of an infinitude of similar changes, and I nevertheless do not know how to compass the infinitude by my imagination, and consequently this conception which I have of the wax is not brought about by the faculty of imagination. What now is this extension? Is it not also unknown? For it becomes greater when the wax is melted, greater when it is boiled, and greater still when the heat increases; and I should not conceive [clearly] according to truth what wax is, if I did not think that even this piece that we are considering is capable of receiving more variations in extension than I have ever imagined. We must then grant that I could not even understand through the imagination what this piece of wax is, and that it is my mind[3] alone which perceives it. I say this piece of wax in particular, for as to wax in general it is yet clearer. But what is this piece of wax which cannot be understood excepting by the [understanding or] mind? It is certainly the same that I see, touch, imagine, and finally it is the same which I have always believed it to be from the beginning. But what must particularly be observed is that its perception is neither an act of vision, nor of touch, nor of imagination, and has never been such although it may have appeared formerly to be so, but only an intuition[4] of the mind, which may be imperfect and confused as it was formerly, or clear and distinct as it is at present, according as my attention is more or less directed to the elements which are found in it, and of which it is composed.

Yet in the meantime I am greatly astonished when I consider [the great feebleness of mind] and its proneness to fall [insensibly] into error; for although without giving expression to my thoughts I consider all this in my own mind, words often impede me and I am almost deceived by the terms of ordinary language. For we say that we see the same wax, if it is present, and not that we simply judge that it is the same from its having the same colour and figure. From this I should conclude that I knew the wax by means of vision and not simply by the intuition of the mind; unless by chance I remember that, when looking from a window and saying I see men who pass in the street, I really do not see them, but infer that what I see is men, just as I say that I see wax. And yet what do I see from the window but hats and coats which may cover automatic machines? Yet I judge these to be men. And similarly solely by the faculty of judgment which rests in my mind, I comprehend that which I believed I saw with my eyes.

A man who makes it his aim to raise his knowledge above the common should be ashamed to derive the occasion for doubting from the forms of speech invented by the vulgar; I prefer to pass on and consider whether I had a more evident and perfect conception of what the wax was when I first perceived it, and when I believed I knew it by means of the external senses or at least by the common sense[5] as it is called, that is to say by the imaginative faculty, or whether my present conception is clearer now that I have most carefully examined what it is, and in what way it can be known. It would certainly be absurd to doubt as to this. For what was there in this first perception which was distinct? What was there which might not as well have been perceived by any of the animals? But when I distinguish the wax from its external forms, and when, just as if I had taken from it its vestments, I consider it quite naked, it is certain that although some error may still be found in my judgment, I can nevertheless not perceive it thus without a human mind.

But finally what shall I say of this mind, that is, of myself, for up to this point I do not admit in myself anything but mind? What then, I who seem to perceive this piece of wax so distinctly, do I not know myself, not only with much more truth and certainty, but also with much more distinctness and clearness? For if I judge that the wax is or exists from the fact that I see it, it certainly follows much more clearly that I am or that I exist myself from the fact that I see it. For it may be that what I see is not really wax, it may also be that I do not possess eyes with which to see anything; but it cannot be that when I see, or (for I no longer take account of the distinction) when I think I see, that I myself who think am nought. So if I judge that the wax exists from the fact that I touch it, the same thing will follow, to wit, that I am; and if I judge that my imagination, or some other cause, whatever it is, persuades me that the wax exists, I shall still conclude the same. And what I have here remarked of wax may be applied to all other things which are external to me [and which are met with outside of me]. And further, if the [notion or] perception of wax has seemed to me clearer and more distinct, not only after the sight or the touch, but also after many other causes have rendered it quite manifest to me, with how much more [evidence] and distinctness must it be said that I now know myself, since all the reasons which contribute to the knowledge of wax, or any other body whatever, are yet better proofs of the nature of my mind! And there are so many other things in the mind itself which may contribute to the elucidation of its nature, that those which depend on body such as these just mentioned, hardly merit being taken into account.

But finally here I am, having insensibly reverted to the point I desired, for, since it is now manifest to me that even bodies are not properly speaking known by the senses or by the faculty of imagination, but by the understanding only, and since they are not known from the fact that they are seen or touched, but only because they are understood, I see clearly that there is nothing which is easier for me to know than my mind. But because it is difficult to rid oneself so promptly of an opinion to which one was accustomed for so long, it will be well that I should halt a little at this point, so that by the length of my meditation I may more deeply imprint on my memory this new knowledge.

Notes

1   Or 'form an image' (effingo).
2   sentire.
3   entendement F., mens L.
4   inspectio.
5   sensus communis.

2

COMMENTARY ON LOCKE

British philosopher John Locke (1632–1704) is generally regarded as the founder of empiricism,[1] but he is as much famed for his political philosophy and his life in politics as for his epistemology. He interspersed his academic work with involvements in the intrigue of British politics, which at one point led him into hiding in Holland.[2] Perhaps no other philosopher since Descartes has influenced the way in which philosophers conceive of "persons" and personal identity, and Locke's account continues to be a mainstay of analytical philosophies of personal identity.

Locke was the first philosopher to insist that philosophy start out from an examination of what we are able to know, that is, from epistemology. He considered that to do otherwise was to engage in fruitless speculation. One such fruitless speculation, in Locke's view, concerned the nature of the soul. He thought that since we could not know whether the soul remained the same over time, we could not know if a person remained the same person over time. This presented serious problems for determining how persons were to be judged for their actions, and rewarded or punished by God. These religious and moral concerns drive Locke's investigations into personal identity.[3] Accordingly, he shifts focus from metaphysical questions concerning the soul to practical questions concerning continuity in a person's identity.

In this excerpt, Locke begins by pointing out that we employ different criteria for identity depending on whether we are talking about substances, animals and vegetables, or persons. The criterion for identity of a substance (even immaterial substance) is that it admits of absolutely no change in size or shape or mass. By contrast, living things such as plants and animals do change their size, shape, and mass, and even their matter, yet are still the "same." According to Locke, a living thing retains its identity by retaining the same organization of its parts, that is, by "participation in the same continued life."[4] Even though the matter that comprises the organism is not identical, its organization is unchanged, and this allows the organism to retain its specific character, or sameness. Things are more complicated when it comes to the identity of persons, partly because Locke is inexact in his use of the terms "person," "self," "soul," "man," and "thinking thing." At times he uses these terms synonymously; at other times he uses their differences as critical wedges.

Locke frames his account by noting that when we ask about a person's identity, we ask if this man is the same man as he was in the past. If, by the word "man" we were just referring to a rational thinking being (the soul), a very clever parrot would have to be considered one, while a very stupid human being could not − a possibility he considers ridiculous. For Locke, to be a "man" necessitates one have a human body. This means that "man" is not equated with "soul." If it was, we would be obliged to concur with the belief that two "men" who lived in vastly different ages could have the same identity because their souls could transmigrate − a view Locke abhorred. However, if "man" is regarded as distinct from the soul, his corporeal identity alone is insufficient to account for the kind of drastic differences that can emerge within a personality over time. Moreover, for Locke, bodily identity cannot provide a basis for moral responsibility because responsibility concerns agency and psychological attributes, not merely bodily appearance.

Locke sets down his definition of "person" as "a thinking intelligent being that has reason and reflection, and can consider itself as itself, the same thinking thing, in different times and places."[5] Here, Locke shares Descartes's conception of consciousness as reflexive and involving only those ideas of which one is explicitly aware: whenever I have an idea I also have an awareness of myself as having that idea. This emphasizes the role of the first person perspective and conceives "person" as the "I" or subject of a temporally continuous existence. Significantly here, when one claims to have a memory one must be able to remember oneself having the experience of which it is a memory. This way of putting things allows Locke to ask: what makes a subject (or "I") of a set of perceptions and actions at one time the same subject of a set of perceptions and actions at another time? Identity, for Locke concerns the continued existence of the "same consciousness" (and much debate concerns exactly how this is to be interpreted). Introducing time and relation, thus difference, into the concept of the subject breaks a radical new ground for thinking about the nature of selfhood and identity of consciousness, a ground on which Hume was to make his indelible mark shortly afterwards.

For Locke, the question of "same consciousness" concerns whether I am the subject of the same perceptions, memories, and actions of an earlier person (a requirement of morality). Put this way, we can see that what really matters for personal identity is *continuity* in consciousness, that is, psychological continuity. The upshot of Locke's account of psychological continuity is that if I were to lose all my memories, I would lose my identity. Even if my friends and family showed me photographs and documents tracing my entire life, this would not help. No amount of external evidence will give me my identity back because the reflexive nature of consciousness requires that *I* have to remember being that person if I am to be the same person; I have to be able to consider myself *as* myself, as "the same thinking thing, in different times and places." In other words, I have to be able to ascribe that existence to myself on the basis of my memory of it. If after suffering amnesia, I go on to develop a new identity with new beliefs and skills, Locke argues that it is legitimate to say that I am a different person (and what we have in this case is two persons in one body).

The psychological approach allows Locke to resolve a question that plagued Descartes: what happens to the soul in cases of interruptions to consciousness, for example, forgetting or sleeping? How can a thinking thing exist where no thinking is going on? According to Locke, such interruptions may cast serious doubt on the identity of the soul/substance, but they present no problem for determining whether or not I am the same person. Here, Locke shifts the philosophical question to an empirical one, which asks instead: is the person who woke up the same person who fell asleep?

There are a number of objections to Locke's argument. I will mention briefly four main criticisms: that the argument is circular, that it is contradictory, that it is too narrow, and that it is too broad. The criticism of circularity, made by Bishop Butler and Thomas Reid, says that by defining personal identity in terms of consciousness of personal identity, Locke has confused *knowledge* of personal identity with what actually *constitutes* personal identity; that is, he has confused an epistemological question with a metaphysical question.[6] I may know who I am by regarding myself as the subject of my memories, but still not know in what my *subjectivity* consists. In this sense, Locke's theory presupposes what it is supposed to explain.

The second objection, made by Reid, argues that Locke's account leads to absurdities because it violates transitivity. A transitive relation is an identity relation, expressed in the following way: if a has it to b, and b has it to c, then a has it to c. For example, if the cereal I ate this morning (a) is the same cereal as I bought at the supermarket yesterday (b), and if the supermarket cereal is the same cereal that was delivered by my brother-in-law (c), then the cereal I ate for breakfast (a) was the same cereal delivered to the supermarket by my brother-in-law (c). Each of these cases expresses an equivalence relation between its terms, and it is in virtue of the transitivity of that relation that the cereal can be said to be the same cereal, that is, numerically identical.

Reid's famous objection asks us to consider this:

> Suppose a brave officer to have been flogged when a boy at school, for robbing an orchard, to have taken a standard from the enemy in his first campaign, and to have been made a general in advanced life. Suppose also . . . that when he took the standard he was conscious of his having been flogged at school, and that when he was made a general he was conscious of taking the standard but had absolutely lost the consciousness of his flogging.[7]

On Locke's view, we are obliged to say that the general is and is not the same person as the boy, and so identity cannot hold. Contemporary analytical accounts of personal identity (Shoemaker's and Parfit's, for example), have endeavored to overcome this criticism by formulating continuity in terms of memory-connectedness that emphasizes degrees of continuity and overlap in memories, rather than the all-or-nothing conditions of Reid's interpretation.

It has also been argued that Locke's account is too narrow a basis for moral responsibility because it limits personal identity to memory. The problem of amnesia demonstrates this clearly. On Locke's view, if one loses sufficient of one's memories such that one does not have any recollection of who one was, one ceases to be that person. The criteria for identity are all "inner" with nothing "outer." To ameliorate this, Leibniz argued that individuals who lack memory of their past can be provided with "a middle bond of consciousness" through the testimony of others.[8] This testimony functions to fill in the gaps and so provides the continuity required for personal identity and accountability. If these amnesiacs could take on those characteristics ascribed to them by others they would have the "same consciousness."

On the other hand, it has been argued that Locke's account is too broad because it allows a person to be held accountable for actions for which the person holds a memory, but which the person did not actually perform.[9] The injustice of this is easily apparent, and borne out by the well-documented experience of children who, in their immature understanding, mistakenly believe themselves to be responsible for their parents' unhappiness. Locke's unconvincing response to the possibility of being held accountable for what one has not done is to appeal to the goodness of God to prevent it.[10]

The full implications of Locke's empiricist approach to personal identity are borne out by David Hume's "bundle theory" of self, which puts to rest (at least temporarily), the idea that "self" is some kind of substance.

Notes

1   Gilbert Ryle points out that the approaches we call "empiricism" and "rationalism" were not mentioned as such until the nineteenth century. See the introduction to I. C. Tipton, *Locke On Human Understanding: Selected Essays* (Oxford: Oxford University Press, 1977).

2   D. J. O'Connor, *John Locke* (London: Penguin, 1952), p. 19.

3   See Raymond Martin, "Locke's Psychology of Personal Identity," *Journal of the History of Philosophy*, 38 (1), 2000, pp. 41–61; also Marya Schechtman, *The Constitution of Selves* (Ithaca, NY: Cornell University Press, 1996), p. 17.

4   Henry Allison, "Locke's Theory of Personal Identity," in I. C. Tipton (ed.), *Locke on Human Understanding* (Oxford: Oxford University Press, 1977), p. 108.

5   John Locke, *An Essay Concerning Human Understanding*, II, ed. Raymond Wilburn, Chapter XXVII (London: Dent and Sons, 1948), p. 9.

6   J. Butler, cited in J. L. Mackie, *Problems From Locke* (Oxford: Clarendon Press, 1976), p. 187.

7   Reid, cited in Allison (1977), p. 113.

8   Leibniz, *New Essays Concerning Human Understanding*, trans. A. G. Langley, 3rd edn (LaSalle, IL: Open Court Press, 1949), p. 246, cited in Allison (1977), p. 117.

9   Antony Flew, "Locke and the Problem of Personal Identity," *Philosophy* 26, 1951, pp. 53–68.

10   Locke (1948), Chapter XXVII, p. 22.

Main Texts by Locke

Peter H. Nidditch (ed. and foreword), *An Essay Concerning Human Understanding* (Oxford: Clarendon Press, 1979).

Peter Gay (ed. and notes), *John Locke on Education* (New York: Bureau of Publications, Teachers College, Columbia University, 1964).

John Harrison and Peter Laslett (eds.), *The Library of John Locke* (Oxford: The Oxford Bibliographical Society, Oxford University Press, 1965).

Mark Goldie (ed.), *Locke: Political Essays* (Cambridge, UK and New York: Cambridge University Press, 1997).

The Works of John Locke (Darmstadt, Germany: Scientia Verlag, 1963).

Further Reading

Ayers, Michael, *Locke: Epistemology and Ontology*, 2 vols (London: Routledge, 1991).

Chappell, Vere (ed.), *The Cambridge Companion to Locke* (Cambridge, UK: Cambridge University Press, 1994).

Cranston, Maurice, *John Locke, A Biography* (Oxford: Oxford University Press, 1985).

Lowe, E. J., *Locke on Human Understanding* (London: Routledge, 1995).

Mackie, J. L., *Problems from Locke* (Oxford: Clarendon Press, 1976).

Tipton, I. C. (ed.), *Locke on Human Understanding: Selected Essays* (Oxford: Oxford University Press, 1977).

Yolton, John, *John Locke and the Way of Ideas* (Oxford: Oxford University Press, 1956).

Yolton, John, *John Locke and the Compass of Human Understanding* (Cambridge, UK: Cambridge University Press, 1970).

"OF IDENTITY AND DIVERSITY"

John Locke

1.   ANOTHER occasion the mind often takes of comparing, is the very being of things, when, considering anything as existing at any determined time and place, we compare it with itself existing at another time, and thereon from the ideas of *identity* and *diversity*. When we see anything to be in any place in any instant of time, we are sure (be it what it will) that it is that very thing, and not another which at that same time exists in another place, how like and undistinguishable soever it may be in all other respects: and in this consists *identity*, when the ideas it is attributed to vary not at all from what they were that moment wherein we consider their former existence, and to which we compare the present. For we never finding, nor conceiving it possible, that two things of the same kind should exist in the same place at the same time, we rightly conclude, that, whatever exists anywhere at any time, excludes all of the same kind, and is there itself alone. When therefore we demand whether anything be the same or no, it refers always to something that existed such a time in such a place, which it was certain, at that instant, was the same with itself, and no other. From whence it follows, that one thing cannot have two beginnings of existence, nor two things one beginning; it being impossible for two things of the same kind to be or exist in the same instant, in the very same place; or one and the same thing in different places. That, therefore, that had one beginning, is the same thing; and that which had a different beginning in time and place from that, is not the same, but diverse. That which has made the difficulty about

From *An Essay Concerning Human Understanding*, abridged and edited by Raymond Wilburn (London: J. M. Dent & Sons, 1947), pp. 162–74.

this relation has been the little care and attention used in having precise notions of the things to which it is attributed.

2.   We have the ideas but of three sorts of substances: (1) *God.* (2) *Finite intelligences.* (3) *Bodies.*

First, *God* is without beginning, eternal, unalterable, and everywhere, and therefore concerning his identity there can be no doubt.

Secondly, *Finite spirits* having had each its determinate time and place of beginning to exist, the relation to that time and place will always determine to each of them its identity, as long as it exists.

Thirdly, The same will hold of every *particle of matter*, to which no addition or subtraction of matter being made, it is the same. For, though these three sorts of substances, as we term them, do not exclude one another out of the same place, yet we cannot conceive but that they must necessarily each of them exclude any of the same kind out of the same place: or else the notions and names of identity and diversity would be in vain, and there could be no such distinctions of substances, or anything else one from another. For example: could two bodies be in the same place at the same time; then those two parcels of matter must be one and the same, take them great or little.

All other things being but modes or relations ultimately terminated in substances, the identity and diversity of each particular existence of them too will be by the same way determined: only as to things whose existence is in succession, such as are the actions of finite beings, v.g. *motion* and *thought*, both which consist in a continued train of succession, concerning their diversity there can be no question: because each perishing the moment it begins, they cannot exist in different times, or in different places, as permanent beings can at different times exist in distant places; and therefore no motion or thought, considered as at different times, can be the same, each part thereof having a different beginning of existence.

3.   From what has been said, it is easy to discover what is so much inquired after, the *principium individuationis*; and that, it is plain, is existence itself; which determines a being of any sort to a particular time and place, incommunicable to two beings of the same kind. This, though it seems easier to conceive in simple substances or modes; yet, when reflected on, is not more difficult in compound ones, if care be taken to what it is applied: v.g. let us suppose an atom, i.e. a continued body under one immutable superficies, existing in a determined time and place; it is evident, that, considered in any instant of its existence, it is in that instant the same with itself. For, being at that instant what it is, and nothing else, it is the same, and so must continue as long as its existence is continued; for so long it will be the same, and no other. In like manner, if two or more atoms be joined together into the same mass, every one of those atoms will be the same, by the foregoing rule: and whilst they exist united together, the mass, consisting of the same atoms, must be the same mass, or the same body, let the parts be ever so differently jumbled. But if one of these atoms be taken away, or one new one added, it is no longer the same mass or the same body. In the state of living creatures, their identity depends not on a mass of the same particles, but on something else. For in them the variation of great parcels of matter alters not the identity: an oak growing from a plant to a great tree, and then lopped, is still the same oak; and a colt grown up to a horse, sometimes fat, sometimes lean, is all the while the same horse: though, in both these cases, there may be a manifest change of the parts; so that truly they are not

either of them the same masses of matter, though they be truly one of them the same oak, and the other the same horse. The reason whereof is, that, in these two cases – a *mass of matter* and a *living body* – identity is not applied to the same thing.

4, 5.   We must therefore consider wherein an oak differs from a mass of matter, and that seems to me to be in this, that the one is only the cohesion of particles of matter any how united, the other such a disposition of them as constitutes the parts of an oak; and such an organization of those parts as is fit to receive and distribute nourishment, so as to continue and frame the wood, bark, and leaves, etc., of an oak, in which consists the vegetable life. For this organization, being at any one instant in any one collection of matter, is in that particular concrete distinguished from all other, and *is* that individual life. The case is not so much different in *brutes* but that any one may hence see what makes an animal and continues it the same.

6.   This also shows wherein the identity of the same *man* consists; viz. in nothing but a participation of the same continued life, by constantly fleeting particles of matter, in succession vitally united to the same organized body. He that shall place the identity of man in anything else but, like that of other animals, in one fitly organized body, taken in any one instant, and from thence continued, under one organization of life, in several successively fleeting particles of matter united to it, will find it hard to make an embryo, one of years, mad and sober, the *same* man, by any supposition that will not make it possible for Seth, Ismael, Socrates, Pilate, St. Austin, and Caesar Borgia, to be the same man. For if the identity of *soul alone* makes the same *man*; and there be nothing in the nature of matter why the same individual spirit may not be united to different bodies, it will be possible that those men, living in distant ages, and of different tempers, may have been the same man: which way of speaking must be from a very strange use of the word man, applied to an idea out of which body and shape are excluded.

7, 8.   It is not therefore unity of substance that comprehends all sorts of identity, or will determine it in every case; but to conceive and judge of it aright, we must consider what idea the word it is applied to stands for: it being one thing to be the same *substance*, another the same *man*, and a third the same *person*, if *person, man*, and *substance* are three names standing for three different ideas – for such as is the idea belonging to that name, such must be the identity. For I presume it is not the idea of a thinking or rational being alone that makes the *idea of a man* in most people's sense: but of a body, so and so shaped, joined to it; and if that be the idea of a man, the same successive body not shifted all at once must, as well as the same immaterial spirit, go to the making of the same man.

9.   To find wherein personal identity consists, we must consider what *person* stands for; which, I think, is a thinking intelligent being, that has reason and reflection, and can consider itself as itself, the same thinking thing, in different times and places; which it does only by that *consciousness* which is inseparable from thinking, and, as it seems to me, essential to it: it being impossible for any one to perceive without *perceiving* that he does perceive. When we see, hear, smell, taste, feel, meditate, or will anything, we know that we do so. Thus it is always as to our present sensations and perceptions: and by this every one is to himself that which he calls *self*.

10.   But it is further inquired, whether it be the same identical substance. That which seems to make the difficulty is this, that *consciousness* being interrupted always by forgetfulness, there being no moment of our lives wherein we have the whole train of all

our past actions before our eyes in one view, but even the best memories losing the sight of one part whilst they are viewing another; and we sometimes, and that the greatest part of our lives, not reflecting on our past selves, being intent on our present thoughts, and in sound sleep having no thoughts at all, or at least none with that consciousness which remarks our waking thoughts – I say, in all these cases, our *consciousness* being interrupted, and we losing the sight of our past selves, doubts are raised whether we are the same thinking thing, i.e. the same *substance*, or no. Which, however reasonable or unreasonable, concerns not *personal* identity at all: the question being what makes the same person; and not whether it be the same identical substance, which always thinks in the same person, which, in this case, matters not at all: different substances, by the same consciousness (where they do partake in it) being united into one person, as well as different bodies by the same life are united into one animal, whose identity is preserved in that change of substances by the unity of one continued life. For, it being the same consciousness that makes a man be himself to himself, personal identity depends on that only, whether it be annexed solely to one individual substance, or can be continued in a succession of several substances.

11.   That this is so, we have some kind of evidence in our very bodies, all whose particles, whilst vitally united to this same thinking conscious self, so that *we feel* when they are touched; and are affected by, and conscious of, good or harm that happens to them, are a part of ourselves; i.e. of our thinking conscious self. Thus, the limbs of his body are to every one a part of himself; he sympathizes and is concerned for them. Cut off a hand, and thereby separate it from that consciousness he had of its heat, cold, and other affections, and it is then no longer a part of that which is himself, any more than the remotest part of matter. Thus, we see the *substance* whereof personal self consisted at one time may be varied at another, without the change of personal identity; there being no question about the same person, though the limbs, which but now were a part of it, be cut off.

12.   But the question is, Whether, if the same substance which thinks be changed, it can be the same person; or, remaining the same, it can be different persons.

And to this I answer: First, This can be no question at all to those who place thought in a purely material animal constitution, void of an immaterial substance. For, whether their supposition be true or no, it is plain they conceive personal identity preserved in something else than identity of substance; as animal identity is preserved in identity of life, and not of substance. And therefore those who place thinking in an immaterial substance only, before they can come to deal with these men, must show why personal identity cannot be preserved in the change of immaterial substances, or variety of particular immaterial substances, as well as animal identity is preserved in the change of material substances, or variety of particular bodies: unless they will say, it is one immaterial spirit that makes the same life in brutes, as it is one immaterial spirit that makes the same person in men; which the Cartesians at least will not admit, for fear of making brutes thinking things too.

13.   But next, as to the first part of the question, whether, if the same thinking substance (supposing immaterial substances only to think) be changed, it can be the same person. I answer: That cannot be resolved but by those who know what kind of substances they are that do think; and whether the consciousness of past actions can be transferred from one thinking substance to another. I grant, were the same

consciousness the same individual action, it could not: but it being a present representation of a past action, why it may not be possible that that may be represented to the
mind to have been which really never was, will remain to be shown. And therefore
how far the consciousness of past actions is annexed to any individual agent, so that
another cannot possibly have it, will be hard for us to determine, till we know what
kind of action it is that cannot be done without a reflex act of perception accompa-
nying it, and how performed by thinking substances, who cannot think without being
conscious of it. But that which we call the same consciousness, not being the same
individual act, why one intellectual substance may not have represented to it, as done
by itself, what *it* never did, and was perhaps done by some other agent – why, I say,
such a representation may not possibly be without reality of matter of fact, as well as
several representations in dreams are, which yet whilst dreaming we take for true – will
be difficult to conclude from the nature of things. And that it never is so, will by us,
till we have clearer views of the nature of thinking substances, be best resolved into the
goodness of God; who, as far as the happiness or misery of any of his sensible creatures
is concerned in it, will not, by a fatal error of theirs, transfer from one to another that
consciousness which draws reward or punishment with it. How far this may be an argument against those who would place thinking in a system of fleeting animal spirits, I
leave to be considered. But yet, to return to the question before us, it must be allowed,
that, if the same consciousness (which, as has been shown, is quite a different thing from
the same numerical figure or motion in body) can be transferred from one thinking
substance to another, it will be possible that two thinking substances may make but one
person. For the same consciousness being preserved, whether in the same or different
substances, the personal identity is preserved.

    14.   As to the second part of the question, whether, the same immaterial substance
remaining, there may be two distinct persons; which question seems to me to be built
on this: whether the same immaterial being, being conscious of the action of its past
duration, may be wholly stripped of all the consciousness of its past existence, and lose
it beyond the power of ever retrieving it again; and so as it were beginning a new
account from a new period, have a consciousness that *cannot* reach beyond this new
state. All those who hold pre-existence are evidently of this mind; since they allow the
soul to have no remaining consciousness of what it did in that pre–existent state, either
wholly separate from body, or informing any other body; and if they should not, it is
plain experience would be against them. So that, personal identity reaching no further
than consciousness reaches, a pre–existent spirit not having continued so many ages in
a state of silence, must needs make different persons. I once met with one who was
persuaded his had been the *soul* of Socrates (how reasonably I will not dispute; this I
know, that in the post he filled, which was no inconsiderable one, he passed for a very
rational man, and the press has shown that he wanted not parts or learning); would any
one say, that he, being not conscious of any of Socrates' actions or thoughts, could be
the same *person* with Socrates? Let any one reflect upon himself, and conclude that he
has in himself an immaterial spirit, which is that which thinks in him, and in the constant change of his body keeps him the same, and is that which he calls *himself*: let him
also suppose it to be the same soul that was in Nestor or Thersites, at the siege of Troy
(for souls being, as far as we know anything of them, in their nature indifferent to any
parcel of matter, the supposition has no apparent absurdity in it), which it may have

been, as well as it is now the soul of any other man: but he now having no consciousness of any of the actions either of Nestor or Thersites, does or can he conceive himself the same person with either of them? Can he be concerned in either of their actions? attribute them to himself, or think them his own, more than the actions of any other men that ever existed? So that, this consciousness not reaching to any of the actions of either of those men, he is no more one *self* with either of them than if the soul or immaterial spirit that now informs him had been created, and began to exist, when it began to inform his present body; though it were never so true, that the same *spirit* that informed Nestor's or Thersites' body were numerically the same that now informs his. For this would no more make him the same person with Nestor, than if some of the particles of matter that were once a part of Nestor were now a part of this man; the same immaterial substance, without the same consciousness, no more making the same person, by being united to any body, than the same particle of matter, without consciousness, united to any body, makes the same person. But let him once find himself conscious of any of the actions of Nestor, he then finds himself the same person with Nestor.

15. And thus may we be able, without any difficulty, to conceive the same person at the resurrection, though in a body not exactly in make or parts the same which he had here – the same consciousness going along with the soul that inhabits it. But yet the soul alone, in the change of bodies, would scarce to any one but to him that makes the soul the man, be enough to make the same man. For should the soul of a prince, carrying with it the consciousness of the prince's past life, enter and inform the body of a cobbler, as soon as deserted by his own soul, every one sees he would be the same *person* with the prince, accountable only for the prince's actions: but who would say it was the same *man*?

16. But though the same immaterial substance or soul does not alone, wherever it be, in whatsoever state, make the same *man*; yet it is plain, consciousness, as far as ever it can be extended – should it be to ages past – unites existences and actions very remote in time into the same *person*, as well as it does the existences and actions of the immediately preceding moment: so that whatever has the consciousness of present and past actions, is the same person to whom they both belong. Had I the same consciousness that I saw the ark and Noah's flood, as that I saw an overflowing of the Thames last winter, or as that I write now, I could no more doubt that I who write this now, that saw the Thames overflowed last winter, and that viewed the flood at the general deluge, was the same *self* – place that self in what *substance* you please – than that I who write this am the same *myself* now whilst I write (whether I consist of all the same substance, material or immaterial, or no) that I was yesterday. For as to this point of being the same self, it matters not whether this present self be made up of the same or other substances – I being as much concerned and as justly accountable for any action that was done a thousand years since, appropriated to me now by this self-consciousness, as I am for what I did the last moment.

17. *Self* is that conscious thinking thing – whatever substance made up of (whether spiritual or material, simple or compounded, it matters not) – which is sensible or conscious of pleasure and pain, capable of happiness or misery, and so is concerned for itself, as far as that consciousness extends. Thus every one finds that, whilst comprehended under that consciousness, the little finger is as much a part of himself as what

is most so. Upon separation of this little finger, should this consciousness go along with the little finger, and leave the rest of the body, it is evident the little finger would be the person, the same person; and self then would have nothing to do with the rest of the body. As in this case it is the consciousness that goes along with the substance, when one part is separate from another, which makes the same person, and constitutes this inseparable self: so it is in reference to substances remote in time. That with which the consciousness of this present thinking thing *can* join itself, makes the same person, and is one self with it, and with nothing else; and so attributes to itself and owns all the actions of that thing as its own, as far as that consciousness reaches, and no further; as every one who reflects will perceive.

18.   In this personal identity is founded all the right and justice of reward and punishment; happiness and misery being that for which every one is concerned for *himself*, and not mattering what becomes of any *substance*, not joined to, or affected with, that consciousness. For, as it is evident in the instance I gave but now, if the consciousness went along with the little finger when it was cut off, that would be the same self which was concerned for the whole body yesterday, as making part of itself, whose actions then it cannot but admit as its own now. Though, if the same body should still live, and immediately from the separation of the little finger have its own peculiar consciousness, whereof the little finger knew nothing, it would not at all be concerned for it, as a part of itself, or could own any of its actions, or have any of them imputed to him.

19.   This may show us wherein personal identity consists: not in the identity of substance, but, as I have said, in the identity of consciousness, wherein if Socrates and the present mayor of Queenborough agree, they are the same person: if the same Socrates waking and sleeping do not partake of the same consciousness, Socrates waking and sleeping is not the same person. And to punish Socrates waking for what sleeping Socrates thought, and waking Socrates was never conscious of, would be no more of right, than to punish one twin for what his brother-twin did, whereof he knew nothing, because their outsides were so like, that they could not be distinguished; for such twins have been seen.

20.   But yet possibly it will still be objected: Suppose I wholly lose the memory of some parts of my life, beyond a possibility of retrieving them, so that perhaps I shall never be conscious of them again; yet am I not the same person that did those actions, had those thoughts that I once was conscious of, though I have now forgot them. To which I answer, that we must here take notice what the word *I* is applied to: which, in this case, is the *man* only. And the same man being presumed to be the same person, I is easily here supposed to stand also for the same person. But if it be possible for the same man to have distinct incommunicable consciousness at different times, it is past doubt the same man would at different times make different persons; which, we see, is the sense of mankind in the solemnest declaration of their opinions, human laws not punishing the mad man for the sober man's actions, nor the sober man for what the mad man did – thereby making them two persons: which is somewhat explained by our way of speaking in English when we say such an one is 'not himself,' or is 'beside himself'; in which phrases it is insinuated, as if those who now, or at least first used them, thought that self was changed; the self-same person was no longer in that man.

21. But yet it is hard to conceive that Socrates, the same individual man, should be two persons. To help us a little in this, we must consider what is meant by Socrates, or the same individual *man*.

First, it must be either the same individual, immaterial, thinking substance; in short, the same numerical soul, and nothing else.

Secondly, or the same animal, without any regard to an immaterial soul.

Thirdly, or the same immaterial spirit united to the same animal.

Now, take which of these suppositions you please, it is impossible to make personal identity to consist in anything but consciousness; or reach any further than that does.

For, by the first of them, it must be allowed possible that a man born of different women, and in distant times, may be the same man. A way of speaking which, whoever admits, must allow it possible for the same man to be two distinct persons, as any two that have lived in different ages without the knowledge of one another's thoughts.

By the second and third, Socrates, in this life and after it, cannot be the same man any way but by the same consciousness; and so making human identity to consist in the same thing wherein we place personal identity, there will be no difficulty to allow the same man to be the same person. But then they who place human identity in consciousness only, and not in something else, must consider how they will make the infant Socrates the same man with Socrates after the resurrection. But whatsoever to some men makes a man, and consequently the same individual man, wherein perhaps few are agreed, personal identity can by us be placed in nothing but consciousness (which is that alone which makes what we call *self*), without involving us in great absurdities.

22. But is not a man drunk and sober the same person? why else is he punished for the fact he commits when drunk, though he be never afterwards conscious of it? Just as much the same person as a man that walks and does other things in his sleep, is the same person, and is answerable for any mischief he shall do in it. Human laws punish both, with a justice suitable to *their* way of knowledge; because, in these cases, they cannot distinguish certainly what is real, what counterfeit: and so the ignorance in drunkenness or sleep is not admitted as a plea. For, though punishment be annexed to personality, and personality to consciousness, and the drunkard perhaps be not conscious of what he did, yet human judicatures justly punish him; because the fact is proved against him, but want of consciousness cannot be proved for him. But in the Great Day, wherein the secrets of all hearts shall be laid open, it may be reasonable to think, no one shall be made to answer for what he knows nothing of; but shall receive his doom, his conscience accusing or excusing him.

23. Nothing but consciousness can unite remote existences into the same person: the identity of substance will not do it; for whatever substance there is, however framed, without consciousness there is no person: and a carcass may be a person, as well as any sort of substance be so, without consciousness.

Could we suppose two distinct incommunicable consciousnesses acting the same body, the one constantly by day, the other by night; and, on the other side, the same consciousness, acting by intervals, two distinct bodies: I ask, in the first case, whether the day and the night man would not be two as distinct persons as Socrates and Plato? And whether, in the second case, there would not be one person in two distinct bodies, as much as one man is the same in two distinct clothings? Nor is it at all material to say, that this same and this distinct consciousness, in the cases above mentioned, is owing to the same and distinct immaterial substances, bringing it with them to those bodies; which, whether true or no, alters not the case: since it is evident the personal identity would equally be determined by the consciousness, whether that consciousness were annexed to some individual immaterial substance or no. For, granting that the thinking substance in man must be necessarily supposed immaterial, it is evident that immaterial thinking thing may sometimes part with its past consciousness, and be restored to it again: as appears in the forgetfulness men often have of their past actions; and the mind many times recovers the memory of a past consciousness, which it had lost for twenty years together. Make these intervals of memory and forgetfulness to take their turns regularly by day and night, and you have two persons with the same immaterial spirit, as much as in the former instance two persons with the same body. So that self is not determined by identity or diversity of substance, which it cannot be sure of, but only by identity of consciousness.

24, 25.   Indeed it may conceive the substance whereof it is now made up to have existed formerly, united in the same conscious being: but, consciousness removed, that substance is no more itself, or makes no more a part of it, than any other substance. For, whatsoever any substance has thought or done, which I cannot recollect, and by my consciousness make my own thought and action, it will no more belong to me, whether a part of me thought or did it, than if it had been thought or done by any other immaterial being anywhere existing. I agree, the more probable opinion is, that this consciousness is annexed to, and the affection of, one individual immaterial substance. Any substance vitally united to the present thinking being is a part of that very same self which now is; anything united to it by a consciousness of former actions, makes also a part of the same self, which is the same both then and now.

26.   *Person*, as I take it, is the name for this self. Wherever a man finds what he calls himself, there, I think, another may say is the same person. It is a forensic term, appropriating actions and their merit; and so belongs only to intelligent agents, capable of a law, and happiness, and misery. This personality extends itself beyond present existence to what is past, only by consciousness; whereby it becomes concerned and accountable; owns and imputes to itself past actions, just upon the same ground and for the same reason as it does the present. All which is founded in a concern for happiness, the unavoidable concomitant of consciousness; that which is conscious of pleasure and pain, desiring that that self that is conscious should be happy. And therefore whatever past actions it cannot reconcile or *appropriate* to that present self by consciousness, it can be no more concerned in than if they had never been done: and to receive pleasure or pain, i.e. reward or punishment, on the account of any such action, is all one as to be made happy or miserable in its first being, without any demerit at all.

3

COMMENTARY ON HUME

Writing some 50 years after Locke, and greatly influenced by him, the Scottish philosopher David Hume (1711–56) is best known as an empiricist. However, only a few of his writings concern epistemology; much of his work concerns moral and political philosophy. Hume was also quite a famed historian during his lifetime. He wrote the *History of England*, which became a standard and went through a staggering 167 posthumous editions.[1] An atheist, Hume was renowned for his formidable attacks on religious beliefs, and is a rare find in a tradition steeped in theological concepts.

Hume addresses himself to the question of the self by refuting Descartes's claim to have discovered through introspection that the "I" is an immaterial, intelligent substance. Hume's method of attack is to pull apart the idea that the self is a kind of substrate underlying our ideas and emotions in order to show that we do not experience such a self, and therefore cannot have knowledge of it. Despite his powerful refutation of a metaphysical self, Hume despaired of what to make of subjectivity or personal identity, declaring "I must confess, I neither know how to correct my former opinions, nor how to render them consistent."[2] Despite the shortcomings of Hume's arguments, his naturalistic approach to psychology continues to be influential in moral philosophy and psychology, especially in the study of artificial intelligence.

Hume adopts Locke's empiricist premise that all knowledge must be founded in some sense perception. He cites as *prima facie* evidence the case that wherever one lacks a perception, one lacks knowledge of its object, for example, a deaf person has no knowledge of sound and a blind person has no knowledge of color. According to Hume, the mind receives sense-impressions from the outside world that, through the agency of imagination, are linked together according to innate principles of association. The systematicity of these associations gives our experiences a regularity that we mistakenly attribute to the external world. The mind habitually associates perceptions on the basis of:

1   Resemblance: perceptions that are like each other;
2   Spatiotemporal contiguity: perceptions that are close together in time or space;
3   Cause and effect: perceptions that tend to follow after each other.

Like other empiricists, Hume takes the view that what I have immediate awareness of is the content of my consciousness and not things as they exist in-themselves independent of the mind. This means that my awareness is directed by the principles of association of the mind. To illustrate, imagine that I see a car run into another car and hear a loud noise. Because the mind tends to associate impressions that are perceived close in succession, my mind will make a strong association between the collision and the loud noise such that I will have the idea that the collision caused the noise. While it is quite reasonable to infer that the collision caused the loud noise (indeed, for Hume, we could not but infer it), the continuity in my thought that links the crash and the noise is no guarantee of the continuity of events in the world independent of my ideas of it. For all I know, that loud noise could be coming from some other object I cannot perceive. The potential mismatch between the nature of the objects of consciousness and the nature of the world as it exists in-itself has earned Hume the title of skeptic.

For Hume, the only basis for knowledge of any thing, including a thinking thing, can be an impression and perception of it. So, if we are to claim knowledge of the self in the manner of Descartes, we should find an impression of it on introspection. However, Hume points out, this never occurs: "I never catch *myself* at any time without a perception, and never can observe anything but the perception."[3] Hume says that all one can ever find in one's mind is a series of constantly changing perceptions of other things, related together in different ways. He argues that if I could empty my mind of all those perceptions of outer objects there would be nothing left, and this demonstrates that we do not have any idea, nor knowledge, of an inner entity, "the self."

Our error in positing an entity "the self" consists in mistaking the connectedness of consciousness (relation) for the existence of a soul (identity): "our propension to confound identity with relation is so great that we are apt to imagine something unknown and mysterious."[4] This propension to confound diversity with identity has its roots in the imagination. Hume regards imagination as a power of making images, and ideas are types of images.[5] Imagination unites the diversity of sense-perceptions to such a high degree that we experience identity: "The relation facilitates the transition of the mind from one object to another, and renders the passage as smooth as if it contemplated one continued object."[6] The seamless transition from perception to perception leads us to mistake the (synthetic) identity of the object in consciousness for the identity of a substance, when in reality consciousness is more like "a kind of theatre, where several perceptions successively make their appearance; pass, repass, glide away, and mingle in an infinite variety of postures and situations."[7]

Another way to describe the error in our thinking about the soul is to say that it arises from the unity of consciousness. It is the unity and continuity in one's perceptions that creates the idea of an enduring substrate underlying those perceptions and holding them together. The principle that unites consciousness is simply the fact that they occur in a single sense-perceiving individual, that is, a single mind, the order and unity of which is effected through the mind's habits of association. This has led commentators to describe Hume's account as the "bundle theory of self": the word "I" has no referent other than the bundle of perceptions that comprise a single mind. For Hume, it does not make any sense to claim that there is a substantial self that remains unchanged during our lives. In that sense, our identities can change as easily as our perceptions (which, after all, may not be so easy when you consider the power of habit).

Hume's target is the "substrate view," a view that was in standard use during his time and which proposed to explain the simplicity and unity of substances, and their identity.[8] On the substrate view, the problem of how a thing can remain the *same* thing despite having different properties at different times, is resolved by making a distinction between properties (*accidens*) and an enduring substrate in which the properties are said to inhere (*substantia*). The same argument is then made in relation to the self: one remains the same thinking thing despite changes in one's perceptions, ideas, and emotions because these are merely properties distinct from the underlying enduring substance. Against this view, Hume argues that we do not have a perception of substance; all our perceptions are of *properties*: sound, color, shape, texture, and so on: "We have therefore, no idea of substance, distinct from that of a collection of particular qualities, nor have we any other meaning when we talk or reason concerning it."[9] In other words, there is no justification for supposing a substrate in relation to either objects or the self.

However, Hume's approach is not entirely consistent. His representational account of knowledge claims that all of our ideas are representations (that is, mental states) which resemble their outer objects. In order to argue successfully that there is no self because we cannot perceive it on introspection, Hume has to apply his representational theory to introspection as well as to sense perception. Recall that for Hume, what we have awareness of are the contents of consciousness. If we applied Hume's theory to introspection, that is, if we employ the representational theory self-reflexively, then we would have to say that awareness of one's own mental states is an awareness of states that represent and resemble other mental states. But this would end up in a vicious regress: *any* mental state would imply another mental state, and so on ad infinitum. If Hume does not consider his representational theory to apply generally to introspection (which seems to be the case), then it does not seem legitimate that he should insist it be applied to the special case of the supposed experience of one's substrate self in introspection.[10]

Hume's account is on surer footing when he takes up the familiar objection of how the soul can exist as a thinking thing when there is no thinking going on, for example, during sleep. Since thinking is the very essence of the thinking thing, if such a thing failed to think it should fail to exist. If it did not cease to exist when it was not thinking we should be obliged to claim that something exists that has no properties.[11] Hume thought that this was a nonsensical idea, and that the identity claims of substrate theory consequently fall down: one cannot be a single substrate-subject during one's life if there are periods when that subject does not exist. Since there are experiencing, self-aware people who are considered to be the single subjects of their entire lives, the everyday sense of "self" cannot mean "selves" in the substrate sense. Hume concludes that the self is merely a fiction that we construct from the illusion of identity in consciousness generated by the imagination.

While Hume's theory labors under the threat of a regress, his psychological view of self, tied to the unity of consciousness, had a huge influence on Kant, who described Hume's work as rousing him from his "dogmatic slumbers." Hume's acute analysis of rationalism forced a serious change of approach to questions of the self, seen in Kant's account of "I" as apperceptive, that is, as a purely formal feature of the unity of consciousness.

Notes

1   Donald Livingstone, "Introduction," in D. Livingstone and M. Martin (eds.), *Hume as Philosopher of Society, Politics and History* (Rochester, NY: University of Rochester Press, 1991).
2   David Hume, *A Treatise of Human Nature*, Book One, ed. D. G. C. Macnabb (London: Fontana/Collins, 1962), p. 328. Hereafter *THN*.
3   *THN*, pp. 301–2.
4   *THN*, p. 304.
5   See Mary Warnock, *Imagination* (London and Boston: Faber and Faber, 1976), p. 15.
6   *THN*, p. 303.
7   *THN*, p. 302.
8   John Bricke, *Hume's Philosophy of Mind* (Princeton, NJ: Princeton University Press, 1980), p. 60.
9   *THN*, p. 60.
10   Bricke (1980), p. 64.
11   Ibid, p. 65.

Main Texts by Hume

L. A. Selby-Bigge (ed.), *Enquiry Concerning Human Understanding*, in *Enquiries Concerning Human Understanding and Concerning the Principles of Morals*, 3rd edn revised by P. H. Nidditch (Oxford: Clarendon Press, 1975).
History of England, 6 vols., foreword by W. B. Todd (Indianapolis: Liberty Fund, 1983).
H. D. Aiken (ed.), *Hume's Moral and Political Philosophy* (New York: Hafner/Macmillan, 1948).
J. Y. T. Greig (ed.), *The Letters of David Hume*, 2 vols (Oxford: Clarendon Press, 1932).
L. A. Selby-Bigge (ed.), *A Treatise of Human Nature*, 2nd edn revised by P. H. Nidditch (Oxford: Clarendon Press, 1975).

Further Reading

Baier, Annette C., *A Progress of Sentiments: Reflections on Hume's Treatise* (Cambridge, MA: Harvard University Press, 1991).
Bricke, John, *Hume's Philosophy of Mind* (Princeton, NJ: Princeton University Press, 1980).
Capaldi, Nicholas, *Hume's Place in Moral Philosophy* (New York: Peter Lang, 1989).
Hall, Roland, *Fifty Years of Hume Scholarship: A Bibliographical Guide* (Edinburgh: Edinburgh University Press, 1978).
Norton, David Fate (ed.), *The Cambridge Companion to Hume* (Cambridge, UK: Cambridge University Press, 1993).
Owen, David, *Hume's Reason* (Oxford: Oxford University Press, 2000).
Pears, David, *Hume's System* (Oxford: Oxford University Press, 1990).
Penelhum, Terence, *Hume* (London: Macmillan, 1975).
Stroud, Barry, *Hume* (London: Routledge and Kegan Paul, 1977).

"OF PERSONAL IDENTITY"

David Hume

There are some philosophers who imagine we are every moment intimately conscious of what we call our *self*, that we feel its existence and its continuance in existence; and are certain, beyond the evidence of a demonstration, both of its perfect identity and simplicity. The strongest sensation, the most violent passion, say they, instead of distracting us from this view, only fix it the more intensely and make us consider their influence on *self* either by their pain or pleasure. To attempt a further proof of this were to weaken its evidence; since no proof can be derived from any fact of which we are so intimately conscious; nor is there anything of which we can be certain if we doubt of this.

Unluckily all these positive assertions are contrary to that very experience which is pleaded for them; nor have we any idea of *self*, after the manner it is here explained. For from what impression could this idea be derived? This question it is impossible to answer without a manifest contradiction and absurdity; and yet it is a question which must necessarily be answered, if we would have the idea of self pass for clear and intelligible. It must be some one impression that gives rise to every real idea. But self or person is not any one impression, but that to which our several impressions and ideas are supposed to have a reference. If any impression gives rise to the idea of self, that impression must continue invariably the same, through the whole course of our lives; since self is supposed to exist after that manner. But there is no impression constant and invariable. Pain and pleasure, grief and joy, passions and sensations succeed each other, and never all exist at the same time. It cannot therefore be from any of these impressions, or from any other, that the idea of self is derived; and consequently there is no such idea.

But further, what must become of all our particular perceptions upon this hypothesis? All these are different, and distinguishable, and separable from each other, and may be separately considered, and may exist separately, and have no need of anything to

From *A Treatise of Human Nature: Being an Attempt to Introduce the Experimental Method of Reasoning into Moral Subjects*, edited with an introduction by D. G. C. Macnabb (Glasgow: Fontana Collins, 1970), pp. 300–12. Reprinted by permission of HarperCollins Publishers Ltd.

support their existence. After what manner therefore do they belong to self, and how are they connected with it? For my part, when I enter most intimately into what I call *myself*, I always stumble on some particular perception or other, of heat or cold, light or shade, love or hatred, pain or pleasure. I never can catch *myself* at any time without a perception, and never can observe anything but the perception. When my perceptions are removed for any time, as by sound sleep, so long am I insensible of *myself*, and may truly be said not to exist. And were all my perceptions removed by death, and could I neither think, nor feel, nor see, nor love, nor hate, after the dissolution of my body, I should be entirely annihilated, nor do I conceive what is further requisite to make me a perfect nonentity. If any one, upon serious and unprejudiced reflection, thinks he has a different notion of *himself*, I must confess I can reason no longer with him. All I can allow him is, that he may be in the right as well as I, and that we are essentially different in this particular. He may, perhaps, perceive something simple and continued, which he calls *himself*, though I am certain there is no such principle in me.

But setting aside some metaphysicians of this kind, I may venture to affirm of the rest of mankind, that they are nothing but a bundle or collection of different perceptions, which succeed each other with an inconceivable rapidity, and are in a perpetual flux and movement. Our eyes cannot turn in their sockets without varying our perceptions. Our thought is still more variable than our sight; and all our other senses and faculties contribute to this change; nor is there any single power of the soul, which remains unalterably the same, perhaps for one moment. The mind is a kind of theatre, where several perceptions successively make their appearance; pass, repass, glide away, and mingle in an infinite variety of postures and situations. There is properly no *simplicity* in it at one time, nor *identity* in different, whatever natural propension we may have to imagine that simplicity and identity. The comparison of the theatre must not mislead us. They are the successive perceptions only, that constitute the mind; nor have we the most distant notion of the place where these scenes are represented, or of the materials of which it is composed.

What then gives us so great a propension to ascribe an identity to these successive perceptions, and to suppose ourselves possessed of an invariable and uninterrupted existence through the whole course of our lives? In order to answer this question we must distinguish betwixt personal identity, as it regards our thought or imagination, and as it regards our passions or the concern we take in ourselves. The first is our present subject; and to explain it perfectly we must take the matter pretty deep, and account for that identity, which we attribute to plants and animals; there being a great analogy betwixt it and the identity of a self or person.

We have a distinct idea of an object that remains invariable and uninterrupted through a supposed variation of time; and this idea we call that of *identity* or *sameness*. We have also a distinct idea of several different objects existing in succession, and connected together by a close relation; and this to an accurate view affords as perfect a notion of *diversity* as if there was no manner of relation among the objects. But though these two ideas of identity, and a succession of related objects, be in themselves perfectly distinct, and even contrary, yet it is certain that, in our common way of thinking, they are generally confounded with each other. That action of the imagination, by which we consider the uninterrupted and invariable object, and that by which we reflect on the succession of related objects, are almost the same to the feeling; nor is there much more effort of thought required in the latter case than in the former. The relation facilitates the transition of the mind from one object to another, and renders its passage as smooth as if it contemplated one continued object. This resemblance is the cause of the confusion and mistake, and makes us substitute the notion of identity, instead of that of related objects. However at one instant we may consider the related succession as variable or interrupted, we are sure the next to ascribe to it a perfect identity, and regard it as invariable and uninterrupted. Our propensity to this mistake is so great from the resemblance above mentioned, that we fall into it before we are aware; and though we incessantly correct ourselves by reflection, and return to a more accurate method of thinking, yet we cannot long sustain our philosophy, or take off this bias from the imagination. Our last resource is to yield to it, and boldly assert that these different related objects are in effect the same, however interrupted and variable. In order to justify to ourselves this absurdity, we often feign some new and unintelligible principle, that connects the objects together, and prevents their interruption or variation. Thus we feign the continued existence of the perceptions of our senses, to remove the interruption; and run into the notion of a *soul*, and *self*, and *substance*, to disguise the variation. But, we may further observe, that where we do not give rise to such a fiction, our propension to confound identity with relation is so great, that we are apt to imagine something unknown and mysterious,[1] connecting the parts, beside their relation; and this I take to be the case with regard to the identity we ascribe to plants and vegetables. And even when this does not take place, we still feel a propensity to confound these ideas, though we are not able fully to satisfy ourselves in that particular, nor find anything invariable and uninterrupted to justify our notion of identity.

Thus the controversy concerning identity is not merely a dispute of words. For when we attribute identity, in an improper sense, to variable or interrupted objects, our mistake is not confined to the expression, but is commonly attended with a fiction, either of something invariable and uninterrupted, or of something mysterious and inexplicable, or at least with a propensity to such fictions. What will suffice to prove this hypothesis to the satisfaction of every fair inquirer, is to show, from daily experience and observation, that the objects which are variable or interrupted, and yet are supposed to continue the same, are such only as consist of a succession of parts, connected together by resemblance, contiguity, or causation. For as such a succession answers evidently to our notion of diversity, it can only be by mistake we ascribe to it an identity; and as the relation of parts, which leads us into this mistake, is really nothing but a quality, which produces an association of ideas, and an easy transition of the imagination from one to another, it can only be from the resemblance, which this act of the mind bears to that by which we contemplate one continued object, that the error arises. Our chief business, then, must be to prove, that all objects, to which we ascribe identity, without observing their invariableness and uninterruptedness, are such as consist of a succession of related objects.

In order to this, suppose any mass of matter, of which the parts are contiguous and connected, to be placed before us; it is plain we must attribute a perfect identity to this mass, provided all the parts continue uninterruptedly and invariable the same, whatever motion or change of place we may observe either in the whole or in any of the parts. But supposing some very *small* or *inconsiderable* part to be added to the mass, or subtracted from it; though this absolutely destroys the identity of the whole, strictly speaking, yet as we seldom think so accurately, we scruple not to pronounce a mass of matter the same, where we find so trivial an alteration. The passage of the thought from the object before the change to the object after it, is so smooth and easy, that we scarce perceive the transition, and are apt to imagine, that it is nothing but a continued survey of the same object.

There is a very remarkable circumstance that attends this experiment; which is, that though the change of any considerable part in a mass of matter destroys the identity of the whole, yet we must measure the greatness of the part, not absolutely, but by its *proportion* to the whole. The addition or diminution of a mountain would not be sufficient to produce a diversity in a planet; though the change of a very few inches would be able to destroy the identity of some bodies. It will be impossible to account for this, but by reflecting that objects operate upon the mind, and break or interrupt the continuity of its actions, not according to their real greatness, but according to their proportion to each other; and therefore, since this interruption makes an object cease to appear the same, it must be the uninterrupted progress of the thought which constitutes the imperfect identity.

This may be confirmed by another phenomenon. A change in any considerable part of a body destroys its identity; but it is remarkable, that where the change is produced *gradually* and *insensibly*, we are less apt to ascribe to it the same effect. The reason can plainly be no other, than that the mind, in following the successive changes of the body, feels an easy passage from the surveying its condition in one moment, to the viewing of it in another, and in no particular time perceives any interruption in its actions. From which continued perception, it ascribes a continued existence and identity to the object.

But whatever precaution we may use in introducing the changes gradually, and making them proportionable to the whole, it is certain, that where the changes are at last observed to become considerable, we make a scruple of ascribing identity to such different objects. There is, however, another artifice, by which we may induce the imagination to advance a step further; and that is, by producing a reference of the parts to each other, and a combination to some *common end* or purpose. A ship, of which a considerable part has been changed by frequent reparations, is still considered as the same; nor does the difference of the materials hinder us from ascribing an identity to it. The common end, in which the parts conspire, is the same under all their variations, and affords an easy transition of the imagination from one situation of the body to another.

But this is still more remarkable, when we add a *sympathy* of parts to their *common end*, and suppose that they bear to each other the reciprocal relation of cause and effect in all their actions and operations. This is the case with all animals and vegetables; where not only the several parts have a reference to some general purpose, but also a mutual dependence on, and connection with, each other. The effect of so strong a relation is, that though every one must allow, that in a very few years both vegetables and animals endure a *total* change, yet we still attribute identity to them, while their form, size, and substance are entirely altered. An oak that grows from a small plant to a large tree is still the same oak, though there be not one particle of matter or figure of its parts the same. An infant becomes a man, and is sometimes fat, sometimes lean, without any change in his identity.

We may also consider the two following phenomena, which are remarkable in their kind. The first is, that though we commonly be able to distinguish pretty exactly betwixt numerical and specific identity, yet it sometimes happens that we confound them, and in our thinking and reasoning employ the one for the other. Thus a man, who hears a noise that is frequently interrupted and renewed, says it is still the same noise, though it is evident the sounds have only a specific identity of resemblance, and there is nothing numerically the same but the cause which produced them. In like manner it may be said, without breach of the propriety of language, that such a church, which was formerly of brick, fell to ruin, and that the parish rebuilt the same church of freestone, and according to modern architecture. Here neither the form nor materials are the same, nor is there anything common to the two objects but their relation to the inhabitants of the parish; and yet this alone is sufficient to make us denominate them the same. But we must observe, that in these cases the first object is in a manner annihilated before the second comes into existence; by which means, we are never presented, in any one point of time, with the idea of difference and multiplicity; and for that reason are less scrupulous in calling them the same.

Secondly, we may remark, that though in a succession of related objects it be in a manner requisite that the change of parts be not sudden nor entire, in order to preserve the identity, yet where the objects are in their nature changeable and inconstant, we admit of a more sudden transition than would otherwise be consistent with that relation. Thus, as the nature of a river consists in the motion and change of parts, though in less than four-and-twenty hours these be totally altered, this hinders not the river from continuing the same during several ages. What is natural and essential to anything is, in a manner, expected; and what is expected makes less impression, and appears of less moment than what is unusual and extraordinary. A considerable change of the former kind seems really less to the imagination than the most trivial alteration of the latter; and by breaking less the continuity of the thought, has less influence in destroying the identity.

We now proceed to explain the nature of *personal identity*, which has become so great a question in philosophy, especially of late years in England, where all the abstruser sciences are studied with a peculiar ardour and application. And here it is evident the same method of reasoning must be continued which has so successfully explained the identity of plants, and animals, and ships, and houses, and of all compounded and changeable productions either of art or nature. The identity which we ascribe to the mind of man is only a fictitious one, and of a like kind with that which we ascribe to vegetable and animal bodies. It cannot therefore have a different origin, but must proceed from a like operation of the imagination upon like objects.

But lest this argument should not convince the reader, though in my opinion perfectly decisive, let him weigh the following reasoning, which is still closer and more immediate. It is evident, that the identity which we attribute to the human mind, however perfect we may imagine it to be, is not able to run the several different perceptions into one, and make them lose their characters of distinction and difference, which are essential to them. It is still true that every distinct perception which enters into the composition of the mind, is a distinct existence, and is different, and distinguishable, and separable from every other perception, either contemporary or successive. But as, notwithstanding this distinction and separability, we suppose the whole train of perceptions to be united by identity, a question naturally arises concerning this relation of identity, whether it be something that really binds our several perceptions together, or only associates their ideas in the imagination; that is, in other words, whether in pronouncing concerning the identity of a person, we observe some real bond among his perceptions, or only feel one among the ideas we form of them. This question we might easily decide, if we would recollect what has been already proved at large, that the understanding never observes any real connection among objects, and that even the union of cause and effect, when strictly examined, resolves itself into a customary association of ideas. For from thence it evidently follows, that identity is nothing really belonging to these different perceptions, and uniting them together, but is merely a quality which we attribute to them, because of the union of their ideas in the imagination when we reflect upon them. Now, the only qualities which can give ideas a union in the imagination, are these three relations above mentioned. These are the uniting principles in the ideal world, and without them every distinct object is separable by the mind, and may be separately considered, and appears not to have any more connection with any other object than if disjoined by the greatest difference and remoteness. It is therefore on some of these three relations of resemblance, contiguity, and causation, that identity depends; and as the very essence of these relations consists in their producing an easy transition of ideas, it follows that our notions of personal identity proceed entirely from the smooth and uninterrupted progress of the thought along a train of connected ideas, according to the principles above explained.

The only question, therefore, which remains is, by what relations this uninterrupted progress of our thought is produced, when we consider the successive existence of a mind or thinking person. And here it is evident we must confine ourselves to resemblance and causation, and must drop contiguity, which has little or no influence in the present case.

To begin with *resemblance*; suppose we could see clearly into the breast of another, and observe that succession of perceptions which constitutes his mind or thinking principle, and suppose that he always preserves the memory of a considerable part of past perceptions, it is evident that nothing could more contribute to the bestowing a relation on this succession amidst all its variations. For what is the memory but a faculty, by which we raise up the images of past perceptions? And as an image necessarily resembles its object, must not be frequent placing of these resembling perceptions in the chain of thought, convey the imagination more easily from one link to another, and make the whole seem like the continuance of one object? In this particular, then, the memory not only discovers the identity, but also contributes to its production, by producing the relation of resemblance among the perceptions. The case is the same, whether we consider ourselves or others.

As to *causation*; we may observe that the true idea of the human mind, is to consider it as a system of different perceptions or different existences, which are linked together by the relation of cause and effect, and mutually produce, destroy, influence, and modify each other. Our impressions give rise to their correspondent ideas; and these ideas, in their turn, produce other impressions. One thought chases another, and draws after it a third, by which it is expelled in its turn. In this respect, I cannot compare the soul more properly to anything than to a republic or commonwealth, in which the several members are united by the reciprocal ties of government and subordination, and give rise to other persons who propagate the same republic in the incessant changes of its parts. And as the same individual republic may not only change its members, but also its laws and constitutions; in like manner the same person may vary his character and disposition, as well as his impressions and ideas, without losing his identity. Whatever changes he endures, his several parts are still connected by the relation of causation. And in this view our identity with regard to the passions serves to corroborate that with regard to the imagination, by the making our distant perceptions influence each other, and by giving us a present concern for our past or future pains or pleasures.

As memory alone acquaints us with the continuance and extent of this succession of perceptions, it is to be considered, upon that account chiefly, as the source of personal identity. Had we no memory, we never should have any notion of causation, nor consequently of that chain of causes and effects, which constitute our self or person. But having once acquired this notion of causation from the memory, we can extend the same chain of causes, and consequently the identity of our persons beyond our memory, and can comprehend times, and circumstances, and actions, which we have entirely forgot, but suppose in general to have existed. For how few of our past actions are there, for which we have any memory? Who can tell me, for instance, what were his thoughts and actions on the first of January 1715, the eleventh of March 1719, and the third of August 1733? Or will he affirm, because he has entirely forgot the incidents of these days, that the present self is not the same person with the self of that time; and by that means overturn all the most established notions of personal identity? In this view, therefore, memory does not so much *produce* as *discover* personal identity, by showing us the relation of cause and effect among our different perceptions. It will be incumbent on those who affirm that memory produces entirely our personal identity, to give a reason why we can thus extend our identity beyond our memory.

The whole of this doctrine leads us to a conclusion, which is of great importance in the present affair, viz. that all the nice and subtile questions concerning personal identity can never possibly be decided, and are to be regarded rather as grammatical than as philosophical difficulties. Identity depends on the relations of ideas; and these relations produce identity, by means of that easy transition they occasion. But as the relations, and the easiness of the transition may diminish by insensible degrees, we have no just standard by which we can decide any dispute concerning the time when they acquire or lose a title to the name of identity. All the disputes concerning the identity of connected objects are merely verbal, except so far as the relation of parts gives rise to some fiction or imaginary principle of union, as we have already observed.

What I have said concerning the first origin and uncertainty of our notion of identity, as applied to the human mind, may be extended with little or no variation to that of *simplicity*. An object, whose different coexistent parts are bound together by a close relation, operates upon the imagination after much the same manner as one perfectly simple and indivisible, and requires not a much greater stretch of thought in order to its conception. From this similarity of operation we attribute a simplicity to it, and feign a principle of union as the support of this simplicity, and the centre of all the different parts and qualities of the object.

Note

1   If the reader is desirous to see how a great genius may be influenced by these seem-
    ingly trivial principles of the imagination, as well as the mere vulgar, let him read my Lord
    Shaftesbury's reasonings concerning the uniting principle of the universe, and the identity
    of plants and animals. See his *Moralists*, or *Philosophical Rhapsody*.

PART II

LATER MODERN PHILOSOPHY

4

COMMENTARY ON KANT

Immanuel Kant (1724–1804) was born in Konigsberg, East Prussia, where he spent an otherwise uneventful life, teaching and writing at the University of Konigsberg from 1755 until his old age. Kant had a great interest in natural science, but was also quite religious; it is said that his aim, in setting out the conditions for and limitations of knowledge in the *Critique of Pure Reason,* was to limit reason to make room for faith. Kant is widely considered to be the paradigmatic Enlightenment thinker. He believed that the Enlightenment heralded human intellectual and moral self-sufficiency through the exercise of reason and rational self-sovereignty. Kant reconstructs Descartes's idea that knowledge is grounded in the human subject, and Hegel later takes it to its peak in his philosophy of *Geist.*

Kant continues the tradition initiated by Locke, of grounding philosophy in what we are able to know. He goes further than empiricism to counter Hume's skepticism by arguing that all experience has as conditions of its possibility, certain universal *a priori* structures that arise, not from things as they are independently of the mind, but from the mind itself. Kant is known as a transcendental idealist because he argues that our faculty of reason is the source of the laws of nature and those aspects of reality previously attributed to matter: space, time, quantity, and cause and effect. Kant is credited with bringing about a "Copernican turn" in philosophy as a result of his response to skepticism. By conceding the skeptic's point that we cannot know objects as they are in-themselves, Kant argues that our knowledge cannot conform to objects, but rather, that objects conform to our knowledge of them – that is, objects appear with forms imposed by the understanding.[1] Thus, the human subject becomes the universal and necessary (and therefore objective) condition of knowledge. The discussion of the paralogisms is part of this greater project.

In the "Paralogisms of Pure Reason" Kant pits his conception of "I" as a formal or logical feature of the unity of consciousness against the claim that we can know the "I" as a thinking thing. Here, like Hume, Kant rejects knowledge of the "I" as substance. However, he does not regard the self as a mere fiction, but as part of the structure of consciousness.

Elsewhere in the *Critique of Pure Reason*, and in his moral philosophy, Kant employs a tripartite distinction within his use of the term "self": first, a purely logical notion of "I" in apperception; second, a "phenomenal self" – one's sense of oneself as one appears to oneself; and third, the "noumenal self" – the necessary *thought* of oneself as the agent of one's own actions, which is implied in morality.[2]

Kant writes, famously, that all knowledge begins with experience, but it does not all arise out of experience.[3] For Kant, knowledge requires two things: (1) *a priori* pure concepts of the mind (*categories*), which organize (2) sensible intuitions or "affections" into our various empirical representations of reality. The categories function as rules according to which sensible intuitions (affections of the mind by "something" outside of the mind) are brought together in a unity (manifold), to form a complex representation. Our understanding and experiences are limited *a priori* to the modes of representation enabled by the categories. Importantly, the categories only produce knowledge (or experience, that is, empirical concepts) when they are applied to intuitions.[4] It is this principle that runs through all of Kant's arguments in the "Paralogisms of Pure Reason."

A paralogism is a fallacious syllogism, a faulty form of reasoning. In the "Paralogisms" Kant identifies a series of syllogisms that draw false inferences about the "I" by the illegitimate application of the category of "substance." For Kant, the category of "substance" is *a rule for uniting intuitions* such that a representation of a logical subject is formed.[5] Kant argues that the "I" that is taken to be the soul is purely logical and involves no intuitions; therefore, no knowledge claims can be made about it.

Apperception is a principle of unity in consciousness that says that all representations in a single consciousness must have a single logical subject.[6] Henry Allison calls this an "identity condition of thought": in any consciousness containing thoughts *a*, *b*, *c*, "I" must be the same "I" who has thought *a*, and thought *b* and thought *c*, and has them *all together*.[7] In other words, although I seem to refer to the same "I" at different times, this "I" is not an enduring entity but simply a logical feature of a unified consciousness. Kant says that the awareness of the apperceptive "I" is not intuited and does not come about through the engagement of any category; rather, it arises from the spontaneous *a priori* unity of consciousness.

The First Paralogism

The first paralogism claims to demonstrate that "I" as thinking thing (soul) am substance. This is Descartes's claim that the nature of the soul can be known immediately through reason. The paralogism says that an "absolute subject" is something that cannot "be employed as the determination of another thing." This was the standard view of substance. However, as Kant points out, this definition is of "substance" *qua* logical subject only, and, as such, can only be legitimately employed as a mode of representation of intuitions. Since we do not have any intuitions of the soul, we cannot conclude that the soul is a substance; in fact, we cannot come to any conclusions whatsoever. The "I" is not, strictly speaking, *represented* at all. For this reason, there is nothing that can be deduced from the supposed "concept" of the immaterial soul.

The Second Paralogism

The second paralogism claims to demonstrate through reason that the soul is a simple (that is, noncomposite) being. This is Descartes's argument that the soul is indivisible. This paralogism mistakes the unity of apperception for the indivisible unity of a non-material substance (soul). This mistake builds upon the first paralogism. The reasoning goes like this: it is impossible that thinking can be composite because if you take a composite thought, for example, a verse of a song, and distribute it among different consciousnesses you lose the song; it does not appear whole in the different beings. As Kant says, the *nervus probandi* (crux of the argument) of this proposition is that a representation with multiple parts requires that all the parts have a single subject. The paralogism mistakenly interprets the singularity of the subject metaphysically, taking apperception for indivisibility. The purported simplicity of the soul is simply "an immediate expression of apperception."[8] Moreover, Kant argues, the simplicity of the soul is not even inferred from the "I think" because it is contained in the concept "I think," and therefore is a tautology.

Kant also eliminates three other possible defenses by demonstrating that the proposition that the soul is simple is neither an analytical proposition, nor a synthetic proposition of either an *a priori* or *a posteriori* type. Since these three types exhaust all the possible forms of propositions by which knowledge can be expressed, the claim that the soul is simple cannot be a knowledge claim.

The Third Paralogism

The third paralogism claims to demonstrate that "I" refers to a person, that is, a substance that has consciousness of its identity over time. This is, essentially, the claim that the soul as immaterial substance constitutes personal identity. The paralogism mistakes the numerical identity of the "I" (the fact that the "I" of apperception is the same "I" at all times), for the permanence of the soul in time. Kant's explanation here is more difficult than the previous two analyses, and presupposes arguments made much earlier in the *Critique*, pertaining to the ideality of time (in the "Transcendental Aesthetic"), and of permanence (in the "Schematism"). It is also one of the most interesting arguments, and one that has been employed in more recent times in defense of a certain views of personal identity.[9]

The crux of Kant's argument concerns the fallacious notion of permanence employed in the paralogism, and the conflation of the inner perspective of apperception with the outer perspective of an object. When Kant says "In my own consciousness . . . identity of person is unfailingly met with" he is referring to the formal numerical identity of the "I" in apperception. On introspection, the same "I" is always encountered because of the apperceptive nature of consciousness. The reason I believe that this same "I" endures over time is because my consciousness extends over time, and so the unity of apperception is also a temporal unity. It is just because of the fact that the term "I" can accompany each of my thoughts at any moment that I can mistake

this formal principle of the (temporal) unity of consciousness for a permanently existing thing, and so come to believe that permanence is a property of "I".

However, the numerical identity of the "I" is not the permanence of substance. Permanence in the Kantian system is actually a "schema," that is, a mediating concept for
bringing intuitions under a category.[10] As such, schema form part of the synthesis in
the understanding by which we form representations of outer objects as existing in
time. In short, the notion of permanence can only be legitimately employed in relation to sensible intuitions. The paralogism confuses the permanence in time of an object
viewed "from the outside" as it were (that is, an empirical concept of permanence) with
the sameness of the "I" of apperception, viewed "from the inside." From the numerical identity of the apperceptive "I," nothing can be inferred or deduced. It can yield
no knowledge of the same *enduring* "I" at different times because only substance can
be said to endure, and this "I" is not a substance. Once again, Kant brings us back to
his central and immovable thesis: the only legitimate employment of the pure concepts
of the understanding is in relation to intuitions; where there is no intuition there is no
knowledge.

Kant's "Copernican turn," with its emphasis on the rational and subjective structures
presupposed by knowledge, gave rise to two distinct philosophical movements – phenomenology and analytical philosophy of language – each of which developed very
different approaches to questions of self and identity, as well as philosophy in general.
It is not until the late twentieth century that those two paths begin to converge, for
example, in the work of people such as Paul Ricoeur.

Notes

1   Immanuel Kant, *Critique of Pure Reason*, trans. Norman Kemp Smith (London: Macmillan,
     1990), hereafter *CPR*; preface to the 2nd edn, Bxvi.
2   See Immanuel Kant, *Groundwork of a Metaphysics of Morals*, translated and edited by Mary
     Gregor (Cambridge, UK: Cambridge University Press, 1998), Section III; also Christine
     Korsgaard, *Creating the Kingdom of Ends* (Cambridge, UK: Cambridge University Press,
     1996).
3   *CPR*, Introduction, B1.
4   *CPR*, A51/B75.
5   *CPR*, B149.
6   *CPR*, B131–2.
7   Henry Allison, *Kant's Transcendental Idealism, An Interpretation and Defense* (New Haven, CT
     and London: Yale University Press, 1983), p. 138.
8   *CPR*, A355.
9   Andrew Brook, *Kant and the Mind* (Cambridge, UK, New York, and Melbourne: Cambridge
     University Press, 1994), pp. 191–207.
10   *CPR*, A143/B183.

Main Texts by Kant

Werner S. Pluhar (trans.), *Critique of Judgment* (Indianapolis: Hackett, 1987).

Mary Gregor (trans.), *Critique of Practical Reason* (New York: Cambridge University Press, 1997).

Norman Kemp Smith (trans.), *Critique of Pure Reason* (Basingstoke and London: Macmillan, 1999).

Mary Gregor (ed. and trans.), *Groundwork of the Metaphysics of Morals* (New York: Cambridge University Press, 1998).

Robert S. Hartman and Wolfgang Schwarz (trans.), *Logic* (New York: Dover Publications, 1974).

James Ellington (trans.), *Metaphysical Foundations of Natural Science* (Indianapolis: Hackett, 1975).

Mary Gregor (trans.), *The Metaphysics of Morals* (New York: Cambridge University Press, 1996).

Gary Hatfield (trans.), *Prolegomena to Any Future Metaphysics* (New York: Cambridge University Press, 1997).

T. M. Greene and H. H. Hudson (trans.), *Religion Within the Limits of Reason Alone* (New York: Harper and Row, 1960).

David Walford and Ralf Meerbote (eds. and trans.), *Theoretical Philosophy* (Cambridge, UK: Cambridge University Press, 1992).

Further Reading

Allison, Henry, *Kant's Transcendental Idealism, An Interpretation and Defense* (New Haven, CT and London: Yale University Press, 1983).

Ameriks, Karl, *Kant's Theory of Mind* (Oxford: Clarendon Press, 1982).

Caygill, Howard, *A Kant Dictionary* (Oxford and Cambridge, MA: Blackwell, 1995).

Collins, Arthur, *Possible Experience: Understanding Kant's Critique of Pure Reason* (Berkeley and Los Angeles: University of California Press, 1999).

Gardiner, Sebastian, *Kant and the Critique of Pure Reason* (London and New York: Routledge, 1999).

Korner, Stephen, *Kant* (London: Penguin, 1955).

Korsgaard, Christine, *Creating the Kingdom of Ends* (Cambridge, UK: Cambridge University Press, 1996).

Strawson, P. F. *The Bounds of Sense: An Essay on Kant's Critique of Pure Reason* (London: Methuen, 1966).

Wolff, R. P. (ed.), *Kant: A Collection of Critical Essays* (Garden City, NY: Doubleday Anchor, 1967).

Zweig, Arnulf (ed. and trans.), *Kant: Philosophical Correspondence 1759–1799* (Chicago: Chicago University Press, 1967).

CRITIQUE OF PURE REASON, "PARALOGISMS OF PURE REASON (A)" (FIRST, SECOND, AND THIRD PARALOGISMS)

Immanuel Kant

First Paralogism: Of Substantiality

That, the representation of which is the *absolute subject* of our judgments and cannot therefore be employed as determination of another thing, is *substance*.

I, as a thinking being, am the *absolute subject* of all my possible judgments, and this representation of myself cannot be employed as predicate of any other thing.

Therefore I, as thinking being (soul), am *substance*.

Critique of the First Paralogism of Pure Psychology

In the analytical part of the Transcendental Logic we have shown that pure categories, and among them that of substance, have in themselves no objective meaning, save in so far as they rest upon an intuition, and are applied to the manifold of this intuition, as functions of synthetic unity. In the absence of this manifold, they are merely functions of a judgment, without content. I can say of any and every thing that it is substance, in the sense that I distinguish it from mere predicates and determinations of things. Now in all our thought the 'I' is the subject, in which thoughts inhere only as determinations; and this 'I' cannot be employed as the determination of another thing. Everyone must, therefore, necessarily regard himself as substance, and thought as [consisting] only [in] accidents of his being, determinations of his state.

But what use am I to make of this concept of a substance? That I, as a thinking being, *persist* for myself, and do not in any natural manner either *arise* or *perish*, can by no means be deduced from it. Yet there is no other use to which I can put the concept of the substantiality of my thinking subject, and apart from such use I could very well dispense with it.

So far from being able to deduce these properties merely from the pure category of substance, we must, on the contrary, take our start from the permanence of an object

From *Critique of Pure Reason*, translated by Norman Kemp Smith (Basingstoke and London: Macmillan, 1990), pp. 333–44. Reprinted by permission of Palgrave Macmillan.

given in experience as permanent. For only to such an object can the concept of *substance* be applied in a manner that is empirically serviceable. In the above proposition, however, we have not taken as our basis any experience; the inference is merely from   A350
the concept of the relation which all thought has to the 'I' as the common subject in which it inheres. Nor should we, in resting it upon experience, be able, by any sure observation, to demonstrate such permanence. The 'I' is indeed in all thoughts, but there is not in this representation the least trace of intuition, distinguishing the 'I' from other objects of intuition. Thus we can indeed perceive that this representation is invariably present in all thought, but not that it is an abiding and continuing intuition, wherein the thoughts, as being transitory, give place to one another.

It follows, therefore, that the first syllogism of transcendental psychology, when it puts forward the constant logical subject of thought as being knowledge of the real subject in which the thought inheres, is palming off upon us what is a mere pretence of new insight. We do not have, and cannot have, any knowledge whatsoever of any such subject. Consciousness is, indeed, that which alone makes all representations to be thoughts, and in it, therefore, as the transcendental subject, all our perceptions must be found; but beyond this logical meaning of the 'I', we have no knowledge of the subject in itself, which as substratum underlies this 'I', as it does all thoughts. The proposition, '*The soul is substance*', may, however, quite well be allowed to stand, if only it be recognised that this concept [of the soul as substance] does not carry us a single step further, and so cannot yield us any of the usual deductions of the pseudo-rational doctrine of   A351
the soul, as, for instance, the everlasting duration of the human soul in all changes and even in death – if, that is to say, we recognise that this concept signifies a substance only in idea, not in reality.

Second Paralogism: Of Simplicity

That, the action of which can never be regarded as the concurrence of several things acting, is *simple*.

Now the soul, or the thinking 'I', is such a being. Therefore, etc.

Critique of the Second Paralogism of Transcendental Psychology

This is the Achilles of all dialectical inferences in the pure doctrine of the soul. It is no mere sophistical play, contrived by a dogmatist in order to impart to his assertions a superficial plausibility, but an inference which appears to withstand even the keenest scrutiny and the most scrupulously exact investigation. It is as follows.

Every *composite* substance is an aggregate of several substances, and the action of a composite, or whatever inheres in it as thus composite, is an aggregate of several actions or accidents, distributed among the plurality of the substances. Now an effect which arises from the concurrence of many acting substances is indeed possible, namely, when   A352
this effect is external only (as, for instance, the motion of a body is the combined motion of all its parts). But with thoughts, as internal accidents belonging to a thinking being, it is different. For suppose it be the composite that thinks: then every part of it would be a part of the thought, and only all of them taken together would contain the whole

thought. But this cannot consistently be maintained. For representations (for instance, the single words of a verse), distributed among different beings, never make up a whole thought (a verse), and it is therefore impossible that a thought should inhere in what is essentially composite. It is therefore possible only in a *single* substance, which, not being an aggregate of many, is absolutely simple.[1]

The so-called *nervus probandi* of this argument lies in the proposition, that if a multiplicity of representations are to form a single representation, they must be contained in the absolute unity of the thinking subject. No one, however, can prove this proposition from *concepts*. For how should he set about the task of achieving this? The proposition, 'A thought can only be the effect of the absolute unity of the thinking being', cannot be treated as analytic. For the unity of the thought, which consists of many representations, is collective, and as far as mere concepts can show, may relate just as well to the collective unity of different substances acting together (as the motion of a body is the composite motion of all its parts) as to the absolute unity of the subject. Consequently, the necessity of presupposing, in the case of a composite thought, a simple substance, cannot be demonstrated in accordance with the principle of identity. Nor will anyone venture to assert that the proposition allows of being known synthetically and completely *a priori* from mere concepts – not, at least, if he understands the ground of the possibility of *a priori* synthetic propositions, as above explained.

It is likewise impossible to derive this necessary unity of the subject, as a condition of the possibility of every thought, from experience. For experience yields us no knowledge of necessity, apart even from the fact that the concept of absolute unity is quite outside its province. Whence then are we to derive this proposition upon which the whole psychological syllogism depends?

It is obvious that, if I wish to represent to myself a thinking being, I must put myself in his place, and thus substitute, as it were, my own subject for the object I am seeking to consider (which does not occur in any other kind of investigation), and that we demand the absolute unity of the subject of a thought, only because otherwise we could not say, '*I* think' (the manifold in one representation). For although the whole of the thought could be divided and distributed among many subjects, the subjective '*I*' can never be thus divided and distributed, and it is this '*I*' that we presuppose in all thinking.

Here again, as in the former paralogism, the formal proposition of apperception, 'I think', remains the sole ground to which rational psychology can appeal when it thus ventures upon an extension of its knowledge. This proposition, however, is not itself an experience, but the form of apperception, which belongs to and precedes every experience; and as such it must always be taken only in relation to some possible knowledge, as a *merely subjective condition* of that knowledge. We have no right to transform it into a condition of the possibility of a knowledge of objects, that is, into a *concept* of thinking being in general. For we are not in a position to represent such being to ourselves save by putting ourselves, with the formula of our consciousness, in the place of every other intelligent being.

Nor is the simplicity of myself (as soul) really *inferred* from the proposition, 'I think'; it is already involved in every thought. The proposition, '*I am simple*', must be regarded as an immediate expression of apperception, just as what is referred to as the Cartesian inference, *cogito, ergo sum*, is really a tautology, since the *cogito* (*sum cogitans*) asserts my

A353

A354

A355

existence immediately. '*I am simple*' means nothing more than that this representation, 'I', does not contain in itself the least manifoldness and that it is absolute (although merely logical) unity.

Thus the renowned psychological proof is founded merely on the indivisible unity of a representation, which governs only the verb in its relation to a person. It is obvious that in attaching 'I' to our thoughts we designate the subject of inherence only transcendentally, without noting in it any quality whatsoever – in fact, without knowing anything of it either by direct acquaintance or otherwise. It means a something in general (transcendental subject), the representation of which must, no doubt, be simple, if only for the reason that there is nothing determinate in it. Nothing, indeed, can be represented that is simpler than that which is represented through the concept of a mere something. But the simplicity of the representation of a subject is not *eo ipso* knowledge of the simplicity of the subject itself, for we abstract altogether from its properties when we designate it solely by the entirely empty expression 'I', an expression which I can apply to every thinking subject.

This much, then, is certain, that through the 'I', I always entertain the thought of an   A356
absolute, but logical, unity of the subject (simplicity). It does not, however, follow that I thereby know the actual simplicity of my subject. The proposition, 'I am substance', signifies, as we have found, nothing but the pure category, of which I can make no use (empirically) *in concreto*; and I may therefore legitimately say: 'I am a simple substance', that is, a substance the representation of which never contains a synthesis of the manifold. But this concept, as also the proposition, tells us nothing whatsoever in regard to myself as an object of experience, since the concept of substance is itself used only as a function of synthesis, without any underlying intuition, and therefore without an object. It concerns only the condition of our knowledge; it does not apply to any assignable object. We will test the supposed usefulness of the proposition by an experiment.

Everyone must admit that the assertion of the simple nature of the soul is of value only in so far as I can thereby distinguish this subject from all matter, and so can exempt it from the dissolution to which matter is always liable. This is indeed, strictly speaking, the only use for which the above proposition is intended, and is therefore generally expressed as 'The soul is not corporeal'. If, then, I can show that, although   A357
we allow full objective validity – the validity appropriate to a judgment of pure reason derived solely from pure categories – to this cardinal proposition of the rational doctrine of the soul (that is, that everything which thinks is a simple substance), we still cannot make the least use of this proposition in regard to the question of its dissimilarity from or relation to matter, this will be the same as if I had relegated this supposed psychological insight to the field of mere ideas, without any real objective use.

In the Transcendental Aesthetic we have proved, beyond all question, that bodies are mere appearances of our outer sense and not things in themselves. We are therefore justified in saying that our thinking subject is not corporeal; in other words, that, inasmuch as it is represented by us as object of inner sense, it cannot, is so far as it thinks, be an object of outer sense, that is, an appearance in space. This is equivalent to saying that thinking beings, *as such*, can never be found by us among outer appearances, and that their thoughts, consciousness, desires, etc., cannot be outwardly intuited. All these belong to inner sense. This argument does, in fact, seem to be so natural and so popular

that even the commonest understanding appears to have always relied upon it, and thus
A358   already, from the earliest times, to have regarded souls as quite different entities from
their bodies.

But although extension, impenetrability, cohesion, and motion – in short, everything
which outer senses can give us – neither are nor contain thoughts, feeling, desire, or
resolution, these never being objects of outer intuition, nevertheless the something
which underlies the outer appearances and which so affects our sense that it obtains
the representations of space, matter, shape, etc., may yet, when viewed as noumenon
(or better, as transcendental object), be at the same time the subject of our thoughts.
That the mode in which our outer sense is thereby affected gives us no intuition of
representations, will, etc., but only of space and its determinations, proves nothing to
the contrary. For this something is not extended, nor is it impenetrable or composite,
since all these predicates concern only sensibility and its intuition, in so far as we are
affected by certain (to us otherwise unknown) objects. By such statements we are not,
however, enabled to know what kind of an object it is, but only to recognise that if it
be considered in itself, and therefore apart from any relation to the outer senses, these
predicates of outer appearances cannot be assigned to it. On the other hand, the predi-
A359   cates of inner sense, representations and thought, are not inconsistent with its nature.
Accordingly, even granting the human soul to be simple in nature, such simplicity by
no means suffices to distinguish it from matter, in respect of the substratum of the latter
– if, that is to say, we consider matter, as indeed we ought to, as mere appearance.

If matter were a thing in itself, it would, as a composite being, be entirely different
from the soul, as a simple being. But matter is mere outer appearance, the substratum
of which cannot be known through any predicate that we can assign to it. I can therefore very well admit the possibility that it is in itself simple, although owing to the
manner in which it affects our sense it produces in us the intuition of the extended
and so of the composite. I may further assume that the substance which in relation to
our outer sense possesses extension is in itself the possessor of thoughts, and that these
thoughts can by means of its own inner sense be consciously represented. In this way,
what in one relation is entitled corporeal would in another relation be at the same time
a thinking being, whose thoughts we cannot intuit, though we can indeed intuit their
signs in the [field of] appearance. Accordingly, the thesis that only souls (as particular
kinds of substances) think, would have to be given up; and we should have to fall back
A360   on the common expression that men think, that is, that the very same being which, as
outer appearance, is extended, is (in itself) internally a subject, and is not composite,
but is simple and thinks.

But, without committing ourselves in regard to such hypotheses, we can make this
general remark. If I understand by soul a thinking being in itself, the question whether
or not it is the same in kind as matter – matter not being a thing in itself, but merely
a species of representations in us – is by its very terms illegitimate. For it is obvious
that a thing in itself is of a different nature from the determinations which constitute
only its state.

If, on the other hand, we compare the thinking 'I' not with matter but with the
intelligible that lies at the basis of the outer appearance which we call matter, we have
no knowledge whatsoever of the intelligible, and therefore are in no position to say
that the soul is in any inward respect different from it.

The simple consciousness is not, therefore, knowledge of the simple nature of the self as subject, such as might enable us to distinguish it from matter, as from a composite being.

If, therefore, in the only case in which this concept can be of service, namely, in the comparison of myself with objects of outer experience, it does not suffice for determining what is specific and distinctive in the nature of the self, then though we may still profess to know that the thinking 'I', the soul (a name for the transcendental object   A361 of inner sense), is simple, such a way of speaking has no sort of application to real objects, and therefore cannot in the least extended our knowledge.

Thus the whole of rational psychology is involved in the collapse of its main support. Here as little as elsewhere can we hope to extend our knowledge through mere concepts – still less by means of the merely subjective form of all our concepts, consciousness – in the absence of any relation to possible experience. For [as we have thus found], even the fundamental concept of a *simple nature* is such that it can never be met with in any experience, and such, therefore, that there is no way of attaining to it, as an objectively valid concept.

Third Paralogism: Of Personality

That which is conscious of the numerical identity of itself at different times is in so far a *person*.

Now the soul is conscious, etc.

Therefore it is a person.

Critique of the Third Paralogism of Transcendental Psychology

If I want to know through experience, the numerical identity of an external object, I   A362 shall pay heed to that permanent element in the appearance to which as subject everything else is related as determination, and note its identity throughout the time in which the determinations change. Now I am an object of inner sense, and all time is merely the form of inner sense. Consequently, I refer each and all of my successive determinations to the numerically identical self, and do so throughout time, that is, in the form of the inner intuition of myself. This being so, the personality of the soul has to be regarded not as inferred but as a completely identical proposition of self-consciousness in time; and this, indeed, is why it is valid *a priori*. For it really says nothing more than that in the whole time in which I am conscious of myself, I am conscious of this time as belonging to the unity of myself; and it comes to the same whether I say that this whole time is in me, as individual unity, or that I am to be found as numerically identical in all this time.

In my own consciousness, therefore, identity of person is unfailingly met with. But if I view myself from the standpoint of another person (as object of his outer intuition), it is this outer observer who first represents *me in time*, for in the apperception *time* is represented, strictly speaking, only *in me*. Although he admits, therefore, the 'I', which accompanies, and indeed with complete identity, all representations at all times   A363 in *my* consciousness, he will draw no inference from this to the objective permanence of myself. For just as the times in which the observer sets me is not the time of my own but of his sensibility, so the identity which is necessarily bound up with my consciousness is not therefore bound up with his, that is, with the consciousness which contains the outer intuition of my subject.

The identity of the consciousness of myself at different times is therefore only a formal condition of my thoughts and their coherence, and in no way proves the numerical identity of my subject. Despite the logical identity of the 'I', such a change may have occurred in it as does not allow of the retention of its identity, and yet we may ascribe to it the same-sounding 'I', which in every different state, even in one involving change of the [thinking] subject, might still retain the thought of the preceding subject and so hand it over to the subsequent subject.[2]

A364   Although the dictum of certain ancient schools, that everything in the world is *in a flux* and nothing is *permanent* and abiding, cannot be reconciled with the admission of substances, it is not refuted by the unity of self-consciousness. For we are unable from our own consciousness to determine whether, as souls, we are permanent or not. Since we reckon as belonging to our identical self only that of which we are conscious, we must necessarily judge that we are one and the same throughout the whole time of which we are conscious. We cannot, however, claim that this judgment would be valid from the standpoint of an outside observer. For since the only permanent appearance which we encounter in the soul is the representation 'I' that accompanies and connects them all, we are unable to prove that this 'I', a mere thought, may not be in the same state of flux as the other thoughts which, by means of it, are linked up with one another.

A365   It is indeed strange that personality, and its presupposition, permanence, and therefore the substantiality of the soul, should have to be proved *at this stage and not earlier.* For could we have presupposed these latter [permanence and substantiality], there would follow, not indeed the continuance of consciousness, yet at least the possibility of a continuing consciousness in an abiding subject, and that is already sufficient for personality. For personality does not itself at once cease because its activity is for a time interrupted. This permanence, however, is in no way given prior to that numerical identity of our self which we infer from identical apperception, but on the contrary is inferred first from the numerical identity. (If the argument proceeded aright, the concept of substance, which is applicable only empirically, would first be brought in after such proof of numerical identity.) Now, since this identity of person [presupposing, as it does, numerical identity] in nowise follows from the identity of the 'I' in the consciousness of all the time in which I know myself, we could not, earlier in the argument, have founded upon it the substantiality of the soul.

Meanwhile we may still retain the concept of personality – just as we have retained the concept of substance and of the simple – in so far as it is merely transcendental, that is, concerns the unity of the subject, otherwise unknown to us, in the determinations of which there is a thoroughgoing connection through apperception. Taken in
A366   this way, the concept is necessary for practical employment and is sufficient for such use; but we can never parade it as an extension of our self-knowledge through pure reason, and as exhibiting to us from the mere concept of the identical self an unbroken continuance of the subject. For this concept revolves perpetually in a circle, and does not help us in respect to any question which aims at synthetic knowledge. What matter may be as a thing in itself (transcendental object) is completely unknown to us, though,

owing to its being represented as something external, its permanence as appearance can indeed be observed. But if I want to observe the mere 'I' in the change of all representations, I have no other *correlatum* to use in my comparisons except again myself, with the universal conditions of my consciousness. Consequently, I can give none but tautological answers to all questions, in that I substitute my concept and its unity for the properties which belong to myself as object, and so take for granted that which the questioner has desired to know.

Notes

1   This proof can very easily be given the customary syllogistic correctness of form. But for my purpose it is suffcient to have made clear, though in popular fashion, the bare ground of proof.
2   An elastic ball which impinges on another similar ball in a straight line communicates to the latter its whole motion, and therefore its whole state (that is, if we take account only of the positions in space). If, then, in analogy with such bodies, we postulate substances such that the one communicates to the other representations together with the consciousness of them, we can conceive a whole series of substances of which the first transmits its state together with its consciousness to the second, the second its own state with that of the preceding substance to the third, and this in turn the states of all the preceding substances together with its own consciousness and with their consciousness to another. The last substance would then be conscious of all the states of the previously changed substances, as being its own states, because they would have been transferred to it together with the consciousness of them. And yet it would not have been one and the same person in all these states.

5

COMMENTARY ON HEGEL

Georg Wilhelm Friedrich Hegel was born in Stuttgart, Germany, in 1770. His thinking was greatly influenced by the Enlightenment, in particular, Kant's *Critique of Pure Reason*, to which much of his work is oriented, if critically. Hegel counted among his friends and colleagues leaders of the German Romantic movement such as Goethe and Schiller. His ideas continue to be enormously influential in schools as diverse as American pragmatism, European existentialism, and British analytic philosophy.

Hegel takes the central idea of transcendental idealism – that objects are constituted by consciousness – to its limits. The key triad of concepts in Hegel's philosophy is *Geist* (spirit), history, and freedom. He tells us that "The history of the world is none other than the progress of the consciousness of freedom."[1] The idea here is that world history is about the progressive development of human spirit to the realization of what it truly is, namely, *Geist*. World history is the history of the development of self-consciousness from its immaturity – manifest in the various forms of partial knowledge that characterize different forms of human life – to the fully fledged realization of its spirit (*Geist*) as universal consciousness (also called "absolute knowledge"). Why Hegel thinks this is so can be understood by reference to his critique of Kantian idealism. Put rather crudely, Hegel thought that noumena could be nothing to us because noumena are nothing. Therefore, all that exists is what we can know. For Hegel, truth consists in agreement of consciousness with itself: the full apprehension and comprehension of itself *in its* objects – in what we know – and not the objects themselves.[2] In this sense, *Geist* is the full realization of self-consciousness.

It is important to understand that for Hegel *Geist* is immanent in the world. It arises from and is tied to the worldly existence of human subjects. That means that self-consciousness is always mediated through the forms of life of thinking subjects. Consequently, the achievement of full self-realization comes only with a certain level of social and political development; this is why it takes time – in other words, is historical. The concept of *Geist* encompasses individual psychological life (subjective spirit) as well as the communal spirit embodied in the laws and customs of that society (objective spirit).[3] *Geist* is not a substrate underlying the self; it is pure, infinite activity, which is why Hegel regards it as synonymous with freedom. As pure activity, it "animates" all periods of human history, articulating successively more rational forms of human existence as it finds expression in the thoughts, actions, and institutions of those societies.

On Hegel's view, over time *Geist* is able to "iron out" problems and tensions in experience because these arise from lack of rational understanding. In this sense, reason is not opposed to nature (or desire), but rather, needs to be more fully reconciled with it. This reconciliation, which is nothing other than freedom itself, takes time because freedom is a practical achievement, an achievement that occurs within the time and by the means of the living world. Freedom, for Hegel, is to be understood both epistemologically and practically. Freedom of thought, for example, is not possible without concrete political structures that allow the full and free expression of self-consciousness. This means that not only individual action, but society as a whole, in its structure and institutions, must be based on rational principles.

Hegel links the realization of freedom with the development of the Christian principle of conscience. According to this principle, a mature individual conscience can operate completely independently of external laws or morality because *as* conscience it contains its principle within itself. Hegel thought that this exemplified *Geist*, and that the Reformation marked a period of maturation in which society had become the kind of place in which the transformation of individual self-consciousness to objective spirit could occur. With this, history arrives at its end as *Geist* realizes itself both in theory (thought) and practice.

Hegel's conception of freedom is heavily indebted to Kant's account of freedom as duty to act in accordance with reason. However, rather than reconciling reason and desire, he thought that Kant placed them in perpetual conflict. Hegel's form of reconciliation is *Sittlichkeit*. This is the concept of an organic community; a community in which the desires of individuals can exist in accord with reason because the society embodies rational principles in the concrete institutions through which individuals achieve their subjectivity. Crucial to *Sittlichkeit* is the mutual recognition of subjects. This principle is central to the "master–slave" dialectic. Like much of Hegel's writing, this piece is obscure and even incomprehensible outside of an understanding of Hegel's overall project. The master–slave is perhaps best known because of Alexandre Kojève's influential interpretation, which emphasized the role of recognition in attaining freedom.

As noted, *Geist* reaches its self-realization when it becomes conscious of itself as freedom. A crucial, if obscure, phase in this progression is the master–slave relationship, which is essentially a description of a struggle for recognition. Hegel's insight here is that subjectivity is mediated through relations with other people; subjectivity is always intersubjectivity. In contrast to the abstract immediacy of the Cartesian *cogito*, for Hegel consciousness is a concrete and mediated achievement.

In order to grasp the significance of this struggle, it needs to be considered within Hegel's understanding of consciousness *per se*. It is of the essence of consciousness that it be consciousness of *something*; that is, that it have an object. For Hegel, the "object" of self-consciousness is consciousness itself. The difficulty this poses is that consciousness is defined in a negative relation to its object – it is a "not-this," in contrast to a determinate "this" of a thing (Sartre's idea of consciousness as nothingness is immediately recognizable). In order to take itself as an object, consciousness must become something *experienced*. It does this by expressing itself as desire.

Consciousness in the mode of desire has two characteristics that create difficulties. First, because its essence is negation, consciousness necessarily destroys its object. This means that in pursuing and satisfying a desire the object of desire is removed (negated) and one is left with nothing. However, to satisfy one's desire for the (certainty of) self the continued existence of the object that it negates is required; self-consciousness needs an object that retains its independence through negation. Put simply, it requires the existence of an object that exists *as* a negation. The only object that fits the bill is another self-consciousness. The desire that a self-consciousness needs to be satisfied in order to be sure of its existence as a subject, is the desire for the desire of another; that is, the desire for *recognition*. Such recognition comes about through a struggle that ensues from the encounter of two self-consciousnesses. The struggle is what Hegel's master–slave relationship describes.

According to Hegel, the encounter of two self-consciousnesses in the world is experienced ambiguously by each as both a threat to, and a promise of, self-certainty. Each sees the other as a kind of object (an "Other") in the external world. However, insofar as the subject is aware of this Other as another subject, one is aware of something that is essentially the same as oneself. In coming to experience another subject of experience, one becomes aware that oneself is also an "Other"; that the Other is also oneself.[4] The subject becomes aware that the Other is constituted in just the same way as itself, namely, as a negation which defines itself by excluding all otherness. At the same time, however, the subject experiences itself as "outside of itself," in the world of externality, in contrast to the inner world of self-certainty. This presents as a threat because the subject is now aware of itself as an external object to the other, and thus vulnerable to negation by that other consciousness.[5] So arises a life and death struggle in the effort to establish self-certainty; the struggle for recognition. Within this struggle, however, subjects realize that their subjectivity is grounded in their existence as living beings, that "life is the natural setting of consciousness,"[6] and so, rather than fight to the death, one subject yields to the other's power. The outcome is a situation where one is the victor (the master) who allows the other (the slave) to live in servitude, and the slave accepts servitude rather than death. Furthermore, if the slave were killed in battle no recognition of the victor's autonomy would be possible, so enslavement of the loser is the price of recognition.

Hegel then introduces a twist: it is the slave, not the master, who has the higher realization of self-consciousness. Hegel provides three reasons for this. First, since each serves as an object (and in this sense, truth) for the other's self-certainty, the slave, having the master as his object, has the superior truth, while the master has the "inessential consciousness" of the slave as his object. Second, since the slave has been shaken to the core by the fear of facing death, he has experienced independent consciousness of himself. Third, the master's satisfaction is fleeting because it lacks the endurance and recognition that the slave enjoys through seeing his will objectified in the objects of his labor. This last point becomes important to Marx's theory of labor and alienation.

The lesson of the master–slave dialectic is that the realization of our capacities as subjects in the world (our freedom) requires the mutual recognition of ourselves as members of a moral community. The ideal outcome of an encounter of two consciousnesses is that each discover in the other a constructive rather than destructive desire for the other's desire. In this way, negation and existence are reconciled nonviolently in the mutual recognition of the subjects' shared need for, and thus affirmation of, the value of each other *as* self-consciousnesses. This idea becomes central to Simone de Beauvoir's philosophy, with its emphasis on the shared nature of the human situation.

Despite its grand metaphysical overtones, Hegel's account turns on the idea that subjectivity and freedom are worldly achievements, mediated through our relations with others. One of Hegel's achievements has been to identify the ways in which forms of political organization can be systematically oppressive through their mediating role in the constitution of subjectivity. These insights have been central to the philosophies of Marx, phenomenology, and existentialism, and they continue to inform not only the utopian politics of some critics of postmodernity, most notably Jürgen Habermas, Axel Honneth, and Seyla Benhabib, but also Anglo-American pragmatists such as John McDowell and Robert Brandom.

Notes

1   Hegel, from "Introduction" to *The Philosophy of History*, cited in Peter Singer, *Hegel* (Oxford: Oxford University Press, 1983), p. 11.
2   Ivan Soll, *An Introduction to Hegel's Metaphysics* (Chicago and London: University of Chicago Press, 1976), p. 11.
3   Michael Inwood, *A Hegel Dictionary* (Oxford: Blackwell, 1992), p. 285.
4   See Ross Poole, "Desire, Fear and the Self," *Dialectic*, 16, 1979, p. 40.
5   This experience is well documented by victims of oppression who find their ideas and feelings wrongly anticipated, appropriated, and thus effectively negated, by oppressive others. When this kind of social encounter is systematic (for example, racism or sexism), selfhood can be progressively eroded.
6   Hegel, *Phenomenology of Spirit*, trans. A. V. Miller, with analysis and foreword by J. N. Findlay (Oxford: Clarendon Press, 1977), p. 114.

Main Texts by Hegel

Allen W. Wood (ed.), H. B. Nisbet (trans.), *Elements of the Philosophy of Right* (Cambridge, UK: Cambridge University Press, 1991).
T. F. Geraets, W. A. Suchting, and H. S. Harris (trans.), *The Encyclopedia Logic: Part 1 of the Encyclopaedia of Philosophical Sciences* (Indianapolis: Hackett, 1991).
A. V. Miller (trans.), *Phenomenology of Spirit* (Oxford: Oxford University Press, 1977).
Laurence Dickey and H. B. Nisbet (eds.), H. B. Nisbet (trans.), *Political Writings* (Cambridge, UK: Cambridge University Press, 1999).

Further Reading

Beiser, Frederick C., *The Cambridge Companion to Hegel* (Cambridge, UK: Cambridge University Press, 1993).
Forster, Michael N., *Hegel's Idea of a Phenomenology of Spirit* (Chicago: University of Chicago Press, 1998).

Houlgate, Stephen, *Freedom, Truth and History: An Introduction to Hegel's Philosophy* (London and New York: Routledge, 1991).

Kojève, Alexandre, *Introduction to the Reading of Hegel*, ed. Allan Bloom, trans. J. H. Nichols, Jr. (New York: Basic Books, 1969).

Pinkard, Terry, *Hegel: A Biography* (Cambridge, UK: Cambridge University Press, 2000).

Pippin, Robert, *Hegel's Idealism: The Satisfactions of Self-consciousness* (Cambridge, UK: Cambridge University Press, 1989).

Stern, Robert, *Routledge Philosophy Guidebook to Hegel and the Phenomenology of Spirit* (London: Routledge, 2002).

Williams, Robert, *Hegel's Ethics of Recognition* (Berkeley: University of California Press, 1997).

PHENOMENOLOGY OF SPIRIT, "SELF-CONSCIOUSNESS: LORDSHIP AND BONDAGE"

G. W. F. Hegel

Independence and Dependence of Self-consciousness: Lordship and Bondage

178.   Self-consciousness exists in and for itself when, and by the fact that, it so exists for another; that is, it exists only in being acknowledged. The Notion of this its unity in its duplication embraces many and varied meanings. Its moments, then, must on the one hand be held strictly apart, and on the other hand must in this differentiation at the same time also be taken and known as not distinct, or in their opposite signifi-cance. The twofold significance of the distinct moments has in the nature of self-consciousness to be infinite, or directly the opposite of the determinateness in which it is posited. The detailed exposition of the Notion of this spiritual unity in its dupli-cation will present us with the process of Recognition.

179.   Self-consciousness is faced by another self-consciousness; it has come *out of itself*. This has a twofold significance: first, it has lost itself, for it finds itself as an *other* being; secondly, in doing so it has superseded the other, for it does not see the other as an essential being, but in the other sees its own self.

180.   It must supersede this otherness of itself. This is the supersession of the first ambiguity, and is therefore itself a second ambiguity. First, it must proceed to supersede the *other* independent being in order thereby to become certain of *itself* as the essen-tial being; secondly, in so doing it proceeds to supersede its *own* self, for this other is itself.

181.   This ambiguous supersession of its ambiguous otherness is equally an ambigu-ous return *into itself*. For first, through the supersession, it receives back its own self, because, by superseding *its* otherness, it again becomes equal to itself; but secondly, the other self-consciousness equally gives it back again to itself, for it saw itself in the other, but supersedes this being of itself in the other and thus lets the other again go free.

From *Phenomenology of Spirit*, translated by A.V. Miller with analysis and foreword by J. N. Findlay (Oxford: Clarendon Press, 1977), pp. 110–19. Reprinted by permission of Oxford University Press.

182.   Now, this movement of self-consciousness in relation to another self-consciousness has in this way been represented as the action of *one* self-consciousness, but this action of the one has itself the double significance of being both its own action and the action of the other as well. For the other is equally independent and self-contained, and there is nothing in it of which it is not itself the origin. The first does not have the object before it merely as it exists primarily for desire, but as something that has an independent existence of its own, which, therefore, it cannot utilize for its own purposes, if that object does not of its own accord do what the first does to it. Thus the movement is simply the double movement of the two self-consciousnesses. Each sees the *other* do the same as it does; each does itself what it demands of the other, and therefore also does what it does only in so far as the other does the same. Action by one side only would be useless because what is to happen can only be brought about by both.

183.   Thus the action has a double significance not only because it is directed against itself as well as against the other, but also because it is indivisibly the action of one as well as of the other.

184.   In this movement we see repeated the process which presented itself as the play of Forces, but repeated now in consciousness. What in that process was *for us*, is true here of the extremes themselves. The middle term is self-consciousness which splits into the extremes; and each extreme is this exchanging of its own determinateness and an absolute transition into the opposite. Although, as consciousness, it does indeed come *out of itself*, yet, though out of itself, it is at the same time kept back within itself, is *for itself*, and the self outside it, is for *it*. It is aware that it at once is, and is not, another consciousness, and equally that this other is *for itself* only when it supersedes itself as being for itself, and is for itself only in the being-for-self of the other. Each is for the other the middle term, through which each mediates itself with itself and unites with itself; and each is for itself, and for the other, an immediate being on its own account, which at the same time is such only through this mediation. They *recognize* themselves as *mutually recognizing* one another.

185.   We have now to see how the process of this pure Notion of recognition, of the duplicating of self-consciousness in its oneness, appears to self-consciousness. At first, it will exhibit the side of the inequality of the two, or the splitting-up of the middle term into the extremes which, as extremes, are opposed to one another, one being only *recognized*, the other only *recognizing*.

186.   Self-consciousness is, to begin with, simple being-for-self, self-equal through the exclusion from itself of everything else. For it, its essence and absolute object is 'I'; and in this immediacy, or in this [mere] being, of its being-for-self, it is an *individual*. What is 'other' for it is an unessential, negatively characterized object. But the 'other' is also a self-consciousness; one individual is confronted by another individual. Appearing thus immediately on the scene, they are for one another like ordinary objects, *independent* shapes, individuals submerged in the being [or immediacy] of *Life* – for the object in its immediacy is here determined as Life. They are, *for each other*, shapes of consciousness which have not yet accomplished the movement of absolute abstraction, of rooting-out all immediate being, and of being merely the purely negative being of self-identical consciousness; in other words, they have not as yet exposed themselves to each other in the form of pure being-for-self, or as self-consciousnesses. Each is indeed

certain of its own self, but not of the other, and therefore its own self-certainty still has no truth. For it would have truth only if its own being-for-self had confronted it as an independent object, or, what is the same thing, if the object had presented itself as this pure self-certainty. But according to the Notion of recognition this is possible only when each is for the other what the other is for it, only when each in its own self through its own action, and again through the action of the other, achieves this pure abstraction of being-for-self.

187.   The presentation of itself, however, as the pure abstraction of self-consciousness consists in showing itself as the pure negation of its objective mode, or in showing that it is not attached to any specific *existence*, not to the individuality common to existence as such, that it is not attached to life. This presentation is a twofold action: action on the part of the other, and action on its own part. In so far as it is the action of the *other*, each seeks the death of the other. But in doing so, the second kind of action, action on its own part, is also involved; for the former involves the staking of its own life. Thus the relation of the two self-conscious individuals is such that they prove themselves and each other through a life-and-death struggle. They must engage in this struggle, for they must raise their certainty of being *for themselves* to truth, both in the case of the other and in their own case. And it is only through staking one's life that freedom is won; only thus is it proved that for self-consciousness, its essential being is not [just] being, not the *immediate* form in which it appears, not its submergence in the expanse of life, but rather that there is nothing present in it which could not be regarded as a vanishing moment, that it is only pure *being-for-self*. The individual who has not risked his life may well be recognized as a *person*, but he has not attained to the truth of this recognition as an independent self-consciousness. Similarly, just as each stakes his own life, so each must seek the other's death, for it values the other no more than itself; its essential being is present to it in the form of an 'other', it is outside of itself and must rid itself of its self-externality. The other is an *immediate* consciousness entangled in a variety of relationships, and it must regard its otherness as a pure being-for-self or as an absolute negation.

188.   This trial by death, however, does away with the truth which was supposed to issue from it, and so, too, with the certainty of self generally. For just as life is the *natural* setting of consciousness, independence without absolute negativity, so death is the *natural* negation of consciousness, negation without independence, which thus remains without the required significance of recognition. Death certainly shows that each staked his life and held it of no account, both in himself and in the other; but that is not for those who survived this struggle. They put an end to their consciousness in its alien setting of natural existence, that is to say, they put an end to themselves, and are done away with as *extremes* wanting to be *for themselves*, or to have an existence of their own. But with this there vanishes from their interplay the essential moment of splitting into extremes with opposite characteristics; and the middle term collapses into a lifeless unity which is split into lifeless, merely immediate, unopposed extremes; and the two do not reciprocally give and receive one another back from each other consciously, but leave each other free only indifferently, like things. Their act is an abstract negation, not the negation coming from consciousness, which supersedes in such a way as to preserve and maintain what is superseded, and consequently survives its own supersession.

189.   In this experience, self-consciousness learns that life is as essential to it as pure self-consciousness. In immediate self-consciousness the simple 'I' is absolute mediation, and has as its essential moment lasting independence. The dissolution of that simple unity is the result of the first experience; through this there is posited a pure self-consciousness, and a consciousness which is not purely for itself but for another, i.e. is a merely *immediate* consciousness, or consciousness in the form of *thinghood*. Both moments are essential. Since to begin with they are unequal and opposed, and their reflection into a unity has not yet been achieved, they exist as two opposed shapes of consciousness; one is the independent consciousness whose essential nature is to be for itself, the other is the dependent consciousness whose essential nature is simply to live or to be for another. The former is lord, the other is bondsman.

190.   The lord is the consciousness that exists *for itself*, but no longer merely the Notion of such a consciousness. Rather, it is a consciousness existing *for itself* which is mediated with itself through another consciousness, i.e. through a consciousness whose nature it is to be bound up with an existence that is independent, or thinghood in general. The lord puts himself into relation with both of these moments, to a *thing* as such, the object of desire, and to the consciousness for which thinghood is the essential characteristic. And since he is (a) *qua* the Notion of self-consciousness an immediate relation of *being-for-self*, but (b) is now at the same time mediation, or a being-for-self which is for itself only through another, he is related (a) immediately to both, and (b) mediately to each through the other. The lord relates himself mediately to the bondsman through a being [a thing] that is independent, for it is just this which holds the bondsman in bondage; it is his chain from which he could not break free in the struggle, thus proving himself to be dependent, to possess his independence in thinghood. But the lord is the power over this thing, for he proved in the struggle that it is something merely negative; since he is the power over this thing and this again is the power over the other [the bondsman], it follows that he holds the other in subjection. Equally, the lord relates himself mediately to the thing through the bondsman; the bondsman, *qua* self-consciousness in general, also relates himself negatively to the thing, and takes away its independence; but at the same time the thing is independent *vis-à-vis* the bondsman, whose negating of it, therefore, cannot go the length of being altogether done with it to the point of annihilation; in other words, he only *works* on it. For the lord, on the other hand, the *immediate* relation becomes through this mediation the sheer negation of the thing, or the enjoyment of it. What desire failed to achieve, he succeeds in doing, viz. to have done with the thing altogether, and to achieve satisfaction in the enjoyment of it. Desire failed to do this because of the thing's independence; but the lord, who has interposed the bondsman between it and himself, takes to himself only the dependent aspect of the thing and has the pure enjoyment of it. The aspect of its independence he leaves to the bondsman, who works on it.

191.   In both of these moments the lord achieves his recognition through another consciousness; for in them, that other consciousness is expressly something unessential, both by its working on the thing, and by its dependence on a specific existence. In neither case can it be lord over the being of the thing and achieve absolute negation of it. Here, therefore, is present this moment of recognition, viz. that the other consciousness sets aside its own being-for-self, and in so doing itself does what the first does to it. Similarly, the other moment too is present, that this action of the second is

the first's own action; for what the bondsman does is really the action of the lord. The latter's essential nature is to exist only for himself; he is the sheer negative power for whom the thing is nothing. Thus he is the pure, essential action in this relationship, while the action of the bondsman is impure and unessential. But for recognition proper the moment is lacking, that what the lord does to the other he also does to himself, and what the bondsman does to himself he should also do to the other. The outcome is a recognition that is one-sided and unequal.

192.   In this recognition the unessential consciousness is for the lord the object, which constitutes the *truth* of his certainty of himself. But it is clear that this object does not correspond to its Notion, but rather that the object in which the lord has achieved his lordship has in reality turned out to be something quite different from an independent consciousness. What now really confronts him is not an independent consciousness, but a dependent one. He is, therefore, not certain of *being-for-self* as the truth of himself. On the contrary, his truth is in reality the unessential consciousness and its unessential action.

193.   The *truth* of the independent consciousness is accordingly the servile consciousness of the bondsman. This, it is true, appears at first *outside* of itself and not as the truth of self-consciousness. But just as lordship showed that its essential nature is the reverse of what it wants to be, so too servitude in its consummation will really turn into the opposite of what it immediately is; as a consciousness forced back into itself, it will withdraw into itself and be transformed into a truly independent consciousness.

194.   We have seen what servitude is only in relation to lordship. But it is a self-consciousness, and we have now to consider what as such it is in and for itself. To begin with, servitude has the lord for its essential reality; hence the *truth* for it is the independent consciousness that is *for itself*. However, servitude is not yet aware that this truth is implicit in it. But it does in fact contain within itself this truth of pure negativity and being-for-self, for it has experienced this its own essential nature. For this consciousness has been fearful, not of this or that particular thing or just at odd moments, but its whole being has been seized with dread. In that experience it has been quite unmanned, has trembled in every fibre of its being, and everything solid and stable has been shaken to its foundations. But this pure universal movement, the absolute melting-away of everything stable, is the simple, essential nature of self-consciousness, absolute negativity, *pure being-for-self*, which consequently is *implicit* in this consciousness. This moment of pure being-for-self is also *explicit* for the bondsman, for in the lord it exists for him as his *object*. Furthermore, his consciousness is not this dissolution of everything stable merely in principle; in his service he *actually* brings this about. Through his service he rids himself of his attachment to natural existence in every single detail; and gets rid of it by working on it.

195.   However, the feeling of absolute power both in general, and in the particular form of service, is only implicitly this dissolution, and although the fear of the lord is indeed the beginning of wisdom, consciousness is not therein aware that it is a being-for-self. Through work, however, the bondsman becomes conscious of what he truly is. In the moment which corresponds to desire in the lord's consciousness, it did seem that the aspect of unessential relation to the thing fell to the lot of the bondsman, since in that relation the thing retained its independence. Desire has reserved to itself the pure negating of the object and thereby its unalloyed feeling of self. But that is the

reason why this satisfaction is itself only a fleeting one, for it lacks the side of objectivity and permanence. Work, on the other hand, is desire held in check, fleetingness staved off; in other words, work forms and shapes the thing. The negative relation to the object becomes its *form* and something *permanent*, because it is precisely for the worker that the object has independence. This *negative* middle term or the formative *activity* is at the same time the individuality or pure being-for-self of consciousness which now, in the work outside of it, acquires an element of permanence. It is in this way, therefore, that consciousness, *qua* worker, comes to see in the independent being [of the object] its *own* independence.

196.   But the formative activity has not only this positive significance that in it the pure being-for-self of the servile consciousness acquires an existence; it also has, in contrast with its first moment, the negative significance of *fear*. For, in fashioning the thing, the bondsman's own negativity, his being-for-self, becomes an object for him only through his setting at nought the existing *shape* confronting him. But this objective *negative* moment is none other than the alien being before which it has trembled. Now, however, he destroys this alien negative moment, posits *himself* as a negative in the permanent order of things, and thereby becomes *for himself*, someone existing on his own account. In the lord, the being-for-self is an 'other' for the bondsman, or is only *for* him [i.e. is not his own]; in fear, the being-for-self is present in the bondsman himself; in fashioning the thing, he becomes aware that being-for-self belongs to *him*, that he himself exists essentially and actually in his own right. The shape does not become something other than himself through being made external to him; for it is precisely this shape that is his pure being-for-self, which in this externality is seen by him to be the truth. Through this rediscovery of himself by himself, the bondsman realizes that it is precisely in his work wherein he seemed to have only an alienated existence that he acquires a mind of his own. For this reflection, the two moments of fear and service as such, as also that of formative activity, are necessary, both being at the same time in a universal mode. Without the discipline of service and obedience, fear remains at the formal stage, and does not extend to the known real world of existence. Without the formative activity, fear remains inward and mute, and consciousness does not become explicitly *for itself*. If consciousness fashions the thing without that initial absolute fear, it is only an empty self-centred attitude; for its form or negativity is not negativity *per se*, and therefore its formative activity cannot give it a consciousness of itself as essential being. If it has not experienced absolute fear but only some lesser dread, the negative being has remained for it something external, its substance has not been infected by it through and through. Since the entire contents of its natural consciousness have not been jeopardized, determinate being still *in principle* attaches to it; having a 'mind of one's own' is self-will, a freedom which is still enmeshed in servitude. Just as little as the pure form can become essential being for it, just as little is that form, regarded as extended to the particular, a universal formative activity, an absolute Notion; rather it is a skill which is master over some things, but not over the universal power and the whole of objective being.

6

COMMENTARY ON NIETZSCHE

Friedrich Wilhelm Nietzsche (1844–1900) was raised in a devoutly religious family and received an extensive classical German education. He enjoyed precocious success in his university career and was appointed professor of classics at the University of Basel at 24 years of age. Nietzsche was very influenced by German Romanticism, especially the idea that reality was underpinned by nonrational forces which were the font of creativity. Sadly, Nietzsche spent a great part of his adult life plagued by poverty and illness and died at the age of 55.

Nietzsche's philosophy is emblematic of the decline of Enlightenment thinking. He despised the Christian morality central to Hegel's thought and he rejected the Enlightenment ideal of progress through reason, with its belief in rational self-sovereignty. Like Freud, who was greatly influenced by him, Nietzsche regarded consciousness as a second-order expression of underlying part-biological, part-social evolutionary urges and instincts. In contrast to Enlightenment thinking, he considered (so-called) truths to be necessarily illusory and the idea of autonomy to be based in a serious misconception of the human condition. Nietzsche took the view that concepts of "mind" (or "soul") and "body" do not refer to distinct entities, but rather, are linguistic strategies we employ in order to speak of different aspects of our lives. He couples a descriptive philosophical method to a Lamarckian-style view of biological life, resulting in a complex and lively, if somewhat menacing, account of human existence. For Nietzsche, there is no soul, no rational "thinking thing." For him "life" is the all-important concept, and consciousness is only ever at the service of life. Under the influence of Nietzsche, subjectivity becomes "decentered" as self-consciousness is shaken from its sovereign certainty by its organic underbelly.

Unlike most of his predecessors, Nietzsche valorizes bodily life, rather than reason.[1] Nietzsche was very influenced by Schopenhauer's metaphysical view of the world as "Will": the idea that behind appearances the world is constituted by an unconscious, striving force ("will") that manifests in the multitude of forms of living things. Accordingly, Nietzsche regarded all living things (including human beings) as animated by urges or impulses that are both creative and destructive. The fundamental characteristic of urges is their capacity to "seize stimuli and transform it"; urges are not merely reactive, but have a transformative energy. This transformative energy is what Nietzsche's calls the "will to power."[2]

The direction that instinctual urges take a human being – that is, the type of behavior exhibited – is a result of a transformative interaction of internal urges with an external environment that facilitates some urges while obstructing others.[3] On this view, human beings have no fixed or determinate characteristics; human traits are all historically contingent, arising from the expression of urges within historically evolving forms of societal life over successive generations. According to Nietzsche, beneath the veneer of rational agency lie generations of sedimented attitudes and practices. In the following century this idea would become central to the genealogical method of Michel Foucault.

Nietzsche's is a holistic embodied view of subjectivity. What we call the self, on his view, is just a unity of urges that compose the living body. It is a "subject unity," rather like the head of a community. However, the head is not one individual of the community, but its entirety. Nietzsche stresses the point that there is no doer behind the deed, no thinker behind the thought; the domain of the self is the entire complex living organism, a living unity of urges. Nietzsche specifically rejects the substrate view of "self," arguing that this view arises from a fundamental confusion where from the fact that something is done (thinking, willing, feeling, etc.), a certain kind of doer is inferred, whose nature consists in just these acts – that is, a thinking, willing, feeling thing.[4]

This view, naturally enough, leads Nietzsche to reject the popular conception of the will. For Nietzsche, there is no separate faculty or agent of volition that causes one to act when one wills it. Within his organic, holistic view of life, the will is, if you like, an orchestration of the organism through the agency of its own impulses. Nietzsche claims that the impression of freedom of the will, and its correlate notion of soul, arises simply from the ability of the organism to subordinate some urges while allowing others to dominate. The more integrated the impulses are, the more effective is the organism's will. A high level of integration gives precision and clarity of direction to action, and that clarity and precision creates the illusion of a single agent of volition. The composite and conflictual nature of the human organism gives us the important capacity to see things from different perspectives.[5] For this reason, Nietzsche urges us to be highly suspicious of "facts" because "facts" are simply expressive of the perspective of a particular dominant complex of urges which, by necessity, suppresses other possible perspectives.

One of Nietzsche's most important criticisms of Enlightenment thinking is his denial that progress is made by increasing our level of consciousness. He thought that consciousness, with its emphasis on universal rationality, was bringing about a degeneration of human creativity and individuality to a common, herd-like way of living.[6] Nietzsche provides a mythic account of the origins of this condition in which he claims that at some stage in human history nomadic or "wild" humans were suddenly brought under the ruthless domination of a conquering horde.[7] The suddenness of this change meant that the urges had no time to develop a satisfactory equilibrium with the external environment, and so became directed inward. The inward turn of the urges gave rise to the inner world of subjectivity from which the concept of the self and the soul emerged. With this development, the inner world became a new source of pain: human

Übermensch
& slave

beings began to suffer from *themselves*. According to Nietzsche, this situation ... provides the ground for the rise of Christian morality.

Nietzsche argues that Christianity is a slave morality borne from an oppressive form of life under the brutal rule of the Roman Empire, and that Christianity is driven by *Ressentiment* (resentment). Resentment is said to arise when impulses are denied expression in the external world and are forced inward for their satisfaction. In the case of slaves, whose bondage effectively denies their will to power free expression, the suffering of bondage produces hatred and fear, but also resentment because slaves cannot act on their feelings. They cannot express their hatred toward their master, and so that hatred is turned inward and directed toward those aspects of life denied to slaves by their slavery. They resent those who are proud, strong, free, and noble, and set store by the meek and poor. For Nietzsche, the will to power is the basis of all our valuations: we regard something as good when it is able to be put to the service of our dominant instincts, and we regard something as bad if it cannot. Under these conditions, slaves' values are determined by those urges that enable their survival, and thus, are suited to slavery. The slave comes to judge certain aspects of slave life to be good, for example, humility, poverty, and self-sacrifice, while judging their opposites to be bad, namely, all that is bold and creative and "living" in life.

According to Nietzsche, Christianity gives rise to the fiction of the moral subject through two means: first, it makes the error of positing the soul, and second, it falsely universalizes the particular situation of slavery. Christianity provides a set of moral rules supposedly grounded in absolute truth, which it uses to justify its resentment. For Nietzsche, the things commonly regarded as good and bad are just habits of the Christian tradition which serve certain inward and deathly impulses. For this reason, a moral philosophy demands that we expose the slavish basis of our inherited morality and reassess *all* of our values.

The development of the inner world of self had an up-side: the urges had a whole new level of existence in which to find expression. For this reason, Nietzsche calls humankind the "still unfixed animal," a being with "no eternal horizons."[8] He thought that these conditions now produced the possibility of overcoming self-suffering to create new and more potent forms of human life: the *Übermensch*, or "overman," sometimes translated, controversially, as "superman." The overman is a human being who puts his inner world to the service of his nonrational impulses in order to create his own authentic, unique existence. This transition to a new form of life is achieved by harnessing the transformative powers of the will to power, and as such, is an aesthetic endeavor. For Nietzsche, the real nature of human subjectivity is aesthetic and consists in the power to create oneself. The way in which such transformation occurs is through the "revaluation of all values."

Nietzsche describes the revaluation of values as a "positive nihilism," a joyful rejection of Christian morality and its systems of meaning. He sends out a call for "free spirits" to turn the "no" of rebellion into the "yes" of new, life-embracing values. The person who can create a new form of life out of the destruction of Christian mores is the overman: "the most exuberant, most living and most world-affirming man."[9]

Nietzsche's ideas continue to influence much of contemporary thought – indirectly through the influence of Freudian psychoanalysis, and more directly through the

application of his core concepts and genealogical method in the work of Michel
Foucault and Judith Butler.

Notes

1   See Friedrich Nietzsche, *The Will to Power*, trans. W. Kaufmann and R. Hollingdale (New
    York: Vintage/Random House, 1968), pp. 341–8; hereafter *WP*.
2   "each moment of our life lets some tentacles of our being grow and some others wither,
    according to the nourishment which the moment does or does not bear in itself." Nietzsche
    quoted in George Morgan, *What Nietzsche Means* (New York and Evanston, IL: Harper and
    Row, 1965), p. 96.
3   *WP*, p. 324.
4   Richard Schacht, *Nietzsche* (London: Routledge and Kegan Paul, 1985), p. 135; See *WP*,
    pp. 267–72.
5   *WP*, p. 271.
6   See *WP*, p. 459 for a taste of Nietzsche's passion on the topic: "the annihilation of the
    decaying races. Decay of Europe. – The annihilation of slavish evaluations. – Dominion over
    the earth as a means of producing a higher type. – The annihilation of the tartuffery called
    'morality' . . ." and so it goes on. At #861 Nietzsche announces that "A declaration of war
    on the masses by higher men is needed!"
7   Morgan (1965), p. 110.
8   Ibid, p. 112.
9   Nietzsche, *Beyond Good and Evil*, trans. R. Hollingdale (London and New York: Penguin,
    1990), #56, p. 82.

Main Texts by Nietzsche

Walter Kaufmann (ed. and trans.), *Beyond Good and Evil* (New York: Random House, 1966).
Walter Kaufmann (ed. and trans.), *Birth of Tragedy and The Case of Wagner* (New York: Random
    House, 1967).
R. J. Hollingdale (ed. and trans.), *Daybreak: Thoughts on the Prejudices of Morality* (Cambridge, UK:
    Cambridge University Press, 1982).
Walter Kaufmann (ed. and trans.), *The Gay Science, with a Prelude of Rhymes and an Appendix of
    Songs* (New York: Random House, 1974).
R. J. Hollingdale (ed. and trans.), *Human, All Too Human: A Book for Free Spirits* (Cambridge, UK:
    Cambridge University Press, 1986).
Walter Kaufmann (ed. and trans.), *On the Genealogy of Morals and Ecce Homo* (New York: Random
    House, 1967).
Marianne Cowan (trans.), *Philosophy in the Tragic Age of the Greeks* (Chicago: Henry Regnery
    Company, 1962).
Daniel Breazeale (ed. and trans.), *Philosophy and Truth: Selections from Nietzsche's Notebooks of the
    Early 1870's* (Atlantic Highlands, NJ: Humanities Press, 1979).
Walter Kaufmann (ed. and trans.), *The Portable Nietzsche* (New York: Viking Press, 1968).
R. J. Hollingdale (ed. and trans.), *Untimely Meditations* (Cambridge, UK: Cambridge University
    Press, 1983).
Walter Kaufmann (ed. and trans.), *The Will to Power* (New York: Random House, 1967).

Further Reading

Allison, David, *Reading the New Nietzsche* (Lanham, MD: Rowman & Littlefield, 2000).

Deleuze, Gilles, *Nietzsche and Philosophy*, trans. Hugh Tomlinson (New York: Columbia University Press, 1983).

Hayman, Ronald, *Nietzsche: A Critical Life* (New York: Oxford University Press, 1980).

Hollingdale, R. J., *Nietzsche* (London and New York: Routledge and Kegan Paul, 1973).

Kaufmann, Walter, *Nietzsche: Philosopher, Psychologist, Antichrist* (Princeton, NJ: Princeton University Press, 1950).

Nehamas, Alexander, *Nietzsche: Life as Literature* (Cambridge, MA: Harvard University Press, 1985).

Oliver, Kelly, *Womanizing Nietzsche: Philosophy's Relation to the "Feminine"* (New York and London: Routledge, 1995).

Parkes, Graham, *Composing the Soul: Reaches of Nietzsche's Psychology* (Chicago and London: University of Chicago Press, 1994).

Schacht, Richard, *Nietzsche* (London: Routledge and Kegan Paul, 1983).

"THE GENEALOGY OF MORALS"

Friedrich Nietzsche

X

The slave revolt in morals begins by rancor turning creative and giving birth to values – the rancor of beings who, deprived of the direct outlet of action, compensate by an imaginary vengeance. All truly noble morality grows out of triumphant self-affirmation. Slave ethics, on the other hand, begins by saying *no* to an "outside," an "other," a non-self, and that *no* is its creative act. This reversal of direction of the evaluating look, this invariable looking outward instead of inward, is a fundamental feature of rancor. Slave ethics requires for its inception a sphere different from and hostile to its own. Physiologically speaking, it requires an outside stimulus in order to act at all; all its action is reaction. The opposite is true of aristocratic valuations: such values grow and act spontaneously, seeking out their contraries only in order to affirm themselves even more gratefully and delightedly. Here the negative concepts, *humble, base, bad*, are late, pallid counterparts of the positive, intense and passionate credo, "We noble, good, beautiful, happy ones." Aristocratic valuations may go amiss and do violence to reality, but this happens only with regard to spheres which they do not know well, or from the knowledge of which they austerely guard themselves: the aristocrat will, on occasion, misjudge a sphere which he holds in contempt, the sphere of the common man, the people. On the other hand we should remember that the emotion of contempt, of looking down, provided that it falsifies at all, is as nothing compared with the falsification which suppressed hatred, impotent vindictiveness, effects upon its opponent, though only in effigy. There is in all contempt too much casualness and nonchalance, too much blinking of facts and impatience, and too much inborn gaiety for it ever to make of its object a downright caricature and monster. Hear the almost benevolent nuances the Greek aristocracy, for example, puts into all its terms for the commoner; how emotions of compassion, consideration, indulgence, sugar-coat these words until, in the end, almost all terms referring to the common man survive as expressions for "unhappy," "pitiable"

From *The Birth of Tragedy* and *The Genealogy of Morals*, translated by Francis Golffing (Garden City, NY: Doubleday Anchor, 1956), pp. 170–3, 177–80, 189–95, 217–21. Used by permission of Doubleday, a division of Random House, Inc.

(cf. *deilos, deilaios, poneros, mochtheros*, the last two of which properly characterize the common man as a drudge and beast of burden); how, on the other hand, the words *bad, base, unhappy* have continued to strike a similar note for the Greek ear, with the timbre "unhappy" preponderating. The "wellborn" really felt that they were also the "happy." They did not have to construct their happiness factitiously by looking at their enemies, as all rancorous men are wont to do, and being fully active, energetic people they were incapable of divorcing happiness from action. They accounted activity a necessary part of happiness (which explains the origin of the phrase *eu prattein*).

All this stands in utter contrast to what is called happiness among the impotent and oppressed, who are full of bottled-up aggressions. Their happiness is purely passive and takes the form of drugged tranquillity, stretching and yawning, peace, "sabbath," emotional slackness. Whereas the noble lives before his own conscience with confidence and frankness (*gennaios* "nobly bred" emphasizes the nuance "truthful" and perhaps also "ingenuous"), the rancorous person is neither truthful nor ingenuous nor honest and forthright with himself. His soul squints; his mind loves hide-outs, secret paths, and back doors; everything that is hidden seems to him his own world, his security, his comfort; he is expert in silence, in long memory, in waiting, in provisional self-depreciation, and in self-humiliation. A race of such men will, in the end, inevitably be cleverer than a race of aristocrats, and it will honor sharp-wittedness to a much greater degree, i.e., as an absolutely vital condition for its existence. Among the noble, mental acuteness always tends slightly to suggest luxury and overrefinement. The fact is that with them it is much less important than is the perfect functioning of the ruling, unconscious instincts or even a certain temerity to follow sudden impulses, court danger, or indulge spurts of violent rage, love, worship, gratitude, or vengeance. When a noble man feels resentment, it is absorbed in his instantaneous reaction and therefore does not poison him. Moreover, in countless cases where we might expect it, it never arises, while with weak and impotent people it occurs without fail. It is a sign of strong, rich temperaments that they cannot for long take seriously their enemies, their misfortunes, their *misdeeds*; for such characters have in them an excess of plastic curative power, and also a power of oblivion. (A good modern example of the latter is Mirabeau, who lacked all memory for insults and meannesses done him, and who was unable to forgive because he had forgotten.) Such a man simply shakes off vermin which would get beneath another's skin – and only here, if anywhere on earth, is it possible to speak of "loving one's enemy." The noble person will respect his enemy, and respect is already a bridge to love. . . . Indeed he requires his enemy for himself, as his mark of distinction, nor could he tolerate any other enemy than one in whom he finds nothing to despise and much to esteem. Imagine, on the other hand, the "enemy" as conceived by the rancorous man! For this is his true creative achievement: he has conceived the "evil enemy," the Evil One, as a fundamental idea, and then as a pendant he has conceived a Good One – himself.

[. . .]

XII

Here I want to give vent to a sigh and a last hope. Exactly what is it that I, especially, find intolerable; that I am unable to cope with; that asphyxiates me? A bad smell. The smell of failure, of a soul that has gone stale. God knows it is possible to endure all kinds of misery – vile weather, sickness, trouble, isolation. All this can be coped with, if one is born to a life of anonymity and battle. There will always be moments of re-emergence into the light, when one tastes the golden hour of victory and once again stands foursquare, unshakable, ready to face even harder things, like a bowstring drawn taut against new perils. But, you divine patronesses – if there are any such in the realm beyond good and evil – grant me now and again the sight of something perfect, wholly achieved, happy, magnificently triumphant, something still capable of inspiring fear! Of a man who will justify the existence of mankind, for whose sake one may continue to believe in mankind! . . . The leveling and diminution of European man is our greatest danger; because the sight of him makes us despond. . . . We no longer see anything these days that aspires to grow greater; instead, we have a suspicion that things will continue to go downhill, becoming ever thinner, more placid, smarter, cosier, more ordinary, more indifferent, more Chinese, more Christian – without doubt man is getting "better" all the time. . . . This is Europe's true predicament: together with the fear of man we have also lost the love of man, reverence for man, confidence in man, indeed the *will to man*. Now the sight of man makes us despond. What is nihilism today if not that?

XIII

But to return to business: our inquiry into the origins of that other notion of good-ness, as conceived by the resentful, demands to be completed. There is nothing very odd about lambs disliking birds of prey, but this is no reason for holding it against large birds of prey that they carry off lambs. And when the lambs whisper among themselves, "These birds of prey are evil, and does not this give us a right to say that whatever is the opposite of a bird of prey must be good?" there is nothing intrinsically wrong with such an argument – though the birds of prey will look somewhat quizzically and say, "*We* have nothing against these good lambs; in fact, we love them; nothing tastes better than a tender lamb." – To expect that strength will not manifest itself as strength, as the desire to overcome, to appropriate, to have enemies, obstacles, and triumphs, is every bit as absurd as to expect that weakness will manifest itself as strength. A quantum of strength is equivalent to a quantum of urge, will, activity, and it is only the snare of lan-guage (of the arch-fallacies of reason petrified in language), presenting all activity as conditioned by an agent – the "subject" – that blinds us to this fact. For, just as popular superstition divorces the lightning from its brilliance, viewing the latter as an activity whose subject is the lightning, so does popular morality divorce strength from its manifestations, as though there were behind the strong a neutral agent, free to mani-fest its strength or contain it. But no such agent exists; these is no "being" behind the doing, acting, becoming; the "doer" has simply been added to the deed by the imagination – the doing is everything. The common man actually doubles the doing by making the lightning flash; he states the same event once as cause and then again as effect. The natural scientists are no better when they say that "energy *moves*," "energy *causes*." For all its detachment and freedom from emotion, our science is still the dupe of linguistic habits; it has never yet got rid of those changelings called "subjects." The atom is one such changeling, another is the Kantian "thing-in-itself." Small wonder, then, that the repressed and smoldering emotions of vengeance and hatred have taken advantage of this superstition and in fact espouse no belief more ardently than that it is within the discretion of the strong to be weak, of the bird of prey to be a lamb. Thus they assume the right of calling the bird of prey to account for being a bird of prey. We can hear the oppressed, downtrodden, violated whispering among themselves with the wily vengefulness of the impotent, "Let us be unlike those evil ones. Let us be good. And the good shall be he who does not do violence, does not attack or retaliate, who leaves vengeance to God, who, like us, lives hidden, who shuns all that is evil, and altogether asks very little of life – like us, the patient, the humble, the just ones." Read in cold blood, this means nothing more than "We weak ones are, in fact, weak. It is a good thing that we do nothing for which we are not strong enough." But this plain fact, this basic prudence, which even the insects have (who, in circumstances of great danger, sham death in order not to have to "do" too much) has tricked itself out in the garb of quiet, virtuous resignation, thanks to the duplicity of impotence – as though the weakness of the weak, which is after all his essence, his natural way of being, his sole and inevitable reality, were a spontaneous act, a meritorious deed. This sort of person requires the belief in a "free subject" able to choose indifferently, out of that instinct of self-preservation which notoriously justifies every kind of lie. It may well be that to this day the subject, or in popular language the soul, has been the most viable of all articles of faith simply because it makes it possible for the majority of mankind – i.e., the weak and oppressed of every sort – to practice the sublime sleight of hand which gives weakness the appearance of free choice and one's natural disposition the distinction of merit.

[. . .]

Second Essay

"Guilt," "Bad Conscience," and Related Matters

I

To breed an animal with the right to make promises – is not this the paradoxical problem nature has set itself with regard to man? and is it not man's true problem? That the problem has in fact been solved to a remarkable degree will seem all the more surprising if we do full justice to the strong opposing force, the faculty of oblivion. Oblivion is not merely a *vis inertiae*, as is often claimed, but an active screening device, responsible for the fact that what we experience and digest psychologically does not, in the stage of digestion, emerge into consciousness any more than what we ingest physically does. The role of this active oblivion is that of a concierge: to shut temporarily the doors and windows of consciousness; to protect us from the noise and agitation with which our lower organs work for or against one another; to introduce a little quiet into our consciousness so as to make room for the nobler functions and functionaries of our organism which do the governing and planning. This concierge maintains order and etiquette in the household of the psyche; which immediately suggests that there can be no happiness, no serenity, no hope, no pride, no *present*, without oblivion. A man in whom this screen is damaged and inoperative is like a dyspeptic (and not merely *like* one): he can't be done with anything. . . . Now this naturally forgetful animal, for whom oblivion represents a power, a form of strong health, has created for itself an opposite power, that of remembering, by whose aid, in certain cases, oblivion may be suspended – specifically in cases where it is a question of promises. By this I do not mean a purely passive succumbing to past impressions, the indigestion of being unable to be done with a pledge once made, but rather an active not wishing to be done with it, a continuing to will what has once been willed, a veritable "memory of the will"; so that, between the original determination and the actual performance of the thing willed, a whole world of new things, conditions, even volitional acts, can be interposed without snapping the long chain of the will. But how much all this presupposes! A man who wishes to dispose of his future in this manner must first have learned to separate necessary from accidental acts; to think causally; to see distant things as though they were near at hand; to distinguish means from ends. In short, he must have become not only calculating but himself calculable, regular even to his own perception, if he is to stand pledge for his own future as a guarantor does.

II

This brings us to the long story of the origin or genesis of responsibility. The task of breeding an animal entitled to make promises involves, as we have already seen, the preparatory task of rendering man up to a certain point regular, uniform, equal among equals, calculable. The tremendous achievement which I have referred to in *Day-break* as "the custom character of morals," that labor man accomplished upon himself over a vast period of time, receives its meaning and justification here – even despite the brutality, tyranny, and stupidity associated with the process. With the help of custom and the social strait-jacket, man was, in fact, made calculable. However, if we place ourselves at the terminal point of this great process, where society and custom finally reveal their true aim, we shall find the ripest fruit of that tree to be the sovereign individual, equal only to himself, all moral custom left far behind. This autonomous, more than moral individual (the terms *autonomous* and *moral* are mutually exclusive) has developed his own, independent, long-range will, which dares to make promises; he has a proud and vigorous consciousness of what he has achieved, a sense of power and freedom, of absolute accomplishment. This fully emancipated man, master of his will, who dares make promises – how should he not be aware of his superiority over those who are unable to stand security for themselves? Think how much trust, fear, reverence he inspires (all three fully *deserved*), and how, having that sovereign rule over himself, he has mastery too over all weaker-willed and less reliable creatures! Being truly free and possessor of a long-range, pertinacious will, he also possesses a scale of values. Viewing others from the center of his own being, he either honors or disdains them. It is natural to him to honor his strong and reliable peers, all those who promise like sovereigns: rarely and reluctantly; who are chary of their trust; whose trust is a mark of distinction; whose promises are binding because they know that they will make them good in spite of all accidents, in spite of destiny itself. Yet he will inevitably reserve a kick for those paltry windbags who promise irresponsibly and a rod for those liars who break their word even in uttering it. His proud awareness of the extraordinary privilege responsibility confers has penetrated deeply and become a dominant instinct. What shall he call that dominant instinct, provided he ever feels impelled to give it a name? Surely he will call it his *conscience*.

III

His conscience? It seems a foregone conclusion that this conscience, which we encounter here in its highest form, has behind it a long history of transformations. The right proudly to stand security for oneself, to approve oneself, is a ripe but also a late fruit; how long did that fruit have to hang green and tart on the tree! Over an even longer period there was not the slightest sign of such a fruit; no one had a right to predict it, although the tree was ready for it, organized in every part to the end of bringing it forth. "How does one create a memory for the human animal? How does one go about to impress anything on that partly dull, partly flighty human intelligence – that incarnation of forgetfulness – so as to make it stick?" As we might well imagine, the means used in solving this age-old problem have been far from delicate: in fact, there is perhaps nothing more terrible in man's earliest history than his mnemotechnics. "A thing is branded on the memory to make it stay there; only what goes on hurting will stick" – this is one of the oldest and, unfortunately, one of the most enduring psychological axioms. In fact, one might say that wherever on earth one still finds solemnity, gravity, secrecy, somber hues in the life of an individual or a nation, one also senses a residuum of that terror with which men must formerly have promised, pledged, vouched. It is the past – the longest, deepest, hardest of pasts – that seems to surge up whenever we turn serious. Whenever man has thought it necessary to create a memory for himself, his effort has been attended with torture, blood, sacrifice. The ghastliest sacrifices and pledges, including the sacrifice of the first-born; the most repulsive mutilations, such as castration; the cruelest rituals in every religious cult (and all religions are at bottom systems of cruelty) – all these have their origin in that instinct which divined pain to be the strongest aid to mnemonics. (All asceticism is really part of the same development: here too the object is to make a few ideas omnipresent, unforgettable, "fixed," to the end of hypnotizing the entire nervous and intellectual system; the ascetic procedures help to effect the dissociation of those ideas from all others.) The poorer the memory of mankind has been, the more terrible have been its customs. The severity of all primitive penal codes gives us some idea how difficult it must have been for man to overcome his forgetfulness and to drum into these slaves of momentary whims and desires a few basic requirements of communal living. Nobody can say that we Germans consider ourselves an especially cruel and brutal nation, much less a frivolous and thriftless one; but it needs only a glance at our ancient penal codes to impress on us what labor it takes to create a nation of thinkers. (I would even say that we are the one European nation among whom is still to be found a maximum of trust, seriousness, insipidity, and matter-of-factness, which should entitle us to breed a mandarin caste for all of Europe.) Germans have resorted to ghastly means in order to triumph over their plebeian instincts and brutal coarseness. We need only recount some of our ancient forms of punishment: stoning (even in earliest legend millstones are dropped on the heads of culprits); breaking on the wheel (Germany's own contribution to the techniques of punishment); piercing with stakes, drawing and quartering, trampling to death with horses, boiling in oil or wine (these were still in use in the fourteenth and fifteenth centuries), the popular flaying alive, cutting out of flesh from the chest, smearing the victim with honey and leaving him in the sun, a prey to flies. By such methods the individual was finally taught to remember five or six "I won'ts" which entitled him to participate in the benefits of society; and indeed, with the aid of this sort of memory, people eventually "came to their senses." What an enormous price man had to pay for reason, seriousness, control over his emotions – those grand human prerogatives and cultural showpieces! How much blood and horror lies behind all "good things"!

IV

But how about the origin of that other somber phenomenon, the consciousness of guilt, "bad conscience"? Would you turn to our genealogists of morals for illumination? Let me say once again, they are worthless. Completely absorbed in "modern" experience, with no real knowledge of the past, no desire even to understand it, no historical instinct whatever, they presume, all the same, to write the history of ethics! Such an undertaking must produce results which bear not the slightest relation to truth. Have these historians shown any awareness of the fact that the basic moral term *Schuld* (guilt) has its origin in the very material term *Schulden* (to be indebted)? Of the fact that punishment, being a *compensation*, has developed quite independently of any ideas about freedom of the will – indeed, that a very high level of humanization was necessary before even the much more primitive distinctions, "with intent," "through negligence," "by accident," *compos mentis*, and their opposites could be made and allowed to weigh in the judgments of cases? The pat and seemingly natural notion (so natural that it has often been used to account for the origin of the notion of justice itself) that the criminal deserves to be punished *because* he could have acted otherwise, is in fact a very late and refined form of human reasoning; whoever thinks it can be found in archaic law grossly misconstrues the psychology of uncivilized man. For an unconscionably long time culprits were not punished because they were felt to be responsible for their actions; not, that is, on the assumption that only the guilty were to be punished; rather, they were punished the way parents still punish their children, out of rage at some damage suffered, which the doer must pay for. Yet this rage was both moderated and modified by the notion that for every damage there could somehow be found an equivalent, by which that damage might be compensated – if necessary in the pain of the doer. To the question how did that ancient, deep-rooted, still firmly established notion of an equivalency between damage and pain arise, the answer is, briefly: it arose in the contractual relation between creditor and debtor, which is as old as the notion of "legal subjects" itself and which in its turn points back to the basic practices of purchase, sale, barter, and trade.
    [. . .]

XVI

I can no longer postpone giving tentative expression to my own hypothesis concerning the origin of "bad conscience." It is one that may fall rather strangely on our ears and that requires close meditation. I take bad conscience to be a deep-seated malady to which man succumbed under the pressure of the most profound transformation he ever underwent – the one that made him once and for all a sociable and pacific creature. Just as happened in the case of those sea creatures who were forced to become land animals in order to survive, these semi-animals, happily adapted to the wilderness, to war, free roaming, and adventure, were forced to change their nature. Of a sudden they found all their instincts devalued, unhinged. They must walk on legs and carry themselves, where before the water had carried them: a terrible heaviness weighed upon them. They felt inapt for the simplest manipulations, for in this new, unknown world they could no longer count on the guidance of their unconscious drives. They were forced to think, deduce, calculate, weigh cause and effect – unhappy people, reduced to their weakest, most fallible organ, their consciousness! I doubt that there has ever been on earth such a feeling of misery, such a leaden discomfort. It was not that those old instincts had abruptly ceased making their demands; but now their satisfaction was rare and difficult. For the most part they had to depend on new, covert satisfactions. All instincts that are not allowed free play turn inward. This is what I call man's interiorization; it alone provides the soil for the growth of what is later called man's *soul*. Man's interior world, originally meager and tenuous, was expanding in every dimension, in proportion as the outward discharge of his feelings was curtailed. The formidable bulwarks by means of which the polity protected itself against the ancient instincts of freedom (punishment was one of the strongest of these bulwarks) caused those wild, extravagant instincts to turn in upon man. Hostility, cruelty, the delight in persecution, raids, excitement, destruction all turned against their begetter. Lacking external enemies and resistances, and confined within an oppressive narrowness and regularity, man began rending, persecuting, terrifying himself, like a wild beast hurling itself against the bars of its cage. This languisher, devoured by nostalgia for the desert, who had to turn *himself* into an adventure, a torture chamber, an insecure and dangerous wilderness – this fool, this pining and desperate prisoner, became the inventor of "bad conscience." Also the generator of the greatest and most disastrous of maladies, of which humanity has not to this day been cured: his sickness of himself, brought on by the violent severance from his animal past, by his sudden leap and fall into new layers and conditions of existence, by his declaration of war against the old instincts that had hitherto been the foundation of this power, his joy, and his awesomeness. Let me hasten to add that the phenomenon of an animal soul turning in upon itself, taking arms against itself, was so novel, profound, mysterious, contradictory, and pregnant with possibility, that the whole complexion of the universe was changed thereby. This spectacle (and the end of it is not yet in sight) required a divine audience to do it justice. It was a spectacle too sublime and paradoxical to pass unnoticed on some trivial planet. Henceforth man was to figure among the most unexpected and breathtaking throws in the game of dice played by Heracleitus' great "child," be he called Zeus or Chance. Man now aroused an interest, a suspense, a hope, almost a conviction – as though in him something were heralded, as though he were not a goal but a way, an interlude, a bridge, a great promise. . . .

[. . .]

XVIII

We should guard against taking too dim a view of this phenomenon simply because it is both ugly and painful. After all, the same will to power which in those violent artists and organizers created polities, in the "labyrinth of the heart" – more pettily, to be sure, and in inverse direction – created negative ideals and humanity's bad conscience. Except that now the material upon which this great natural force was employed was man himself, his old animal self – and not, as in that grander and more spectacular phenomenon – his fellow man. This secret violation of the self, this artist's cruelty, this urge to impose on recalcitrant matter a form, a will, a distinction, a feeling of contradiction and contempt, this sinister task of a soul divided against itself, which makes itself suffer for the pleasure of suffering, this most energetic "bad conscience" – has it not given birth to a wealth of strange beauty and affirmation? Has it not given birth to beauty itself? Would beauty exist if ugliness had not first taken cognizance of itself, not said to itself, "I am ugly"? This hint will serve, at any rate, to solve the riddle of why contradictory terms such as *selflessness, self-denial, self-sacrifice* may intimate an ideal, a beauty. Nor will the reader doubt henceforth that the *joy* felt by the self-denying, self-sacrificing, selfless person was from the very start a *cruel* joy. – So much for the origin of altruism as a moral value. Bad conscience, the desire for self-mortification, is the wellspring of all altruistic values.

PART III

PHENOMENOLOGY AND EXISTENTIALISM

7

COMMENTARY ON SARTRE

Jean-Paul Sartre (1905–80) is popularly regarded as the exemplar existentialist. He is noted for his range of talents (novelist, playwright, and political activist), as well as for the influence of his work and the extraordinary times in which he wrote. He was awarded, but refused to accept, the Nobel Prize for Literature in 1962. Sartre's closest influence was Simone de Beauvoir, and the two were intimate collaborators during their entire adult lives. The originator of the central idea of "The Look" is now widely held to have been Beauvoir.[1]

Existentialism is generally considered to have begun with Søren Kierkegaard, who challenged the Enlightenment faith in reason. Put crudely, he thought it was personal revelation, not reason, that led to truth. Once revealed, truth could be chosen or not. In choosing truth one chooses who and what one becomes. On this view, the task of philosophy is met, not by the universality of reason, but through a distinctly personal effort to know one's *own* nature, the "strange inaccessible self."[2] In the case of Sartre, it is the denial of God that drives his philosophy. Sartre argued that the belief that human nature consisted in the rational soul was a by-product of the popular conception of God as a craftsman of humankind.[3] Reversing this view, Sartre declared that humankind's existence *precedes* its essence: "there is no human nature because there is no God to have a conception of it. . . . Man is nothing else but that which he makes of himself. . . . man will only attain existence when he is what he purposes to be."[4] Behind this claim are a number of the ideas that made their first appearance in Sartre's early essay, "The Transcendence of the Ego." There he distinguished two modes of consciousness: a prereflective *cogito* and a reflective *cogito*, arguing that Descartes failed to realize that his *cogito* was not immediate and self-transparent but reflective: the consciousness that says "I am" is not the same consciousness that thinks. The former is the expression of consciousness that has been reflected upon, whereas the latter is an anonymous and spontaneous prereflective consciousness.

For Sartre, prereflective consciousness does not express a particular "I," but simply a general consciousness of something. The "I" (or "me" or "Ego") forms when prereflective consciousness is reflected upon (by itself) and becomes explicit consciousness. When reflection occurs, consciousness becomes aware of its objects as being related according to an ideal unity, a perspectival unity. This ideal unity is what Sartre calls the Ego. For Sartre, there is no "self" in the Cartesian sense; there is only consciousness, which is comprised of the ideal unity of the Ego constituted through the particular reflective activity of a prereflective consciousness. The Ego is a product of the power of reflection (consciousness) directed toward its own activity. Although Sartre refers to the Ego as an object of consciousness, strictly speaking reflective consciousness does not give rise to the self or Ego as an object. Rather, it produces a fresh way of being conscious of the objects given in prereflective consciousness.

In *Being and Nothingness* Sartre classifies consciousness as one of two basic types of existence, being-in-itself or *en-soi* (objects) and being-for-itself or *pour-soi* (consciousness).[5] Sartre describes being-for-itself as nothingness, or nihilation (very close to Hegel's conception). Consciousness is not an entity, but simply "not-this," not the objects of which there is consciousness. Hazel Barnes explains that the idea here is that there are things – a world – for us only because there is consciousness. In a universe without consciousness there would be being, but no "thing," because "thing" (or "object") is a concept and, as such, is something only for a subject. Consciousness adds nothing to the universe but nevertheless creates a world of objects.[6]

From this conception of consciousness comes Sartre's contentious account of freedom. As a power of negation, being-for-itself can have projects and plans because it can always say "no" to its situation (here, Sartre equates negation with choosing). This gives one the power to exceed the givenness (or "facticity") of one's situation, which, for Sartre, is freedom (or "transcendence"). This view underpins Sartre's claim that human existence precedes its essence. As pure negation, freedom undermines the idea of a determinate "human nature." Rather, as the power of negation (or choice), human beings are free to create the meaning of their own existences; moreover, they are human beings *only* when they do so.

Sartre famously argues that we are "condemned to be free," and cannot evade the responsibility for our own lives because we are only what we make of ourselves, "the rest is self-deception or cowardice"[7] – or what Sartre calls "bad faith." Sartre goes as far as claiming that although I may not be able to realize my aims in action, for example, because I am imprisoned, I am nevertheless free because I can form the intention to act and the values that motivate it. In essence, Sartre's conception of choice is negative: I am never in the situation where I cannot choose and cannot be responsible for my choices; I can always say "no" to my captors. Simone de Beauvoir criticized Sartre for failing to appreciate the significance of the differences in power that characterize and circumscribe the lives of men and women – a point that has been central to contemporary accounts of psychological oppression.

The account of "the look" as the means by which the unity of one's Ego and consequently one's sense of self is penetrated by another consciousness, is one of the most interesting aspects of existentialism. It has been extremely influential, for example, in Michel Foucault's work on power, which has itself influenced a generation of philosophers. In this section of *Being and Nothingness*, Sartre not so much resolves the problem of how we can know other minds as dissolves it. In brief, he argues that my relation to another person (the Other) is not an epistemological issue, that is, not a matter of *knowing* the Other, but rather, an "absolute event," an ontological datum.

Sartre's account of the interpersonal encounter is modeled upon the conflictual relations of the Hegelian master–slave dialectic: it is an experience of annihilation of one's subjectivity. This occurs, says Sartre, when another person perceives me. On being looked at, for example, I feel myself to be reduced to an object in the person's perceptual field. This induces in me an acute awareness that I am something other than the center of the whole world; I am an object in a world in which the Other's consciousness is the center. This is why, in his discussion of being in the park, Sartre describes the world as "fleeing" from him when another person comes on the scene. The appearance of the Other acts like a new gravitational field, drawing into its own orbit the objects which were orbiting me. Worse still, I feel myself pulled into an orbit around the Other, and lose entirely my special status as a center of the universe as I am compelled to inhabit a world organized around the Other's perspective.

Unlike Hegel, Sartre argues that the encounter with an Other is not a question of cognition of something *in* my world because it is not a question of a relation to an object. The crucial point is that the presence of the Other transforms my entire world. In this, my relation to the Other is revealed as an ontological state, not a relation of knowledge. If my relation to the Other was a special instance of a relation to an object, when I sense a person in my vicinity I should, as Sartre says, comprehend that person as occupying a certain spatial location and relation to the other objects in my vicinity. But that is not the case. The Other does not merely add to my situation: he or she fundamentally alters the orientation of the objects in my world and effects a reorganization of my experiential field.

Sartre argues that not only does the Other's presence alter my relation to objects, the Other's regard of me alters my relation to myself. When the Other perceives me I no longer regard myself as a free agent who determines the world in relation to my chosen projects, but, instead, as a physical body propelled into a project determined by an Other. In this way, says Sartre, my freedom is annihilated. Sartre claims that our only alternatives in responding to "the Look" are fear, shame, or pride. I either succumb to the power of the Other's freedom or assert my own by returning the gaze and threatening the Other with annihilation. As far as Sartre is concerned, the conflict can never be resolved once and for all; there can only be assertion and counter-assertion, and all interpersonal relations are of this type. Sartre claims that in dealing with the emotions induced by the Other's gaze, we resort to a variety of strategies which all rest upon bad faith: vanity, seduction, sadism, masochism, indifference, and even love. They all fail as attempts to escape the bondage of the Other's nihilating power because, being ontological, it cannot be evaded. As a result, the Other's Ego (or perspective) becomes enmeshed with my own sense of self – the gaze of the Other is internalized, as Foucault later puts it.

Marjorie Grene notes that Sartre's analysis lacks any trace of "original togetherness," even of the originary togetherness of the maternal relation (which becomes important for later feminist scholars such as Luce Irigaray). Instead, he presents his readers with a distorted abstraction in which "solitary inwardness" is taken as the whole of subjective life.[8] We will find a much less conflictual account of intersubjectivity in the philosophies of Merleau-Ponty and Simone de Beauvoir.

Notes

1   In 1959 Sartre's English translator, Hazel Barnes, noted that the ideas presented in *Being and Nothingness* had been systematically depicted in Beauvoir's novel *L'Invitée* (translated as *She Came to Stay*), published in the same year (see Kate Fullbrook and Edward Fullbrook, "de Beauvoir," in Simon Critchley and William Schroeder (eds.), *A Companion to Continental Philosophy* (Oxford and Malden, MA: Blackwell, 1998), pp. 269–80). As late as 1986 Ronald Hayman claimed that Beauvoir "made excellent use . . . of his [Sartre's] ideas, his categories, his attitudes, while he benefited from seeing them in both her life and her books" (Hayman, *Writing Against: A Biography of Sartre* (London: George Weidenfeld and Nicolson Limited, 1986), p. 80). It seems that these commentators simply assumed that it was Sartre who had influenced Beauvoir, until Beauvoir claimed authorship in 1979. See Kate and Edward Fullbrook (1998); also Dermot Moran, "Jean Paul Sartre: Passionate Description," in *Introduction to Phenomenology* (London and New York: Routledge, 2000, pp. 354–90).
2   Marjorie Grene, *Introduction to Existentialism* (London: University of Chicago, 1959), p. 24.
3   Sartre, "Existentialism is a Humanism," in Walter Kaufman (ed.), *Existentialism from Dostoyevsky to Sartre* (New York: Meridian, 1989), p. 349.
4   Ibid, p. 349. Sartre does not provide an argument in his defense. Grene notes that he could have argued against Aristotle, who does not assume that the absence of God entails the absence of a human essence. See Grene (1959), p. 44.
5   Being-for-itself contains a subcategory of being-for-Others (*être-pour-autrui*), which refers to the way "in which my Self exists outside as an object for others" – essentially, a state of constant conflict with others. Jean-Paul Sartre, *Being and Nothingness*, trans. Hazel Barnes (New York: Washington Square/Pocket Books, 1966), p. 800.
6   See Hazel Barnes's "Translator's Introduction" to *Being and Nothingness*, p. xxiv.
7   Sartre cited in Robert Solomon, *Continental Philosophy since 1750, The Rise and Fall of the Self* (Oxford and New York: Oxford University Press, 1988), p. 178.
8   Grene (1959), p. 88.

Main Texts by Sartre

Hazel Barnes (trans.), *Being and Nothingness* (New York: Washington Square Books, 1966).
John Matthews (trans.), *Between Existentialism and Marxism* (London: New Left Books, 1974).
David Pellauer (trans.), *Notebook for an Ethics* (Chicago: University of Chicago Press, 1992).
Forrest Williams and Robert Kirkpatrick (trans.), *The Transcendence of the Ego* (New York: Noonday Press, 1962).

Further Reading

Busch, T., *The Power of Consciousness and the Force of Circumstances in Sartre's Philosophy* (Bloomington, IN: Indiana University Press, 1990).
Beauvoir, Simone de, *Adieux: A Farewell to Sartre*, trans. Patrick O'Brien (New York: Pantheon Books, 1984).
Catalano, J., *A Commentary on Sartre's "Being and Nothingness"* (New York: Harper and Row, 1974).

Howells, C., *Sartre: The Necessity of Freedom* (Cambridge UK: Cambridge University Press, 1988).

Howells, C. (ed.), *The Cambridge Companion to Sartre* (Cambridge, UK: Cambridge University Press, 1992).

Schilpp, P., *The Philosophy of Jean-Paul Sartre*, The Library of Living Philosophers (LaSalle, IL: Open Court, 1981).

"THE LOOK"

Jean-Paul Sartre

This woman whom I see coming toward me, this man who is passing by in the street, this beggar whom I hear calling before my window, all are for me *objects* – of that there is no doubt. Thus it is true that at least one of the modalities of the Other's presence to me is *object-ness*. But we have seen that if this relation of object-ness is the fundamental relation between the Other and myself, then the Other's existence remains purely conjectural. Now it is not only conjectural but *probable* that this voice which I hear is that of a man and not a song on a phonograph; it is infinitely *probable* that the passerby whom I see is a man and not a perfected robot. This means that without going beyond the limits of probability and indeed because of this very probability, my apprehension of the Other as an object essentially refers me to a fundamental apprehension of the Other in which he will not be revealed to me as an object but as a "presence in person." In short, if the Other is to be a probable object and not a dream of an object, then his object-ness must of necessity refer not to an original solitude beyond my reach, but to a fundamental connection in which the Other is manifested in some way other than through the knowledge which I have of him. The classical theories are right in considering that every perceived human organism *refers* to something and that this to which it refers is the foundation and guarantee of its probability. Their mistake lies in believing that this reference indicates a separate existence, a consciousness which would be behind its perceptible manifestations as the noumenon is behind the Kantian *Empfindung*. Whether or not this consciousness exists in a separate state, the face which I see does not refer to it; it is not this consciousness which is the *truth* of the probable object which I perceive. In actual fact the reference is to a twin upsurge in which the Other is presence for me to a "being-in-a-pair-with-the-Other," and this is given outside of knowledge proper even if the latter be conceived as an obscure and unexpressible form on the order of intuition. In other words, the problem of Others has generally been treated as if the primary relation by which the Other is discovered is

From *Being and Nothingness*, translated and introduced by Hazel E. Barnes (New York: Washington Square Press, 1966), pp. 340–51 (part 3, ch. 1, section IV). Reproduced by permission of the Philosophical Library, New York.

object-ness; that is, as if the Other were first revealed – directly or indirectly – to our perception. But since this perception by its very nature *refers* to something other than to itself and since it can refer neither to an infinite series of appearances of the same type – as in idealism the perception of the table or of the chair does – nor to an isolated entity located on principle outside my reach, its essence must be to refer to a primary relation between my consciousness and the Other's. This relation, in which the Other must be given to me directly as a subject although in connection with me, is the fundamental relation, the very type of my being-for-others.

Nevertheless the reference here cannot be to any mystic or ineffable experience. It is in the reality of everyday life that the Other appears to us, and his probability refers to everyday reality. The problem is precisely this: there is in everyday reality an original relation to the Other which can be constantly pointed to and which consequently can be revealed to me outside all reference to a religious or mystic unknowable. In order to understand it I must question more exactly this ordinary appearance of the Other in the field of my perception; since this appearance refers to that fundamental relation, the appearance must be capable of revealing to us, at least as a reality aimed at, the relation to which it refers.

I am in a public park. Not far away there is a lawn and along the edge of that lawn there are benches. A man passes by those benches. I see this man; I apprehend him as an object and at the same time as a man. What does this signify? What do I mean when I assert that this object *is a man*?

If I were to think of him as being only a puppet, I should apply to him the categories which I ordinarily use to group temporal-spatial "things." That is, I should apprehend him as being "beside the benches, two yards and twenty inches from the lawn, as exercising a certain pressure on the ground, *etc.* His relation with other objects would be of the purely additive type; this means that I could have him disappear without the relations of the other objects around him being perceptibly *changed*. In short, no new relation would appear *through him* between those things in my universe: grouped and synthesized *from my point of view* into instrumental complexes, they would *from his* disintegrate into multiplicities of indifferent relations. Perceiving him as a *man*, on the other hand, is not to apprehend an additive relation between the chair and him; it is to register an organization *without distance* of the things in my universe around that privileged object. To be sure, the lawn remains two yards and twenty inches away from him, but it is also *as a lawn* bound to him in a relation which at once both transcends distance and contains it. Instead of the two terms of the distance being indifferent, interchangeable, and in a reciprocal relation, the distance *is unfolded starting from* the man whom I see and *extending up to* the lawn as the synthetic upsurge of a univocal relation. We are dealing with a relation which is without *parts*, given at one stroke, inside of which there unfolds a spatiality which is not *my* spatiality; for instead of a grouping *toward me* of the objects, there is now an orientation *which flees from me*.

Of course this relation without distance and without parts is in no way that original relation of the Other to me which I am seeking. In the first place, it concerns only the man and the things in the world. In addition it is still an object of knowledge; I shall express it, for example, by saying that this man sees the lawn, or that in spite of the prohibiting sign he is preparing to walk on the grass, *etc.* Finally it still retains a pure character of probability: First, it is *probable* that this object is a man. Second, even granted that he is a man, it remains only probable that he sees the lawn at the moment that I perceive him; it is possible that he is dreaming of some project without exactly being aware of what is around him, or that he is blind, *etc., etc.* Nevertheless this new relation of the object-man to the object-lawn has a particular character; it is simultaneously given to me as a whole, since it is there in the world as an object which I can know (it is, in fact, an objective relation which I express by saying: Pierre has glanced at this watch, Jean has looked out the window, *etc.*), and at the same time it entirely escapes me. To the extent that the man-as-object is the fundamental term of this relation, to the extent that the relation *reaches toward him*, it escapes me. I can not put myself at the center of it. The distance which unfolds between the lawn and the man across the synthetic upsurge of this primary relation is a negation of the distance which I establish – as a pure type of external negation – between these two objects. The distance appears as a pure *disintegration* of the relations which I apprehend between the objects of my universe. It is not I who realize this disintegration; it appears to me as a relation which I aim at emptily across the distances which I originally established between things. It stands as a background of things, a background which on principle escapes me and which is conferred on them from without. Thus the appearance among the objects of *my* universe of an element of disintegration in that universe is what I mean by the appearance of a man in my universe.

The Other is first the permanent flight of things toward a goal which I apprehend as an object at a certain distance from me but which escapes me inasmuch as it unfolds about itself its own distances. Moreover this disintegration grows by degrees; if there exists between the lawn and the Other a relation which is without distance and which creates distance, then there exists necessarily a relation between the Other and the statue which stands on a pedestal *in the middle of* the lawn, and a relation between the Other and the big chestnut trees which border the walk; there is a total space which is grouped around the Other, and this space is made *with my space*; there is a regrouping in which I take part but which escapes me, a regrouping of all the objects which people my universe. This regrouping does not stop there. The grass is something qualified; it is *this* green grass which exists for the Other; in this sense the very quality of the object, its deep, raw green is in direct relation to this man. This green turns toward the Other a face which escapes me. I apprehend the relation of the green to the Other as an objective relation, but I can not apprehend the green *as* it appears to the Other. Thus suddenly an object has appeared which has stolen the world from me. Everything is in place; everything still exists for me; but everything is traversed by an invisible flight and fixed in the direction of a new object. The appearance of the Other in the world corresponds therefore to a fixed sliding of the whole universe, to a decentralization of the world which undermines the centralization which I am simultaneously effecting.

But the *Other* is still an object *for me*. He belongs to *my distances*; the man is there, twenty paces from me, he is turning his back on me. As such he is again two yards, twenty inches from the lawn, six yards from the statue; hence the disintegration of my universe is contained within the limits of this same universe; we are not dealing here with a flight of the world toward nothingness or outside itself. Rather it appears that the world has a kind of drain hole in the middle of its being and that it is perpetually flowing off through this hole. The universe, the flow, and the drain hole are all once again recovered, reapprehended, and fixed as an object. All this is there *for me* as a partial structure of the world, even though the total disintegration of the universe is involved. Moreover these disintegrations may often be contained within more narrow limits. There, for example, is a man who is reading while he walks. The disintegration of the universe which he represents is purely virtual: he has ears which do not hear, eyes which see nothing except his book. Between his book and him I apprehend an undeniable relation without distance of the same type as that which earlier connected the walker with the grass. But this time the form has closed in on itself. There is a full object for me to grasp. In the midst of the world I can say "man-reading" as I could say "cold stone," "fine rain." I apprehend a closed "Gestalt" in which the *reading* forms the essential quality; for the rest, it remains blind and mute, lets itself be known and perceived as a pure and simple temporal-spatial thing, and seems to be related to the rest of the world by a purely indifferent externality. The quality "man-reading" as the relation of the man to the book is simply a little particular crack in my universe. At the heart of this solid, visible form he makes himself a particular emptying. The form is massive only in appearance; its peculiar meaning is to be – in the midst of my universe, at ten paces from me, at the heart of that massivity – a closely consolidated and localized flight.

None of this enables us to leave the level on which the Other is an *object*. At most we are dealing with a particular type of objectivity akin to that which Husserl designated by the term *absence* without, however, his noting that the Other is defined not as the absence of a consciousness in relation to the body which I see but by the absence of the world which I perceive, an absence discovered at the very heart of my perception of this world. On this level the Other is an object in the world, an object which can be defined by the world. But this relation of flight and of absence on the part of the world in relation to me is only probable. If it is this which defines the objectivity of the Other, then to what original presence of the Other does it refer? At present we can given this answer: if the Other-as-object is defined in connection with the world as the object which sees what I see, then my fundamental connection with the Other-as-subject must be able to be referred back to my permanent possibility of *being seen* by the Other. It is in and through the revelation of my being-as-object for the Other that I must be able to apprehend the presence of his being-as-subject. For just as the Other is a probable object for me-as-subject, so I can discover myself in the process of becoming a probable object for only a certain subject. This revelation can not derive from the fact that *my universe is an object for the Other-as-object, as if* the Other's look after having wandered over the lawn and the surrounding objects came following a definite path to place itself on me. I have observed that I can not be an object for an object. A radical conversion of the Other is necessary if he is to escape objectivity. Therefore I can not consider the look which the Other directs on me as one of the possible manifestations of his objective being; the Other can not look at *me* as he looks at the grass. Furthermore my objectivity can not itself derive *for me* from the objectivity of the world since I am precisely the one by whom *there is* a world; that is, the one who on principle can not be an object for himself.

Thus this relation which I call "being-seen-by-another," far from being merely one of the relations signified by the word *man*, represents an irreducible fact which can not be deduced either from the essence of the Other-as-object, or from my being-as-subject. On the contrary, if the concept of the Other-as-object is to have any meaning, this can be only as the result of the conversion and the degradation of that original relation. In a word, my apprehension of the Other in the world as *probably being* a man refers to my permanent possibility of *being-seen-by-him*; that is, to the permanent possibility that a subject who sees me may be substituted for the object seen by me. "Being-seen-by-the-Other" is the *truth* of "seeing-the-Other." Thus the notion of the Other can not under any circumstances aim at a solitary, extra-mundane consciousness which I can not even think. The man is defined by his relation to the world and by his relation to myself. He is that object in the world which determines an internal flow of the universe, an internal hemorrhage. He is the subject who is revealed to me in that flight of myself toward objectivation. But the original relation of myself to the Other is not only an absent truth aimed at across the concrete presence of an object in my universe; it is also a concrete, daily relation which at each instant I experience. At each instant the Other *is looking at me*. It is easy therefore for us to attempt with concrete examples to describe this fundamental connection which must form the basis of any theory concerning the Other. If the Other is on principle the *one who looks at me*, then we must be able to explain the meaning of the Other's look.

Every look directed toward me is manifested in connection with the appearance of a sensible form in our perceptive field, but contrary to what might be expected, it is not connected with any determined form. Of course what *most often* manifests a look is the convergence of two ocular globes in my direction. But the look will be given just as well on occasion when there is a rustling of branches, or the sound of a footstep followed by silence, or the slight opening of a shutter, or a light movement of a curtain. During an attack men who are crawling through the brush apprehend as a *look to be avoided*, not two eyes, but a white farmhouse which is outlined against the sky at the top of a little hill. It is obvious that the object thus constituted still manifests the look as being probable. It is only probable that behind the bush which has just moved there is someone hiding who is watching me. But this probability need not detain us for the moment; we shall return to this point later. What is important first is to define the look in itself. Now the bush, the farmhouse are not the look; they only represent the *eye*, for the eye is not at first apprehended as a sensible organ of vision but as the support for the look. They never refer therefore to the actual eye of the watcher hidden behind the curtain, behind a window in the farmhouse. In themselves they are already eyes. On the other hand neither is the look one quality among others of the object which functions as an eye, nor is it the total form of that object, nor a "worldly" relation which is established between that object and me. On the contrary, far from perceiving the look *on* the objects which manifest it, my apprehension of a look turned toward me appears on the ground of the destruction of the eyes which "look at me." If I apprehend the look, I cease to perceive the eyes; they are there, they remain in the field of my perception as pure *presentations*, but I do not make any use of them; they are neutralized, put out of play; they are no longer the object of a thesis but remain in that state of "disconnection"[1] in which the world is put by a consciousness practicing the phenomenological reduction prescribed by Husserl. It is never when eyes are looking at you that you can find them beautiful or ugly, that you can remark on their color. The Other's look hides his eyes; he seems to go *in front of them*. This illusion stems from the fact that eyes as objects of my perception remain at a precise distance which unfolds from me to them (in a word, I am present to the eyes without distance, but they are distant from the place where I "find myself") whereas the look is upon me without distance while at the same time it holds me at a distance – that is, its imme-diate presence to me unfolds a distance which removes me from it. I can not therefore direct my attention on the look without at the same stroke causing my perception to decompose and pass into the background. There is produced here something analogous to what I attempted to show elsewhere in connection with the subject of the imagi-nation.[2] We can not, I said then, perceive and imagine simultaneously; it must be either one or the other. I should willingly say here: we can not perceive the world and at the same time apprehend a look fastened upon us; it must be either one or the other. This is because to perceive is to *look at*, and to apprehend a look is not to apprehend a look-as-object in the world (unless the look is not directed upon us); it is to be conscious of *being looked at*. The look which the *eyes* manifest, no matter what kind of eyes they are, is a pure reference to myself. What I apprehend immediately when I hear the branches crackling behind me is not that *there is someone there*; it is that I am vulnera-ble, that I have a body which can be hurt, that I occupy a place and that I can not in any case escape from the space in which I am without defense – in short, that I *am seen*. Thus the look is first an intermediary which refers from me to myself. What is the nature of this intermediary? What does *being seen* mean for me?

Let us imagine that moved by jealousy, curiosity, or vice I have just glued my ear to the door and looked through a keyhole. I am alone and on the level of a non–thetic self-consciousness. This means first of all that there is no self to inhabit my conscious-ness, nothing therefore to which I can refer my acts in order to qualify them. They are in no way *known*; I *am my acts* and hence they carry in themselves their whole justifi-cation. I am a pure consciousness *of* things, and things, caught up in the circuit of my selfness, offer to me their potentialities as the proof of my non–thetic consciousness (of) my own possibilities. This means that behind that door a spectacle is presented as "to be seen," a conversation as "to be heard." The door, the keyhole are at once both instru-ments and obstacles; they are presented as "to be handled with care"; the keyhole is given as "to be looked through close by and a little to one side," *etc.* Hence from this moment "I do what I have to do." No transcending view comes to confer upon my acts the character of a *given* on which a judgment can be brought to bear. My con-sciousness sticks to my acts, it *is* my acts; and my acts are commanded only by the ends to be attained and by the instruments to be employed. My attitude, for example, has no "outside"; it is a pure process of relating the instrument (the keyhole) to the end to be attained (the spectacle to be seen), a pure mode of losing myself in the world, of causing myself to be drunk in by things as ink is by a blotter in order that an instrumental-complex oriented toward an end may be synthetically detached on the ground of the world. The order is the reverse of causal order. It is the end to be attained which organizes all the moments which precede it. The end justifies the means; the means do not exist for themselves and outside the end.

Moreover the ensemble exists only in relation to a free project of my possibilities. Jealousy, as the possibility which I *am*, organizes this instrumental complex by tran-scending it toward itself. But I *am* this jealousy; I do not *know* it. If I contemplated it instead of making it, then only the worldly complex in instrumentality could teach it to me. This ensemble in the world with its double and inverted determination (there is a spectacle to be seen behind the door only because I am jealous, but my jealousy is nothing except the simple objective fact that *there is* a sight *to be seen* behind the door) – this we shall call *situation*. This situation reflects to me at once both my facticity and my freedom; on the occasion of a certain objective structure of the world which surrounds me, it refers my freedom to me in the form of tasks to be freely done. There is no constraint here since my freedom eats into my possibles and since correlatively the potentialities of the world indicate and offer only themselves. Moreover I can not truly define myself as *being* in a situation: first because I am not a positional consciousness of myself; second because I am my own nothingness. In this sense – and since I am what I am not and since I am not what I am – I can not even define myself as truly *being* in the process of listening at doors. I escape this provisional definition of myself by means of all my transcendence. There as we have seen is the origin of bad faith. Thus not only am I unable to *know* myself, but my very being escapes – although I *am* that very escape from my being – and I am absolutely nothing. There is nothing *there* but a pure nothingness encircling a certain objective ensemble and throwing it into relief outlined upon the world, but this ensemble is a real system, a disposition of means in view of an end.

But all of a sudden I hear footsteps in the hall. Someone is looking at me! What does this mean? It means that I am suddenly affected in my being and that essential modifications appear in my structure – modifications which I can apprehend and fix conceptually by means of the reflective *cogito*.

First of all, I now exist as *myself* for my unreflective consciousness. It is this irruption of the self which has been most often described: I see *myself* because *somebody* sees me – as it is usually expressed. This way of putting it is not wholly exact. But let us look more carefully. So long as we considered the for-itself in its isolation, we were able to maintain that the unreflective consciousness can not be inhabited by a self; the self was given in the form of an object and only for the reflective consciousness. But here the self comes to haunt the unreflective consciousness. Now the unreflective consciousness is a consciousness *of* the world. Therefore for the unreflective consciousness the self exists on the level of objects in the world; this role which devolved only on the reflective consciousness – the making-present of the self – belongs now to the unreflective consciousness. Only the reflective consciousness has the self directly for an object. The unreflective consciousness does not apprehend the *person* directly or as *its* object; the person is presented to consciousness *in so far as the person is an object for the Other*. This means that all of a sudden I am conscious of myself as escaping myself, not in that I am the foundation of my own nothingness but in that I have my foundation outside myself. I am for myself only as I am a pure reference to the Other.

Nevertheless we must not conclude here that the object is the Other and that the *Ego* present to my consciousness is a secondary structure or a meaning of the Other-as-object; the Other is not an object here and can not be an object, as we have shown, unless by the same stroke *my* self ceases to be an object-for-the-Other and vanishes. Thus I do not aim at the Other as an object nor at my *Ego* as an object for myself; I do not even direct an empty intention toward that *Ego* as toward an object presently out of my reach. In fact it is separated from me by a nothingness which I can not fill since I apprehend it *as not being for me* and since on principle it exists for the *Other*. Therefore I do not aim at it as if it could someday be given me but on the contrary in so far as it on principle flees from me and will never belong to me. Nevertheless I *am that Ego*; I do not reject it as a strange image, but it is present to me as a self which I *am* without *knowing* it; for I discover it in shame and, in other instances, in pride. It is shame or pride which reveals to me the Other's look and myself at the end of that look. It is the shame or pride which makes me *live*, not *know* the situation of being looked at.

Now, shame [. . .] is shame of *self*; it is the *recognition* of the fact that I *am* indeed that object which the Other is looking at and judging. I can be ashamed only as my freedom escapes me in order to become a *given* object. Thus originally the bond between my unreflective consciousness and my *Ego*, which is being looked at, is a bond not of knowing but of being. Beyond any knowledge which I can have, I am this self which another knows. And this self which I am – this I am in a world which the Other has made alien to me, for the Other's look embraces my being and correlatively the walls, the door, the keyhole. All these instrumental-things, in the midst of which I am, now turn toward the Other a face which on principle escapes me. Thus I am my *Ego* for the Other in the midst of a world which flows toward the Other. Earlier we were able to call this internal hemorrhage the flow of *my* world toward the Other-as-object. This was because the flow of blood was trapped and localized by the very fact that I fixed as an object in my world that Other toward which this world was bleeding. Thus not a drop of blood was lost; all was recovered, surrounded, localized although in a being which I could not penetrate. Here on the contrary the flight is without limit; it is lost externally; the world flows out of the world and I flow outside myself. The Other's look makes me be beyond my being in this world and puts me in the midst of the world which is at once *this world* and beyond this world. What sort of relations can I enter into with this being which I am and which shame reveals to me?

In the first place there is a relation of being. I *am* this being. I do not for an instant think of denying it; my shame is a confession. I shall be able later to use bad faith so as to hide it from myself, but had faith is also a confession since it is an effort to flee the being which I am. But I am this being, neither in the mode of "having to be" nor in that of "was"; I do not found it in its being; I can not produce it directly. But neither is it the indirect, strict effect of my acts as when my shadow on the ground or my reflection in the mirror is moved in correlation with the gestures which I make. This being which I am preserves a certain indetermination, a certain unpredictability. And these new characteristics do not come only from the fact that I can not *know* the Other; they stem also and especially from the fact that the Other is free. Or to be exact and to reverse the terms, the Other's freedom is revealed to me across the uneasy indetermination of the being which I am for him. Thus this being is not my possible; it is not always in question at the heart of my freedom. On the contrary, it is the limit of my freedom, its "backstage" in the sense that we speak of "behind the scenes." It is given to me as a burden which I carry without ever being able to turn back to know it, without even being able to realize its weight. If it is comparable to my shadow, it is like a shadow which is projected on a moving and unpredictable material such that no table of reference can be provided for calculating the distortions resulting from these movements. Yet we still have to do with *my* being and not with an image of my being. We are dealing with my being as it is written in and by the Other's freedom. Everything takes place as if I had a dimension of being from which I was separated by a radical nothingness; and this nothingness is the Other's freedom. The Other has to make my being-for-him *be* in so far as he has to be his being. Thus each of my free conducts engages me in a new environment where the very stuff of my being is the unpredictable freedom of another. Yet by my very shame I claim as mine that freedom of another. I affirm a profound unity of consciousness, not that harmony of monads which has some-times been taken as a guarantee of objectivity but a unity of being; for I accept and wish that others should confer upon me a being which I recognize.

Notes

1   Tr. Literally, "put out of circuit" (*mise hors circuit*).
2   *L'Imaginaire*. 1940.

8

COMMENTARY ON MERLEAU-PONTY

Maurice Merleau-Ponty was born in Rochefort-sur-Mer, France, in 1908, and died unexpectedly in 1961. He studied at the École Normale Supérieure in Paris, where he became friends with Sartre and de Beauvoir. Sartre wrote that Merleau-Ponty confessed to having had an incomparably happy childhood, and was deeply attached to his mother whose death left him devastated. Sartre considered these early experiences to be formative of Merleau-Ponty's philosophy, with its desire to return to the beginnings of life, and a relation to the world that is intimate, enveloping, and nurturing. Besides these personal influences, Merleau-Ponty was heavily influenced by Husserlian phenomenology and Heidegger's concept of being-in-the-world, as well as with the structuralist thought of Claude Lévi-Strauss. Merleau-Ponty's philosophical aim was always to get behind rationality to expose the original processes by which we become aware of the world. He considered these processes to be bodily or "carnate." Merleau-Ponty rejected naïve realism in favor of a world the form and significance of which is centered around the presupposition of the human form.

Merleau-Ponty was influenced early on by Gestalt theory, popular in psychology. He thought that, in contrast to the problematic dichotomies of empiricism, Gestalt theory provided a holistic theoretical framework by which he could better grasp the nature of human experience as it is lived. Gestalt theory is the view that organization and meaning are intrinsic to the perceptual field. Empiricism argued that complex perceptions are formed from the aggregation of "atomistic" sensations. By contrast, Gestalt theory argued that sensations always already appear within a context of meaning such that perceptions always exhibit a given structure and form. The basic structure of perception, on this view, is a foreground/background (or "theme/horizon") relation: an object is always perceived against a background. The foregrounding of an object endows it with significance (or theme), but that significance is articulated only against an unthematized background (or horizon). Merleau-Ponty notes that this structure cannot be broken down further, even in the most simple of perceptions, for example, perceiving a white patch on a homogeneous background of contrasting color.[1] He concludes that foreground/background rather than atomism is the most basic structure of experience. This raises the question of how one's very first perceptions – that is, infantile perceptions – can be given as meaningful, considering the infant's total lack of expe-rience. Merleau-Ponty's answer is that it is one's body that functions as a background against which objects are perceived. One's carnate, living body endows objects of perception with a *practical* significance.

The Phenomenology of Perception is a treatise on embodied subjectivity in which Merleau-Ponty identifies the ways in which one's body structures prereflective con-sciousness through its ability to organize the perceptual field with practical meaning. He believed that a lot of the work that was routinely attributed to reflective con-sciousness went on at this prior prereflective level. Unlike dualist philosophies that regarded the body as a distorting and even unruly obstacle between the mind and truth, Merleau-Ponty insists that it is only through one's own body that one is, quite liter-ally, in contact and communication with reality. Thus it is through one's bodily involve-ment with the world that meaning is primarily established. This basic idea leads Merleau-Ponty to argue that the meaning of the world is articulated bodily, and that the origins of our understandings of the world can be traced to our bodily capacities, amongst which he counts the gestural basis of language. This thesis lies behind Merleau-Ponty's interest in the cognitive deficits of patients such as Schneider.

As a result of a brain lesion, Schneider had his capacity to function abstractly severely impaired. He had immense difficulty in carrying out any instructions because it required that he conceptualize a task prior to performing it. Even with his eyes open Schneider could not touch his nose with a ruler when requested. Nevertheless, Schneider had retained the capacity to spontaneously act purposively in complex and habitual ways. For example, he could immediately locate the spot where he is bitten by an insect, find a handkerchief and blow his nose, and his level of performance at work was reported to be not far below normal.

Merleau-Ponty explains that although Schneider had great difficulty acting on the basis of what he *thought*, the world did not cease to be meaningful for him, and his actions did not cease to be purposeful. The actions that Schneider could perform with ease were activities involving situations to which he was habituated or which involved his immediate feelings, that is, situations that had an immediate practical significance for him. Merleau-Ponty argued that this demonstrated the existence of a prereflective *cogito*, a primordial and practical *cogito*. It shows, he argued, that prior to the "I am" there exists an "I can." For Merleau-Ponty, prior to abstract thought there is a kind of natural affinity between the world as a set of possibilities and one's body as the means of actualizing them. Schneider's lesion, which affects his abstract capacities, has left intact this prior basic affinity of body and world that underwrites the capacity to act.

Reasoning from Schneider's situation, Merleau-Ponty argues that the basic struc-tures of the experiential world are laid down through one's body such that the world exhibits features that reflect the powers of one's own body. This is no idealism; such a situation is possible only if the body is continuous with the world, part of the "flesh" of the world. This carnate power to organize the perceptual field is what Merleau-Ponty and others have called the body-schema.[2] The body-schema is a kind of inter-face of oneself and the world, or an immanent topography of the experiential field. The idea here is that one's body, precisely because it not detached and alien like an immaterial ego, but enmeshed with the world, is able to articulate a perspective on the world. For example, we experience the world in terms of qualities such as color, shape, texture, size, and sound, because we have visual, tactile, and auditory capacities. Similarly, with my eyes on the front of my face looking out in the same direction that my arms and legs propel me, I experience the world in terms of "front" and "behind." Furthermore, I can correlate limitations in my judgments of objects with the limitations of my experiences of my own body; for example, I cannot see behind me because my eyes are on the front of my face. All this allows me to experience the world in certain ways by structuring the field of possible action that I can inhabit. This is why Merleau-Ponty describes the world as a "prolongation" of the body, and consciousness as a kind of "internal double" of the world.

The reality is a little more complicated, as Merleau-Ponty describes at length in the *Phenomenology*, because the body is not only an apparatus of perception, but perceives through the medium of its own sensate flesh. In other words, the body is both a "sensible" – something that can be felt and perceived, like other things in the world – and a subject of sensation, a perceiver; and it is both of these *simultaneously*. This structures all experience with an ineliminable ambiguity, which grounds the need for an interpretative, or hermeneutic, epistemology.

For Merleau-Ponty, the continuity between the world and the body allows each to give form to the other. On this view, I understand the world through the kind of practical engagements it affords my body; and at the same time, the ways in which the world accommodates aspects of my bodily capacities gives form and meaning to my body. There is a constant backward and forward relatedness of meanings between one's body and one's situation. This I–world relation is a two-way street, a constant dynamic through which meaning is produced. Merleau-Ponty describes this as "reversibility." In his later work, *The Visible and the Invisible*, he develops reversibility into the more complex notion of "chiasm."

As well as undercutting the dichotomies of dualism, Merleau-Ponty's philosophy of embodiment also provides a response to the problem of other minds. Merleau-Ponty argues that I am able to understand other people because they have an immediate practical significance for me in virtue of our common bodily form.[3] He argues that I recognize another person through a kind of identification of the bodily powers I feel myself to possess with those I find expressed in the bodies of others. Initially this is an unreflective process that begins with the bodily intimacy of the mother–child relation and becomes more sophisticated as one's body develops, especially with the acquisition of language.[4]

The acquisition of language is one particular use of the body that has a pivotal role in our relations with others because it marks my entry as an "I" into the social and conceptual realms. For Merleau-Ponty, discourse is a kind of "dual being," a shared activity in which interlocutors create mutual understanding through their participation in a common meaning-making activity. Here, discourse is not merely the exchange of information but the mutual creation of meaning, a collaboration within a practical field.[5] This view has none of the violence of Sartrean intersubjectivity. Hostility is possible, and real, of course, but it is by no means the totality of interpersonal relations. Merleau-Ponty gives primacy to a productive, and even benevolent, reciprocity, and regards hostility between persons as a breakdown of that primal relation.

Interest in Merleau-Ponty's work on the importance of embodiment has increased in recent years as philosophers explore the impact of technology, especially technologies of the body. His work has been taken up by feminist philosopher, Judith Butler, to explore gender identity, as well as by analytical philosophers with interests in epistemology and autonomy.[6]

Notes

1   Maurice Merleau-Ponty, *Phenomenology of Perception*, trans. Colin Smith (London: Routledge, 1992) (hereafter *PP*), p. 4.

2   Merleau-Ponty refers to "body-image" (see *PP*, p.141 and p. 99 fn.) but translators use the term "body-schema" to avoid a psychological interpretation of the concept. The exposition of the notion of the body-schema appears in Part One, Section 3, entitled "The Spatiality of One's Own Body and Motility." For a clear exposition of this notion, see Douwe Tiemersma, "'Body-image' and 'Body-schema' in the Existential Phenomenology of Merleau-Ponty," *Journal of the British Society of Phenomenology*, 13 (3), 1982, pp. 246–55.

3   See "Other Selves and the Human World" in *PP*, especially pp. 348–52.

4   See "The Body as Expression, and Speech" in *PP*, pp. 174–99.

5   *PP*, p. 354.

6   See Jose Luis Bermúdez, Anthony Marcel, and Naomi Eilan (eds.), *The Body and the Self* (Cambridge, MA: MIT Press, 1998); also Moira Gatens, *Imaginary Bodies: Ethics, Power, and Corporeality* (New York: Routledge, 1996); Catriona Mackenzie, "On Bodily Autonomy," in S. K. Toombs (ed.), *Philosophy and Medicine, Vol. 68: Handbook of Phenomenology and Medicine* (Dordrecht: Kluwer Academic Press, 2001), pp. 417–39.

Main Texts by Merleau-Ponty

Alden Fisher (trans.), *Adventures of the Dialectic* (Evanston IL: Northwestern University Press, 1973).

John O'Neill (trans.), *Humanism and Terror* (Boston, MA: Beacon Press, 1969).

Colin Smith (trans.), *Phenomenology of Perception* (London: Routledge, 1992).

James Edie (trans.), *The Primacy of Perception* (Evanston IL: Northwestern University Press, 1964).

John O'Neill (trans.), *The Prose of the World* (Evanston IL: Northwestern University Press, 1973).

H. L. Dreyfus and P. A. Dreyfus (trans.), *Sense and Nonsense* (Evanston IL: Northwestern University Press, 1964).

Richard McCleary (trans.), *Signs* (Evanston IL: Northwestern University Press, 1964).

Alden Fisher (trans.), *The Structure of Behavior* (Boston, MA: Beacon Press, 1963).

Alphonso Lingis (trans.), *The Visible and The Invisible* (Evanston IL: Northwestern University Press, 1968).

Further Reading

Cataldi, Sue, *Emotion, Depth and Flesh. A Study of Sensitive Space: Reflections on Merleau-Ponty's Philosophy of Embodiment* (Albany, NY: SUNY Press, 1993).

Dillon, M. C., *Merleau-Ponty's Ontology* (Bloomington, IN: Indiana University Press, 1988).

Gillan, Garth (ed.), *Horizons of the Flesh: Critical Perspectives on the Thought of Merleau-Ponty* (Carbondale, IL: Northwestern University Press, 1990).

Langer, Monika, *Merleau-Ponty's Phenomenology of Perception: A Guide and Commentary* (London: Macmillan, 1989).

Madison, Gary, *The Phenomenology of Merleau-Ponty* (Athens, OH: Ohio University Press, 1981).

Marcel, Gabriel, *The Mystery of Being: 1. Reflection and Mystery* (Chicago: Henry Regnery, 1960).

Marcel, Gabriel, *Being and Having: An Existentialist Diary* (New York: Harper and Row, 1965).

Stewart, Jon (ed.), *The Debate Between Sartre and Merleau-Ponty* (Evanston, IL: Northwestern University Press, 1998).

Whitford, Margaret, *Merleau-Ponty's Critique of Sartre's Philosophy* (Lexington, KY: French Forum, 1982).

"THE SPATIALITY OF ONE'S OWN BODY AND MOTILITY"

Maurice Merleau-Ponty

Let us first of all describe the spatiality of my own body. If my arm is resting on the table I should never think of saying that it is *beside* the ash-tray in the way in which the ash-tray is beside the telephone. The outline of my body is a frontier which ordinary spatial relations do not cross. This is because its parts are inter-related in a peculiar way: they are not spread out side by side, but enveloped in each other. For example, my hand is not a collection of points. In cases of allocheiria,[1] in which the subject feels in his right hand stimuli applied to his left hand, it is impossible to suppose that each of the stimulations changes its spatial value on its own account.[2] The various points on the left hand are transferred to the right as relevant to a total organ, a hand without parts which has been suddenly displaced. Hence they form a system and the space of my hand is not a mosaic of spatial values. Similarly my whole body for me is not an assemblage of organs juxtaposed in space. I am in undivided possession of it and I know where each of my limbs is through a *body image* in which all are included. But the notion of body image is ambiguous, as are all notions which make their appearance at turning points in scientific advance. They can be fully developed only through a reform of methods. At first, therefore, they are used only in a sense which falls short of their full sense, and its is their immanent development which bursts the bounds of methods hitherto used. 'Body image' was at first understood to mean a *compendium* of our bodily experience, capable of giving a commentary and meaning to the internal impressions and the impression of possessing a body at any moment. It was supposed to register for me the positional changes of the parts of my body for each movement of one of them, the position of each local stimulus in the body as a whole, an account of the movements performed at every instant during a complex gesture, in short a continual translation into visual language of the kinaesthetic and articular impressions of the moment. When the term body image was first used, it was thought that nothing more was being introduced than a convenient name for a great many associations of images, and it was

From "The Spatiality of One's Own Body and Motility," in *Phenomenology of Perception*, translated by Colin Smith (London: Routledge, 1992), pp. 98–106.

intended merely to convey the fact that these associations were firmly established and constantly ready to come into play. The body image was supposed gradually to show itself through childhood in proportion as the tactile, kinaesthetic and articular contents were associated among themselves or with visual contents, and more easily evoked them. Its physiological representation could then be no more than a focus of images in the classical sense. Yet in the use made of it by psychologists, it is clear that the body image does not fit into this associationist definition. For example, in order that the body image may elucidate allocheiria, it is not enough that each sensation of the left hand should take its place among generic images of all parts of the body acting in association to form around the left hand, as it were, a superimposed *sketch* of the body; these associations must be constantly subject to a unique law, the spatiality of the body must work downwards from the whole to the parts, the left hand and its position must be implied in a comprehensive bodily *purpose* and must originate in that purpose, so that it may at one stroke not only be superimposed on or cleave to the right hand, but actually become the right hand. When we try[3] to elucidate the phenomenon of the phantom limb by relating it to the body image of the subject, we add to the accepted explanations, in terms of cerebral tracks and recurrent sensations, only if the body image, instead of being the residue of habitual cenesthesis, becomes the law of its constitution. If a need was felt to introduce this new word, it was in order to make it clear that the spatial and temporal unity, the inter-sensory or the sensori-motor unity of the body is, so to speak, *de jure*, that it is not confined to contents actually and fortuitously associated in the course of our experience, that it is in some way anterior to them and makes their association possible. We are therefore feeling our way towards a second definition of the body image: it is no longer seen as the straightforward result of associations established during experience, but a total awareness of my posture in the intersensory world, a 'form' in the sense used by Gestalt psychology. But already this second definition too is superseded by the analyses of the psychologists. It is inadequate to say that my body is a form, that is to say a phenomenon in which the totality takes precedence over the parts. How is such a phenomenon possible? Because a form, compared to the mosaic of a physico-chemical body or to that of 'cenesthesis', is a new type of existence. The fact that the paralysed limb of the anosognosic no longer counts in the subject's body image, is accounted for by the body image's being neither the mere copy nor even the global awareness of the existing parts of the body, and by its active integration of these latter only in proportion to their value to the organism's projects. Psychologists often say that the body image is *dynamic*. Brought down to a precise sense, this term means that my body appears to me as an attitude directed towards a certain existing or possible task. And indeed its spatiality is not, like that of external objects or like that of 'spatial sensations', a *spatiality of position*, but a *spatiality of situation*. If I stand in front of my desk and lean on it with both hands, only my hands are stressed and the whole of my body trails behind them like the tail of a comet. It is not that I am unaware of the whereabouts of my shoulders or back, but these are simply swallowed up in the position of my hands, and my whole posture can be read so to speak in the pressure they exert on the table. If I stand holding my pipe in my closed hand, the position of my hand is not determined discursively by the angle which it makes with my forearm, and my forearm with my upper arm, and my upper arm with my trunk, and my trunk with the ground. I know indubitably where my pipe is, and thereby I know where my

hand and my body are, as primitive man in the desert is always able to take his bear-
ings immediately without having to cast his mind back, and add up distances covered
and deviations made since setting off. The word 'here' applied to my body does not
refer to a determinate position in relation to other positions or to external co-
ordinates, but the laying down of the first co-ordinates, the anchoring of the active
body in an object, the situation of the body in face of its tasks. Bodily space can be
distinguished from external space and envelop its parts instead of spreading them out,
because it is the darkness needed in the theatre to show up the performance, the background of somnolence or reserve of vague power against which the gesture and its aim
stand out, the zone of not being *in front of which* precise beings, figures and points can
come to light. In the last analysis, if my body can be a 'form' and if there can be, in
front of it, important figures against indifferent backgrounds, this occurs in virtue of its
being polarized by its tasks, of its *existence towards* them, of its collecting together of
itself in its pursuit of its aims; the body image is finally a way of stating that my body
is in-the-world.[4] As far as spatiality is concerned, and this alone interests us at the
moment, one's own body is the third term, always tacitly understood, in the
figure–background structure, and every figure stands out against the double horizon of
external and bodily space. One must therefore reject as an abstraction any analysis of
bodily space which takes account only of figures and points, since these can neither be
conceived nor be without horizons.

It will perhaps be replied that the figure–background structure or the point-horizon
structure themselves presuppose the notion of objective space; that in order to experience a display of dexterity as a figure *against* the massive background of the body, the
hand and the rest of the body must be linked by this relationship of objective spatiality, so that the figure–background structure becomes once again one of the contingent
contents of the universal form of space. But what meaning could the word 'against'
have for a subject not placed by his body face to face with the world? It implies the
distinction of a top and a bottom, or an 'orientated space'. When I say that an object
is *on* a table, I always mentally put myself either in the table or in the object, and I
apply to them a category which theoretically fits the relationship of my body to external objects. Stripped of this anthropological association, the word *on* is indistinguishable from the word 'under' or the word 'beside'. Even if the universal form of space
is that without which there would be for us no bodily space, it is not that by which
there is one. Even if the form is not the *setting in which*, but the *means whereby* the
content is posited, it is not the sufficient means of this act of positing as far as bodily
space is concerned, and to this extent the bodily content remains, in relation to it,
something opaque, fortuitous and unintelligible. The only solution along this road
would be to acknowledge that the body's spatiality has no meaning of its own to distinguish it from objective spatiality, which would do away with the content as a phenomenon and hence with the problem of its relation to form. But can we pretend to
discover no distinctive meaning in the words 'on', 'under', 'beside', or in the dimensions of orientated space? Even if analysis discovers in all these relationships the universal relation of externality, the self-evidentness of top and bottom, right and left, for
the person who has his being in space, prevents us from treating all these distinctions
as nonsense, and suggests to us that we should look beneath the explicit meaning of
definitions for the latent meaning of experiences. The relationships between the two

spaces would therefore be as follows: as soon as I try to posit bodily space or bring out its meaning I find nothing in it but intelligible space. But at the same time this intelligible space is not extracted from orientated space, it is merely its explicit expression, and, when separated from that root has no meaning whatsoever. The truth is that homogeneous space can convey the meaning of orientated space only because it is from the latter that it has received that meaning. In so far as the content can be really subsumed under the form and can appear as the content *of* that form, it is because the form is accessible only through the content. Bodily space can really become a fragment of objective space only if within its individuality as bodily space it contains the dialectical ferment to transform it into universal space. This is what we have tried to express by saying that the point–horizon structure is the foundation of space. The horizon or background would not extend beyond the figure or round about it, unless they partook of the same kind of being as the figure, and unless they could be converted into points by a transference of the gaze. But the point–horizon structure can teach me what a point is only in virtue of the maintenance of a hither zone of corporeality from which to be seen, and round about it indeterminate horizons which are the counterpart of this seeing. The multiplicity of points or 'heres' can in the nature of things be constituted only by a chain of experiences in which on each occasion one and no more of them is presented as an object, and which is itself built up in the heart of this space. And finally, far from my body's being for me no more than a fragment of space, there would be no space at all for me if I had no body.

If bodily space and external space form a practical system, the first being the background against which the object as the goal of our action may stand out or the void in front of which it may *come to light*, it is clearly in action that the spatiality of our body is brought into being, and an analysis of one's own movement should enable us to arrive at a better understanding of it. By considering the body in movement, we can see better how it inhabits space (and, moreover, time) because movement is not limited to submitting passively to space and time, it actively assumes them, it takes them up in their basic significance which is obscured in the commonplaceness of established situations. We should like to analyse closely an example of morbid motility which clearly shows the fundamental relations between the body and space.

A patient whom traditional psychiatry would class among cases of psychic blindness is unable to perform 'abstract' movements with his eyes shut; movements, that is, which are not relevant to any actual situation, such as moving arms and legs to order, or bending and straightening a finger. Nor can he describe the position of his body or even his head, or the passive movements of his limbs. Finally, when his head, arm or leg is touched, he cannot identify the point on his body; he cannot distinguish two points of contact on his skin even as much as three inches apart; and he cannot recognize the size or shape of objects placed against his body. He manages the abstract movements only if he is allowed to watch the limb required to perform them, or to go through preparatory movements involving the whole body. The localization of stimuli, and recognition of objects by touch also become possible with the aid of the preparatory movements. Even when his eyes are closed, the patient performs with extraordinary speed and precision the movements needed in living his life, provided that he is in the habit of performing them: he takes his handkerchief from his pocket and blows his nose, takes a match out of a box and lights a lamp. He is employed in the manufacture of wallets and his production rate is equal to three quarters of that of a normal workman. He can even without any preparatory movement, perform these 'concrete' movements to order. In the same patient, and also in cerebellar cases, one notices a dissociation of the act of pointing from reactions of taking or grasping: the same subject who is unable to point to order to a part of his body, quickly moves his hand to the point where a mosquito is stinging him. Concrete movements and acts of grasping therefore enjoy a privileged position for which we need to find some explanation.

Let us examine the question more closely. A patient, asked to point to some part of his body, his nose for example, can only manage to do so if he is allowed to take hold of it. If the patient is set the task of interrupting the movement before its completion, or if he is allowed to touch his nose only with a wooden ruler, the action becomes impossible. It must therefore be concluded that 'grasping' or 'touching', even for the body, is different from 'pointing'. From the outset the grasping movement is magically at its completion; it can begin only by anticipating its end, since to disallow taking hold is sufficient to inhibit the action. And it has to be admitted that a point on my body can be present to me as one to be taken hold of without being given in this antici- pated grasp as a point to be indicated. But how is this possible? If I know where my nose is when it is a question of holding it, how can I not know where it is when it is a matter of pointing to it? It is probably because knowledge of where something is can be understood in a number of ways. Traditional psychology has no concept to cover these varieties of consciousness of place because consciousness of place is always, for such psychology, a positional consciousness, a representation, *Vor-stellung*, because as such it gives us the place as a determination of the objective world and because such a rep- resentation either is or is not, but, if it is, yields the object to us quite unambiguously and as an end identifiable through all its appearances. Now here, on the other hand, we have to create the concepts necessary to convey the fact that bodily space may be given to me in an intention to take hold without being given in an intention to know. The patient is conscious of his bodily space as the matrix of his habitual action, but not as an objective setting; his body is at his disposal as a means of ingress into a familiar surrounding, but not as the means of expression of a gratuitous and free spatial thought. When ordered to perform a concrete movement, he first of all repeats the order in a questioning tone of voice, then his body assumes the general position required for the task; finally he goes through the movement. It is noticeable that the whole body is involved in it, and that the patient never cuts it down, as a normal subject would, to the strict minimum. To the military salute are added the other external marks of respect. To the right hand pantomime of combing the hair is added, with the left, that of holding a mirror; when the right hand pretends to knock in a nail, the left pretends to hold the nail. The explanation is that the order is taken quite seriously and that the patient manages to perform these concrete movements to order only provided that he places himself mentally in the actual situation to which they correspond. The normal subject, on giving, to order, a military salute, sees in it no more than an experimental situation, and therefore restricts the movement to its most important elements and does not throw himself into it. He is using his body as a means to play acting; he finds it entertaining to pretend to be a soldier; he escapes from reality in the rôle of the soldier[5] just as the actor slips his real body into the 'great phantom'[6] of the character to be played. The normal man and the actor do not mistake imaginary situations for reality, but extricate their real bodies from the living situation to make them breathe, speak and, if need be, weep in the realm of imagination. This is what our patient is no longer able to do. In the course of living, he says 'I experience the movements as being a result of the situation, of the sequence of events themselves; myself and my movements are, so to speak, merely a link in the whole process and I am scarcely aware of any voluntary initiative . . . It all happens independently of me.' In the same way, in order to make a movement to order he places himself 'in the affective situation as a whole, and it is from this that the movement flows, as in real life'.[7] If his performance is interrupted and he has the experimental situation recalled to him, all his dexterity disappears. Once more kinetic initiative becomes impossible, the patient must first of all 'find' his arm, 'find', by the preparatory movements, the gesture called for, and the gesture itself loses the melodic character which it presents in ordinary life, and becomes manifestly a collection of partial movements strung laboriously together. I can therefore take my place, through the medium of my body as the potential source of a certain number of familiar actions, in my environment conceived as a set of *manipulanda* and without, moreover, envisaging my body or my surrounding as objects in the Kantian sense, that is, as systems of qualities linked by some intelligible law, as transparent entities, free from any attachment to a specific place or time, and ready to be named or at least pointed out. There is my arm seen as sustaining familiar acts, my body as giving rise to determinate action having a field or scope known to me in advance, there are my surroundings as a collection of possible points upon which this bodily action may operate, – and there is, furthermore, my arm as a mechanism of muscles and bones, as a contrivance for bending and stretching, as an articulated object, the world as a pure spectacle into which I am not absorbed, but which I contemplate and point out. As far as bodily space is concerned, it is clear that there is a knowledge of place which is reducible to a sort of co-existence with that place, and which is not simply nothing, even though it cannot be conveyed by a description or even by the mute reference of a gesture. A patient of the kind discussed above, when stung by a mosquito, does not need to look for the place where he has been stung. He finds it straight away, because for him there is no question of locating it in relation to axes of co-ordinates in objective space, but of reaching with his phenomenal hand a certain painful spot on his phenomenal body, and because between the hand as a scratching potentiality and the place stung as a spot to be scratched a directly experienced relationship is presented in the natural system of one's own body. The whole operation takes place in the domain of the phenomenal; it does not run through the objective world, and only the spectator, who lends his objective representation of the living body to the acting subject, can believe that the sting is perceived, that the hand moves in objectives space, and consequently find it odd that the same subject should fail in experiments requiring him to point things out. Similarly the subject, when put in front of his scissors, needle and familiar tasks, does not need to look for his hands or his fingers, because they are not objects to be discovered in objective space: bones, muscles and nerves, but potentialities already mobilized by the perception of scissors or needle, the central end of those 'intentional threads' which link him to the objects given. It is never our objective body that we move, but our phenomenal body, and there is no mystery in that, since our body, as the potentiality of this or that part of the world, surges towards objects to be grasped and perceives them.[8] In the same way the patient has no need to look for a theatre of action and a space in which to deploy these concrete movements: the space is given to him in the form of the world at this moment; it is the piece of leather 'to be cut up'; it is the lining 'to be sewn'. The bench, scissors, pieces of leather offer themselves to the subject as poles of action; through their combined values they delimit a certain situation, an open situation moreover, which calls for a certain mode of resolution, a certain kind of work. The body is no more than an element in the system of the subject and his world, and the task to be performed elicits the necessary movements from him by a sort of remote attraction, as the phenomenal forces at work in my visual field elicit from me, without any calculation on my part, the motor reactions which establish the most effective balance between them, or as the conventions of our social group, or our set of listeners, immediately elicit from us the words, attitudes and tone which are fitting. Not that we are trying to conceal our thoughts or to please others, but because we are literally what others think of us and what our world is. In the concrete movement the patient has a positing awareness neither of the stimulus nor of his reaction: quite simply he is his body and his body is the potentiality of a certain world.

Notes

1   A disorder of sensation in which sensations are referred to the wrong part of the body (Translator's note).
2   We have discussed the notion of the local signal in *La Structure du Comportement* (Paris: Presses Universitaires de France, 1942), pp. 102 and ff.
3   As for example Lhermitte, *L'Image de notre Corps* (Paris: Nouvelle Revue Critique, 1939).
4   [. . .] [T]he phantom limb, which is a modality of the body image, is understood in terms of the general movement of being-in-the-world.
5   J. P. Sartre, *L'Imaginaire* (Paris: Gallimard, 1943), p. 243.
6   Diderot, *Paradoxe sur le Comédien* (Paris: Gallimard, 1994).
7   K. Goldstein, *Über die Abhängigkeit der Bewegungen von optischen Vorgängen* (Monatschrift für Psychiatrie und Neurologie, Festschrift Liepmann, 1923), pp. 175–6.
8   It is not a question of how the soul acts on the objective body, since it is not on the latter that it acts, but on the phenomenal body. So the question has to be reframed, and we must ask why there are two views of me and of my body: my body for me and my body for others, and how these two systems can exist together. It is indeed not enough to say that the objective body belongs to the realm of 'for others', and my phenomenal body to that of 'for me', and we cannot refuse to pose the problem of their relations, since the 'for me' and the 'for others' coexist in one and the same world, as is proved by my perception of an other who immediately brings me back to the condition of an object for him.

9

COMMENTARY ON HEIDEGGER

Martin Heidegger (1889–1976) was born into an actively religious Catholic family in rural Germany. He pursued an unremarkable academic career until the publication of *Being and Time* in 1927 whereupon he was given a full professorship at Marburg. A year later when his mentor Edmund Husserl retired, Heidegger was awarded the chair of philosophy at Freiburg University. The reception of Heidegger's work continues to be marred by his involvement with the Nazi Party. Heidegger joined the Party in the early 1930s and under the regime he rose to the position of Rector of Freiburg University, during which time he actively oversaw the Nazification of the University and the departure of several Jewish academics. Following Germany's defeat in World War II, and as a result of his Nazi association, Heidegger was forbidden to teach from 1946 until 1949. He never resigned from the Party.

Despite his dubious political associations, philosophers of the Left in France, notably Jean-Paul Sartre, Maurice Merleau-Ponty, and Simone de Beauvoir, eagerly adopted his antiessentialism and his practically orientated account of human existence. Heidegger also gave a fresh impetus to hermeneutics (notably in the work of Hans-Georg Gadamer and Paul Ricoeur), and his critique of metaphysics has been a driving force in postmodernism, informing the work of Jacques Derrida. Heidegger has also attracted strong critics – among them the political philosopher and activist, Jürgen Habermas – for his Nietzschean-style notion of authenticity and his distaste for the lives of "ordinary" people (the much derided "*das Man*").

Heidegger acknowledges a deep indebtedness to Husserl. Whereas Husserl's method of bracketing, or *epoche,* aimed at establishing purely logical foundations of meaning, Heidegger sought the foundations of meaning in the structures of things as they are encountered in everyday life. Despite the highly abstract appearance of the work, *Being and Time* is oriented to the practical basis of human understanding. Heidegger considered the fundamental task of philosophy was to bring to light the nonphilosophical sources of philosophical concepts in order to then be able to "ask into the meaning of the Being of the sort of entities with which it deals."[1]

The success of this grand plan turns upon the success of a more basic enquiry into what it means to be, *per se*. Heidegger opens his philosophical opus with an enquiry into the entity whose Being consists in asking just this question, namely, ourselves, or "*Dasein.*" Dasein concerns the being of human beings. However, it is wiser to use "Dasein" to indicate "selfhood" rather than the being of human beings, simply because the class of human beings includes babies and nonconscious people, whereas in its explication it is clear that Dasein properly refers only to those beings with explicitly reflective self-awareness.

Heidegger sets out to identify the ontological structures of Dasein through an analysis of the nature of self-conscious experience. His method is phenomenological, focused on the way in which we encounter objects in our practical experiences. Heidegger's analysis reveals that one always already finds oneself encountering a world wherein one is aware of one's existence in that world *as* self-aware, that is, as having an orientation to, and concern for, one's existence. This mode of existence is "Dasein."[2] Dasein is made up of two concepts, "to be" (*zu sein*) and "there" (*da*), meaning "to be there" in the world. In this sense Dasein belongs to, or is made for, the world, hence Heidegger's other famous expression "being-in-the world." In a nutshell, Dasein is "an entity for which, intimately involved in its being-in-the world, this very being is at issue."[3] This statement is a rather formal way of describing a being which is essentially practical and self-reflective: Dasein is the kind of being that can enquire into its own existence *as* an enquirer. For Heidegger, this describes selfhood.

Heidegger insists that Dasein is not to be regarded as an object or substance. It is more like a power or potency, a mode of existence constitutive of those beings whose existence is an issue for them, namely ourselves (that is, the readers of *Being and Time*). According to Heidegger, subjectivity consists in living this self-concernfulness; there is no other human essence, no soul, no *telos* determining what one is or will be. Heidegger's insight here is that since human being lacks an essential nature, it can be characterized only by potentiality. Heidegger then goes on to draw out the kind of structures implicit in the idea of an existence that is sheer potentiality.

As potentiality, one's existence is a question, the question of what *to be*, and this is necessarily a personal question: what am *I* going to make of myself? Dasein sets for each of us the task of becoming who we will be, that is, the task of self-determination through self-interpretation. The meaning of one's existence, one's life as a whole, is not a function of either nature or God, but can only be our own self-activity as we each take up the enquiry into our own being.

Heidegger's view is innovative in that he regards understanding as primordially practical and arising from our worldly involvements. This is a point that Merleau-Ponty later develops into his account of bodily intentionality. Heidegger describes a holistic understanding of the world built up not as an accretion of concepts of objects, but through practical encounters with things that are meaningful in terms of the purposes, or task, to which we can put them (what he calls "equipment"). Dasein always already finds itself in a world structured with practical significance. This state is the state of "being-in-the-world," and, for Heidegger, this state is ontological.

The idea of being-in-the world makes subjectivity essentially temporal because my orientation to my existence is given in terms of a past, present, and future. Heidegger says that the unity of temporal orientations ("*ecstases*") is the primordial structure of Dasein: one is always already in the world in time, or, as he puts it, Dasein is a "being-within-timeness."[4] The temporal unity of past, present, and future grounds the unity of self by configuring my experiences into a temporal order. Thus, conceptual unity is underpinned by the (ontological) temporal unity of consciousness.

For Heidegger, because Dasein is sheer potentiality, each individual person must actively take up the question of his or her existence and determine who he or she is going to *be*. Heidegger describes the alternative – the unreflected life of "*das Man*" – as mere "idling," the kind of herd-like existence so despised by Nietzsche. To exist as *das Man* is to be a nobody, to lack individuality and self-determination and, thus, to live "inauthentically." For Heidegger, like Nietzsche, this is a degenerate form of existence.

Heidegger connects the idea of authenticity to Dasein's temporality through his concept of "being-toward-death." This expression describes a double experience. First, it describes the experience of confronting one's mortality: I realize that at some time in the future I am going to die and that my existence is finite. That realization sets off another realization, namely, the insight that one can suffer another kind of "death": the failure to make one's life one's own. Common to both senses of "death" is the idea of an existential limit to Dasein's existence. In this sense, death is, specifically, a failure of self-determination, the failure to make Dasein *mine*.[5] Death is a finitude that is not merely a chronological limit on the life span, but the extreme negative end of the spectrum of possibilities of my existence: "the condition of not being able to be anybody in particular."[6]

Being-toward-death has a special role to play in the psychological and practical processes of self-determination and "authenticity." Heidegger argues that Dasein, in grasping itself as potentiality for being, realizes that it must make itself *something*, else face the meaninglessness of being nothing in particular (death). The threat of meaningless induces the dread and anxiety of existential *angst*, and this precipitates the processes of self-determination. Knowing that I am going to "die" brings with it awareness that my life is mine, and that only I die with me. The correlative thought is that only I can live my life, and only I can be responsible for the meaning that my life has for me. Heidegger says that in this realization of my life as mine I am able to grasp my existence as a whole, to see myself extended over the entirety of my life.[7] In this way, one is able to posit oneself as the subject of a whole life, a life of one's own.

For Heidegger, without the basic ability to self-interpret I cannot become anyone. A self-interpretation is achieved when one forms an understanding of oneself that is historical, that is, in which there is a chronological and conceptual continuity of one's past, present, and future. Borrowing from Dilthey, Heidegger calls this *Zusammenhang des Lebens*, or the "connectedness of life."[8] I take responsibility for the meaning of my life when I take responsibility for the connectedness of my life. For Heidegger, one must become a kind of author of one's life, and every activity one undertakes earns its significance in the context of one's self-interpretations – a view echoed in narrative accounts of identity.

The notion of authenticity is controversial, not least for its radical individualism, but also for the shadow it casts over supposedly inauthentic lives. Heidegger's account falls foul of the same kind of criticisms made against that philosophical tradition that counts only fully rational beings among the members of the moral community. Nevertheless, Heidegger's conception of Dasein and being-in-the-world has influenced almost all phenomenological and existentialist accounts of selfhood and identity since.

Notes

1 John Caputo, "Heidegger," in Simon Critchley and William Schroeder (eds.), *A Companion to Continental Philosophy* (Malden, MA: Blackwell, 1998), p. 225.

2 Martin Heidegger, *Being and Time*, translated by John Macquarrie and Edward Robinson (New York: Harper and Row, 1962) (hereafter *BT*), p. 12. All page numbers refer to German pagination.

3 Martin Heidegger, *The History of the Concept of Time*, trans. Theodore Kisiel (Bloomington: Indiana University Press, 1992), p. 294. See also *BT*, p. 7.

4 *BT*, p. 333.

5 Heidegger does base death in the extinction of life in the biological sense, although he concedes it is "a certainty which is 'only' empirical." He says, " So far as one knows, all men 'die' " (*BT*, p. 257).

6 William Blattner, "Existence and Self-Understanding in *Being and Time*," *Philosophy and Phenomenological Research*, LVI (1), 1996, p. 108.

7 The idea of one's death allows Dasein to grasp its existence as a totality because it "finalizes my past, cuts off my future, and invades my present as the perspective from which Dasein is seen in its wholeness and conclusive meaning." Heidegger quoted in Hans Kellner, " 'As Real As It Gets . . .' Ricoeur and Narrativity," *Philosophy Today*, 34, Fall 1990, p. 231.

8 *BT*, p. 373.

Main Texts by Heidegger

David Krell (ed.), *Basic Writings* (New York: Harper and Row, 1992).

John Macquarrie and Edward Robinson (trans.), *Being and Time* (New York: Harper and Row, 1962).

Theodore Kisiel (trans.), *The History of the Concept of Time* (Bloomington: Indiana University Press, 1992).

Richard Polt and Gregory Fried (trans.), *Introduction to Metaphysics* (New Haven, CT: Yale University Press, 2000).

Reginald Lilly (trans.), *The Principle of Reason* (Bloomington: Indiana University Press, 1991).

W. Lovitt (trans.), *The Question Concerning Technology and Other Essays* (New York: Harper and Row, 1977).

Further Reading

Biemel, Walter, *Martin Heidegger: An Illustrated Study*, trans. J. Mehta (New York: Harcourt Brace/Janovich, 1976).

Dreyfus, Hubert, *Being-in-the World: A Commentary on Heidegger's Being and Time, Division I* (Cambridge, MA: MIT Press, 1991).

Olafson, Frederick, *Heidegger and the Ground of Ethics: A Study of Mitsein* (Cambridge, UK and New York: Cambridge University Press, 1998).

Ott, Hugo, *Martin Heidegger: A Political Life*, trans. Allan Blunden (New York: Basic Books, 1993).

Polt, Richard, *Heidegger: An Introduction* (Ithaca, NY: Cornell University Press, 1999).

Richardson, William, *Heidegger: Through Phenomenology to Thought* (The Hague: Martinus Nijhoff, 1963).

Sluga, Hans, *Heidegger's Crisis: Philosophy and Politics in Nazi Germany* (Cambridge, MA: Harvard University Press, 1993).

"EXPOSITION OF THE TASK OF A PREPARATORY ANALYSIS OF DASEIN"

Martin Heidegger

The Theme of the Analytic of Dasein

We are ourselves the entities to be analysed. The Being of any such entity is *in each case mine*. These entities, in their Being, comport themselves towards their Being. As enti-   42
ties with such Being, they are delivered over to their own Being. *Being* is that which is an issue for every such entity. This way of characterizing Dasein has a double consequence:

1.   The "essence" ["Wesen"] of this entity lies in its "to be" [Zu-sein]. Its Being-what-it-is [Was-sein] (*essentia*) must, so far as we can speak of it at all, be conceived in terms of its Being (*existentia*). But here our ontological task is to show that when we choose to designate the Being of this entity as "existence" [Existenz], this term does not and cannot have the ontological signification of the traditional term "*existentia*"; ontologically, *existentia* is tantamount to *Being-present-at-hand*, a kind of Being which is essentially inappropriate to entities of Dasein's character. To avoid getting bewildered, we shall always use the Interpretative expression "*presence-at-hand*" for the term "*existentia*", while the term "existence", as a designation of Being, will be allotted solely to Dasein.

   The essence of Dasein lies in its existence. Accordingly those characteristics which can be exhibited in this entity are not "properties" present-at-hand of some entity which "looks" so and so and is itself present-at-hand; they are in each case possible ways for it to be, and no more than that. All the Being-as-it-is [So-sein] which this entity possesses is primarily Being. So when we designate this entity with the term "Dasein", we are expressing not its "what" (as if it were a table, house or tree) but its Being.

2.   That Being which is an *issue* for this entity in its very Being, is in each case mine. Thus Dasein is never to be taken ontologically as an instance or special case of some genus of entities as things that are present-at-hand. To entities such as these, their

From *Being and Time*, translated by John Macquarrie and Edward Robinson (Oxford: Blackwell, 1962), pp. 67–77.

Being is "a matter of indifference"; or more precisely, they "are" such that their Being can be neither a matter of indifference to them, nor the opposite. Because Dasein has *in each case mineness* [*Jemeinigkeit*], one must always use a *personal* pronoun when one addresses it: "I am", "you are".

Furthermore, in each case Dasein is mine to be in one way or another. Dasein has always made some sort of decision as to the way in which it is in each case mine [je meines]. That entity which in its Being has this very Being as an issue, comports itself towards its Being as its ownmost possibility. In each case Dasein *is* its possibility, and it "has" this possibility, but not just as a property [eigenschaftlich], as something present-at-hand would. And because Dasein is in each case essentially its own possibility, it *can*, in its very Being, "choose" itself and win itself; it can also lose itself and never win itself; or only "seem" to do so. But only in so far as it is essentially something which can be *authentic* – that is, something of its own – can it have lost itself and not yet won itself. As modes of Being, *authenticity* and *inauthenticity* (these expressions have been chosen terminologically in a strict sense) are both grounded in the fact that any Dasein whatsoever is characterized by mineness. But the inauthenticity of Dasein does not signify any "less" Being or any "lower" degree of Being. Rather it is the case that even in its fullest concretion Dasein can be characterized by inauthenticity – when busy, when excited, when interested, when ready for enjoyment.

The two characteristics of Dasein which we have sketched – the priority of "*existentia*" over *essentia*, and the fact that Dasein is in each case mine [die Jemeinigkeit] – have already indicated that in the analytic of this entity we are facing a peculiar phenomenal domain. Dasein does not have the kind of Being which belongs to something merely present-at-hand within the world, nor does it ever have it. So neither is it to be presented thematically as something we come across in the same way as we come across what is present-at-hand. The right way of presenting it is so far from self-evident that to determine what form it shall take is itself an essential part of the ontological analytic of this entity. Only by presenting this entity in the right way can we have any understanding of its Being. No matter how provisional our analysis may be, it always requires the assurance that we have started correctly.

In determining itself as an entity, Dasein always does so in the light of a possibility which it *is* itself and which, in its very Being, it somehow understands. This is the formal meaning of Dasein's existential constitution. But this tells us that if we are to Interpret this entity *ontologically*, the problematic of its Being must be developed from the existentiality of its existence. This cannot mean, however, that "Dasein" is to be construed in terms of some concrete possible idea of existence. At the outset of our analysis it is particularly important that Dasein should not be Interpreted with the differentiated character [Differenz] of some definite way of existing, but that it should be uncovered [aufgedeckt] in the undifferentiated character which is has proximally and for the most part. This undifferentiated character of Dasein's everydayness is *not nothing*, but a positive phenomenal characteristic of this entity. Out of this kind of Being – and back into it again – is all existing, such as it is. We call this everyday undifferentiated character of Dasein "*averageness*" [*Durchschnittlichkeit*].

And because this average everydayness makes up what is ontically proximal for this entity, it has again and again been *passed over* in explicating Dasein. That which is ontically closest and well known, is ontologically the farthest and not known at all; and its ontological signification is constantly overlooked. When Augustine asks: "*Quid autem propinquius meipso mihi?*" and must answer: "*ego certe laboro hic et laboro in meipso: factus sum mihi terra difficultatis et sudoris nimii*", this applies not only to the ontical and preontological opaqueness of Dasein but even more to the ontological task which lies ahead; for not only must this entity not be missed in that kind of Being in which it is phenomenally closest, but it must be made accessible by a positive characterization.

Dasein's average everydayness, however, is not to be taken as a mere "aspect". Here too, and even in the mode of inauthenticity, the structure of existentiality lies *a priori*. And here too Dasein's Being is an issue for it in a definite way; and Dasein comports itself towards it in the mode of average everydayness, even if this is only the mode of fleeing *in the face of it* and forgetfulness *thereof*.

But the explication of Dasein in its average everydayness does not give us just average structures in the sense of a hazy indefiniteness. Anything which, taken ontically, *is* in an average way, can be very well grasped ontologically in pregnant structures which may be structurally indistinguishable from certain ontological characteristics [Bestimmungen] of an *authentic* Being of Dasein.

All *explicata* to which the analytic of Dasein gives rise are obtained by considering Dasein's existence-structure. Because Dasein's characters of Being are defined in terms of existentiality, we call them "*existentialia*". These are to be sharply distinguished from what we call "*categories*" – characteristics of Being for entities whose character is not that of Dasein. Here we are taking the expression "category" in its primary ontological signification, and abiding by it. In the ontology of the ancients, the entities we encounter within the world are taken as the basic examples for the interpretation of Being. Νοεῖν (or the λόγος, as the case may be) is accepted as a way of access to them. Entities are encountered therein. But the Being of these entities must be something which can be grasped in a distinctive kind of λέγειν (letting something be seen), so that this Being becomes intelligible in advance as that which it is – and as that which it is already in every entity. In any discussion (λόγος) of entities, we have previously addressed ourselves to Being; this addressing is κατηγορεῖσθαι. This signifies, in the first instance, making a public accusation, taking someone to task for something in the presence of everyone. When used ontologically, this term means taking an entity to task, as it were, for whatever it is as an entity – that is to say, letting everyone see it in its Being. The κατηγορίαι are what is sighted and what is visible in such a seeing. They include the various ways in which the nature of those entities which can be addressed and discussed in a λόγος may be determined *a priori*. *Existentialia* and categories are the two basic possibilities for characters of Being. The entities which correspond to them require different kinds of primary interrogation respectively: any entity is either a "*who*" (existence) or a "*what*" (presence-at-hand in the broadest sense). The connection between these two modes of the characters of Being cannot be handled until the horizon for the question of Being has been clarified.

In our introduction we have already intimated that in the existential analytic of Dasein we also make headway with a task which is hardly less pressing than that of the question of Being itself – the task of laying bare that *a priori* basis which must be visible before the question of "what man is" can be discussed philosophically. The existential analytic of Dasein comes *before* any psychology or anthropology, and certainly before any biology. While these too are ways in which Dasein can be investigated, we can define the theme of our analytic with greater precision if we distinguish it from these. And at the same time the necessity of that analytic can thus be proved more incisively.

How the Analytic of Dasein is to be Distinguished from Anthropology, Psychology, and Biology

After a theme for investigation has been initially outlined in positive terms, it is always important to show what is to be ruled out, although it can easily become fruitless to discuss what is not going to happen. We must show that those investigations and formulations of the question which have been aimed at Dasein heretofore, have missed the real *philosophical* problem (notwithstanding their objective fertility), and that as long as they persist in missing it, they have no right to claim that they *can* accomplish that for which they are basically striving. In distinguishing the existential analytic from anthropology, psychology, and biology, we shall confine ourselves to what is in principle the ontological question. Our distinctions will necessarily be inadequate from the standpoint of "scientific theory" simply because the scientific structure of the above-mentioned disciplines (not, indeed, the "scientific attitude" of those who work to advance them) is today thoroughly questionable and needs to be attacked in new ways which must have their source in ontological problematics.

46   Historiologically, the aim of the existential analytic can be made plainer by considering Descartes, who is credited with providing the point of departure for modern philosophical inquiry by his discovery of the "*cogito sum*". He investigates the "*cogitare*" of the "*ego*", at least within certain limits. On the other hand, he leaves the "*sum*" completely undiscussed, even though it is regarded as no less primordial than the *cogito*. Our analytic raises the ontological question of the Being of the "*sum*". Not until the nature of this Being has been determined can we grasp the kind of Being which belongs to *cogitationes*.

At the same time it is of course misleading to exemplify the aim of our analytic historiologically in this way. One of our first tasks will be to prove that if we posit an "I" or subject as that which is proximally given, we shall completely miss the phenomenal content [Bestand] of Dasein. *Ontologically*, every idea of a "subject" – unless refined by a previous ontological determination of its basic character – still posits the *subjectum* (ὑποκείμενον) along with it, no matter how vigorous one's ontical protestations against the "soul substance" or the "reification of consciousness". The Thinghood itself which such reification implies must have its ontological origin demonstrated if we are to be in a position to ask what we are to understand *positively* when we think of the unreified *Being* of the subject, the soul, the consciousness, the spirit, the person. All these terms refer to definite phenomenal domains which can be "given form" ["ausformbare"]: but they are never used without a notable failure to see the need for inquiring about the Being of the entities thus designated. So we are not being terminologically arbitrary when we avoid these terms – or such expressions as "life" and "man" – in designating those entities which we are ourselves.

On the other hand, if we understand it rightly, in any serious and scientifically-minded "philosophy of life" (this expression says about as much as "the botany of plants") there lies an unexpressed tendency towards an understanding of Dasein's Being.

What is conspicuous in such a philosophy (and here it is defective in principle) is that here "life" itself as a kind of Being does not become ontologically a problem.

The researches of Wilhelm Dilthey were stimulated by the perennial question of "life". Starting from "life" itself as a whole, he tried to understand its "Experiences" in their structural and developmental inter-connections. His *"geisteswissenschaftliche Psychologie"* is one which no longer seeks to be oriented towards psychical elements and atoms or to piece the life of the soul together, but aims rather at *"Gestalten"* and "life as a whole". Its philosophical relevance, however, is not to be sought here, but rather in the fact that in all this he was, *above all*, on his way towards the question of "life".   47 To be sure, we can also see here very plainly how limited were both his problematic and the set of concepts with which it had to be put into words. These limitations, however, are found not only in Dilthey and Bergson but in all the "personalitic" movements to which they have given direction and in every tendency towards a philosophical anthropology. The phenomenological Interpretation of personality is in principle more radical and more transparent; but the question of the Being of Dasein has a dimension which this too fails to enter. No matter how much Husserl and Scheler may differ in their respective inquiries, in their methods of conducting them, and in their orientations towards the world as a whole, they are fully in agreement on the negative side of their Interpretations of personality. The question of "personal *Being*" itself is one which they no longer raise. We have chosen Scheler's Interpretation as an example, not only because it is accessible in print, but because he emphasizes personal Being explicitly as such, and tries to determine its character by defining the specific Being of acts as contrasted with anything "psychical". For Scheler, the person is never to be thought of as a Thing or a substance; the person "is rather the *unity* of living-through [Er-lebens] which is immediately experienced in and with our Experiences – not a Thing merely thought of behind and outside what is immediately Experienced". The person is no Thinglike and substantial Being. Nor can the Being of a person be entirely absorbed in being a subject of rational acts which follow certain laws.

The person is not a Thing, not a substance, not an object. Here Scheler is emphasizing what Husserl suggests when he insists that the unity of the person must have a   48 Constitution essentially different from that required for the unity of Things of Nature. What Scheler says of the person, he applies to acts as well: "But an act is never also an object; for it is essential to the Being of acts that they are Experienced only in their performance itself and given in reflection." Acts are something nonpsychical. Essentially the person exists only in the performance of intentional acts, and is therefore essentially *not* an object. Any psychical Objectification of acts, and hence any way of taking them as something psychical, is tantamount to depersonalization. A person is in any case given as a performer of intentional acts which are bound together by the unity of a meaning. Thus psychical Being has nothing to do with personal Being. Acts get performed; the person is a performer of acts. What, however, is the ontological meaning of "performance"? How is the kind of Being which belongs to a person to be ascertained ontologically in a positive way? But the critical question cannot stop here. It must face the Being of the whole man, who is customarily taken as a unity of body, soul, and spirit. In their turn "body", "soul", and "spirit" may designate phenomenal domains which can be detached as themes for definite investigations; within certain limits their ontological indefiniteness may not be important. When, however, we come to the question of man's Being, this is not something we can simply compute by adding together those kinds of Being which body, soul, and spirit respectively possess – kinds of Being whose nature has not as yet been determined. And even if we should attempt such an ontological procedure, some idea of the Being of the whole must be presupposed. But what stands in the way of the basic question of Dasein's Being (or leads it off the track) is an orientation thoroughly coloured by the anthropology of Christianity and the ancient world, whose inadequate ontological foundations have been overlooked both by the philosophy of life and by personalism. There are two important elements in this traditional anthropology:

1. "Man" is here defined as a ζῷον λόγον ἔχον, and this is Interpreted to mean an *animal rationale*, something living which has reason. But the kind of Being which belongs to a ζῷον is understood in the sense of occurring and Being-present-at-hand. The λόγος is some superior endowment; the kind of Being which belongs to it, however, remains quite as obscure as that of the entire entity thus compounded.

2. The second clue for determining the nature of man's Being and essence is a *theological* one καὶ εἶπεν ὁ Θεός. ποιήσωμεν ἄνθρωπον κατ᾽ εἰκόνα ἡμετέραν καὶ καθ᾽ ὁμοίωσιν – "*faciamus hominem ad imaginem nostram et similitudinem*". With this as its point of departure, the anthropology of Christian theology, taking with it the ancient definition, arrives at an interpretation of that entity which we call "man". But just as the Being of God gets Interpreted ontologically by means of the ancient ontology, so does the Being of the *ens finitum*, and to an even greater extent. In modern times the Christian definition has been deprived of its theological character. But the idea of "transcendence" – that man is something that reaches beyond himself – is rooted in Christian dogmatics, which can hardly be said to have made an ontological problem of man's Being. The idea of transcendence, according to which man is more than a mere something endowed with intelligence, has worked itself out with different variations. The following quotations will illustrate how these have originated: "*His praeclaris dotibus excelluit prima hominis conditio, ut ratio, intelligentia, prudentia, judicium non modo ad terrenae vitae gubernationem suppeterent, sed quibus t r a n s c e n d e r e t usque ad Deum et aeternam felicitatem.*" "*Denn dass der mensch sin u f s e h e n hat uf Gott und sin wort, zeigt er klarlich an, dass er nach siner natur etwas Gott näher anerborn, etwas mee n a c h s c h l ä g t, etwas z u z u g s z u im hat, das alles on zwyfel darus flüsst, dass er nach dem b i l d n u s Gottes geschaffen ist*".

The two sources which are relevant for the traditional anthropology – the Greek definition and the clue which theology has provided – indicate that over and above the attempt to determine the essence of "man" as an entity, the question of his Being has remained forgotten, and that this Being is rather conceived as something obvious or "self-evident" in the sense of the *Being-present-at-hand* of other created Things. These two clues become intertwined in the anthropology of modern times, where the *res cogitans*, consciousness, and the interconnectedness of Experience serve as the point of departure for methodical study. But since even the *cogitationes* are either left ontologically undetermined, or get tacitly assumed as something "self-evidently" "given" whose "Being" is not to be questioned, the decisive ontological foundations of anthropological problematics remain undetermined.

This is no less true of "*psychology*", whose anthropological tendencies are today unmistakable. Nor can we compensate for the absence of ontological foundations by taking anthropology and psychology and building them into the framework of a general *biology*. In the order which any possible comprehension and interpretation must follow, biology as a "science of life" is founded upon the ontology of Dasein, even if not entirely. Life, in its own right, is a kind of Being; but essentially it is accessible only in Dasein. The ontology of life is accomplished by way of a privative Interpretation; it determines what must be the case if there can be anything like mere-aliveness [Nur–noch–leben]. Life is not a mere Being-present-at-hand, nor is it Dasein. In turn, Dasein is never to be defined ontologically by regarding it as life (in an ontologically indefinite manner) plus something else.

In suggesting that anthropology, psychology, and biology all fail to give an unequivocal and ontologically adequate answer to the question about the *kind of Being* which belongs to those entities which we ourselves are, we are not passing judgment on the positive work of these disciplines. We must always bear in mind, however, that these ontological foundations can never be disclosed by subsequent hypotheses derived from empirical material, but that they are always "there" already, even when that empirical material simply gets *collected*. If positive research fails to see these foundations and holds them to be self-evident, this by no means proves that they are not basic or that they are not problematic in a more radical sense than any thesis of positive science can ever be.

The Existential Analytic and the Interpretation of Primitive Dasein. The Difficulties of Achieving a "Natural Conception of the World"

The Interpretation of Dasein in its everydayness, however, is not identical with the describing of some primitive stage of Dasein with which we can become acquainted empirically through the medium of anthropology. *Everydayness does not coincide with primitiveness*, but is rather a mode of Dasein's Being, even when that Dasein is active in a highly developed and differentiated culture – and precisely then. Moreover, even primitive Dasein has possibilities of a Being which is not of the everyday kind, and it has a specific everydayness *of its own*. To orient the analysis of Dasein towards the "life of primitive peoples" can have positive significance [Bedeutung] as a method because "primitive phenomena" are often less concealed and less complicated by extensive self-interpretation on the part of the Dasein in question. Primitive Dasein often speaks to us more directly in terms of a primordial absorption in "phenomena" (taken in a pre-phenomenological sense). A way of conceiving things which seems, perhaps, rather clumsy and crude from our standpoint, can be positively helpful in bringing out the ontological structures of phenomena in a genuine way.

But heretofore our information about primitives has been provided by ethnology. And ethnology operates with definite preliminary conceptions and interpretations of human Dasein in general, even in first "receiving" its material, and in sifting it and working it up. Whether the everyday psychology or even the scientific psychology and sociology which the ethnologist brings with him can provide any scientific assurance that we can have proper access to the phenomena we are studying, and can interpret them and transmit them in the right way, has not yet been established. Here too we

are confronted with the same state of affairs as in the other disciplines we have discussed. Ethnology itself already presupposes as its clue an inadequate analytic of Dasein.
But since the positive sciences neither "can" nor should wait for the ontological labours
of philosophy to be done, the further course of research will not take the form of an
"advance" but will be accomplished by *recapitulating* what has already been ontically
discovered, and by purifying it in a way which is ontologically more transparent.

52   No matter how easy it may be to show how ontological problematics differ formally
from ontical research there are still difficulties in carrying out an existential analytic,
especially in *making a start*. This task includes a *desideratum* which philosophy has long
found disturbing but has continually refused to achieve: *to work out the idea of a "natural
conception of the world"*. The rich store of information now available as to the most exotic
and manifold cultures and forms of Dasein seems favourable to our setting about this
task in a fruitful way. But this is merely a semblance. At bottom this plethora of information can seduce us into failing to recognize the real problem. We shall not get a
genuine knowledge of essences simply by the syncretistic activity of universal comparison and classification. Subjecting the manifold to tabulation does not ensure any
actual understanding of what lies there before us as thus set in order. If an ordering
principle is genuine, it has its own content as a thing [Sachgehalt], which is never to
be found by means of such ordering, but is already presupposed in it. So if one is to
put various pictures of the world in order, one must have an explicit idea of the world
as such. And if the "world" itself is something constitutive for Dasein, one must have
an insight into Dasein's basic structures in order to treat the world-phenomenon
conceptually.

        In this chapter we have characterized some things positively and taken a negative
stand with regard to others; in both cases our goal has been to promote a correct understanding of the tendency which underlies the following Interpretation and the kind of
questions which it poses. Ontology can contribute only indirectly towards advancing
the positive disciplines as we find them today. It has a goal of its own, even if, beyond
the acquiring of information about entities, the question of Being is the spur for all
scientific seeking.

PART IV

ANALYTIC PHILOSOPHY

10

COMMENTARY ON STRAWSON

Sir Peter Strawson (born 1919) was professor of philosophy at Oxford from 1968 until 1987. During that time he was part of the transition within Anglo-American philosophy from a predominantly linguistic-oriented approach to a concern with more broadly metaphysical issues.[1] In contrast to the historicist and social constructivist approaches of much contemporary European philosophy, Strawson considers metaphysics to be concerned not only with concepts (which change over time), but with the "massive central core of human thinking which has no history" and "those categories and concepts which, in their most fundamental character, change not at all."[2] Metaphysics, in this sense, concerns the description of the basic structure of material existence, which Strawson calls "basic particulars." Basic particulars are the fundamental entities presupposed in all our concepts of reality. Consistent with materialism, he considers basic particulars to be individual material bodies upon which the identification and reidentification of all other things rest.[3] Interestingly, Strawson counts "persons" among basic particulars, but refrains from reducing "person" to "body." He argues that a person is a basic material entity to which are ascribed *both* physical and mental predicates. The concept of "person" is logically primitive in the sense that we cannot employ properties or predicates of persons (such as "mind" and "body") without presupposing the concept of "person." This argument runs counter to mainstream analytical approaches to personal identity.

According to Strawson, the truly strange thing is that persons should have mental states at all given that we are material beings. Furthermore, he asks, why should I ascribe mental states to the very same thing that I ascribe physical states? Why do I say, for example, that *I* have long toes and a short temper? Strawson considers the possibility that if we understood enough about the body we might be able to see how and why we ascribe consciousness to it. However, he rejects the claim that mental states are predicates of the body.[4] While facts about the body explain certain things, such as why I should feel a special attachment to my body and regard it as unique, what they do not explain is just why we ascribe mental states to *exactly the same thing* to which we ascribe physical states.

Strawson argues that there is a basic confusion in the way in which philosophers have thought about notions of "person," "body," and "mind." The two main culprits in this respect are a skeptical form of argument he calls the "no-ownership view" and Cartesianism. The first regards the body as logically primitive, and the latter, the mind. Strawson proceeds to show that each of these views implicitly deploys his own concept of "person" despite attempts to argue otherwise.

The No-ownership Argument

Strawson argues that this theory surreptitiously employs a concept that it overtly denies (a ploy he identifies with all skeptical arguments), namely the possessive force of the term "my."

The view of the no-ownership theorist is that there is no entity who "owns" one's mental states; there is only the body in which those states are realized. Like Hume, the theorist argues that it is the individuality of the body that gives rise to the idea that one's experiences can be ascribed to or are possessed by some thing such as a self. To say that something is owned is to say that the thing is "logically transferable." That is, something that is owned is not a *necessary* part of the thing that owns it. That is why we do not really say that we own our bodies, although we might say we own some of our body parts, for example, blood and tissue that can be transferred to another person or place. If I owned my body I would have to be logically separable from my body, which just seems impossible (Descartes's difficulties are instructive here), and *a fortiori* from my experiences. The only way that an experience can be owned, says the no-ownership theorist, is in "the dubious sense" of being causally dependent upon the state of a particular body. In other words, we say, loosely speaking, that we "own" our experiences because they are causally dependent upon the particular body in which those experiences are expressed, namely, "my own" body. On this view, employing the concept of "ownership" is really a category mistake. What we are invoking is a causal relationship between the body and its experiential states.

This now requires the no-ownership theorist to demonstrate the redundancy of the terms "my" and "mine" because on that view, experiences (mental states) are to be understood as physical states that are contingent upon (caused by) a particular physical body. Strawson argues that this is not possible because the relation between "my" and "my experiences" is a necessary one, while the relation between an experience and the body upon which it is causally contingent is clearly not: if mental states are contingent physical states then they can be produced in *any* human body, not simply in *the* body that is alone capable of any particular mental state. On a causal account, there is nothing unique or necessary about the relation between my experiences and my body – mental states are simply instantiations of a general law of physics. For this reason, the no-ownership theorist must be able to describe my experiences without reference to their being *my* experiences.

However, Strawson claims that the no-ownership theorists are in a jam. On the one hand they cannot make their case without using the word "my" because if they do not use it, their theory turns the relationship into a necessary one. The no-ownership theorists have to say something like "all my experiences are had by body B" (where "had" means causally dependent upon that body), because if they leave out the "my" they must say "*all* experiences are had by body B." This is not only no longer contingent, it is false; it is clearly untrue that all experiences are causally contingent upon body B. On the other hand, if they do use "my" they have given away their ground. To be precise, argues Strawson, the no-ownership theorist must "be speaking of some class of experiences of the members of which it is in fact contingently true that they are dependent upon body B. The defining characteristic of this class is in fact that they are '*my* experiences' or 'the experiences *of* some person'."[5]

The jam here is that, in defining the class of experiences that fits their theory, the no-ownership theorists must include only those experiences that are had by one's own body. This means that they cannot but employ "my" or a similar term that expresses the possessive force they wish to deny. This is simply because the experiences at issue (experiences that are contingent upon a certain body) are *those that one ascribes to oneself,* and their being *self-ascriptions* is what delineates them as the contingent class.

Strawson points out that what this shows is that states of consciousness "*owe* their identity as particulars to the identity of the person whose states or experiences they are."[6] In identifying those experiences *as* contingent, it is a condition that those experiences are the ones that I self-ascribe and which, precisely because they are not another's, distinguish me from another person and so constitute my individuality. But this is just what the theorist denies. Strawson explains:

> From this it follows immediately that if they can be identified as particular states or experiences at all, they must be possessed or ascribable in just that way which the no-ownership ridicules, i.e. in such a way that it is logically impossible that a particular state or experience in fact possessed by someone should have been possessed by anyone else.[7]

The upshot is that in order to identify mental states at all prior to any theorizing, the no-ownership theorist must presuppose the Strawsonian concept of "person."

The Cartesian Argument

Having argued that the body is not a basic particular, Strawson sets out to show that neither are mental states. The Cartesian claims that the "I" to which mental states are ascribed is a nonmaterial ego that is entirely private: the "I" of the *cogito* is given only in the first person. Unlike the publicly observable nature of objects (*res extensa*), only *I* can perceive my inner subjective states. Because Cartesian egos are completely "inner" and unobservable, I cannot know if another body has a mind. This is the familiar problem of other minds. However, this also gives rise to a particular difficulty for the Cartesian: given the totally interior nature of the mind, how is it to be identified in order that it meet the description of a basic particular?

Strawson quickly disposes of the standard response, which has been to draw an analogy from one's own case to "the subject that stands to that body in the same special relation as I stand in this one."[8] In other words, I might ascribe mental states to another body on the basis of an analogy with my own self-ascription. However, this is not an option for the Cartesian for the very simple reason that the Cartesian ego does not self-ascribe; its subjective states are given immediately and privately. Because the Cartesian ego does not ascribe, neither does it employ any process of identification (and, consequently, neither can there be any question of whether an experience is its own or not). Therefore, it cannot identify another ego: "One can ascribe states of consciousness to oneself only if one can ascribe them to others. One can ascribe them to others only if one can identify other subjects of experience. And one cannot identify others if one can identify them only as subjects of experience, possessors of states of consciousness."[9]

This brings us to the question of why we should ascribe states of consciousness to anything at all. If a subject of experience really was a Cartesian ego and the Cartesian ego was primitive, I should never have occasion to identify other subjects – just as I should never have occasion to identify myself, and so the question of the existence of other subjects of experience should never arise. Strawson argues that because the Cartesian argument does grant the existence of other minds it implicitly relies upon a conception of a subject of ascription, and in doing so, deploys the Strawsonian conception of a person: a subject of both mental and physical predicates.

One of the advantages of Strawson's nonreductionist argument is that it retains the possibility of a moral vocabulary. One of the problems of psychophysical reductionism and eliminative materialism is that all human activity becomes redescribed in terms of the indifferent laws of physics. This indifference fails to capture the nature of moral life, which is characterized by evaluation and agency. Nevertheless, Strawson's concept of person has drawn heavy criticism from Harry Frankfurt because it does not go far enough in drawing out the implications of self-ascription for moral agency in the concept of "person."

Notes

1   In a recent interview, Mary Midgley suggests that the seeds of the regrowth of metaphysics were sown at Oxford during World War II when many of the philosophers of language became involved in intelligence operations, especially decoding efforts at Bletchley, which left teaching staff with expertise in metaphysics. See Julian Baggini and Jeremy Stangroom, *What Philosophers Think* (London and New York: Continuum, 2003), p. 126.
2   Peter Strawson, *Individuals, An Essay in Descriptive Metaphysics* (London: Methuen, 1977), p. 10.
3   Ibid, p. 87.
4   Ibid, p. 92.
5   Ibid, p. 97.
6   Ibid, p. 97.
7   Ibid, p. 97
8   Ibid, p. 101.
9   Ibid, p. 100.

Main Texts by Strawson

The Bounds of Sense: An Essay on Kant's Critique of Pure Reason (London: Methuen, 1966).
Freedom and Resentment, and Other Essays (London: Methuen, 1974).
Individuals: An Essay in Descriptive Metaphysics (London: Methuen, 1977).

Further Reading

Armstrong, David, *A Materialist Theory of the Mind* (London: Routledge, 1968).
Bermúdez, José Luis, Anthony Marcel, and Naomi Eilan (eds.), *The Body and the Self* (Cambridge, MA: MIT Press, 1995).
Gale, Richard M. (ed.), *Blackwell Guide to Metaphysics* (Oxford: Blackwell, 2002).
Lowe, E. J., *Subjects of Experience* (Cambridge, UK: Cambridge University Press, 1996).
Penelhum, Terence, *Survival and Disembodied Existence* (London: Routledge, 1970).
Sen, P. B. and R. R. Verma (eds.), *The Philosophy of P. F. Strawson* (New Delhi: India Council of Philosophical Research, 1995).
Van Straaten, Zak (ed.), *Philosophical Subjects: Essays Presented to P. F. Strawson* (Oxford: Clarendon Press, 1980).

"PERSONS"

P. F. Strawson

What we have to acknowledge [. . .] is the primitiveness of the concept of a person. What I mean by the concept of a person is the concept of a type of entity such that *both* predicates ascribing states of consciousness *and* predicates ascribing corporeal characteristics, a physical situation &c. are equally applicable to a single individual of that single type. What I mean by saying that this concept is primitive can be put in a number of ways. One way is to return to those two questions I asked earlier: viz. (1) why are states of consciousness ascribed to anything at all? and (2) why are they ascribed to the very same thing as certain corporeal characteristics, a certain physical situation &c.? I remarked at the beginning that it was not to be supposed that the answers to these questions were independent of each other. Now I shall say that they are connected in this way: that a necessary condition of states of consciousness being ascribed at all is that they should be ascribed to the *very same things* as certain corporeal characteristics, a certain physical situation &c. That is to say, states of consciousness could not be ascribed at all, *unless* they were ascribed to persons, in the sense I have claimed for this word. We are tempted to think of a person as a sort of compound of two kinds of subjects: a subject of experiences (a pure consciousness, an ego) on the one hand, and a subject of corporeal attributes on the other. Many questions arise when we think in this way. But, in particular, when we ask ourselves how we come to frame, to get a use for, the concept of this compound of two subjects, the picture – if we are honest and careful – is apt to change from the picture of two subjects to the picture of one subject and one non-subject. For it becomes impossible to see how we could come by the idea of different, distinguishable, identifiable subjects of experiences – different consciousnesses – *if this idea is thought of as logically primitive*, as a logical ingredient in the compound-idea of a person, the latter being composed of two subjects. For there could never be any question of assigning an experience, as such, to any subject other than oneself; and therefore never any question of assigning it to oneself either, never any question of ascribing it to a subject at all. So the concept of the pure individual consciousness – the pure ego – is a concept that cannot exist; or, at least, cannot exist

From *Individuals* (London: Methuen, 1964), pp. 101–12.

as a primary concept in terms of which the concept of a person can be explained or analysed. It can exist only, if at all, as a secondary, non-primitive concept, which itself is to be explained, analysed, in terms of the concept of a person. It was the entity corresponding to this illusory primary concept of the pure consciousness, the ego-substance, for which Hume was seeking, or ironically pretending to seek, when he looked into himself, and complained that he could never discover himself without a perception and could never discover anything but the perception. More seriously – and this time there was no irony, but a confusion, a Nemesis of confusion for Hume – it was this entity of which Hume vainly sought for the principle of unity, confessing himself perplexed and defeated; sought vainly because there is no principle of unity where there is no principle of differentiation. It was this, too, to which Kant, more perspicacious here than Hume, accorded a purely formal ('analytic') unity: the unity of the 'I think' that accompanies all my perceptions and therefore might just as well accompany none. Finally it is this, perhaps, of which Wittgenstein spoke, when he said of the subject, first that there is no such thing, and then that it is not a part of the world, but its limit.

So, then, the word 'I' never refers to this, the pure subject. But this does not mean, as the no-ownership theorist must think, that 'I' in some cases does not refer at all. It refers; because I am a person among others; and the predicates which would, *per impossible* belong to the pure subject if it could be referred to, belong properly to the person to which 'I' does refer.

The concept of a person is logically prior to that of an individual consciousness. The concept of a person is not to be analysed as that of an animated body or of an embodied anima. This is not to say that the concept of a pure individual consciousness might not have a logically secondary existence, if one thinks, or finds, it desirable. We speak of a dead person – a body – and in the same secondary way we might at least think of a disembodied person. A person is not an embodied ego, but an ego might be a disembodied person, retaining the logical benefit of individuality from having been a person.

It is important to realize the full extent of the acknowledgement one is making in acknowledging the logical primitiveness of the concept of a person. Let me rehearse briefly the stages of the argument. There would be no question of ascribing one's own states of consciousness, or experiences, to anything, unless one also ascribed, or were ready and able to ascribe, states of consciousness, or experiences, to other individual entities of the same logical type as that thing to which one ascribes one's own states of consciousness. The condition of reckoning oneself as a subject of such predicates is that one should also reckon others as subjects of such predicates. The condition, in turn, of this being possible, is that one should be able to distinguish from one another, to pick out or identify, different subject of such predicates, i.e. different individuals of the type concerned. The condition, in turn, of this being possible is that the individuals concerned, including oneself, should be of a certain unique type: of a type, namely, such that to each individual of that type there must be ascribed, or ascribable, *both* states of consciousness *and* corporeal characteristics. But this characterization of the type is still very opaque and does not at all clearly bring out what is involved. To bring this out, I must make a rough division, into two, of the kinds of predicates properly applied to individuals of this type. The first kind of predicate consists of those which are also properly applied to material bodies to which we would not dream of applying predicates ascribing states of consciousness. I will call this first kind M-predicates: and they include things like 'weighs 10 stone', 'is in the drawing-room' and so on. The second kind consists of all the other predicates we apply to persons. These I shall call P-predicates. P-predicates, of course, will be very various. They will include things like 'is smiling', 'is going for a walk', as well as things like 'is in pain', 'is thinking hard', 'believes in God' and so on.

So far I have said that the concept of a person is to be understood as the concept of a type of entity such that *both* predicates ascribing states of consciousness *and* predicates ascribing corporeal characteristics, a physical situation &c. are equally applicable to an individual entity of that type. All I have said about the meaning of saying that this concept is primitive is that it is not to be analysed in a certain way or ways. We are not, for example, to think of it as a secondary kind of entity in relation to two primary kinds, viz. a particular consciousness and a particular human body. I implied also that the Cartesian error is just a special case of the more general error, present in a different form in theories of the no-ownership type, of thinking of the designations, or apparent designations, of persons as *not* denoting precisely the same thing or entity for all kinds of predicate ascribed to the entity designated. That is, if we are to avoid the general form of this error, we must *not* think of 'I' or 'Smith' as suffering from type-ambiguity. Indeed, if we want to locate type-ambiguity somewhere, we would do better to locate it in certain predicates like 'is in the drawing-room' 'was hit by a stone' &c., and say they mean one thing when applied to material objects and another when applied to persons.

This is all I have so far said or implied about the meaning of saying that the concept of a person is primitive. What has to be brought out further is what the implications of saying this are as regards the logical character of those predicates with which we ascribe states of consciousness. For this purpose we may well consider P-predicates in general. For though not all P-predicates are what we should call 'predicates ascribing states of consciousness' (e.g. 'going for a walk' is not), they may be said to have this in common, that they imply the possession of consciousness on the part of that to which they are ascribed.

What then are the consequences of the view as regards the character of P-predicates? I think they are these. Clearly there is no sense in talking of identifiable individuals of a special type, a type, namely, such that they possess both M-predicates and P-predicates, unless there is in principle some way of telling, with regard to any individual of that type, and any P-predicate, whether that individual possesses that P-predicate. And, in the case of at least some P-predicates, the ways of telling must constitute in some sense logically adequate kinds of criteria for the ascription of the P-predicate. For suppose in no case did these ways of telling constitute logically adequate kinds of criteria. Then we should have to think of the relation between the ways of telling and what the P-predicate ascribes, or a part of what it ascribes, always in the following way: we should have to think of the ways of telling as *signs* of the presence, in the individual concerned, of this different thing, viz. the state of consciousness. But then we could only know that the way of telling was a sign of the presence of the different thing ascribed by the P-predicate, by the observation of correlations between the two. But this observation we could each make only in one case, viz. our own. And now we are back in the position of the defender of Cartesianism, who thought our way with it was too short. For what, now, does 'our own case' mean? There is no sense in the idea of ascribing states of consciousness to oneself, or at all, unless the ascriber already knows how to ascribe at least some states of consciousness to others. So he cannot argue in general 'from his own case' to conclusions about how to do this; for unless he already knows how to do this, he has no conception of *his own case*, or any *case*, i.e. any subject of experiences. Instead, he just has evidence that pain &c. may be expected when a certain body is affected in certain ways and not when others are. If he speculated to the contrary, his speculations would be immediately falsified.

The conclusion here is not, of course, new. What I have said is that one ascribes P-predicates to others on the strength of observation of their behaviour; and that the behaviour-criteria one goes on are not just signs of the presence of what is meant by the P-predicate, but are criteria of a logically adequate kind for the ascription of the P-predicate. On behalf of this conclusion, however, I am claiming that it follows from a consideration of the conditions necessary for any ascription of states of consciousness to anything. The point is not that we must accept this conclusion in order to avoid scepticism, but that we must accept it in order to explain the existence of the conceptual scheme in terms of which the sceptical problem is stated. But once the conclusion is accepted, the sceptical problem does not arise. So with many sceptical problems: their statement involves the pretended acceptance of a conceptual scheme and at the same time the silent repudiation of one of the conditions of its existence. That is why they are, in the terms in which they are stated, insoluble.

But this is only one half of the picture about P-predicates. For of course it is true of some important classes of P-predicates, that when one ascribes them *to oneself*, one does not do so on the strength of observation of those behaviour criteria on the strength of which one ascribes them to others. This is not true of all P-predicates. It is not, in general, true of those which carry assessments of character or capability: these, when self-ascribed, are in general ascribed on the same kind of basis as that on which they are ascribed to others. Even of those P-predicates of which it is true that one does not generally ascribe them to oneself on the basis of the criteria on the strength of which one ascribes them to others, there are many of which it is also true that their ascription is liable to correction by the self-ascriber on this basis. But there remain many cases in which one has an entirely adequate basis for ascribing a P-predicate to oneself, and yet in which this basis is quite distinct from those on which one ascribes the predicate to another. Thus one says, reporting a present state of mind or feeling: 'I feel tired, am depressed, am in pain'. How can this fact be reconciled with the doctrine that the criteria on the strength of which one ascribes P-predicates to others are criteria of a logically adequate kind for this ascription?

The apparent difficulty of bringing about this reconciliation may tempt us in many directions. It may tempt us, for example, to deny that these self-ascriptions are really ascriptive at all, to *assimilate* first-person ascriptions of states of consciousness to those other forms of behaviour which constitute criteria on the basis of which one person ascribes P-predicates to another. This device seems to avoid the difficulty; it is not, in all cases, entirely inappropriate. But it obscures the facts; and is needless. It is merely a sophisticated form of failure to recognize the special character of P-predicates, or, rather, of a crucial class of P-predicates. For just as there is not in general one primary process of learning, or teaching oneself, an inner private meaning for predicates of this class, then another process of learning to apply such predicates to others on the strength of a correlation, noted in one's own case, with certain forms of behaviour, so – and equally – there is not in general one primary process of learning to apply such predicates to others on the strength of behaviour criteria, and then another process of acquiring the secondary technique of exhibiting a new form of behaviour, viz. first–person P–utterances. Both these pictures are refusals to acknowledge the unique logical character of the predicates concerned. Suppose we write 'Px' as the general form of propositional function of such a predicate. Then, according to the first picture, the expression which primarily replaces 'x' in this form is 'I', the first person singular pronoun: its uses with other replacements are secondary, derivative and shaky. According to the second picture, on the other hand, the primary replacements of 'x' in this form are 'he', 'that person', &c., and its use with 'I' is secondary, peculiar, not a true ascriptive use. But it is essential to the character of these predicates that they have both first- and third–person ascrip-tive uses, that they are both self-ascribable otherwise than on the basis of observation of the behaviour of the subject of them, and other-ascribable on the basis of behaviour criteria. To learn their use is to learn both aspects of their use. In order to *have* this type of concept, one must be both a self-ascriber and an other-ascriber of such predicates, and must see every other as a self-ascriber. In order to *understand* this type of concept, one must acknowledge that there is a kind of predicate which is unambiguously and adequately ascribable *both* on the basis of observation of the subject of the predicate *and* not on this basis, i.e. independently of observation of the subject: the second case is the case where the ascriber is also the subject. If there were no concepts answering to the characterization I have just given, we should indeed have no philosophical problem about the soul; but equally we should not have our concept of a person.

To put the point – with a certain unavoidable crudity – in terms of one particular concept of this class, say, that of depression. We speak of behaving in a depressed way (of depressed behaviour) and we also speak of feeling depressed (of a feeling of depres-sion). One is inclined to argue that feelings can be felt but not observed, and behav-iour can be observed but not felt, and that therefore there must be room here to drive in a logical wedge. But the concept of depression spans the place where one wants to drive it in. We might say: in order for there to be such a concept as that of X's depres-sion, the depression which X has, the concept must cover both what is felt, but not observed, by X, and what may be observed, but not felt, by others than X (for all values of X). But it is perhaps better to say: X's depression *is* something, one and the same thing, which is felt, but not observed, by X, and observed, but not felt, by others than X. (Of course, what can be observed can also be faked or disguised.) To refuse to accept this is to refuse to accept the *structure* of the language in which we talk about depres-sion. That is, in a sense, all right. One might give up talking or devise, perhaps, a dif-ferent structure in terms of which to soliloquize. What is not all right is simultaneously to pretend to accept that structure and to refuse to accept it; i.e. to couch one's rejec-tion in the language of that structure.

It is in this light that we must see some of the familiar philosophical difficulties in the topic of the mind. For some of them spring from just such a failure to admit, or fully to appreciate, the character which I have been claiming for at least some P–predicates. It is not seen that these predicates could not have either aspect of their use, the self-ascriptive or the non–self-ascriptive, without having the other aspect. Instead, one aspect of their use is taken as self-sufficient, which it could not be, and then the other aspect appears as problematical. So we oscillate between philosophical scepticism and philosophical behaviourism. When we take the self-ascriptive aspect of the use of some P-predicates, say 'depressed', as primary, then a logical gap seems to open between the criteria on the strength of which we say that another is depressed, and the actual state of being depressed. What we do not realize is that if this logical gap is allowed to open, then it swallows not only his depression, but our depression as well. For if the logical gap exists, then depressed behaviour, however much there is of it, is no more than a sign of depression. But it can only become a sign of depression because of an observed correlation between it and depression. But whose depression? Only mine, one is tempted to say. But if *only* mine, then *not* mine at all. The sceptical position customarily represents the crossing of the logical gap as at best a shaky inference. But the point is that not even the syntax of the premises of the inference exists, if the gap exists.

If, on the other hand, we take the other-ascriptive uses of these predicates as primary or self-sufficient, we may come to think that all there is in the meaning of these predicates, as predicates, is the criteria on the strength of which we ascribe them to others. Does this not follow from the denial of the logical gap? It does not follow. To think that it does is to forget the self-ascriptive use of these predicates, to forget that we have to do with a class of predicates to the meaning of which it is essential that they should be both self-ascribable and other-ascribable to the same individual, where self-ascriptions are not made on the observational basis on which other-ascriptions are made, but on another basis. It is not that these predicates have two kinds of meaning. Rather, it is essential to the single kind of meaning that they do have, that both ways of ascribing them should be perfectly in order.

If one is playing a game of cards, the distinctive markings of a certain card constitute a logically adequate criterion for calling it, say, the Queen of Hearts; but, in calling it this, in the context of the game, one is ascribing to it properties over and above the possession of these markings. The predicate gets its meaning from the whole structure of the game. So with the language in which we ascribe P-predicates. To say that the criteria on the strength of which we ascribe P-predicates to others are of a logically adequate kind for this ascription, is not to say that all there is to the ascriptive meaning of these predicates is these criteria. To say this is to forget that they are P-predicates, to forget the rest of the language-structure to which they belong.

Now our perplexities may take a different form, the form of the question: 'But how can one ascribe to oneself, not on the basis of observation, the very same thing that others may have, on the basis of observation, reasons of a logically adequate kind for ascribing to one?' This question may be absorbed in a wider one, which might be phrased: 'How are P-predicates possible?' or: 'How is the concept of a person possible?' This is the question by which we replace those two earlier questions, viz.: 'Why are states of consciousness ascribed at all, ascribed to anything?' and 'Why are they ascribed to the very same thing as certain corporeal characteristics &c.?' For the answer to these two initial questions is to be found nowhere else but in the admission of the primitiveness of the concept of a person, and hence of the unique character of P-predicates. So residual perplexities have to frame themselves in this new way. For when we have acknowledged the primitiveness of the concept of a person, and, with it, the unique character of P-predicates, we may still want to ask what it is in the natural facts that makes it intelligible that we should have this concept, and to ask this in the hope of a nontrivial answer, i.e. in the hope of an answer which does not *merely* say: 'Well, there are people in the world'. I do not pretend to be able to satisfy this demand at all fully. But I may mention two very different things which might count as beginnings or fragments of an answer.

First, I think a beginning can be made by moving a certain class of P-predicates to a central position in the picture. They are predicates, roughly, which involve doing something, which clearly imply intention or a state of mind or at least consciousness in general, and which indicate a characteristic pattern, or range of patterns, of bodily movement, while not indicating at all precisely any very definite sensation or experience. I mean such things as 'going for a walk', 'coiling a rope', 'playing ball', 'writing a letter'. Such predicates have the interesting characteristic of many P-predicates, that one does not, in general, ascribe them to oneself on the strength of observation, whereas one does ascribe them to others on the strength of observation. But, in the case of these predicates, one feels minimal reluctance to concede that what is ascribed in these two different ways is the same. This is because of the marked dominance of a fairly definite pattern of bodily movement in what they ascribe, and the marked absence of any distinctive experience. They release us from the idea that the only things we can know about without observation or inference, or both, are private experiences; we can know, without telling by either of these means, about the present and future movements of a body. Yet bodily movements are certainly also things we can know about by observation and inference. Among the things that we observe, as opposed to the things we know about without observation, are the movements of bodies similar to that about which we have knowledge not based on observation. It is important that we should understand such movements, for they bear on and condition our own; and in fact we understand them, we interpret them, only by seeing them as elements in just such plans or schemes of action as those of which we know the present course and future development without observation of the relevant present movements. But this is to say that we see such movements as *actions*, that we interpret them in terms of intention, that we see them as movements of individuals of a type to which also belongs that individual whose present and future movements we know about without observation; it is to say that we see others as self-ascribers, not on the basis of observation, of what we ascribe to them on this basis.

These remarks are not intended to suggest how the 'problem of other minds' could be solved, or our beliefs about others given a general philosophical 'justification'. I have already argued that such a 'solution' or 'justification' is impossible, that the demand for it cannot be coherently stated. Nor are these remarks intended as *a priori* genetic psychology. They are simply intended to help to make it seem intelligible to us, at this stage in the history of the philosophy of this subject, that we have the conceptual scheme we have. What I am suggesting is that it is easier to understand how we can see each other, and ourselves, as persons, if we think first of the fact that we act, and act on each other, and act in accordance with a common human nature. Now 'to see each other as persons' is a lot of things, but not a lot of separate and unconnected things. The class of P-predicates that I have moved into the centre of the picture are not unconnectedly there, detached from others irrelevant to them. On the contrary, they are inextricably bound up with the others, interwoven with them. The topic of the mind does not divide into unconnected subjects.

11

COMMENTARY ON FRANKFURT

Harry Frankfurt (born 1929) is a distinguished professor of moral philosophy at Princeton University. Much of his philosophical working life has been concerned with the moral and conceptual aspects of "persons," but he is probably best known for his work on moral responsibility. Frankfurt's account of moral responsibility turns on a "critical" notion of freedom of the will. In his famous essay, "Freedom of the Will and the Concept of a Person," he argues that freedom of the will consists in the capacity to impose a structure on one's will through identification with, or endorsement of, certain of one's values and beliefs (what he calls "second-order volitions"). These endorsements then determine the motives for those actions for which one can be said to be morally responsible. Frankfurt claims that individuals who do not structure their wills in this way lack an essential attribute of personhood. He calls such individuals "wantons."

Frankfurt's essay opens with a criticism of Strawson. He argues that Strawson's concept of "person" is far too general to capture what is specific about persons; many animals, for example, can meet the definition of a being to whom both mental and physical predicates can be ascribed. For Frankfurt, what distinguishes persons from non-persons is not the ascription of both mental and physical predicates, but the structure of the will. Frankfurt's views stand in stark opposition to those of philosophers such as Derek Parfit, who argues that we can do away entirely with the concept of a "person" because it does not add anything to our moral or epistemic vocabulary. Frankfurt thinks that most philosophers are very confused about what a person is, and this confusion "gratuitously diminishes our philosophical vocabulary."[1] That this is so, he says, can be seen by the fact that the problem of personhood "is so generally neglected that it has been possible to make off with its very name almost without being noticed."[2]

Frankfurt is writing in that tradition of philosophy, dating from the Ancient Greeks, which takes as its central motif the value of the examined life. Here critical self-reflection and self-determination are inextricable from a morally valuable life: a life that can be said to be "one's own," and, for that reason, is worth living. Frankfurt also continues a line of thought originating in Kant's *Groundwork for a Metaphysics of Morals*.[3] There, Kant argued that persons are unlike other animals insofar as they have reason, which enables them to intervene in their desires and impulses to direct their actions.

Famously, Kant says that the role of reason is not to make us happy; reason has an altogether different purpose, which is to produce a good will. The purpose of reason, writes Kant, is morality, because it allows us to bring our actions under the directive of our rational wills. The good will is a self-legislating will: one chooses to have one's actions directed by rational motives alone, and in this way, one is autonomous. Similarly, Frankfurt regards freedom of the will as the defining characteristic of a person. However, while he believes that rationality has a key role, his conception of volition is more complex than Kantian good will. For Frankfurt, the process whereby one comes to endorse certain values and beliefs is partly driven by emotions and desires; it is a process driven by *what one cares about*. Having one's intentions and actions driven by what one cares about distinguishes a "person" from a wanton.

Frankfurt describes the difference between wantons and persons in terms of first-order and second-order desires and volitions. First-order desires are those desires that arise spontaneously from one's situation and are typically unreflective. First-order desires may be expressed in actions (but not necessarily), the motives of which one does not reflect on in a critically evaluative way. If there is evaluation here at all, it is characteristically instrumental and concerns only how one is to obtain what one wants in the most efficient or satisfying way. At the level of first-order desires, one does not stop to consider which, if any, of one's desires one wants to have. Many animals besides human beings have first-order desires, but, according to Frankfurt, only human beings are capable of second-order desires.

Second-order desires arise from reflection upon one's first-order desires; they are desires about desires. Having reason, we have the capacity to reflect upon, scrutinize, and evaluate our first-order desires. When we reflect upon and evaluate our first-order desires, selecting those desires we want to motivate us, we develop second-order desires.

Second-order desires often (but not necessarily) give rise to reasons upon which one acts. When this occurs, Frankfurt calls these "second-order volitions": "Someone has a desire of the second order either when he wants simply to have a certain desire or when he wants a certain desire to be his will. In situations of the latter kind I shall call his second-order desires 'second-order volitions'."[4]

Frankfurt distinguishes second-order desires from second-order volitions in this way: a second-order desire is the desire to have a certain desire. However, one may want that desire but not want to act on it. It is only if one also wants to act on that desire that it becomes a volition. To illustrate, he gives the example of a doctor investigating drug addiction. The doctor may want to experience the craving that addicts feel, so that he will understand their situation better. That is, he desires to have the desire for the drug. This is a second-order desire. However, he does not want to take the drug for which he has a desire – he does not have a first-order desire for the drug. That is, he does not want to act on the desire; he does not want his will to accord with that desire. He wants his actions determined by a different set of desires: a desire to be a good doctor, a knowledgeable researcher, and a nonaddict. Because these are the second-order desires on which he wishes to act, these desires constitute his second-order *volitions*.

Being a person on Frankfurt's terms means being the kind of entity who reflects upon their desires and aversions, and chooses (endorses or identifies with) the desires and aversions by which they will be motivated to act. Anyone who does not attempt this, according to Frankfurt, is a "wanton": "The essential characteristic of a wanton is that he does not care about his will."[5] Wantons can have second-order desires, but unless their wills are actually structured by those desires they will not be persons because they will not have enacted their freedom. Wantons can exercise reason, but do not have freedom of the will because they exercise only instrumental reason, not critical evaluation. On this view, until one critically reflects upon one's desires, the life one leads will not be genuinely one's own because it will not be something for which one can be said to be genuinely responsible. The distinction between first-order and second-order volitions raises the question of how the evaluative processes attached to each level are to be explained. Watson, for example, criticizes Frankfurt for not distinguishing adequately between an agent's motivational and valuational structures.[6]

On this view, only persons are moral agents, and so only persons are members of the moral community. The view that only critically reflective beings can belong to a moral community has attracted much criticism from people such as Peter Singer and Mary Midgley, for example,[7] on the grounds that it is too limited a view of ethics to do justice to environmental and animal ethics. While there is an immediate appeal in the importance Frankfurt places on critical reflection, his view may be too narrow even for human beings. An unintended but possible implication of his account might be that certain individuals, for example, the brain-damaged, might be excluded from the category of "person" or membership of the moral community. It is important to note that "person" is also a legalistic concept that brings with it a whole train of rights, privileges, and obligations, not to mention respect. To exclude a group of human beings from the category of "person" is to exclude them from this constellation of discourses through which significant aspects of one's identity and self-worth are formed. This point has been made in recent work by feminist philosophers, and philosophers influenced by the critical theory of the Frankfurt School,[8] who have argued that the capacity for critical reflection is not a given, but is mediated through interpersonal and social relations.[9] This work, which emphasizes the composite and mediated character of one's sense of self, also problematizes the ease with which distinctions between first-order and second-order desires can be made. Theorizing from an intersubjective and relational conception of "persons," these accounts call into question the interpretation of critical reflection presupposed by classical conceptions of autonomy conceived as rational self-sovereignty.

To demonstrate what is at issue in the idea that the formation of first-order and second-order desires are socially mediated, consider Peter Singer's example:[10] there is a society in which people sweat a lot, and a certain degree of body odor is accepted as normal. Then someone invents a chemical that will eliminate body odor. Given the level of acceptance of body odor, one would not anticipate a great demand for this novel product. However, the inventor embarks upon a massive publicity campaign designed to make people anxious about just how much they sweat and whether their body odor might be offensive to their friends. The campaign is a success and a lot of people develop a desire for the product, which is sold cheaply enough for this desire to be easily satisfied.

On Frankfurt's model of freedom of the will I act autonomously when I form a second-order volition by reflecting upon my desire concerning body odor: I can know that a certain degree of body odor is "natural" (that is, inevitable, inoffensive, and universal), and also believe that the advertising companies and deodorant manufacturers are motivated by profit alone, but nevertheless choose to buy deodorant. Just so long as I choose to eradicate my body odor in the light of this knowledge, I act autonomously.

The difficulty with Frankfurt's account is that it does not seem to capture the idea that my choices (the exercise of my will) may be expressions of a self-conception that is the product of an oppressive ideology. Unless the background conditions under which one's self-conception is formed are fair and undistorted, one's choices will almost inevitably reflect the distortions of those initial conditions. It is not enough to employ the will to peer behind particular desires to better understand the nature of one's choices, although this is clearly vitally essential to autonomy. One must also peer behind the will itself to its conditions of formation.[11] These conditions include, importantly, the role of emotions – note the role that anxiety plays in Singer's example. This work, in critical reflection and the emotions, is currently being developed in feminist moral philosophy to provide a richer and more critical conception of freedom.

Notes

1   Harry Frankfurt, "Freedom of the Will and the Concept of a Person," *The Journal of Philosophy*, LXVIII (1), 1971, p. 6.
2   Ibid.
3   Kant, *Groundwork of the Metaphysics of Morals*, ed. and trans. Mary Gregor with an introduction by Christine Korsgaard (Cambridge, UK: Cambridge University Press, 1998), pp. 1–10 (esp. 8–10).
4   Frankfurt (1971), p. 10.
5   Ibid, p. 11.
6   See Gary Watson, "Volitional Necessities," in Sarah Buss and Lee Overton (eds.), *Contours of Agency: Essays on Themes from Harry Frankfurt* (Cambridge, MA: Bradford/MIT Press, 2002), pp. 129–59.
7   Mary Midgley, "Duties Concerning Islands," in Robert Elliot (ed.), *Environmental Ethics* (New York: Oxford University Press, 1995), pp. 89–103; also Peter Singer, *Practical Ethics* (Cambridge, UK: Cambridge University Press, 1993).
8   The Frankfurt School was a group of left-wing philosophers and social theorists who were associated with the University of Frankfurt's Institute for Social Research. They included Max Horkheimer, Theodor Adorno, Herbert Marcuse, and Walter Benjamin. See Rolf Wiggershaus, *The Frankfurt School: Its History, Theories and Significance*, translated by Michael Roberston (Cambridge, UK: Polity Press, 1994).
9   For example, Catriona Mackenzie, "Critical Reflection, Self-knowledge and the Emotions," *Philosophical Explorations: An International Journal for the Philosophy of Mind and Action*, 5 (3), 2002, pp. 186–206; also Seyla Benhabib, "The Generalized and the Concrete Other: The Kohlberg–Gilligan Controversy and Moral Theory," in Eva Kittay and Diana T. Meyers (eds.), *Women and Moral Theory* (Totowa, NJ: Rowan and Littlefield, 1987), pp. 154–77.
10 Peter Singer, *Hegel: A Very Short Introduction* (Oxford and New York: Oxford University Press, 1983), p. 27.
11 See Seyla Benhabib, "Autonomy, Modernity, and Community: Communitarian and Critical Social Theory in Dialogues," in Axel Honneth, Thomas McCarthy, Claus Offe, and Albrecht Wellmer (eds.), *Cultural-Political Interventions in the Unfinished Project of Enlightenment* (Cambridge, MA: MIT Press, 1992), pp. 35–59.

Main Texts by Frankfurt

"The Dear Self," *Philosopher's Imprint*, 1 (0), 2001 <www.philosophersimprint.org/001000>.
The Importance of What We Care About (New York: Cambridge University Press, 1988).
Necessity, Volition, and Love (New York: Cambridge University Press, 1999).

Further Reading

Buss, Sarah and Lee Overton (eds), *Contours of Agency: Essays on Themes from Harry Frankfurt* (Cambridge, MA: Bradford Books/MIT Press, 2002).
Dennett, Daniel, *Elbow Room: The Varieties of Free Will Worth Wanting* (Cambridge, MA: MIT Press, 1990).
Honneth, Axel, Thomas McCarthy, Claus Offe, and Albrecht Wellmer (eds.), *Cultural-Political Interventions in the Unfinished Project of Enlightenment* (Cambridge, MA: MIT Press, 1992).
Kane, Robert (ed.), *The Oxford Handbook of Free Will* (New York: Oxford University Press, 2002).
Mackenzie, Catriona, "Critical Reflection, Self-knowledge and the Emotions," *Philosophical Explorations*, 5 (3), 2002, pp. 186–206.
Watson, Gary (ed.), *Free Will* (Oxford: Oxford University Press, 1983).

"FREEDOM OF THE WILL AND THE CONCEPT OF A PERSON"

Harry Frankfurt

What philosophers have lately come to accept as analysis of the concept of a person is not actually analysis of *that* concept at all. Strawson, whose usage represents the current standard, identifies the concept of a person as "the concept of a type of entity such that *both* predicates ascribing states of consciousness *and* predicates ascribing corporeal characteristics . . . are equally applicable to a single individual of that single type."[1] But there are many entities besides persons that have both mental and physical properties. As it happens – though it seems extraordinary that this should be so – there is no common English word for the type of entity Strawson has in mind, a type that includes not only human beings but animals of various lesser species as well. Still, this hardly justifies the misappropriation of a valuable philosophical term.

Whether the members of some animal species are persons is surely not to be settled merely by determining whether it is correct to apply to them, in addition to predicates ascribing corporeal characteristics, predicates that ascribe states of consciousness. It does violence to our language to endorse the application of the term "person" to those numerous creatures which do have both psychological and material properties but which are manifestly not persons in any normal sense of the word. This misuse of language is doubtless innocent of any theoretical error. But although the offense is "merely verbal," it does significant harm. For it gratuitously diminishes our philosophical vocabulary, and it increases the likelihood that we will overlook the important area of inquiry with which the term "person" is most naturally associated. It might have been expected that no problem would be of more central and persistent concern to philosophers than that of understanding what we ourselves essentially are. Yet this problem is so generally neglected that it has been possible to make off with its very name almost without being noticed and, evidently, without evoking any widespread feeling of loss.

There is a sense in which the word "person" is merely the singular form of "people" and in which both terms connote no more than membership in a certain biological

From *The Journal of Philosophy*, 68:1 (1971), pp. 5–16. Reproduced by permission of *The Journal of Philosophy* and the author.

species. In those senses of the word which are of greater philosophical interest, however, the criteria for being a person do not serve primarily to distinguish the members of our own species from the members of other species. Rather, they are designed to capture those attributes which are the subject of our most humane concern with ourselves and the source of what we regard as most important and most problematical in our lives. Now these attributes would be of equal significance to us even if they were not in fact peculiar and common to the members of our own species. What interests us most in the human condition would not interest us less if it were also a feature of the condition of other creatures as well.

Our concept of ourselves as persons is not to be understood, therefore, as a concept of attributes that are necessarily species-specific. It is conceptually possible that members of novel or even of familiar nonhuman species should be persons; and it is also conceptually possible that some members of the human species are not persons. We do in fact assume, on the other hand, that no member of another species is a person. Accordingly, there is a presumption that what is essential to persons is a set of characteristics that we generally suppose – whether rightly or wrongly – to be uniquely human.

It is my view that one essential difference between persons and other creatures is to be found in the structure of a person's will. Human beings are not alone in having desires and motives, or in making choices. They share these things with the members of certain other species, some of whom even appear to engage in deliberation and to make decisions based upon prior thought. It seems to be peculiarly characteristic of humans, however, that they are able to form what I shall call "second-order desires" or "desires of the second order."

Besides wanting and choosing and being moved *to do* this or that, men may also want to have (or not to have) certain desires and motives. They are capable of wanting to be different, in their preferences and purposes, from what they are. Many animals appear to have the capacity for what I shall call "first-order desires" or "desires of the first order," which are simply desires to do or not to do one thing or another. No animal other than man, however, appears to have the capacity for reflective self-evaluation that is manifested in the formation of second-order desires.[2]

I

The concept designated by the verb "to want" is extraordinarily elusive. A statement of the form "*A* wants to *X*" – taken by itself, apart from a context that serves to amplify or to specify its meaning – conveys remarkably little information. Such a statement may be consistent, for example, with each of the following statements: (a) the prospect of doing *X* elicits no sensation or introspectible emotional response in *A*; (b) *A* is unaware that he wants to *X*; (c) *A* believes that he does not want to *X*; (d) *A* wants to refrain from *X*-ing; (e) *A* wants to *Y* and believes that it is impossible for him both to *Y* and to *X*; (f) *A* does not "really" want to *X*; (g) *A* would rather die than *X*; and so on. It is therefore hardly sufficient to formulate the distinction between first-order and second-order desires, as I have done, by suggesting merely that someone has a first-order desire when he wants to do or not to do such-and-such, and that he has a second-order desire when he wants to have or not to have a certain desire of the first order.

As I shall understand them, statements of the form "*A* wants to *X*" cover a rather broad range of possibilities.[3] They may be true even when statements like (a) through (g) are true: when *A* is unaware of any feelings concerning *X*-ing, when he is unaware that he wants to *X*, when he deceives himself about what he wants and believes falsely that he does not want to *X*, when he also has other desires that conflict with his desire to *X*, or when he is ambivalent. The desires in question may be conscious or unconscious, they need not be univocal, and *A* may be mistaken about them. There is a further source of uncertainty with regard to statements that identify someone's desires, however, and here it is important for my purposes to be less permissive.

Consider first those statements of the form "*A* wants to *X*" which identify first-order desires – that is, statements in which the term "to *X*" refers to an action. A statement of this kind does not, by itself, indicate the relative strength of *A*'s desire to *X*. It does not make it clear whether this desire is at all likely to play a decisive role in what *A* actually does or tries to do. For it may correctly be said that *A* wants to *X* even when his desire to *X* is only one among his desires and when it is far from being paramount among them. Thus, it may be true that *A* wants to *X* when he strongly prefers to do something else instead; and it may be true that he wants to *X* despite the fact that, when he acts, it is not the desire to *X* that motivates him to do what he does. On the other hand, someone who states that *A* wants to *X* may mean to convey that it is this desire that is motivating or moving *A* to do that he is actually doing or that *A* will in fact be moved by this desire (unless he changes his mind) when he acts.

It is only when it is used in the second of these ways that, given the special usage of "will" that I propose to adopt, the statement identifies *A*'s will. To identify an agent's will is either to identify the desire (or desires) by which he is motivated in some action he performs or to identify the desire (or desires) by which he will or would be motivated when or if he acts. An agent's will, then, is identical with one or more of his first-order desires. But the notion of the will, as I am employing it, is not coextensive with the notion of first-order desires. It is not the notion of something that merely inclines an agent in some degree to act in a certain way. Rather, it is the notion of an *effective* desire – one that moves (or will or would move) a person all the way to action. Thus the notion of the will is not coextensive with the notion of what an agent intends to do. For even though someone may have a settled intention to do *X*, he may nonetheless do something else instead of doing *X* because, despite his intention, his desire to do *X* proves to be weaker or less effective than some conflicting desire.

Now consider those statements of the form "*A* wants to *X*" which identify second-order desires – that is, statements in which the term "to *X*" refers to a desire of the first order. There are also two kinds of situation in which it may be true that *A* wants to want to *X*. In the first place, it might be true of *A* that he wants to have a desire to *X* despite the fact that he has a univocal desire, altogether free of conflict and ambivalence, to refrain from *X*-ing. Someone might want to have a certain desire, in other words, but univocally want that desire to be unsatisfied.

Suppose that a physician engaged in psychotherapy with narcotics addicts believes that his ability to help his patients would be enhanced if he understood better what it is like for them to desire the drug to which they are addicted. Suppose that he is led in this way to want to have a desire for the drug. If it is a genuine desire that he wants, then what he wants is not merely to feel the sensations that addicts characteristically feel when they are gripped by their desires for the drug. What the physician wants, insofar as he wants to have a desire, is to be inclined or moved to some extent to take the drug.

It is entirely possible, however, that, although he wants to be moved by a desire to take the drug, he does not want this desire to be effective. He may not want it to move him all the way to action. He need not be interested in finding out what it is like to take the drug. And insofar as he now wants only to *want* to take it, and not to *take* it, there is nothing in what he now wants that would be satisfied by the drug itself. He may now have, in fact, an altogether univocal desire *not* to take the drug; and he may prudently arrange to make it impossible for him to satisfy the desire he would have if his desire to want the drug should in time be satisfied.

It would thus be incorrect to infer, from the fact that the physician now wants to desire to take the drug, that he already does desire to take it. His second-order desire to be moved to take the drug does not entail that he has a first-order desire to take it. If the drug were now to be administered to him, this might satisfy no desire that is implicit in his desire to want to take it. While he wants to want to take the drug, he may have *no* desire to take it; it may be that *all* he wants is to taste the desire for it. That is, his desire to have a certain desire that he does not have may not be a desire that his will should be at all different than it is.

Someone who wants only in this truncated way to want to X stands at the margin of preciosity, and the fact that he wants to want to X is not pertinent to the identification of his will. There is, however, a second kind of situation that may be described by "A wants to want to X" and when the statement is used to describe a situation of this second kind, then it does pertain to what A wants his will to be. In such cases the statement means that A wants the desire to X to be the desire that moves him effectively to act. It is not merely that he wants the desire to X to be among the desires by which, to one degree or another, he is moved or inclined to act. He wants this desire to be effective – that is, to provide the motive in what he actually does. Now when the statement that A wants to want to X is used in this way, it does entail that A already has a desire to X. It could not be true both that A wants the desire to X to move him into action and that he does not want to X. It is only if he does want to X that he can coherently want the desire to X not merely to be one of his desires but, more decisively, to be his will.[4]

Suppose a man wants to be motivated in what he does by the desire to concentrate on his work. It is necessarily true, if this supposition is correct, that he already wants to concentrate on his work. This desire is now among his desires. But the question of whether or not his second-order desire is fulfilled does not turn merely on whether the desire he wants is one of his desires. It turns on whether this desire is, as he wants it to be, his effective desire or will. If, when the chips are down, it is his desire to concentrate on his work that moves him to do what he does, then what he wants at that time is indeed (in the relevant sense) what he wants to want. If it is some other desire that actually moves him when he acts, on the other hand, then what he wants at that time is not (in the relevant sense) what he wants to want. This will be so despite the fact that the desire to concentrate on his work continues to be among his desires.

II

Someone has a desire of the second order either when he wants simply to have a certain desire or when he wants a certain desire to be his will. In situations of the latter kind, I shall call his second-order desires "second-order volitions" or "volitions of the second order." Now it is having second-order volitions, and not having second-order desires generally, that I regard as essential to being a person. It is logically possible, however unlikely, that there should be an agent with second-order desires but with no volitions of the second order. Such a creature, in my view, would not be a person. I shall use the term "wanton" to refer to agents who have first-order desires but who are not persons because, whether or not they have desires of the second order, they have no second-order volitions.[5]

The essential characteristic of a wanton is that he does not care about his will. His desires move him to do certain things, without its being true of him either that he wants to be moved by those desires or that he prefers to be moved by other desires. The class of wantons includes all nonhuman animals that have desires and all very young children. Perhaps it also includes some adult human beings as well. In any case, adult humans may be more or less wanton; they may act wantonly, in response to first-order desires concerning which they have no volitions of the second order, more or less frequently.

The fact that a wanton has no second-order volitions does not mean that each of his first-order desires is translated heedlessly and at once into action. He may have no opportunity to act in accordance with some of his desires. Moreover, the translation of his desires into action may be delayed or precluded either by conflicting desires of the first order or by the intervention of deliberation. For a wanton may possess and employ rational faculties of a high order. Nothing in the concept of a wanton implies that he cannot reason or that he cannot deliberate concerning how to do what he wants to do. What distinguishes the rational wanton from other rational agents is that he is not concerned with the desirability of his desires themselves. He ignores the question of what his will is to be. Not only does he pursue whatever course of action he is most strongly inclined to pursue, but he does not care which of his inclinations is the strongest.

Thus a rational creature, who reflects upon the suitability to his desires of one course of action or another, may nonetheless be a wanton. In maintaining that the essence of being a person lies not in reason but in will, I am far from suggesting that a creature without reason may be a person. For it is only in virtue of his rational capacities that a person is capable of becoming critically aware of his own will and of forming volitions of the second order. The structure of a person's will presupposes, accordingly, that he is a rational being.

The distinction between a person and a wanton may be illustrated by the difference between two narcotics addicts. Let us suppose that the physiological condition accounting for the addiction is the same in both men, and that both succumb inevitably to their periodic desires for the drug to which they are addicted. One of the addicts hates his addiction and always struggles desperately, although to no avail, against its thrust. He tries everything that he thinks might enable him to overcome his desires for the drug. But these desires are too powerful for him to withstand, and invariably, in the end, they conquer him. He is an unwilling addict, helplessly violated by his own desires.

The unwilling addict has conflicting first-order desires: he wants to take the drug, and he also wants to refrain from taking it. In addition to these first-order desires, however, he has a volition of the second order. He is not a neutral with regard to the conflict between his desire to take the drug and his desire to refrain from taking it. It is the latter desire, and not the former, that he wants to constitute his will; it is the latter desire, rather than the former, that he wants to be effective and to provide the purpose that he will seek to realize in what he actually does.

The other addict is a wanton. His actions reflect the economy of his first-order desires, without his being concerned whether the desires that move him to act are desires by which he wants to be moved to act. If he encounters problems in obtaining the drug or in administering it to himself, his responses to his urges to take it may involve deliberation. But it never occurs to him to consider whether he wants the relations among his desires to result in his having the will he has. The wanton addict may be an animal, and thus incapable of being concerned about his will. In any event he is, in respect of his wanton lack of concern, no different from an animal.

The second of these addicts may suffer a first-order conflict similar to the first-order conflict suffered by the first. Whether he is human or not, the wanton may (perhaps due to conditioning) both want to take the drug and want to refrain from taking it. Unlike the unwilling addict, however, he does not prefer that one of his conflicting desires should be paramount over the other; he does not prefer that one first-order desire rather than the other should constitute his will. It would be misleading to say that he is neutral as to the conflict between his desires, since this would suggest that he regards them as equally acceptable. Since he has no identity apart from his first-order desires, it is true neither that he prefers one to the other nor that he prefers not to take sides.

It makes a difference to the unwilling addict, who is a person, which of his conflicting first-order desires wins out. Both desires are his, to be sure; and whether he finally takes the drug or finally succeeds in refraining from taking it, he acts to satisfy what is in a literal sense his own desire. In either case he does something he himself wants to do, and he does it not because of some external influence whose aim happens to coincide with his own but because of his desire to do it. The unwilling addict identifies himself, however, through the formation of a second-order volition, with one rather than with the other of his conflicting first-order desires. He makes one of them more truly his own and, in so doing, he withdraws himself from the other. It is in virtue of this identification and withdrawal, accomplished through the formation of a second-order volition, that the unwilling addict may meaningfully make the analytically puzzling statements that the force moving him to take the drug is a force other than his own, and that it is not of his own free will but rather against his will that this force moves him to take it.

The wanton addict cannot or does not care which of his conflicting first-order desires wins out. His lack of concern is not due to his inability to find a convincing basis for preference. It is due either to his lack of the capacity for reflection or to his mindless indifference to the enterprise of evaluating his own desires and motives.[6] There is only one issue in the struggle to which his first-order conflict may lead: whether the one or the other of his conflicting desires is the stronger. Since he is moved by both desires, he will not be altogether satisfied by what he does no matter which of them is effective. But it makes no difference *to him* whether his craving or his aversion gets the upper hand. He has no stake in the conflict between them and so, unlike the unwilling addict, he can neither win nor lose the struggle in which he is engaged. When a *person* acts, the desire by which he is moved is either the will he wants or a will he wants to be without. When a *wanton* acts, it is neither.

III

There is a very close relationship between the capacity for forming second-order volitions and another capacity that is essential to persons – one that has often been considered a distinguishing mark of the human condition. It is only because a person has volitions of the second order that he is capable both of enjoying and of lacking freedom of the will. The concept of a person is not only, then, the concept of a type of entity that has both first-order desires and volitions of the second order. It can also be construed as the concept of a type of entity for whom the freedom of its will may be a problem. This concept excludes all wantons, both infrahuman and human, since they fail to satisfy an essential condition for the enjoyment of freedom of the will. And it excludes those suprahuman beings, if any, whose wills are necessarily free.

Just what kind of freedom is the freedom of the will? This question calls for an identification of the special area of human experience to which the concept of freedom of the will, as distinct from the concepts of other sorts of freedom, is particularly germane. In dealing with it, my aim will be primarily to locate the problem with which a person is most immediately concerned when he is concerned with the freedom of his will.

According to one familiar philosophical tradition, being free is fundamentally a matter of doing what one wants to do. Now the notion of an agent who does what he wants to do is by no means an altogether clear one: both the doing and the wanting, and the appropriate relation between them as well, require elucidation. But although its focus needs to be sharpened and its formulation refined, I believe that this notion does capture at least part of what is implicit in the idea of an agent who *acts* freely. It misses entirely, however, the peculiar content of the quite different idea of an agent whose *will* is free.

We do not suppose that animals enjoy freedom of the will, although we recognize that an animal may be free to run in whatever direction it wants. Thus, having the freedom to do what one wants to do is not a sufficient condition of having a free will. It is not a necessary condition either. For to deprive someone of his freedom of action is not necessarily to undermine the freedom of his will. When an agent is aware that there are certain things he is not free to do, this doubtless affects his desires and limits the range of choices he can make. But suppose that someone, without being aware of it, has in fact lost or been deprived of his freedom of action. Even though he is no longer free to do what he wants to do, his will may remain as free as it was before. Despite the fact that he is not free to translate his desires into actions or to act according to the determinations of his will, he may still form those desires and make those determinations as freely as if his freedom of action had not been impaired.

When we ask whether a person's will is free we are not asking whether he is in a position to translate his first-order desires into actions. That is the question of whether he is free to do as he pleases. The question of the freedom of his will does not concern the relation between what he does and what he wants to do. Rather, it concerns his desires themselves. But what question about them is it?

It seems to me both natural and useful to construe the question of whether a person's will is free in close analogy to the question of whether an agent enjoys freedom of action. Now freedom of action is (roughly, at least) the freedom to do what one wants to do. Analogously, then, the statement that a person enjoys freedom of the will means (also roughly) that he is free to want what he wants to want. More precisely, it means that he is free to will what he wants to will, or to have the will he wants. Just as the question about the freedom of an agent's action has to do with whether it is the action he wants to perform, so the question about the freedom of his will has to do with whether it is the will he wants to have.

It is in securing the conformity of his will to his second-order volitions, then, that a person exercises freedom of the will. And it is in the discrepancy between his will and his second-order volitions, or in his awareness that their coincidence is not his own doing but only a happy chance, that a person who does not have this freedom feels its lack. The unwilling addict's will is not free. This is shown by the fact that it is not the will he wants. It is also true, though in a different way, that the will of the wanton addict is not free. The wanton addict neither has the will he wants nor has a will that differs from the will he wants. Since he has no volitions of the second order, the freedom of his will cannot be a problem for him. He lacks it, so to speak, by default.

People are generally far more complicated than my sketchy account of the structure of a person's will may suggest. There is as much opportunity for ambivalence, conflict, and self-deception with regard to desires of the second order, for example, as there is with regard to first-order desires. If there is an unresolved conflict among someone's second-order desires, then he is in danger of having no second-order volition; for unless this conflict is resolved, he has no preference concerning which of his first-order desires is to be his will. This condition, if it is so severe that it prevents him from identifying himself in a sufficiently decisive way with *any* of his conflicting first-order desires, destroys him as a person. For it either tends to paralyze his will and to keep him from acting at all, or it tends to remove him from his will so that his will operates without his participation. In both cases he becomes, like the unwilling addict though in a different way, a helpless bystander to the forces that move him.

Notes

1   P. F. Strawson, *Individuals* (London: Methuen, 1959), pp. 101–2. Ayer's usage of "person" is similar: "it is characteristic of persons in this sense that besides having various physical properties . . . they are also credited with various forms of consciousness" [A. J. Ayer, *The Concept of a Person* (New York: St. Martin's, 1963), p. 82]. What concerns Strawson and Ayer is the problem of understanding the relation between mind and body, rather than the quite different problem of understanding what it is to be a creature that not only has a mind and a body but is also a person.

2   For the sake of simplicity, I shall deal only with what someone wants or desires, neglecting
    related phenomena such as choices and decisions. I propose to use the verbs "to want" and
    "to desire" interchangeably, although they are by no means perfect synonyms. My motive in
    forsaking the established nuances of these words arises from the fact that the verb "to want",
    which suits my purposes better so far as its meaning is concerned, does not lend itself so
    readily to the formation of nouns as does the verb "to desire". It is perhaps acceptable, albeit
    graceless, to speak in the plural of someone's "wants." But to speak in the singular of
    someone's "want" would be an abomination.

3   What I say in this paragraph applies not only to cases in which "to X" refers to a possible
    action or inaction. It also applies to cases in which "to X" refers to a first-order desire and
    in which the statement that "A wants to X" is therefore a shortened version of a statement
    – "A wants to want to X" – that identifies a desire of the second order.

4   It is not so clear that the entailment relation described here holds in certain kinds of cases,
    which I think may fairly be regarded as nonstandard, where the essential difference between
    the standard and the nonstandard cases lies in the kind of description by which the first-
    order desire in question is identified. Thus, suppose that A admires B so fulsomely that, even
    though he does not know what B wants to do, he wants to be effectively moved by what-
    ever desire effectively moves B; without knowing what B's will is, in other words, A wants
    his own will to be the same. It certainly does not follow that A already has, among his desires,
    a desire like the one that constitutes B's will. I shall not pursue here the questions of whether
    there are genuine counterexamples to the claim made in the text or of how, if there are, that
    claim should be altered.

5   Creatures with second-order desires but no second-order volitions differ significantly from
    brute animals, and, for some purposes, it would be desirable to regard them as persons. My
    usage, which withholds the designation "person" from them, is thus somewhat arbitrary. I
    adopt it largely because it facilitates the formulation of some of the points I wish to make.
    Hereafter, whenever I consider statements of the form "A wants to want to X," I shall have
    in mind statements identifying second-order volitions and not statements identifying second-
    order desires that are not second-order volitions.

6   In speaking of the evaluation of his own desires and motives as being characteristic of a
    person, I do not mean to suggest that a person's second-order volitions necessarily manifest
    a *moral* stance on his part toward his first-order desires. It may not be from the point of view
    of morality that the person evaluates his first-order desires. Moreover, a person may be capri-
    cious and irresponsible in forming his second-order volitions and give no serious consider-
    ation to what is at stake. Second-order volitions express evaluations only in the sense that
    they are preferences. There is no essential restriction on the kind of basis, if any, upon which
    they are formed.

12

COMMENTARY ON SHOEMAKER

Sydney Shoemaker (born 1931) is a professor of philosophy at Cornell University. His interests range across metaphysics and the philosophy of mind, including causation, functionalist theories of mind, the nature of sense experience, and problems of self-knowledge. *Personal Identity*, which he coauthored with Richard Swinburne in 1984, is arguably his most widely read work. Shoemaker's account of personal identity has a central place in analytical accounts of personal identity. Almost every other contemporary theorist refers to it.

Shoemaker begins the chapter from which this extract is taken by spelling out exactly what he means by "identity," in order to clarify the way in which identity (sameness) is logically compatible with change (difference). Like philosophers before him, Shoemaker is concerned with numerical identity, that is, with an account according to which we can say that a person at one time *is* the person identified at another time.

Shoemaker is specifically concerned to provide an account of identity that does not violate transitivity (recall Reid's objection to Locke concerning the case of the old general). Shoemaker's first step in solving this problem is to propose that we think of persons as temporally extended, four-dimensional beings. On this view, persons do not exist at a single point in time, but extend over the entire period of their lives; a person exists as a temporal whole. A person can then be divided into temporal parts or "time slices" (also called "person-stages") which are the sets of properties attributable to a person at any specified time. A person is the totality or unity relation holding between all his or her person stages. The unity of a person, then, has two aspects: unity over time and unity at a particular time (diachronic unity and synchronic unity). The two types of unity relations are also said to be "copersonal," to express the idea of different properties or person-stages existing together as part of the same person.

Shoemaker reminds us that, for Locke, having the same consciousness (on this interpretation, memory) requires that one be able to remember "from the inside," that is, from the perspective of actually having undergone the experience that one claims to remember. This requires that we distinguish between remembering *that* certain events occurred and actually remembering the event itself. Put in four-dimensionalist terminology, "two person-stages belong to the same person if and only if the later contains memories (from the inside) of experiences etc., contained in the earlier one. . . . Let us say that two person–stages so related are memory-connected."[1]

This description opens the way to overcome the transitivity problem by articulating continuity of identity in terms of memory-*connectedness*. We no longer have to establish that there is an identical whole consciousness at each stage of a person's life, but rather that there is continuity of memory that connects the various person–stages in a single life. The appropriate kind of memory connectedness must be such that it preserves one's memory "from the inside." It will not be enough, for example (in Reid's objection to Locke), that the general looks over pictures of himself as a boy, or hears the testimony of witnesses. The unity relation must preserve the first-person perspective aspect of memory (or at least its possibility in the case of faded memories). Shoemaker argues that this is achieved if we insist that memory-connectedness be causal, that is, that the memories one has are caused by the events of which they are memories. This distinguishes memories acquired through dreaming, hypnotic suggestion, or unintentional error from identical memories acquired by the experience of which they are memories.

The solution to the transitivity problem is also the solution to the problem of circularity. If we accept that memories must be caused by actual events then we have an objective criterion for establishing memory continuity (and sameness of identity) independently of knowing whose memory it is. At the same time Shoemaker has preserved the first-person perspective central to Locke's sense of "same consciousness" without needing to rely solely on the subjective criterion of its conscious subject. Since personal identity consists in memory continuity, the identity of the person cannot be determined until the unity relation established by the application of the objective causal criterion has been determined.

Shoemaker's defense of the causal criterion is not without its problems. In the example where Brown's brain is transplanted into Robinson's body, we are told that the identity of the resulting person (called Brownson) can be established by reference to the causal chain that underlies his having certain memories, namely, the memories of Brown's life. We know that there is the appropriate causal chain because we know that the person has Brown's brain. However, rather than resolving the problem of circularity it seems to have merely pushed the problem back a stage. We know that this person has Brown's memories because we know that the brain he was given was Brown's. In other words we know this person has Brown's identity (who he is) because we know that he has Brown's identity (brain). It is not simply that the brain provides causal continuity but that the brain already *is* an identity, namely Brown. We do not have any criterion for knowing the identity of this brain and, by extension, for knowing who Brownson is, independently of knowing whose memories the brain has. Shoemaker's suggestion does eliminate the circularity from the question of Brownson's identity, but it reappears at the level of Brown's brain.

Shoemaker points out that not everything about personal identity hangs on memory continuity, and the account so far needs to be broadened to encompass causal continuity in personality traits: one's interests, tastes, dispositions, and so forth. A person has continuity in identity when that person has continuity in memory and personality, in other words, psychological continuity. Shoemaker's innovative move in this respect is to connect psychological continuity to a functionalist model of mind: "Functionalism is a causal theory of mind. In functionalist terms, a psychological state is definable in terms of its relations (primarily its causal relations) to sensory inputs, behavioural outputs, and (especially) other functional states."[2]

Take for example a situation where I step on a rusty nail. The experience is to be understood by reference to the physical stimulus caused by the nail (pain), which is causally related to other mental states, for example, worrying about contracting tetanus, and which are causally related to my behavior, such as crying out, rubbing my foot, and looking for other rusty nails. These states in combination can also give rise to other mental states and beliefs such as deciding to tidy up the backyard or going to the doctor. The integrated nature of the functionalist model makes it particularly suitable for explaining how states are copersonal: a mental state causes its effects in conjunction with mental states of the same person, and it is just the having of states in this integrated way that makes them states of the *same* person; in other words, that circumscribes the identity of a person.

Central to the integrative character of the functionalist model is the idea that mental states tend to give rise to other mental states that are coherent with them. On Shoemaker's view, because a person exists over time mental states are also temporal. That means that mental states can evolve into other states with different but related content ("successor states"). The experience of being bullied at school, for example, can give rise to a successor state such as the belief that people are mainly motivated by personal power. This belief can then play a central role in the production and coherence of other mental states and behavior. For this reason, Shoemaker construes psychological continuity as the relation of successor states. There is logical and/or semantic continuity between one's psychological states, memories, dispositions, and behavior, all of which are related causally and are given "from the inside," that is, in the first-person perspective.

Shoemaker notes that any person can have greater or lesser degrees of internal coherence. Persons with a highly integrated identity are those whose thoughts and behavior are highly consistent. These individuals seldom act in ways that conflict with their professed values and beliefs, or that conflict with their actions in relevantly similar contexts. The functionalist explanation says that these are persons who have a high degree of causal interaction between their mental states. On the other hand, persons who display "compartmentalization" have thoughts and behavior that are inconsistent and that conflict with previous actions in relevantly similar contexts. Such individuals have a lower level of interaction between their mental states such that spheres of mental activity are cut off from the influence of other mental states. Shoemaker suggests that in the extreme this condition characterizes multiple personality disorder.

Shoemaker does not pretend that functionalism has all the answers, or even that it is a developed theory. However, he proposes functionalism as a coherent and economical view to take on the connection between identity and psychology that is neutral with respect to metaphysical or epistemological questions concerning the intrinsic nature of mental states and persons. It is, he says, "compatible with materialism without entailing it."[3] Finally, Shoemaker commends functionalism because it throws much needed light on the problem of other minds: "Because it individuates states by their causal, or explanatory, roles, it makes intelligible that we can know of such states in other persons, as we seem to do, by 'inferences to the best explanation' based on behaviour."[4]

A significant criticism of the causal model of continuity underpinning the functionalist approach comes from Marya Schechtman, who, drawing on the work of Harry Frankfurt, proposes a narrative model of continuity in identity. She argues that the importance we place on psychological continuity as a criteria for identity is not abstract and causal, but rather is driven by our orientation to basic practical concerns about self-interest, survival, compensation, and moral responsibility.[5] On Schechtman's view, the kind of coherence needed at this level involves much more than the extrinsic relations of causation; it requires intrinsic relations of self-constitution, such as are employed in the narrative view.

Despite these criticisms, it is worth remembering that Shoemaker's view is not reductionist. He is mindful that the first-person perspective and the notion of "person" have a certain conceptual priority that theory must accord with. The philosophical question that remains, however, is how a casual model is to do justice to these priorities.

Notes

1   Shoemaker, "Personal Identity: A Materialist's Account," in Sydney Shoemaker and Richard Swinburne, *Personal Identity* (Oxford: Blackwell, 1984), p. 81.
2   Ibid, p. 78.
3   Ibid, p. 92.
4   Ibid, p. 93.
5   Marya Schechtman, *The Constitution of Selves* (Ithaca, NY: Cornell University Press, 1996), p. 2.

Main Texts by Shoemaker

The First-Person Perspective, and Other Essays (Cambridge, UK and New York: Cambridge University Press, 1996).
Identity, Cause and Mind: Philosophical Essays (Cambridge, UK: Cambridge University Press, 1984).
Self-knowledge and Self-identity (Ithaca, NY: Cornell University Press, 1963).

Further Reading

Braddon-Mitchell, David and Frank Jackson, *The Philosophy of Mind and Cognition* (Oxford, UK and Cambridge, MA: Blackwell Publishers, 1996).
Lewis, David, *Philosophical Papers*, vol. 1 (Oxford: Oxford University Press, 1983).
Noonan, Harold W., *Personal Identity* (London: Routledge, 1989).
Perry, John (ed.), *Personal Identity* (Berkeley: University of California Press, 1975).
Rorty, Amelie Oksenberg (ed.), *The Identities of Persons* (Berkeley: University of California Press, 1976).
Schechtman, Marya, *The Constitution of Selves* (Ithaca, NY: Cornell University Press, 1996).
Smith, Peter and O. R. Jones, *The Philosophy of Mind: An Introduction* (Cambridge, UK: Cambridge University Press, 1986).
Wilkes, Kathleen V., *Real People: Personal Identity Without Thought Experiments* (New York: Oxford University Press, 1988).

"PERSONAL IDENTITY: A MATERIALIST'S ACCOUNT"

Sydney Shoemaker

Personal Identity as Psychological Continuity

This requires us to consider something we would have had to consider anyhow, namely the role *vis-à-vis* personal identity of kinds of psychological continuity other than memory continuity – I mean continuity with respect to the sorts of traits . . . : interests, tastes, talents, and traits of personality and character.[1] Let us return to the Brown–Brownson case. If Brownson's possession of Brown's brain makes it plausible that he will have memories from the inside of Brown's past life, it makes it equally plausible that he will resemble Brown psychologically in all of the ways one expects a person on one day to resemble himself as he was the day before, and this resemblance would certainly be part of our reason for regarding Brownson as the same person as Brown. Suppose just for the moment that while Brownson's memories-from-the-inside are all of Brown's past, his personality and character traits are those of the old Robinson; I think that in this case (which would be physiologically unintelligible, and perhaps psychologically unintelligible as well) we would be much more hesitant about identifying Brownson with Brown.

We know, of course, that different people can share personality and character traits. And this may seem a reason for saying that Brownson's similarity to Brown with respect to such traits could not be part of what constitutes his identity with Brown, even though it might be evidence for it. This may suggest that, conceptually speaking, memory continuity is much more intimately related to personal identity than is similarity and continuity of personality. But all of this ignores the fact that what we have in the Brown–Brownson case is not merely similarity of personality and character. Brownson does not merely have the same personality traits as Brown did; he has those traits *because* Brown's life was such as to lead him to acquire such traits. The fact that Brownson has Brown's brain gives us reason to suppose that there is a relationship of causal or counterfactual dependence between Brownson's traits subsequent to the brain transfer and

From Sydney Shoemaker and Richard Swinburne, *Personal Identity* (Oxford: Blackwell, 1984), pp. 89–97. Reprinted by permission of Blackwell Publishing.

Brown's traits prior to it – we have reason to think that if Brown's traits had been different, Brownson's traits would have been different in corresponding ways. It is precisely when the circumstances are such that evidence of similarity is evidence of such a causal or counterfactual dependence that evidence of similarity is evidence of identity. Indeed, it is for the same reason that the nature of Brownson's memories is evidence that he is Brown; we have reason to think that if Brown's life had been different, Brownson's memories would have been correspondingly different, and thus that Brownson's memories are causally and counterfactually dependent on Brown's past life. Thus the status of similarity and continuity of personality traits as evidence of personal identity seems no different than that of memory continuity; both are evidence only in so far as they include, or are evidence for, causal relations between earlier and later states.

Henceforth I shall use the term 'psychological continuity' to cover both of these sorts of causally grounded continuity. The memory continuity account of personal identity thus gives way to a more general psychological continuity account.[2] Memory continuity is now seen as just a special case of psychological continuity, and it is in psychological continuity that personal identity is now held to consist. Reverting to the 'person-stage' terminology, two person-stages will be directly connected, psychologically, if the later of them contains a psychological state (a memory impression, personality trait, etc.) which stands in the appropriate relation of causal dependence to a state contained in the earlier one; and two stages belong to the same person if and only if (1) they are connected by a series of stages such that each member of the series is directly connected, psychologically, to the immediately preceding member, and (2) no such series of stages which connects them 'branches' at any point, i.e., contains a member which is directly connected, psychologically, to two different stages occurring at the same time.

It is not peculiar to persons that their identity over time involves there being relationships of causal or counterfactual dependence between successive stages. The same is true of continuants generally. It is, I think, a point in favour of the psychological continuity account of personal identity that it can be seen as applying to the special case of personal identity an account of identity through time – call it the 'causal continuity account' – which holds of continuants generally.[3]

But the psychological continuity account as so far presented is extremely sketchy. Very little has been said about what constitutes the 'appropriate' causal connections between mental states involved in such continuity. I think that the best way of getting additional light on this is to draw on other parts of the philosophy of mind. What I propose to do now is to consider a widely held (and widely disputed) theory about the nature of mental states, a theory that has been held on grounds having nothing to do with personal identity, and to see what that theory implies about the nature of personal identity. What it implies seems to me a version of the psychological continuity view, and one that puts the notion of an 'appropriate causal connection' in a new and interesting light.

Functionalism and Personal Identity

This account of mind is what has come to be called 'functionalism'. What the various versions of it hold in common is that every mental state is a 'functional state', i.e., a state which is definable in terms of its relations (primarily its causal relations) to sensory inputs, behavioural outputs, and (especially) other functional states. A mental state is individuated, and constituted as being the particular mental state it is, by its place in a complex causal network of states. Take, for example, the belief that it is raining. It is characteristic of this state that it is apt to be brought about by certain sense-experiences (but only if the person has certain background beliefs), that in combination with certain other beliefs (e.g., the belief that umbrellas keep off rain) and certain desires (e.g., the desire to keep dry) it leads to certain behaviour (e.g., taking an umbrella if one goes out), and that in combination with certain other beliefs (e.g., the belief that if it is raining then the streets are wet) it leads to still other beliefs (e.g., the belief that the streets are wet). On the functional view, if this characterization were suitably expanded and refined, then no state would count as the belief that it is raining unless it satisfied this characterization, and any state that satisfied it would automatically count as that belief (or, as it is sometimes put, as a 'realization' of that belief). To believe that it is raining, on this view, just *is* to have a state which can be caused to exist in these ways, and which has these sorts of effects when combined with such-and-such other states. And every mental state will have such a functional characterization – one such that a state is a realization of that mental state just in case it satisfies that characterization.[4]

I can indicate only very briefly the considerations that have recommended this view to those who have held it. First, it is compatible with materialism without entailing it. Since the functional characterization of a mental state describes it solely in terms of its causal relations to other states, it leaves open what the 'intrinsic' nature of such a state is. It may be (and this is what most functionalists believe) that what stand in these networks of causal relations – what 'play these functional roles' – are neurophysiological states of the brain. In that case the states are realized physically; and if all such states are realized physically, materialism is true. But it is also compatible with the functional characterizations that the states should be realized non-physically; thus a mind–body dualist can agree with the functional characterizations without being committed to materialism. The issue of whether materialism or dualism is true is, on this view, an empirical one. This allows the materialist to concede the intelligibility of the dualist view, and even the logical possibility of its being true, while maintaining that it is in fact false.

Second, and closely related to this, functionalism is compatible with, and provides a way of reconciling materialism with, the widely held view that creatures can share the same mental states while differing radically in their internal physical make-ups. The 'abstractness' of functional characterizations allows the same functional state to be realized in a variety of different ways, and if mental states are functional states there is no a priori reason why the same mental state cannot be realized in very different physical states in creatures of different species (humans and dolphins, or, more radically, humans and Martians). In computer jargon, the same 'software' (the same program) can be realized in different 'hardware'.

Finally, functionalism helps with the problem of other minds. Because it individuates states by their causal, or explanatory, roles, it makes it intelligible that we can know of such states in other persons, as we seem to do, by 'inferences to the best explanation' based on behaviour.

Now let us return to the topic of personal identity. What the functionalist view claims is that it is of the essence of a mental state to be caused in certain ways, and to produce, in conjunction with other mental states, certain effects (behaviour or other mental states). But of course, it is in conjunction with other mental states *of the same person* that a mental state produces the effects it does; and its immediate effects, those the having of which is definitive of its being the mental state it is, will be states (or behaviour) on the part of the *very same person* who had the mental state in question. Thus there is, on the functionalist view, a very intimate connection between the question 'What is the nature of the various mental states?' and the question 'How must different mental states be causally connected in order to be 'copersonal', i.e., to belong to one and the same person?'[5]

Unlike the psychological continuity view characterized earlier, the functionalist account of mind has implications concerning the synchronic unity of minds. It is only when the belief that it is raining and the desire to keep dry are copersonal that they tend (in conjunction with other mental states) to lead to such effects as the taking of an umbrella; if the belief is mine and the desire is yours, they will not directly produce any joint effects. And it seems that if a belief and desire to produce (in conjunction with other mental states) just those effects which the functional characterizations of them say they ought to produce if copersonal, then in virtue of this they are copersonal. We can make sense of the idea that a single body might be simultaneously 'animated' by two different minds or consciousnesses; the phenomena that would make it reasonable to believe that this had happened would be similar to, but more extreme than, the phenomena observed in 'split-brain' patients that have led some investigators to think that splitting the brain results in splitting the mind. Whether different mental states that are realized in such a body should count as belonging to the same person, or mind, would seem to turn precisely on whether they are so related that they will jointly have the functionally appropriate sorts of effects.

But one cannot formulate these conditions for synchronic unity of mental states without invoking the notion of diachronic unity. Mental states are synchronically unified in virtue of what they jointly cause or are capable of causing, and what they cause will be something later in time with which they are diachronically unified. Although the effects will include behaviour, I shall focus here on the role of mental states in producing other mental states.

Most functional accounts make it central to the functional nature of mental states that they tend to bring about effects which they, in conjunction with other mental states of the same person, 'rationalize', i.e., make it rational for the person to do (in the case of behaviour) or have (in the case of mental states). A clear case of this is that in which a person's beliefs lead, through reasoning, to other beliefs which they entail or otherwise support, or in which beliefs and desires give rise, through deliberation, to a decision which they make reasonable. But we have an instance of it even in what can naturally be regarded as the mere retention of a mental state. I form the intention to do something tomorrow, and when tomorrow comes I do it, from that intention. But while there is a sense in which I retained the same intention throughout, there is also a sense in which the content of my intention was constantly changing; it began as the intention to do something twenty-four hours hence, evolved into the intention to do it twenty-three hours hence, and eventually became the intention to do it *now*. And of course the nature of this change was determined in part by my other mental states, in particular my belief at each point about how much time had passed since the initial formation of the intention. The same thing happens with expectations and with memories.

Instead of speaking of mental states 'evolving into' states having somewhat different contents, let us speak of them as giving rise to 'successor states' having these contents. While the content of a person's mental state (belief, intention, etc.) will to a certain extent depend on the nature of all of his states at earlier times, there will often be a particular state at an earlier time on whose content its content especially depends – and it is of that state that we will call it the 'successor state'. (In some cases, including beliefs expressed by what Quine calls 'eternal sentences', the successor states will have the very same content as their predecessor states; the successor states of my belief that there is no highest prime number will be other tokens of the belief that there is no highest primer number.) On the functionalist view, a mental state is defined in part in terms of what successor states it is liable to give rise to in combination with various other states.

Viewed in this light, what I earlier called 'psychological continuity' is just the playing out over time of the functional natures of the mental states characteristic of persons. To the extent that it consists in psychological similarity between different person-stages, this is due to the fact that in many cases what is required as the successor state of a mental state is just another token of the same state. To the extent that it consists in 'memory-continuity', this is because it belongs to the nature of certain states (sense experiences and intentional actions) that they give rise to successor states of the sort I have called memories from the inside, and because it belongs to the nature of these to perpetuate themselves, i.e., to produce successor states having the same or closely related contents. But psychological continuity is constituted no more by these than it is by the evolution and execution of plans of action, by deliberation and reasoning, and by count-less other mental processes. (It should be observed that the 'states' here need not be conscious; most of them will exist in the way my beliefs about Argentina exist when I am giving no thought to Argentina, or in the way my memories of my schooldays exist when I am sound asleep. Also, included under 'states' here are psychological capacities of all kinds; so psychological continuity as here understood will occur even in the case of a newborn infant, although there it will be mainly a matter of retaining psychological capacities that have not yet begun to be exercised.)

Let me return to the point that the functional natures of mental states determine not only the conditions for their diachronic unity but also the conditions for their syn-chronic unity. It is a commonplace that our minds are sometimes 'compartmentalized'; that they contain subsystems of beliefs, desires and values which are internally coher-ent but do not cohere well with one another. Thus, for example, there is the man who lives by one set of moral precepts in his private life and quite another in his business dealings, and is unable to see the discrepancy. In such a case the determinants of a person's actions on any given occasion will normally be beliefs and desires belonging to the same 'compartment'; mental states from different compartments either do not combine to influence action at all, or, if they do, result in behaviour which seems inco-herent or irrational. The opposite of compartmentalization is 'integration'; a mind is integrated to the extent that the different mental states in it form a consistent set of beliefs and a coherent set of values, and, what goes with this, that what the person does can be seen as rational in the light of all of his beliefs and values, rather than only in the light of some subset of them. As a rough approximation, the unity relation holds between mental states just in case there is at least the possibility of their being integrated into a single set. If the states of what we initially suppose to be one mind were compartmentalized to the extent that it was impossible that states from different compartments should jointly produce effects which they jointly rationalized, then we might speak of there being two 'consciousnesses' there, or perhaps of there being two minds or even two persons, even if the states were all realized in a single human body. There are of course actual cases, cases of 'multiple personality', that approximate to this condition. If we resist saying that there are really two minds or two persons in such cases, this is not (I think) because we are wedded to the principle 'one body, one person'; it is because in the cases that actually occur the compartmentalization is not complete (e.g., one of the personalities will sometimes have memories 'from the inside' of the deeds of the other), and because we think that there is the possibility of integration being at least partially restored.

Notes

1   Shoemaker is interested in exploring some of the objections to (and possible defenses of) Locke's account of personal identity in terms of 'remembering from the inside.' He notes that some readers who may not be persuaded of a distinction between personal identity and bodily identity by Locke's account of soul swapping may nevertheless be persuaded by a case of brain-swapping:

> Suppose then, that by a surgical blunder (of rather staggering proportions!) Brown's brain gets into Robinson's head. When the resulting person, call him 'Brownson,' regains consciousness, he claims to be Brown, and exhibits detailed knowledge of Brown's past life, always reporting Brown's deeds and experiences in the first person. It is hard to resist the conclusion that we, viewing the case from the outside, ought to accept Brownson's claim to be Brown, precisely on the basis of the evidence that he remembers Brown's life from the inside. (Shoemaker, 'Personal Identity: A Materialist's Account,' p. 78) [KA]

2   A psychological continuity account is given in Anthony Quinton, 'The Soul,' *Journal of Philosophy*, 59, 1962, pp. 393–403.
3   See Sydney Shoemaker, 'Identities, Properties and Causality,' *Midwest Studies in Philosophy*, 4, 1979, pp. 341–2.
4   See Hilary Putnam, 'The Nature of Mental States,' in Putnam, *Mind, Language and Reality, Philosophical Papers*, vol. 2, 1975, Cambridge University Press; David Lewis, 'An Argument for the Identity Theory,' *Journal of Philosophy*, 63, 1966, pp. 17–25, and 'Psychophysical and Theoretical Identification,' *Australasian Journal of Philosophy*, 50, 1972, pp. 249–58.
5   See Shoemaker (1979), and Patricia Kitcher, 'Kant on Self-Identity,' *The Philosophical Review*, 91, 1982, pp. 41–72.

13

COMMENTARY ON WILLIAMS

Sir Bernard Williams (1929–2003) was one of Britain's most highly regarded philosophers, holding prestigious positions at Oxford and Cambridge as well as in the United States. The greatest volume of his work is in moral philosophy, where he embraced pluralism and the value of the "good life," but his scholarship also encompasses a broad sweep of epistemology, metaphysics, philosophy of mind, personal identity, and political philosophy.

Although Williams could argue with the best of them in the abstract language of Anglo-American analytical philosophy, he resisted the tendency to treat moral philosophy as a matter of logical, ahistorical concepts. He thought that moral values and beliefs were embedded in history, culture, and ways of life inextricably linked to our emotions and desires. At the same time he embraced much of the Enlightenment aspiration to scientific objectivity, and his style of argument and defense always displays the highest rigor. His book, *Problems of the Self*, is a collection of essays in which he defends the importance of understanding a person's life as a whole, and of doing justice to the role of the human body in personal identity. It is his view that the absurdities that arise in theoretical models of identity are the result of a neglect of such attitudes.

In this excerpt, Williams responds to a criticism of an argument he made in an earlier publication. There, he argued that because the standard Lockean view of identity leads to an absurdity it should be abandoned. His respondent, Robert Coburn, claimed to have a counterexample that showed that Williams's criticism was wrong. Williams now shows that Coburn's case fails because it lacks the kind of a criterion for identity that can only be provided by reference to the body. While this essay may seem a little dated (it was first published in 1972), William's argument continues to be a powerful criticism of current mainstream analytical accounts that fail to grasp the implications of embodiment for identity.

Williams's original argument claimed that on the standard Lockean account of personal identity, if person (A) acquires a character exactly like a person known to have existed in the past (B) and sincerely claims to have B's memories, then A = B. However, it is quite possible and involves no contradiction that another person C also makes the same claims to be B on the same basis. Because A and C are separate persons they clearly cannot be *numerically* identical. In other words, using memory as the sole criterion for identity leads to an absurdity: both A and C are B, which violates transitivity. Furthermore, there is nothing that could justify allowing either A or C to be B, rather than the other. Williams's conclusion is that we should not accept even the original proposition that A = B because the normal account of identity is grounded in erroneous reasoning.

Coburn objects by providing a counterexample designed to show that if we did abandon the memory-criterion of personal identity we would be required to abandon our real life practices of reidentification. In Coburn's example, a man called George suddenly disappears and "a moment later an individual begins to exist who is in all discernible respects exactly similar to George (say George★)."[1] According to Coburn, if we took Williams's advice we could not say that George★ is George, despite the fact that this describes the ordinary situation of reidentification and many important consequences hinge upon it, such as punishment for a crime.

Williams agrees that it matters that we be able to reidentify people for purposes such as legal and moral responsibility, but he does not think that the standard view can do the job without the support of criteria for bodily continuity. In reply to Coburn, Williams aims to show that unless Coburn incorporates certain spatiotemporal restrictions for reidentifying George his example is not an example of personal identity. If Coburn does incorporate the restrictions then his example is not a counterexample to Williams's. So, either way, Williams will have defused Coburn's objection.

Williams begins by pointing out that we need to formulate Coburn's example – the case of George and George★ – in the terms of the logical relation proper to numerical identity: a "one–one" relation, or a relation that is described by a "uniquely referring expression."[2] In other words, the relation between George and George★ is a one–one relation when it holds only between those two and when there is no other person or entity that could be in that relation to George or George★. By contrast, a "one–many" relation is a relation that could hold between a type and a number of others who instantiate that type. For example, "being Penelope Fitzgerald's daughter" is a relation that holds between me, Kim Atkins, and my mother, Penelope Fitzgerald. But it also refers to four other people, namely my sisters. Williams argues that on the standard view of identity, having the same character and memory as another person is a "many–many" relation. There are many people who could have the same character and memories as many other people. This type of relation is too broad to express numerical identity, and so cannot function as a criterion for personal identity.

In order to describe the case of George and George★ as a one–one relation, and in order for the stipulations of appearing a moment later and being "in all discernible respects exactly similar to George" to operate as criteria for identity, some additional restrictions are required. Williams says that the duration of time between George's disappearance and George★'s appearance is a crucial consideration. If the period of time is extremely short then the one–one relation can be established, but if a longer period of time passes too many other people would be able to meet Coburn's criteria for being

George. If we assume a very brief time span the following modification of appearing a moment later and being "in all discernible respects exactly similar to George" will protect identity: "being in all respects similar to, and appearing as the first subsequent occupant of the place vacated by the disappearance of, the individual"[3] with the following conditions on the expression " 'the place vacated by . . .': first, that it should be so restricted that it will not be possible for two persons simultaneously to occupy that place, and, second, that it should be sufficiently determinate not to leave in doubt which of the two places, so restricted, is the place in question."[4]

The effect of these restrictions is to allow us to specify an exact and unique time and place where George disappears and George★ reappears. Furthermore it allows that the unique spatiotemporal coordinates so specified could not be met by more than one person. In contrast, as Williams points out, if we said that George was last seen in his bed, that is not specific enough because, for example, the bed could have since been moved to another room and this increases the number of candidates for fitting the description "the place vacated by George." This also creates the possibility that more than one person could be said to have occupied "the place vacated by George." What Williams's restrictions come down to is that, when applied correctly, they specify a unique spatiotemporal continuity between George and George★ and in doing so establish a unique relation. Moreover, such spatiotemporal specifications can only be met by reference to George's body. He concludes that to be sufficiently determinate and unambiguous, there has to be bodily continuity between George and George★. Williams argues that unless Coburn adopts these restrictions, Coburn's description cannot function as a criterion for identity. Once Coburn does adopt these restrictions the case of George and George★ ceases to be a counterexample to Williams's view, and Coburn will have effectively acceded to the view that personal identity requires bodily continuity.

There is a further advantage to adopting Williams's position. Applying the restrictions as he specifies them provides what he calls "a certain sort of historical enquiry" which will allow us to avoid the kind of absurdity noted at the beginning of the chapter. By "historical enquiry" he means that the process of reidentification involves tracing spatiotemporal continuity. Answering the identity question involves "two expressions each of which picks out an object of a certain type under a description containing, in each case, a different time-reference."[5] If carried out fully, charting the temporal path, for example, from George to George★, should provide a description of the entire history of the object or person in question. Going back to the case of persons A, B, and C discussed at the beginning of the chapter, there is an unexplained gap between the disappearance of A and the appearance of B, and the disappearance of A and the appearance of C. Williams points out that this absence seems to have been tolerated by the mistaken application to these imaginary cases of our normal presumptions of the continued existence of people we cannot perceive. But this will not do; there needs to be a justification of such a presumption. That is, the theory of identity has to account for the temporal gaps. The superiority of Williams's account lies in its ability to fill those temporal gaps. Because his model of historical enquiry provides criteria for determining unambiguously spatiotemporal continuity, it can give the entire history of the identity at issue. This means that if there was, for example, a case of fission where a person is replicated, this fact would be included in the account of identity. The advantage of this is that, unlike the situation with the standard account, a case of a person being replicated does not imperil the theory. Instead, the digression in spatiotemporal continuity that occurs in fission would provide an answer in the negative to the question of identity. In other words, where there is a case of A being divided into B and C – for example, through brain bisection and transplantation into two bodies – we cannot establish the determinations specified in Williams's criteria because of the interruption to bodily continuity. Therefore his criteria of personal identity determines that neither A nor B nor C are the same persons.

Williams's account of identity in terms of historical enquiry influenced a generation of philosophers and has been given critical support in both analytical and European schools, for example, in the narrative models of identity of Marya Schechtman, Alasdair MacIntyre, and Paul Ricoeur. The most serious challenge has come from Derek Parfit who, in *Reasons and Persons*, dismisses the necessity of numerical identity altogether in favor of qualitative identity, and takes issue with the way in which Williams conceives bodily continuity. For Parfit all that is necessary is that one have *a* body and brain, not that one have the numerically identical brain and body. On the argument that Williams has given in this chapter it is not immediately obvious that only a numerically identical body would satisfy the restrictions he places on identity. Williams's account needs to be supplemented by an argument that draws an internal necessity between identity and bodily continuity. This kind of argument has been proposed by philosophers in recent years, drawing upon Merleau-Pontian-type accounts of embodiment.[6]

Notes

1   Bernard Williams, "Bodily Continuity and Personal Identity," in *Problems of the Self* (Cambridge, UK: Cambridge University Press, 1973), p. 19.
2   Ibid, p. 21.
3   Ibid.
4   Ibid.
5   Ibid, p. 24.
6   Quassim Cassam, "Introspection and Bodily Self-ascription," in J. Bermúdez, A. Marcel, and N. Eilan (eds.), *The Body and the Self* (Cambridge, MA: MIT Press, 1995), pp. 311–36.

Main Texts by Williams

"Identity and Identities," in Henry Harris (ed.), *Identity: Essays Based on Herbert Spencer Lectures Given in the University of Oxford* (Oxford and New York: Oxford University Press, 1995).
Making Sense of Humanity and Other Philosophical Papers, 1982–1993 (New York: Cambridge University Press, 1995).
Moral Luck: Philosophical Papers 1973–1980 (Cambridge, UK: Cambridge University Press, 1982).
Problems of the Self: Philosophical Papers 1956–1972 (Cambridge, UK: Cambridge University Press, 1973).
"Seminar with Bernard Williams," *Ethical Perspectives*, 6 (3–4), 1999, pp. 243–65.

Further Reading

Altham, J. E. J. and Ross Harrison (eds.), *World, Mind, and Ethic: Essays on the Ethical Philosophy of Bernard Williams* (Cambridge, UK and New York: Cambridge University Press, 1995).

Ameriks, Karl, "Criteria of Personal Identity," *Canadian Journal of Philosophy*, 7, 1977, pp. 47–69.

Bermúdez, José Luis, Anthony Marcel, and Naomi Eilan (eds.), *The Body and the Self* (Cambridge, MA: MIT Press, 1995).

Campbell, John, *Past, Space, and Self* (Cambridge, MA: MIT Press, 1994).

Cassam, Quassim, *Self and World* (Oxford: Oxford University Press, 1997).

Parfit, Derek, "How We Are Not What We Believe," in *Reasons and Persons* (Oxford: Clarendon Press, 1984), pp. 219–44.

"BODILY CONTINUITY AND PERSONAL IDENTITY"[1]

Bernard Williams

The argument which Coburn criticises runs like this. Suppose a person A to undergo a sudden change, and to acquire a character exactly like that of some person known to have lived in the past, B. Suppose him further to make sincere memory claims which entirely fit the life of B. We might think these conditions sufficient for us to identity A (as he now is) with B. But they are not. For another contemporary person, C, might undergo an exactly similar change at the same time as A, and if the conditions were sufficient to say that A = B, they would be sufficient to say that C = B as well. But it cannot be the case both that A = B and C = B, for, where it so, it would follow that A = C, which is absurd. One can avoid this absurdity by abandoning one or both of the assertions A = B and C = B. But it would be vacuous to assert one of these and abandon the other, since there is nothing to choose between them; hence the rational course is to abandon both. Therefore, I argued, it would be just as vacuous to make the identification with B even if only one contemporary person were involved.

Coburn claims that this argument can be applied just as well to another case in which it gives unacceptable results. He supposes the case of a man George who suddenly disappears; 'a moment later an individual begins to exist who is in all discernible respects exactly similar to George (say, George$\star$)'.[2] Coburn argues that to this case, too, my argument would apply, with the result that it would be vacuous to identify George$\star$ with George. But this, he argues, is unacceptable: such an identification would certainly not be vacuous, since much would depend on it (concerning e.g. punishment for George's crimes). Moreover it is an identification that we should justifiably accept. Hence my argument is called into doubt.

First, a point about 'vacuity'. In saying that an identification of A with B in the imagined circumstances was 'vacuous', I did not mean that no consequences would follow from it. If the identification were taken seriously, consequences of the kind Coburn mentions could as well follow in my sort of case as in his. My use of the term 'vacuous' concerned not the consequences, but the grounds, of such an identification,

From *Problems of the Self: Philosophical Papers 1956–1972* (Cambridge, UK: Cambridge University Press, 1973), pp. 19–25. Reprinted by permission of Mrs P. Williams.

my argument being meant to show that there would be in principle for such a case no grounds to justify a judgement of identity as against a judgement of exact similarity. I agree that the term 'vacuous' is misleading, in that it suggests that there would be no difference at all between the two judgements, and this, in terms of consequences, is false.

My argument can be put in another way to incorporate this point. Where there is a difference in the consequences, in this sense, of two judgements, there should all the more be a difference in their grounds, for it is unreasonable that there should be no more grounds for applying one of a pair of judgements to a situation rather than the other, and yet one judgement carry consequences not carried by the other. On the thesis that similarity of character and of memory claims is a sufficient condition of personal identity, there would be no difference in the grounds of two judgements, that of identity and that of exact similarity, one of which does carry consequences not carried by the other. Hence that thesis is to be rejected. (What is meant by 'exact similarity' here is '*mere* exact similarity', an assertion of which would entail the denial of identity.)

More important than this point about vacuity is the conclusion which Coburn states, or rather implies, that we should in fact in a case such as he describes identify George★ with George, and be justified in so doing. If this conclusion is correct, and it is also correct that my reduplication argument would apply as well to this case, my argument must be defective. Now Coburn does not make entirely clear the circumstances of his imagined case. He does not say whether George★ appears in the same place as that from which George disappeared; and while he says that George★ appears 'a moment later', he does not say whether he regards the shortness of the interval as essential to his example or not. If Coburn allows distant places and long intervals of time for the appearance of George★, his case would in fact approximate to my original one, with physical resemblance added to the resemblances of character and memory claims. If, on the other hand, a short interval of time and reappearance in the same place are essential to Coburn's example, it is worth asking why this should be so.

I shall argue that if Coburn's example is to provide a case of identity, it must be restricted in this way; but that when it is restricted in this way, it is not a counter-example to my argument. The principle of my argument is, very roughly put, that identity is a one–one relation, and that no principle can be a criterion of identity for things of type T if it relies only on what is logically a one–many or many–many relation between things of type T. What is wrong with the supposed criterion of identity for persons which relies only on memory claims is just that '. . . being disposed to make sincere memory claims which exactly fit the life of . . .' is not a one–one, but a many–one, relation, and hence cannot possibly be adequate in logic to constitute a criterion of identity. (There are well-known difficulties about speaking of identity as a relation at all. The point being made here can be expressed more rigorously in terms of the sense and reference of uniquely referring expressions, but I hope it is clear enough in this rough, and shorter, form.)

This principle states a necessary condition of anything's serving as a criterion of identity. It clearly does not state a sufficient condition; still less does it state a sufficient condition of anything's being, for a given type of thing T, a philosophically satisfactory criterion of identity for Ts. In particular (and this was the basis of the later part of my original argument), no principle P will be a philosophically satisfactory criterion of identity for Ts if the only thing that saves P from admitting many–one relations among Ts is a quite arbitrary provision.

Returning now to Coburn's example, it can be seen that if it is taken as quite unrestricted, the criterion of identity suggested by it will not pass the test just stated, any more than the bare memory and character criteria do; for the relation '. . . being in all respects similar to, and appearing somewhere at some time after the disappearance of, the individual . . .' is many–one, and could not suffice to do what a criterion of identity is required to do, viz. enable us to identify uniquely the thing that is identical with the thing in question. However, if the principle is restricted in certain ways, this difficulty can be avoided. If, for instance, it is modified to: '. . . being in all respects similar to, and appearing as the first subsequent occupant of the place vacated by the disappearance of, the individual . . .', it will pass the test, so long at least as two, slightly different, conditions are satisfied about the application of the expression 'the place vacated by . . .': first, that it should be so restricted that it will not be possible for two persons simultaneously to occupy that place, and, second, that it should be sufficiently determinate not to leave it in doubt which of two or more places, so restricted, is the place in question.

It is perhaps this latter condition, among others, that introduces the consideration, not mentioned in the criteria as so far stated, but mentioned in Coburn's example, of the length of the lapse of time between disappearance and appearance. One reason at least why one might be moved to introduce a very brief lapse of time into Coburn's example is this: that if the lapse of time is very short, it is very much clearer what 'the same place' will be. Granted a longer time, in which various changes can take place, it may become less clear and determinate what 'the same place' will be. For instance, if George had been in bed in his bedroom when he disappeared, and the bed, before George★ appears, is moved into another room or another house, where must George★ appear in order to appear in the place vacated by George? Difficulties of this kind could be multiplied indefinitely. One motive for the introduction of a brief lapse of time is, then, perhaps this: that it makes the application of 'same place' more determinate than it might otherwise be.

However, there is perhaps another motive for thinking in terms of a brief lapse of time: that it is only this that makes a criterion of identity in terms of 'same place' plausible *at all*. For if the appearance of George★ happens some substantial time after the disappearance of George, why should his appearance in precisely the place vacated by George be privileged in giving an answer to the identity question? Here we have a dilemma: on the one hand some such restriction is needed, to make the principle implied in the example into a criterion of identity at all; on the other hand, it seems equally to be in these circumstances quite arbitrary.

One reason for the latter is that in thinking about the imagined case we are in fact using a model drawn from the real world and our normal identification of persons: a model in which the disappeared George, though 'immaterial', in some sense goes on existing, and in particular can move from one place to another. This model contains an illusion, no doubt; but to see that there is an illusion should lead one, not to stick unthinkingly to a criterion of identity to which identity of place is essential, but to conclude that the application of criteria of personal identity to these imagined cases of disappearance is a far less certain and indisputable buisiness than may at first sight appear.

Now Coburn himself cannot consistently have in mind a restricted principle as the criterion of identity presupposed in his example, since he says that in his example reduplication would be possible. If the criterion presupposed in his example were restricted in the ways I have been discussing, no reduplication would be possible, since it could not be the case that two persons could both be the first subsequent occupants of the place (in the required sense) vacated by the disappearance of George.

It seems, then, that Coburn has in mind as suggested by his example a principle unrestricted in space and time. If so, I do not see how it can satisfy the logical requirements of being a criterion of identity. If, on the other hand, the principle were restricted in space and time, it would be a possible criterion of identity, in the sense at least that it satisfied the logical requirements of such a criterion; but in that case, the possibility of reduplication could not exist, and his case would not be a counter-example to my argument, which was directed against supposed criteria of identity which did not satisfy the requirements. If, again, the principle were restricted in space but not in time, it might still satisfy the logical requirements (though there would be systematic doubts about its application), but it would scarcely seem a plausible or philosophically satisfactory sort of criterion. Whether, granted this point, the fully restricted criterion would be plausible or satisfactory, is a question I shall not pursue here, though I think the answer is in fact 'no'.

It may be objected to this argument that I have set too high the standard for a principle's serving as a criterion of identity, by requiring that it guard against the logical possibility of reduplication such as I have discussed. No criterion can guard against this, it may be said; and this can be seen from the fact that even a criterion of identity in terms of spatio-temporal continuity, on which I lay the weight for personal identity, is itself not immune to this possibility. It is possible to imagine a man splitting, amoeba-like, into two simulacra of himself. If this happened, it must of course follow from my original argument that it would not be reasonable to say that either of the resultant men was identical with the original one: they could not both be, because they are not identical with each other, and it should not be reasonable to choose one rather than the other to be identical with the original. Hence it would seem that by my requirements, not even spatio-temporal continuity would serve as a criterion of identity: hence the requirements are too high.[3]

I do not think, however, that this case upsets the principle of my argument. There is a vital difference between this sort of reduplication, with the criterion of spatio-temporal continuity, and the other sorts of case. This emerges when one considers what it is to apply the criterion of spatio-temporal continuity. To apply this criterion – for instance, in trying to answer the question whether a certain billiard ball now in my hand is the billiard ball that was at a certain position at the start of the game – is to engage in a certain sort of historical enquiry. The identity-question contains two expressions each of which picks out an object of a certain type under a description containing, in each case, a different time-reference; to answer the question is to chart an historical course which starts from the situation given by one of the descriptions, in order to see whether this course does or does not lead to the situation given by the other. This procedure, ideally carried out, will give the entire history in question; and in particular, if there were any reduplication of the kind under discussion, *it would inevitably reveal it*. This consideration puts the spatio-temporal continuity criterion into a different situation from the others discussed; for in this case, but evidently not in others, a thorough application of the criterion would itself reveal the existence of the reduplication situation, and so enable us to answer (negatively) the original identity question. To enable us to answer such questions is the point of a criterion of identity. Thus, in this case, but not in the others, the logical possibility of reduplication fails to impugn the status of the criterion of identity.

I think that these considerations perhaps suffice for us to say that in a case of fission, such as that of an amoeba, the resultant items are not, in the strict sense, spatio-temporally continuous with the original. The justification for saying this would be that the normal application of the concept of continuity is interfered with by the fact of fission, a fact which would itself be discovered by the verification procedure tied to the application of the concept. There would be a motive for saying this, moreover, in that we might want to insist that spatio-temporal continuity, in the strict sense, was transitive. But for the present issue, nothing immediately turns on our decision on this point.

It may be said that for most sorts of objects to which spatio-temporal continuity applies, we do not in fact pursue our identity enquiries in this thorough-going histor-ical way. This is true, but nothing to the point; because, for most sorts of objects, we have the strongest empirical reasons for disbelieving in reduplication. Where we have not such reasons – for instance with amoebae – one would indeed (in the unlikely event of one's wanting to answer an identity question) have to watch out for redupli-cation, by constant observation or otherwise.

I conclude, then, that this sort of case, because of its special nature, does not tell against my general position; which is that in order to serve as a criterion of identity, a principle must provide what I have called a one–one relation and not a one–many rela-tion. Unless there is some such requirement, I cannot see how one is to preserve and explain the evident truth that the concepts of identity and of exact similarity are different concepts.

Notes

1   *Note* 1972. This was a reply to criticisms made by Robert C. Coburn (*Analysis*, 20.5, 1960) of an argument which I used in 'Personal identity and individuation' [*Problems of the Self*, pp. 1–18] to try to show that bodily continuity was a necessary condition of personal identity, and more particularly that similarity of memory claims and personal characteristics could not be a sufficient condition of it. There is some more about the 'reduplication' argument discussed here, in 'Are persons bodies?' [*Problems of the Self*, pp. 77ff.].

2   *Analysis* 20.5, p. 118.

3   This sort of case has been discussed in his contribution to this topic by C. B. Martin (*Analy-sis* 18.4, March 1958). Martin's own criticism, however, seems merely to confuse identity with the quite different concept of 'having the same life-history as', where this is defined to suit the amoeba-like case. To say that (putatively) two amoebae are identical is to say that *pro tanto* I have only one amoeba; to say that they share the same life-history is not. Cf. G. C. Nerlich, *Analysis* 18.6, June 1958, on this point.

14

COMMENTARY ON PARFIT

Derek Parfit (born 1942) is a Fellow of All Souls College, Oxford. He specializes in ethics and philosophy of mind, and his extremely influential work, *Reasons and Persons*, is largely concerned with the relation between rationality, morality, and personal identity. In this chapter from *Reasons and Persons* he briefly sets out the standard views of personal identity in order to clarify his own. Like Shoemaker, Parfit considers personal identity to consist in memory-connectedness. However, Parfit takes a reductionist view, arguing that we can do away entirely with the concept of "person."

Parfit uses the example of the case of teletransportation and replication to illustrate what he takes to be the incoherence of some of the ways we commonly think about personal identity – specifically, our ideas about "persons." The teletransportation scenario prompts the question: do I die or do I survive? The question seems unanswerable because the reference of "I" becomes impossible to pin down; it is impossible to say where "I" am. Parfit thinks that this puzzlement forces us to confront the incoherence of *personal* identity. Our confusion, he says, results from the belief that a self or person is some kind of special entity over and above one's body and thoughts, like a Cartesian ego.

Against this view Parfit proposes his own reductionist view. He says:

(1) . . . the fact of a person's identity over time just consists in the holding of certain more particular facts,

(2) . . . these facts can be described without either presupposing the identity of this person, or explicitly claiming that the experiences in this person's life are had by this person, or even explicitly claiming that this person exists. These facts can be described in an *impersonal* way.[1]

This is his "impersonality thesis." It claims that a full account of personal identity can be given without presupposing the existence of particular persons and without imputing experiences to any particular person. "Persons" for Parfit are comprised by "the existence of our brains and bodies, and the doing of our deeds and the thinking of our thoughts and the occurrence of certain other physical and mental events."[2] In other words, the concept of "persons" refers to states of affairs that can be described wholly impersonally.

Parfit is not saying that the human beings we ordinarily call persons do not exist, but rather that we can replace the word "person" with a set of purely objective data and not miss out on any facts about selves or persons. It follows from this that there is no reason to be *self*-interested. Parfit takes the view that the whole of reality is actually a giant complicated set of objective facts, and "person" is simply a subset of reality – a subset of facts within a wider complex of facts. We can, then, refer to both personal identity and reality without ever using the word "person." He thinks that the advantage of adopting this impersonal language deliberately and consciously is that it protects us from inadvertently sliding into a Cartesian view of persons as entities existing separately from our physical existences.

In a big break with tradition, Parfit abandons the requirement that identity be transitive. On his view, continued existence entails qualitative identity rather than numerical identity. Whereas for Shoemaker, psychological continuity consists in having memory and psychological traits that are connected causally in the "appropriate way" to maintain numerical identity, Parfit argues that the "right kind of cause" could be any cause. This means that one's continued existence (personal identity) does not require that one have a numerically identical brain and body, but merely that one has *a* brain and body.

According to Parfit I survive when there is psychological continuity between the person I am now and the person who is me at a later time. For example, I care that the Kim Atkins who wakes up in my skin tomorrow morning has the same beliefs, hopes, and aspirations as me. I do not want the person who is me to despise my mother, or dislike reading, or be indifferent to her health. It is no comfort to me to know that I will be the same body and brain tomorrow if I am psychologically utterly different from me now. On Parfit's view, I do not care that tomorrow's Kim Atkins is numerically identical with me; I just care that she is qualitatively identical with me. In fact, Parfit thinks that we will happily acquire new bodies but will never happily acquire new consciousnesses; we will always value psychological continuity and qualitative identity over numerical identity or bodily continuity.

Parfit calls this kind of continuity in identity R-relation.[3] There is overlapping memory when I remember some of my experiences from the previous day. Among those experiences I recall will be recollections of experiences that happened in the days before yesterday, and among those, memories of earlier days, and so on. Parfit says that even though not every one of my experiences is carried forward in memory in this way, there is ordinarily sufficient overlap of earlier memories as time goes on to constitute psychological continuity. Normally, each day I have a direct psychological connection to the psychological states of the previous day. When I am directly connected to a lot of my previous overlapping psychological states I have a strong connection; when I am directly connected to few overlapping states I have a weak connection. There is psychological continuity, or R-relatedness, when I enjoy overlapping chains of strong connectedness. If the connectedness is very weak (for example, I can recall few experiences from my childhood or my daily life since), or there is very little overlap (for example, I can recall everything that happened in the last few hours but nothing prior), there is little psychological continuity.

Parfit claims that sometimes the question of personal identity does not have a "yes" or "no" answer. Consider the case of teletransportation with replication. The statement "I am going to die" is neither true nor false. If you believe that personal identity consists in numerical identity, I die, although there is the inconvenient fact that I also continue to exist (on Mars). So, I neither survive nor die, it seems. Parfit concludes that this shows that identity is not what matters. What matters is just the same thing that matters, for example, in the survival of a club: continuity. What I care about when I care about my identity is not numerical identity but simply the survival of the relation between my "members," my beliefs, intentions, desires, and memories. In other words, I care about the R–relation. Parfit insists that the method of acquiring memories does not matter. Just so long as the memories *are* the original person's memories, the replica will have psychological continuity with that person. On Parfit's view, if you care about your survival you will care about your replica's survival. Your survival *is* your replica's survival.

Parfit's arguments in *Reasons and Persons* have been a source of considerable debate. Susan Wolf, for example, has argued that Parfit is mistaken in believing that the care we have toward persons is driven by our metaphysical beliefs concerning persons. In Wolf's words, it is Parfit's view that "whereas we currently form attachments to particular persons, we rationally ought to form attachments to the very R–related beings with whom these persons largely coincide."[4] Wolf then notes some undesirable practical implications of forming attachments to R–relations. For example, she argues that parent–child relations would be seriously adversely affected because babies are barely psychologically connected at all, and so there might not be very much there to care about. On the other hand, given that any child will only be weakly R–related to the adult he or she becomes, the parents may have a greater reason to love the child rather than the adult that the child grows into. Furthermore, she claims, adult relationships would be expected to weaken as personalities change over time, and this would have the effect of severely narrowing the kind of development within close relationships that we generally regard as healthy.

There are also concerns about Parfit's treatment of the first person perspective, specifically, his lack of appreciation of the apperceptive nature of consciousness. Quassim Cassam, for example, points out that, as Kant has argued, the unity of consciousness – the having of copersonal states – rests upon the possibility of one ascribing those states to oneself as their single logical subject, as the "I" whose thoughts they are.[5] The proof that all of my thoughts belong to a single experiential subject cannot be observed from an "outside" objective perspective but is a practical proof, established from an "inside" subjective or first person perspective. In other words, an important part of the kind of continuity (copersonality) that Parfit is endeavoring to describe in impersonal terms is established in the first and only instance by reference to the first person.

Cassam notes that when we are concerned with the identity of persons, there are really two questions at issue.[6] There is an internal question which asks "What, *within* a given mental life underpins experience?," and there is an external question which asks "What does the unity of consciousness in a given life consist in?" The answer to the first is not just "the unity of consciousness" but "self-ascription," and self-ascription does not fit a causal model in the manner that Parfit assumes. The external perspective deployed by the second question is more amenable to an answer given in terms of causal continuities. Parfit's error lies in drawing a distinction between two kinds of *external* questions (between the unity of consciousness at time *t*, and the unity of consciousness over a duration of time) instead of between internal and external questions.

On a different front, Christine Korsgaard takes the view that Parfit has failed to appreciate the fact that as practical beings – beings who act – we cannot avoid making choices, and so we necessarily regard ourselves from two distinct standpoints: as objects of theoretical understanding and as the originators of our actions (agents).[7] This conception of ourselves as agents arises without reference to metaphysical or theoretical facts. As can be seen in the range of responses to Parfit's work, the question of the nature of psychological continuity and its relation to the body has become an important concern to philosophers across the different schools of contemporary philosophy.

Notes

1 Derek Parfit, *Reasons and Persons* (Oxford: Clarendon Press, 1984), p. 210.
2 Ibid, p. 216.
3 See pp. 215–17. Parfit argues that contrary to standard views of personal identity, what really matters for persons is not continuity in numerical identity – for example, existing as the same "person" over time – but rather, enjoying both unity of one's thoughts and continuity in one's life. This is what he means by the "R-relation" (p. 215). As long as memories and psychological states are connected by some cause (in fact, any cause), and those connections overlap sufficiently from day to day, then continuity in one's life (and unity within one's consciousness at any particular time) will be secured, even if identity is not.
4 Susan Wolf, "Self-Interest and Interest in Selves," *Ethics*, 96, July 1986, p. 710.
5 Quassim Cassam, "Kant and Reductionism," *Review of Metaphysics*, 43, 1989, pp. 72–106. See Immanuel Kant, *Critique of Pure Reason*, trans. Norman Kemp Smith (Basingstoke and London: Macmillan, 1999), B131–2.
6 Cassam (1989), p. 103.
7 Christine Korsgaard, *Creating the Kingdom of Ends* (Cambridge, UK: Cambridge University Press, 1996), pp. 377–80.

Main Texts by Parfit

"Commentator: 'Pluralism and the Standard of Living'," in Martha Nussbaum and Amartya Sen (eds.), *The Quality of Life* (New York: Oxford University Press, 1993), pp. 410–16.
"Comments on Susan Wolf's 'Self-Interest and Interest in Selves,'" *Ethics*, 96, 1986, pp. 832–8.
"Reasons and Motivation" (with John Broome), *Proceedings of the Aristotelian Society*, 1997 (Supplement, 71), pp. 98–146.
Reasons and Persons (Oxford: Clarendon Press, 1984).
"The Unimportance of Identity," in Henry Harris (ed.), *Identity: Essays Based on Herbert Spencer Lectures Given in the University of Oxford* (Oxford and New York: Oxford University Press, 1995), pp. 13–45.

Further Reading

Atkins, Kim, "Personal Identity and the Importance of One's Own Body," *International Journal of Philosophical Studies*, 8 (3), 2000, pp. 329–49.

Cassam, Quassim, "Reductionism and First Person Thinking," in D. Charles and K. Lennon (eds.), *Reductionism, Explanation and Realism* (Oxford: Clarendon Press, 1992), pp. 362–80.

Cassam, Quassim, "Parfit on Persons," *Proceedings of the Aristotelian Society*, 1993, pp. 17–37.

Cassam, Quassim, *Self-Knowledge* (Oxford: Oxford University Press, 1994).

Dancy, Jonathan (ed.), *Reading Parfit* (Oxford: Blackwell, 1997).

Korsgaard, Christine, "Personal Identity and the Unity of Agency: A Kantian Response to Parfit," in *Creating the Kingdom of Ends* (Cambridge, UK: Cambridge University Press, 1996), pp. 363–97.

Noonan, Harold W., *Personal Identity* (London: Routledge, 1989).

Perring, Christian, "Degrees of Personhood," *The Journal of Medicine and Philosophy*, 22 (2), 1997, pp. 228–40.

Perry, John (ed.), *Personal Identity* (Berkeley: University of California Press, 1975).

Rorty, Amelie Oksenberg (ed.), *The Identities of Persons* (Berkeley: University of California Press, 1976).

Wilkes, Kathleen V., *Real People: Personal Identity Without Thought Experiments* (New York: Oxford University Press, 1988).

Wolf, Susan, "Self-Interest and Interest in Selves," *Ethics*, 96, July 1986, pp. 704–20.

REASONS AND PERSONS, "WHAT WE BELIEVE OURSELVES TO BE"

Derek Parfit

I enter the Teletransporter. I have been to Mars before, but only by the old method, a space-ship journey taking several weeks. This machine will send me at the speed of light. I merely have to press the green button. Like others, I am nervous. Will it work? I remind myself what I have been told to expect. When I press the button, I shall lose consciousness, and then wake up at what seems a moment later. In fact I shall have been unconscious for about an hour. The Scanner here on Earth will destroy my brain and body, while recording the exact states of all of my cells. It will then transmit this information by radio. Travelling at the speed of light, the message will take three minutes to reach the Replicator on Mars. This will then create, out of new matter, a brain and body exactly like mine. It will be in this body that I shall wake up.

Though I believe that this is what will happen, I still hesitate. But then I remember seeing my wife grin when, at breakfast today, I revealed my nervousness. As she reminded me, she has been often teletransported, and there is nothing wrong with *her*. I press the button. As predicted, I lose and seem at once to regain consciousness, but in a different cubicle. Examining my new body, I find no change at all. Even the cut on my upper lip, from this morning's shave, is still there.

Several years pass, during which I am often Teletransported. I am now back in the cubicle, ready for another trip to Mars. But this time, when I press the green button, I do not lose consciousness. There is a whirring sound, then silence, I leave the cubicle, and say to the attendant: 'It's not working. What did I do wrong?'

'It's working', he replies, handing me a printed card. This reads: 'The New Scanner records your blueprint without destroying your brain and body. We hope that you will welcome the opportunities which this technical advance offers.'

The attendant tells me that I am one of the first people to use the New Scanner. He adds that, if I stay for an hour, I can use the Intercom to see and talk to myself on Mars.

From *Reasons and Persons* (Oxford: Clarendon Press, 1984), pp. 199–213. Reprinted by permission of Oxford University Press.

'Wait a minute', I reply, 'If I'm here I can't *also* be on Mars'.

Someone politely coughs, a white-coated man who asks to speak to me in private. We go to his office, where he tells me to sit down, and pauses. Then he says: 'I'm afraid that we're having problems with the New Scanner. It records your blueprint just as accurately, as you will see when you talk to yourself on Mars. But it seems to be damaging the cardiac systems which it scans. Judging from the results so far, though you will be quite healthy on Mars, here on Earth you must expect cardiac failure within the next few days.'

The attendant later calls me to the Intercom. On the screen I see myself just as I do in the mirror every morning. But there are two differences. On the screen I am not left-right reversed. And, while I stand here speechless, I can see and hear myself, in the studio on Mars, starting to speak.

What can we learn from this imaginary story? Some believe that we can learn little. This would have been Wittgenstein's view.[1] And Quine writes: 'The method of science fiction has its uses in philosophy, but . . . I wonder whether the limits of the method are properly heeded. To seek what is 'logically required' for sameness of person under unprecedented circumstances is to suggest that words have some logical force beyond what our past needs have invested them with.'[2]

This criticism might be justified if, when considering such imagined cases, we had no reactions. But these cases arouse in most of us strong beliefs. And these are beliefs, not about our words, but about ourselves. By considering these cases, we discover what we believe to be involved in our own continued existence, or what it is that makes us now and ourselves next year the same people. We discover our beliefs about the nature of personal identity over time. Though our beliefs are revealed most clearly when we consider imaginary cases, these beliefs also cover actual cases, and our own lives. [. . .]

Simple Teletransportation and the Branch–Line Case

At the beginning of my story, the Scanner destroys my brain and body. My blueprint is beamed to Mars, where another machine makes an organic *Replica* of me. My Replica thinks that he is me, and he seems to remember living my life up to the moment when I pressed the green button. In every other way, both physically and psychologically, my Replica is just like me. If he returned to Earth, everyone would think that he was me.

Simple Teletransportation, as just described, is a common feature in science fiction. And it is believed, by some readers of this fiction, merely to be the fastest way of travelling. They believe that my Replica *would* be *me*. Other science fiction readers, and some of the characters in this fiction, take a different view. They believe that, when I press the green button, I die. My Replica is *someone else*, who has been made to be exactly like me.

This second view seems to be supported by the end of my story. The New Scanner does not destroy my brain and body. Besides gathering the information, it merely damages my heart. While I am in the cubicle, with the green button pressed, nothing seems to happen. I walk out, and learn that in a few days I shall die. I later talk, by two-way television, to my Replica on Mars. Let us continue the story. Since my Replica knows that I am about to die, he tries to console me with the same thoughts with which I recently tried to console a dying friend. It is sad to learn, on the receiving end, how unconsoling these thoughts are. My Replica then assures me that he will take up my life where I leave off. He loves my wife, and together they will care for my children. And he will finish the book that I am writing. Besides having all of my drafts, he has all of my intentions. I must admit that he can finish my book as well as I could. All these facts console me a little. Dying when I know that I shall have a Replica is not quite as bad as, simply, dying. Even so, I shall soon lose consciousness, forever.

In Simple Teletransportation, I do not co-exist with my Replica. This makes it easier to believe that this *is* a way of travelling – that my Replica *is* me. At the end of my story, my life and that of my Replica overlap. Call this the *Branch-Line Case*. In this case, I cannot hope to travel on the *Main Line*, waking up on Mars with forty years of life ahead. I shall remain on the Branch-Line, on Earth, which ends a few days later. Since I can talk to my Replica, it seems clear that he is *not* me. Though he is exactly like me, he is one person, and I am another. When I pinch myself, he feels nothing. When I have my heart attack, he will again feel nothing. And when I am dead he will live for another forty years.

If we believe that my Replica is not me, it is natural to assume that my prospect, on the Branch Line, is almost as bad as ordinary death. I shall deny this assumption. As I shall argue later, I ought to regard having a Replica as being about as good as ordinary survival. I can best defend this claim, and the view that supports it, after briefly discussing part of the past debate about personal identity.

Qualitative and Numerical Identity

There are two kinds of sameness, or identity. I and my Replica are *qualitatively identical*, or exactly alike. But we may not be *numerically identical*, or one and the same person. Similarly, two white billiard balls are not numerically but may be qualitatively identical. If I paint one of these balls red, it will not now be qualitatively identical to itself yesterday. But the red ball that I see now and the white ball that I painted red are numerically identical. They are one and the same ball.

We might say, of someone, 'After his accident, he is no longer the same person'. This is a claim about both kinds of identity. We claim that *he*, the same person, is *not* now the same person. This is not a contradiction. We merely mean that this person's character has changed. This numerically identical person is now qualitatively different.

When we are concerned about our future, it is our numerical identity that we are concerned about. I may believe that, after my marriage, I shall not be the same person. But this does not make marriage death. However much I change, I shall still be alive if there will be some person living who is numerically identical with me.

The philosophical debate is about the nature both of persons and of personal identity over time. It will help to distinguish these questions:

(1)   What is the nature of a person?

(2)   What is it that makes a person at two different times one and the same person?

(3)   What is necessarily involved in the continued existence of each person over time?

The answer to (2) can take this form: '*X* today is one and the same person as *Y* at some past time *if and only if* . . .' This answer states the *necessary and sufficient conditions* for personal identity over time. And the answer to (2) provides the answer to (3). Each person's continued existence has the *same* necessary and sufficient conditions.

In answering (2) and (3) we shall also partly answer (1). The necessary features of our continued existence depend upon our nature. And the simplest answer to (1) is that, to be a person, a being must be self-conscious, aware of its identity and its continued existence over time.

We can also ask

(4)   What is in fact involved in the continued existence of each person over time?

Since our continued existence has features that are not necessary, the answer to (3) is only part of the answer to (4). Being happy, for our example, is not necessary to our continued existence, but it may be part of what someone's continued existence in fact involves.

Though question (2) is about numerical rather than qualitative identity, this does not imply that qualitative changes do not matter. On one view, certain kinds of qualitative change destroy numerical identity. If certain things happened to me, the truth may not be that I become a very different person. The truth may be that I cease to exist, and the resulting person is someone else.

The Physical Criterion of Personal Identity

Many writers use the ambiguous phrase 'the criterion of identity over time'. Some mean by this 'our way of telling whether some present object is identical with some past object'. But I shall mean *what this identity necessarily involves, or consists in.*

In the case of most physical objects, on what I call the *standard view*, the criterion of identity over time is the spatio-temporal physical continuity of this object. This is something that we all understand, even if we fail to understand the description I shall now give. In the simplest case of physical continuity, like that of the Pyramids, an apparently static object continues to exist. In another simples case, like that of the Moon, an object moves in a regular way. Many objects move in less regular ways, but they still trace physically continuous spatio–temporal paths. Suppose that the billiard ball that I painted red is the same as the white ball with which last year I made a winning shot. On the standard view, this is true only if this ball traced such a continuous path. It must be true (1) that there is a line through space and time, starting where the white ball rested before I made my winning shot and ending where the red ball now is, (2) that at every point on this line there was a billiard ball, and (3) that the existence of a ball at each point on this line was in part caused by the existence of a ball at the immediately preceding point.[3]

Some kinds of thing continue to exist even though their physical continuity involves great changes. A Camberwell Beauty is first an egg, then a caterpillar, then a chrysalis, then a butterfly. These are four stages in the physically continuous existence of a single organism. Other kinds of thing cannot survive such great changes. Suppose that an artist paints a self-portrait and then, by repainting, turns this into a portrait of his father. Even though these portraits are more similar than a caterpillar and a butterfly, they are not stages in the continued existence of a single painting. The self-portrait is a painting that the artist destroyed. In a general discussion of identity, we would need to explain why the requirement of physical continuity differs in such ways for different kinds of thing. But we can ignore this here.

Can there be gaps in the continued existence of a physical object? Suppose that I have the same gold watch that I was given as a boy even though, for a month, it lay disassembled on a watch-repairer's shelf. On one view, in the spatio-temporal path traced by this watch there was not at every point a watch, so my watch does not have a history of full physical continuity. But during the month when my watch was disassembled, and did not exist, all of its parts had histories of full continuity. On another view, even when it was disassembled, my watch existed.

Another complication again concerns the relation between a complex thing and the various parts of which it is composed. It is true of some of these things, though not true of all, that their continued existence need not involve the continued existence of their components. Suppose that a wooden ship is repaired from time to time while it is floating in harbour, and that after fifty years it contains none of the bits of wood out of which it was first built. It is still one and the same ship, because, as a ship, it has displayed throughout these fifty years full physical continuity. This is so despite the fact that it is now composed of quite different bits of wood. These bits of wood might be qualitatively identical to the original bits, but they are not one and the same bits. Something similar is partly true of a human body. With the exception of some brain cells, the cells in our bodies are replaced with new cells several times in our lives.

I have now described the physical continuity which, on the standard view, makes a physical object one and the same after many days or years. This enables me to state one of the rival views about personal identity. On this view, what makes me the same person over time is that I have the same brain and body. The criterion of my identity over time – or what this identity involves – is the physical continuity, over time, of my brain and body. I shall continue to exist if and only if this particular brain and body continue both to exist and to be the brain and body of a living person.

This is the simplest version of this view. There is a better version. This is

The Physical Criterion: (1) What is necessary is not the continued existence of the whole body, but the continued existence of *enough* of the brain to be the brain of a living person. X today is one and the same person as Y at some past time if and only if (2) enough of Y's brain continued to exist, and is now X's brain, and (3) there does not exist a different person who also has enough of Y's brain. (4) Personal identity over time just consists in the holding of facts like (2) and (3).

(1) is clearly needed in certain actual cases. Some people continue to exist even though they lose much of their bodies, perhaps including their hearts and lungs if they are on Heart-Lung Machines. The need for (3) will be clear later.

Those who believe in the Physical Criterion would reject Teletransportation. They would believe this to be a way, not of travelling, but of dying. They would also reject, as inconceivable, reincarnation. They believe that someone cannot have a life after death, unless he lives this life in a resurrection of the very same, physically continuous body. Some of the Christians who believe this insist that they be buried. They believe that if, like Greek and Trojan heroes, they were burnt on funeral pyres, and their ashes scattered, not even God could bring them to life again. God could create only a Replica, someone else who was exactly like them. Other Christians believe that God could resurrect *them* if He reassembled their bodies out of the bits of matter that, when they were last alive, made up their bodies. This view is like the first of the views about the reassembly of my gold watch.[4]

The Psychological Criterion

Some people believe in a kind of psychological continuity that resembles physical continuity. This involves the continued existence of a purely mental *entity*, or thing – a soul, or spiritual substance. I shall return to this view. But I shall first explain another kind of psychological continuity. This is less like physical continuity, since it does not consist in the continued existence of some entity. But this other kind of psychological continuity involves only facts with which we are familiar.

What has been most discussed is the continuity of memory. This is because it is memory that makes most of us aware of our own continued existence over time. The exceptions are the people who are suffering from amnesia. Most amnesiacs lose only two sets of memories. They lose all of their memories of having particular past experiences – or, for short, their *experience memories*. They also lose some of their memories about facts, those that are about their own past lives. But they remember other facts, and they remember how to do different things, such as how to speak, or swim.

Locke suggested that experience-memory provides the criterion of personal identity.[5] Though this is not, on its own, a plausible view, I believe that it can be part of such a view. I shall therefore try to answer Locke's critics.

Locke claimed that someone cannot have committed some crime unless he now remembers doing so. We can understand a reluctance to punish people for crimes that they cannot remember. But, taken as a view about what is involved in a person's continued existence, Locke's claim is clearly false. If it was true, it would not be possible for someone to forget any of the things that he once did, or any of the experiences that he once had. But this *is* possible. I cannot now remember putting on my shirt this morning.

There are several ways to extend the experience-memory criterion so as to cover such cases. I shall appeal to the concept of an overlapping chain of experience-memories. Let us say that, between X today and Y twenty years ago, there are *direct memory connections* if X can now remember having some of the experiences that Y had twenty years ago. On Locke's view, this makes X and Y one and the same person. Even if there are *no* such direct memory connections, there may be *continuity of memory* between X now and Y twenty years ago. This would be so if between X now and Y at that time there has been an overlapping chain of direct memories. In the case of most people who are over twenty three, there would be such an overlapping chain. In each day within the last twenty years, most of these people remembered some of their experiences on the previous day. On the revised version of Locke's view, some present person X is the same as some past person Y if there is between them continuity of memory.

This revision meets one objection to Locke's view. We should also revise the view so that it appeals to other facts. Besides direct memories, there are several other kinds of direct psychological connection. One such connection is that which holds between an intention and the later act in which this intention is carried out. Other such direct connections are those which hold when a belief, or a desire, or any other psychological feature, continues to be had.

I can now define two general relations:

Psychological connectedness is the holding of particular direct psychological connections

Psychological continuity is the holding of overlapping chains of *strong* connectedness.

Of these two general relations, connectedness is more important both in theory and in practice. Connectedness can hold to any degree. Between X today and Y yesterday there might be several thousand direct psychological connections, or only a single connection. If there was only a single connection, X and Y would not be, on the revised Lockean View, the same person. For X and Y to be the same person, there must be over every day *enough* direct psychological connections. Since connectedness is a matter of degree, we cannot plausibly define precisely what counts as enough. But we can claim that there is enough connectedness if the number of connections, over any day, is *at least half* the number of direct connections that hold, over every day, in the lives of nearly every actual person.[6] When there are enough direct connections, there is what I call *strong* connectedness.

This relation cannot be the criterion of personal identity. A relation *F* is *transitive* if it is true that, if *X* is F-related to *Y*, and Y is F-related to *Z*, X and Z *must* be F-related. Personal identity is a transitive relation. If Bertie was one and the same person as the philosopher Russell, and Russell was one and the same person as the author of *Why I Am Not a Christian*, this author and Bertie must be one and the same person.

Strong connectedness is *not* a transitive relation. I am now strongly connected to myself yesterday, when I was strongly connected to myself two days ago, when I was strongly connected to myself three days ago, and so on. It does not follow that I am now strongly connected to myself twenty years ago. And this is not true. Between me now and myself twenty years ago there are many fewer than the number of direct psychological connections that hold over any day in the lives of nearly all adults. For example, while these adults have many memories of experiences that they had in the previous day, I have few memories of experiences that I had twenty years ago.

By 'the criterion of personal identity over time' I mean what this identity *necessarily involves or consists in*. Because identity is a transitive relation, the criterion of identity must be a transitive relation. Since strong connectedness is not transitive, it cannot be the criterion of identity. And I have just described a case in which this is shown. I am the same person as myself twenty years ago, though I am not now strongly connected to myself then.

Though a defender of Locke's view cannot appeal to psychological connectedness, he can appeal to psychological continuity, which *is* transitive. He can appeal to

> *The Psychological Criterion*: (1) There is *psychological continuity* if and only if there are overlapping chains of strong connectedness. X today is one and the same person as Y at some past time if and only if (2) X is psychologically continuous with Y, (3) this continuity has the right kind of cause, and (4) there does not exist a different person who is also psychologically continuous with Y. (5) Personal identity over time just consists in the holding of facts like (2) to (4).

As with the Physical Criterion, the need for (4) will be clear later.

There are three versions of the Psychological Criterion. These differ over the question of what is the *right* kind of cause. On the *Narrow* version, this must be the *normal* cause. On the *Wide* version, this could be *any reliable* cause. On the *Widest* version, the cause could be *any* cause.

The Narrow Psychological Criterion uses words in their ordinary sense. Thus I remember having an experience only if

(1)   I seem to remember having an experience,

(2)   I did have this experience,

and

(3)   my apparent memory is causally dependent, in the normal way, on this past experience.

That we need condition (3) can be suggested with an example. Suppose that I am knocked unconscious in a climbing accident. After I recover, my fellow–climber tells me what he shouted just before I fell. In some later year, when my memories are less clear, I might seem to remember the experience of hearing my companion shout just before I fell. And it might be true that I did have just such an experience. But though conditions (1) and (2) are met, we should not believe that I am remembering that past experience. It is a well-established fact that people can never remember their last few experiences before they were knocked unconscious. We should therefore claim that my apparent memory of hearing my companion shout is not a real memory of that past experience. This apparent memory is not causally dependent in the right way on that past experience. I have this apparent memory only because my companion later told me what he shouted.[7]

Similar remarks apply to the other kinds of continuity, such as continuity of character. On the Narrow Psychological Criterion, even if someone's character radically changes, there is continuity of character if these changes have one of several normal causes. Some changes of character are deliberately brought about; others are the natural consequence of growing older; others are the natural response to certain kinds of experience. But there would not be continuity of character if radical and unwanted changes were produced by abnormal interference, such as direct tampering with the brain.

Though it is memory that makes us aware of our own continued existence over time, the various other continuities have great importance. We may believe that they have enough importance to provide personal identity even in the absence of memory. We shall then claim, what Locke denied, that a person continues to exist even if he suffers from complete amnesia. I would rather suffer amnesia than have surgery that would give me a quite different and obnoxious character.

Besides the Narrow version, I described the two Wide versions of the Psychological Criterion. These versions extend the senses of several words. On the ordinary sense of 'memory', a memory must have its normal cause. The two Wide Psychological Criteria appeal to a wider sense of 'memory', which allows either any reliable cause, or any cause. Similar claims apply to the other kinds of direct psychological connection. To simplify my discussion of these three Criteria, I shall use 'psychological continuity' in its widest sense, that allows this continuity to have *any* cause.

If we appeal to the Narrow Version, which insists on the normal cause, the Psychological Criterion coincides in most cases with the Physical Criterion. The normal causes of memory involve the continued existence of the brain. And some or all of our psychological features depend upon states or events in our brains. The continued existence of a person's brain is at least part of the normal cause of psychological continuity. On the Physical Criterion, a person continues to exist if and only if (*a*) there continues to exist *enough* of this person's brain so that it remains the brain of a living person, and (*b*) no different person ever has enough of this person's brain. (*a*) and (*b*) are claimed to be the necessary and sufficient conditions for this person's identity, or continued existence, over time. On the Narrow Psychological Criterion, (*a*) is necessary, but not sufficient. A person continues to exist if and only if (*c*) there is psychological continuity, (*d*) this continuity has its normal cause, and (*e*) there does not exist a different person who is also psychologically continuous with this person. (*a*) is required as part of the normal cause of psychological continuity.

I shall argue that the two Wide Psychological Criteria are both better than the Narrow Criterion. A partial analogy may suggest why. Some people go blind because of damage to their eyes. Scientists are now developing artificial eyes. These involve a glass or plastic lens, and a microcomputer which sends through the optic nerve electrical patterns like those that are sent through this nerve by a natural eye. When such artificial eyes are more advanced, they might give to someone who has gone blind visual experiences just like those that he used to have. What he seems to see would correspond to what is in fact before him. And his visual experiences would be causally dependent, in this new but reliable way, on the light-waves coming from the objects that are before him.

Would this person be *seeing* these objects? If we insist that seeing must involve the normal cause, we would answer No. But even if this person cannot see, what he has is *just as good as* seeing, both as a way of knowing what is within sight, and as a source of visual pleasure. If we accept the Psychological Criterion, we could make a similar claim. If psychological continuity does not have its normal cause, some may claim that it is *not* true psychological continuity. We can claim that, even if this is so, this kind of continuity is *just as good as* ordinary continuity.

Reconsider the start of my imagined story, where my brain and body are destroyed. The Scanner and the Replicator produce a person who has a new but exactly similar brain and body, and who is psychologically continuous with me as I was when I pressed the green button. The cause of this continuity is, though unusual, reliable. On both the Physical Criterion and the Narrow Psychological Criterion, my Replica would *not* be me. On the two Wide Criteria, he *would* be me.

The Other Views

I am asking what is the criterion of personal identity over time – what this identity involves, or consists in. I first described the spatio-temporal physical continuity that, on the standard view, is the criterion of identity of physical objects. I then described two views about personal identity, the Physical and Psychological Criteria.

There is a natural but false assumption about these views. Many people believe in what is called *Materialism*, or *Physicalism*. This is the view that that there are no purely mental objects, states, or events. On one version of Physicalism, every mental event is just a physical event in some particular brain and nervous system. There are other versions. Those who are not Physicalists are either *Dualists* or *Idealists*. Dualists believe that mental events are *not* physical events. This can be so even if all mental events are causally dependent on physical events in a brain. Idealists believe that all states and events are, when understood correctly, purely mental. Given these distinctions, we may assume that Physicalists must accept the Physical Criterion of personal identity.

This is not so. Physicalists could accept the Psychological Criterion. And they could accept the version that allows any reliable cause, or any cause. They could thus believe that, in Simple Teletransportation, my Replica would be me. They would here be rejecting the Physical Criterion.[8]

These criteria are not the only views about personal identity. I shall now describe the other views that are either sufficiently plausible, or have enough supporters, to be worth considering. This description will be too abstract to be fully understood, before the details are filled out in later chapters. But it is worth giving this description, both for later reference, and to provide a rough idea of what lies ahead. If much of this summary seems, on a first reading, either obscure or trivial, *do not worry*.

I start with a new distinction. On the Physical Criterion, personal identity over time just involves the physically continuous existence of enough of a brain so that it remains the brain of a living person. On the Psychological Criterion, personal identity over time just involves the various kinds of psychological continuity, with the right kind of cause. These views are both *Reductionist*. They are Reductionist because they claim

(1)   that the fact of a person's identity over time just consists in the holding of certain more particular facts,

and

> (2)   that these facts can be described without either presupposing the identity
> of this person, or explicitly claiming that the experiences in this person's life are
> had by this person, or even explicitly claiming that this person exists. These facts
> can be described in an *impersonal* way.

It may seem that (2) could not be true. When we describe the psychological continuity that unifies some person's mental life, we must mention this person, and many other
people, in describing the *content* of many thoughts, desires, intentions, and other mental
states. But mentioning this person in this way does not involve either asserting that
these mental states are had by this person, or asserting that this person exists. A similar
claim applies to the Physical Criterion. These claims need further arguments, which I
shall later give.

Our view is *Non-Reductionist* if we reject either or both of the two Reductionist claims.
    Many Non-Reductionists hold what I call the view that *we are separately existing enti-
ties*. On this view, personal identity over time does not just consist in physical and/or
psychological continuity. It is a separate, further fact. A person is a separately existing
entity, distinct from his brain and body, and his experiences. On the best-known version
of this view, a person is a *purely mental* entity: a Cartesian Pure Ego, or spiritual substance. But we might believe that a person is a separately existing *physical* entity, of a
kind that is not yet recognised in the theories of contemporary physics.
    There is another Non-Reductionist View. This view denies that we are separately
existing entities, distinct from our brains and bodies, and our experiences. But this view
claims that, though we are not separately existing entities, personal identity *is* a further
fact, which does not just consist in physical and/or psychological continuity. I call this
the *Further Fact View*.

The Physical and Psychological Criteria are versions of the Reductionist View. And
there are two versions of each Criterion. As I have said, what is *necessarily* involved in
a person's continued existence is less than what is *in fact* involved. Believers in the
Reductionist Criteria disagree when considering imaginary cases. But they would agree
about what is in fact involved in the existence of actual people. They would start to
disagree only if, for example, people began to be Teleported.
    On the Reductionist View, each person's existence just involves the existence of a
brain and body, the doing of certain deeds, the thinking of certain thoughts, the occurrence of certain experiences, and so on. It will help to extend the ordinary sense of
the word 'event'. I shall use 'event' to cover even such *boring* events as the continued
existence of a belief, or a desire. This use makes the Reductionist View simpler to
describe. And it avoids what a Reductionist believes to be the misleading implications
of the words 'mental state'. While a state must be a state *of* some entity, this is not
true of an event. Given this extended use of the word 'event', all Reductionists would
accept

> (3)   A person's existence just consists in the existence of a brain and body, and
> the occurrence of a series of interrelated physical and mental events.

Some Reductionists claim

(4)   A person *just is* a particular brain and body, and such a series of interrelated events.

(4) uses the *is of composition*, as in the claim that a statue is a piece of bronze. This is not the *is of identity*. A statue and a piece of bronze are not one and the same thing. This is shown by the fact that, if we melt the statue, we destroy the statue but do not destroy the piece of bronze. Such a statue is composed of a piece of bronze. In the same sense, (4) claims that a person is composed of a particular brain and body, and a series of inter-related physical and mental events.

Other Reductionists claim

(5)   A person is an entity that is *distinct* from a brain and body, and such a series of events.

On this version of the Reductionist View, a person is not merely a composite object, with these various components. A person is an entity that *has* a brain and body, and *has* particular thoughts, desires, and so on. But, though (5) is true, a person is not a *separately existing* entity. Though (5) is true, (3) is also true.

This version of Reductionism may seem self-contradictory. (3) and (5) may seem to be inconsistent. It may help to consider Hume's analogy: 'I cannot compare the soul more properly to anything than to a republic, or commonwealth.'[9] Most of us are Reductionists about nations. We would accept the following claims: Nations exist. Ruritania does not exist, but France does. Though nations exist, a nation is not an entity that exists separately, apart from its citizens and its territory. We would accept

(6)   A nation's existence just involves the existence of its citizens, living together in certain ways, on its territory.

Some claim

(7)   A nation just *is* these citizens and this territory.

Others claim

(8)   A nation is an entity that is distinct from it citizens and its territory.

We may believe that (8) and (6) are not inconsistent. If we believe this, we may accept that there is no inconsistency between the corresponding claims (3) and (5). We may thus agree that the version of Reductionism expressed in (3) and (5) is a consistent view. If this version is consistent, as I believe, it is the better version. It uses our actual concept of a person. In most of what follows, we can ignore the difference between these two versions. But at one point this difference may have great importance.[10]

Besides claiming (1) and (2), Reductionists would also claim

(9)   Though persons exist, we could give a *complete* description of reality *without* claiming that persons exist.

I call this the view *that a complete description could be impersonal.*

This view may also seem to be self-contradictory. If persons exist, and a description of what exists fails to mention persons, how can this description be complete?

A Reductionist could give the following reply. Suppose that an object has two names. This is true of the planet that is called both *Venus* and the *Evening Star.* In our description of what exists, we could claim that Venus exists. Our description could then be complete even though we do not claim that the Evening Star exists. We need not make this claim because, using its other name, we have already claimed that this object exists.

A similar claim applies when some fact can be described in two ways. Some Reductionists accept (4), the claim that a person just is a particular brain and body, and a series of interrelated physical and mental events. If this is what a person *is*, the same fact can be described in two ways. We can claim either

(10)   that there exists a particular brain and body, and a particular series of inter-related physical and mental events.

or

(11)   that a particular person exists,

If (10) and (11) are two ways of describing the *same* fact, a complete description need not make *both* claims. In a complete description we could claim (10), and fail to claim (11). Though this person exists, a complete description need not claim that he exists. The fact that he exists has already been reported in claim (10).

Other Reductionists accept (5), the claim that a person is distinct from his brain and body, and his acts, thoughts, and other physical and mental events. On this version of Reductionism, claim (10) does not describe the very same fact that claim (11) describes. But claim (10) *implies* or *entails* claim (11). More weakly, given our understanding of the concept of a person, if we know that (10) is true, we shall know that (11) is true. These Reductionists can say that, if our description of reality either states or implies or would enable us to know that existence of everything that exists, our description is complete. This claim is not as clearly true as the claim that a complete description need not give two descriptions of the same fact. But this claim seems plausible. If it is justified, and the Reductionist View is true, these Reductionists can completely describe reality without claiming that persons exist.[11]

Notes

1   See, for example, *Zettel*, ed. by G. Anscombe and G. von Wright, and translated by G. Anscombe, Blackwell, 1967, Proposition 350: 'It is as if our concepts involve a scaffolding of facts . . . If you imagine certain facts otherwise . . . then you can no longer imagine the application of certain concepts.'

2 W. V. Quine, reviewing Milton K. Munitz, ed., *Identity and Individuation*, in *The Journal of Philosophy*, 69, 1972, p. 490.

3 This states a necessary condition for the continued existence of a physical object. Saul Kripke has argued, in lectures, that this condition is not sufficient. Since I missed these lectures, I cannot discuss this argument.

4 On this view, it could be fatal to live in what has long been a densely populated area, such as London. It may here be true of many bits of matter that they were part of the bodies of many different people, when they were last alive. These people could not all be resurrected, since there would not be enough such matter to be reassembled. Some hold a version of this view which avoids this problem. They believe that a resurrected body needs to contain only one particle from the original body.

5 Locke, *Essay Concerning Human Understanding*, Chapter 27, Section 16.

6 This suggestion would need expanding, since there are many ways to count the number of direct connections. And some kinds of connection should be given more importance than others. As I suggest later, more weight should be given to those connections which are distinctive, or different in different people. All English-speakers share a vast number of undistinctive memories of how to speak English.

7 I follow C. B. Martin and M. Deutscher, 'Remembering', *Philosophical Review*, 75, 1966.

8 A. Quinton defends this view in J. Perry, ed., *Personal Identity* (University of California Press, 1975).

9 Hume, *A Treatise of Human Nature*, Part IV, Section 6.

10 Sections 96 and 98–9, and Chapter 14.

11 Reductionism raises notoriously difficult questions. I am influenced by these remarks in S. Kripke, 'Naming and Necessity', in G. Harman and D. Davidson, eds., *Semantics of Natural Language* (Dordrecht, Reidel, 1972), p. 271:

> Although the statement that England fought Germany in 1943 perhaps cannot be *reduced* to any statement about individuals, nevertheless in some sense it is not a fact 'over and above' the collection of all facts about persons, and their behavior over history. The sense in which facts about nations are not facts 'over and above' those about persons can be expressed in the observation that a description of the world mentioning all facts about persons but omitting those about nations can be a *complete* description of the world, from which the facts about nations follow. Similarly, perhaps facts about material objects are not facts 'over and above' facts about their constituent molecules. We may then ask, given a description of a non-actualized possible situation in terms of people, whether England still exists in that situation . . . Similarly, given certain counterfactual vicissitudes in the history of the molecules of a table, *T*, one may ask whether *T* would exist, in that situation, or whether a certain bunch of molecules, which in that situation would constitute a table, constitute the very same table *T*. In each case, we ask criteria of identity across possible worlds for certain particulars in terms of those for other, more 'basic', particulars. If statements about nations (or tribes [tables?]) are not *reducible* to those about other more 'basic' constituents, if there is some 'open texture' in the relationship between them, we can hardly expect to give hard and fast identity criteria; nevertheless in concrete cases we may be able to answer whether a certain bunch of molecules would still constitute table *T*, though in some cases the answer may be indeterminate. I think similar remarks apply to the problem of identity over time . . .

Given the non-reducibility of the statement about England, I am inclined to weaken the word 'follow' at the end of Kripke's second sentence. The central question about personal identity I believe to be whether these remarks apply, not only to nations and tables, but also to people.

PART V

POST-STRUCTURALISM

15

COMMENTARY ON FREUD

Sigmund Freud was born in Freiberg, Moravia, in 1856. He based his work and studies in Vienna until he fled the Nazi regime for England in 1938. He died in London in 1939.

Freud's work represents an unusual confluence of Romantic and scientific thought, combining the idea of powerful and arational forces with a rigorous science. Freud's is a naturalistic materialist theory of the mind in which the traditional primacy of immediate consciousness is radically undermined by the supposition of underlying arational biological instincts of which we can never become conscious (the instinctual drives) and, as a consequence, over which we have no control.

Freud's conception of the mind contrasts with Descartes's in just about every respect. Where Descartes regarded the mind as nonbodily, transparent, simple, a distinct substance, and the guarantee of truth, Freud regards it as bodily, composite, inherently obscure, and conflictual. One of the interesting features that Freud's conception of the mind shares with Descartes's, however, is a principle of suspicion: both Descartes and Freud make doubting a central apparatus of their investigative methods. The theory of psychoanalysis treats consciousness as a question that is put through the structures of a naturalistic architecture. Psychoanalysis is itself a means of reflection, a process in which the subject is constituted and rediscovers itself. And what it discovers itself as is a decentered and partial power, prone to the pretensions of omniscience and immortality.[1] Although Freud does not discuss the "subject" or the "self" as such, his account "decenters" subjectivity through its conception of a mind divided between its multiple agencies (the id, ego, and superego). Freud's naturalist conception of the divided mind has informed all accounts of subjectivity in the tradition since, not least because it provided the first thoroughgoing materialist alternative to spiritualist conceptions of mind.

Freud depicts psychological life as a function of a multileveled biological energy system, the health and behavior of which is determined by the organism's ability to both discharge and store energy within certain homeostatically controlled parameters.[2] Energy is experienced as either pleasure or unpleasure and can be tracked as such in human behavior, which can thus be understood in terms of economies of energy and pleasure. Although Freud eventually gave up the attempt to demonstrate the neurological basis of psychological states, he never gave up his belief in that neurological basis.

Freud argued that the main energy source for the mind arises from within the body in the form of instinctual energy or drives called "libido." This energy is not confined to the cellular functioning of bodily organs but also traverses the mind or "psychical apparatus." In short, the psyche is a kind of second-order expression of the body's functioning. The instinctual drives are often referred to as sexual instincts; however, Freud uses "sexual" in a technical sense to refer to bodily processes associated with self-preservation and the perpetuation of the species. Thus his theory of sexuality is closely tied to his theory of energy: the sexual instincts are expressed through the desire to acquire and maintain bodily pleasure, which is underwritten by an energy economy in the service of the species.

Since Freud's theory of the mind is developmental, he accordingly provides an account of the successive stages of the development and organization of the sexual drives from infancy to maturity. These stages begin with the oral and anal stages of infancy – where the infant derives pleasure from suckling and defecating – through to the complex emotions of the Oedipal stage characterized by intense desire for the mother, fear of castration, and hostility toward the father; and finally to the mature phallic stage, where desire is regulated according to a heterosexual model under the primacy of the genitals. At every stage there is parental or social interference with the individual's pursuit of bodily pleasure, and in this way social norms come to regulate the expression (or repression) of instinctual drives. This makes the developmental process essentially conflictual, and Freud believed that mental health depended upon the successful resolution of each stage of conflict. On this view, individuals will exhibit different subjectivities depending upon the person's success in resolving the normal succession of conflicts, as well as other traumatic experiences incurred along the way.

"The Ego and the Id" is a relatively late piece of work. In it Freud fine-tunes some of his earlier ideas concerning the distinction between the unconscious and conscious systems. These terms do not refer to two different types of mind, or to two distinct divisions within the mind. Rather, they relate to different functional aspects of the three main structures of the mind: the id, the ego, and the superego. The instinctual drives comprise the id, and so the id is fully and permanently unconscious. The ego has the most complexity because it relates to the entirety of mental life incorporating aspects of the preconscious, conscious, and unconscious systems. Arising originally from the perceptual system, the ego can be described as a kind of repository of all our sensations (relating to experiential states and memories). The superego is probably best described as the "conscience." It is an unconscious, socially acquired mechanism that controls thought and behavior, a kind of censor, or "moralizer" of the mind.

Within this triumvirate, the ego has the most onerous task and becomes the center of conscious life – which is perhaps why it has been equated with the "self" for so long. The ego is charged with reconciling the conflicting demands of the unconscious drives with the demands of external, social reality to produce meaningful and practically oriented ideas and actions.[3] In doing so, the ego also mediates between the urges of the id and the proscriptions of the superego. An unconscious impulse from the id can find conscious expression (satisfaction) only after undergoing the permutations wrought upon it by the dynamic interactions of the ego and the superego. The outcome of this is an (optimally) coherent and socially integrated personality, a human subject.

In its mediatory role, the ego stands between the instinctual drives and their satisfaction through action (including speech and writing). It is the ego that finally transforms energy into specific action and behavior in the material world – action that, ideally, produces pleasure. The ego is able to fill this role because of its bodily origins in the perceptual system, that is, because it is located at the interface of internal and external domains of the body. For Freud, the entire human body acts as an integrated sensory organ that extends in two directions: to the internal domain animated by the instinctual drives of the id, and to external reality. This double sensory role, Freud says, allows the body to produce a mental projection of its surface, which becomes the ego. In other words, the body–ego functions as a kind of grid that coordinates the organic, psychic, and social regions of reality.

As the gatekeeper for behavior, the ego is responsible for repression. Repression is the central defense mechanism that keeps essentially dangerous (that is, violent and self-destructive) impulses from direct conscious expression in thoughts, feelings, or actions. Such threatening impulses are aroused in the usual course of psychic development, specifically during the Oedipal stage where the child is said to desire the death of the father. But they can also be aroused as a result of emotionally powerfully experiences such as violence or sexual activity. In a robust psyche, such experiences will be managed through the mechanism of repression, rather than overwhelming the person and causing neurosis.

According to psychoanalysis, when the ego represses an instinctual drive it confines its direct expression to the unconscious in an effort to avoid the unpleasure arising from the conflict between the demands of the impulse and reality. However, despite repression, an impulse can continue to exert a force upon the conscious mind, and, if powerful enough, can give rise to neurotic symptoms. This is what happens, for example, in the case of an inconclusive resolution of the Oedipus conflict, or in the case of post-traumatic disorders.[4]

As the domain of reason and explicit consciousness linked to action, the ego is also the domain of moral agency, free will, and choice. Thus, for Freud, the traditional conceptions of subjectivity in terms of self-awareness, bodily and moral agency, rational thought, and mental organization remain relevant, but the legitimacy of these concepts is dramatically reduced. The authority of the traditionally conceived subject is displaced (decentered) by the powerful forces of the id and its natural antagonist, the superego.

These considerations lead to the central question of "The Ego and the Id": how can something unconscious be made conscious? The question goes to the heart of the nature of thought itself: how do we become aware of what we think? Freud describes thought processes as "displacements of mental energy . . . as this energy proceeds on its way towards action."[5] In other words, the question is directly concerned with how bodily processes (drives) are converted to ideas. Indirectly, the question revisits the scientific premise of psychoanalysis, namely, the causal link between neurology (cellular biology) and psychological life (what we think and do).

Freud's response is to argue two points. First, he makes the general claim that for anything from the unconscious to become conscious it must take on the form of an external perception, since consciousness arises from and is coextensive with the

perceptual system. Second, some of what is unconscious is able to enter the preconscious (and thus be rendered capable of becoming conscious) by being attached to
"word-presentations" which correspond to it. The idea here is that word-presentations
are (primarily verbal) memory traces, traces of external perceptions, namely, perceptions of the sounds of words. The proximity of the perceptual-consciousness system to
the unconscious allows memory traces of words to be energized or "cathected" by
impulses from the unconscious. This allows a memory trace to be endowed with the
liveliness of a regular external perception. In this way repressed ideas can find their way
into consciousness through intermediary links established through the activation of
verbal residues. This manifests, for example, in the case of so-called "Freudian slips."

Freud says that the interposition of word-presentations between the energy source
of the unconscious and the representational structure of consciousness allows "internal
thought processes" to be turned into perceptions and thus made conscious: "When a
hypercathexis of the process of thinking takes place, thoughts are *actually* perceived –
as if they came from without – and are consequently held to be true."[6] This is supposed to explain normal psychology as well as the therapeutic effects of the "talking
cure," where normal psychological mechanisms are put to specific work in the clinical
setting through such techniques as free association.

The scientific status of the theory of psychoanalysis has long been debated. For
example, Karl Popper claimed that psychoanalysis failed the test of falsifiability because
the theory was compatible with every possible state of affairs in human psychology and
behavior.[7] Other philosophers, notably Paul Ricoeur and Jürgen Habermas, have down-
played the scientific status of psychoanalysis, and regard its significance to lie in its function as a hermeneutic enterprise.[8] More pointed criticism has come from feminists who
argue that Freud's theory is premised on the model of the male, and either cannot
account for female sexual desire or rules out its very possibility. However, this has not
prevented its feminist critics from working with some of the central insights of psychoanalysis, for example, Julia Kristeva's concept of the semiotic and *jouissance* in infantile life, and Irigaray's notion of maternal debt.[9]

Notes

1   See Paul Ricoeur, *Freud and Philosophy: An Essay on Interpretation*, trans. Denis Savage (New
    Haven, CT and London: Yale University Press, 1970), p. 422.
2   Freud was clearly influenced by Ernst Brücke, his laboratory supervisor in Vienna, who had
    published on the application of Helmholtz's theory to neurophysiology. See Sigmund Freud,
    On Metapsychology, trans. James Strachey (London and New York: Penguin, 1991), p. 19; here-
    after *OM*.
3   *OM*, p. 355.
4   See Freud's Twenty-Fourth Lecture: "Ordinary Nervousness," and Eighteenth Lecture:
    "Fixation Upon Traumas: The Unconscious," in *A General Introduction to Psychoanalysis*, ed.
    and trans. Joan Riviere (New York: Washington Square Press, 1960).
5   *OM*, p. 357.
6   *OM*, p. 361.
7   Karl Popper, *Conjectures and Refutations: The Growth of Scientific Knowledge* (New York: Basic
    Books, 1962).

8 See Ricoeur (1970) and Jürgen Habermas, *Knowledge and Human Interest*, trans. J. Shapiro (Boston: Beacon Press, 1971).
9 See Julia Kristeva, *Tales of Love*, trans. Leon S. Roudiez (New York: Columbia University Press, 1987); Luce Irigaray, *Speculum of the Other Woman*, trans. Gillian Gill (Ithaca, NY: Cornell University Press, 1985).

Main Texts by Freud

Marie Bonaparte, Anna Freud, and Ernst Kris (eds.), *The Origins of Psychoanalysis: Letters to Wilhelm Fleiss, Drafts and Notes, 1887–1902*, trans. Eric Mosbacher and James Strachey (New York: Basic Books, 1954).

James Strachey (ed. and trans.), *The Standard Edition of Complete Psychological Works of Sigmund Freud* (London: Hogarth Press, 1953–71).

Further Reading

Deigh, John, *The Sources of Moral Agency: Essays in Moral Psychology and Freudian Theory* (Cambridge, UK: Cambridge University Press, 1996).

Jones, Ernest, *The Life and Work of Sigmund Freud* (New York: Basic Books, 1957).

Klein, Melanie, *Contributions to Psycho-analysis, 1921–1945*, with an introduction by Ernest Jones (London: Hogarth Press, 1973).

Kristeva, Julia, *Powers of Horror: An Essay on Abjection*, trans. Leon Roudiez (New York: Columbia University Press, 1982).

Lacan, Jacques, *Ecrits, A Selection*, trans. A. Sheridan (London: Tavistock, 1977).

Mitchell, Juliet, *Psychoanalysis and Feminism* (London: Allen Lane, 1974).

Neu, Jerome (ed.), *The Cambridge Companion to Freud* (Cambridge, UK: Cambridge University Press, 1991).

Robinson, Paul, *Freud and His Critics* (Berkeley: University of California Press, 1993).

"THE EGO AND THE ID"

Sigmund Freud

Pathological research has directed our interest too exclusively to the repressed. We should like to learn more about the ego, now that we know that it, too, can be unconscious in the proper sense of the word. Hitherto the only guide we have had during our investigations has been the distinguishing mark of being conscious or unconscious; we have finally come to see how ambiguous this can be.

Now all our knowledge is invariably bound up with consciousness. We can come to know even the *Ucs.* only by making it conscious. But stop, how is that possible? What does it mean when we say 'making something conscious'? How can that come about?

We already know the point from which we have to start in this connection. We have said that consciousness is the *surface* of the mental apparatus; that is, we have ascribed it as a function to a system which is spatially the first one reached from the external world – and spatially not only in the functional sense but, on this occasion, also in the sense of anatomical dissection.[1] Our investigations too must take this perceiving surface as a starting-point.

All perceptions which are received from without (sense-perceptions) and from within – what we call sensations and feelings – are *Cs.* from the start. But what about those internal processes which we may – roughly and inexactly – sum up under the name of thought-processes? They represent displacements of mental energy which are effected somewhere in the interior of the apparatus as this energy proceeds on its way towards action. Do they advance to the surface, which causes consciousness to be generated? Or does consciousness make its way to them? This is clearly one of the difficulties that arise when one begins to take the spatial or 'topographical' idea of mental life seriously. Both these possibilities are equally unimaginable; there must be a third alternative.[2]

From *On Metapsychology: The Theory of Psychoanalysis* (London: Penguin, 1991), pp. 357–66. © by the Institute of Psychoanalysis and the Hogarth Press; reprinted by permission of the Random House Group Ltd. from *The Standard Edition of the Complete Psychological Works of Sigmund Freud*, translated and edited by James Strachey.

I have already, in another place,[3] suggested that the real difference between a *Ucs.* and a *Pcs.* idea (thought) consists in this: that the former is carried out on some material which remains unknown, whereas the latter (the *Pcs.*) is in addition brought into connection with *word-presentations*. This is the first attempt to indicate distinguishing marks for the two systems, the *Pcs.* and the *Ucs.*, other than their relation to consciousness. The question, 'How does a thing become conscious?' would thus be more advantageously stated: 'How does a thing become preconscious?' And the answer would be: 'Through becoming connected with the word-presentations corresponding to it.'

These word-presentations are residues of memories; they were at one time perceptions, and like all mnemic residues they can become conscious again. Before we concern ourselves further with their nature, it dawns upon us like a new discovery that only something which has once been a *Cs.* perception can become conscious, and that anything arising from within (apart from feelings) that seeks to become conscious must try to transform itself into external perceptions: this becomes possible by means of memory-traces.

We think of the mnemic residues as being contained in systems which are directly adjacent to the system *Pcpt.–Cs.*, so that the cathexes of those residues can readily extend from within on to the elements of the latter system. We immediately think here of hallucinations, and of the fact that the most vivid memory is always distinguishable both from a hallucination and from an external perception but it will also occur to us at once that when a memory is revived the cathexis remains in the mnemic system, whereas a hallucination, which is not distinguishable from a perception, can arise when the cathexis does not merely spread over from the memory-trace on to the *Pcpt.* element, but passes over to it entirely.

Verbal residues are derived primarily from auditory perceptions, so that the system *Pcs.* has, as it were, a special sensory source. The visual components of word-presentations are secondary, acquired through reading, and may to begin with be left on one side; so may the motor images of words, which, except with deaf-mutes, play the part of auxiliary indications. In essence a word is after all the mnemic residue of a word that has been heard.

We must not be led, in the interests of simplification perhaps, to forget the importance of optical mnemic residues, when they are of *things*, or to deny that it is possible for thought-processes to become conscious through a reversion to visual residues, and that in many people this seems to be the favoured method. The study of dreams and of preconscious phantasies as shown in Varendonck's observations[4] can give us an idea of the special character of this visual thinking. We learn that what becomes conscious in it is as a rule only the concrete subject-matter of the thought, and that the relations between the various elements of this subject-matter, which is what specially characterizes thoughts, cannot be given visual expression. Thinking in pictures is, therefore, only a very incomplete form of becoming conscious. In some way, too, it stands nearer to unconscious processes than does thinking in words, and it is unquestionably older than the latter both ontogenetically and phylogenetically.

To return to our argument: if, therefore, this is the way in which something that is in itself unconscious becomes preconscious, the question how we make something that is repressed (pre)conscious would be answered as follows. It is done by supplying *Pcs.*

intermediate links through the work of analysis. Consciousness remains where it is, therefore; but, on the other hand, the *Ucs.* does not rise into the *Cs.*

Whereas the relation of *external* perceptions to the ego is quite perspicuous, that of *internal* perceptions to the ego requires special investigation. It gives rise once more to a doubt whether we are really right in referring the whole of consciousness to the single superficial system *Pcpt.–Cs.*

Internal perceptions yield sensations of processes arising in the most diverse and certainly also in the deepest strata of the mental apparatus. Very little is known about these sensations and feelings; those belonging to the pleasure–unpleasure series may still be regarded as the best examples of them. They are more primordial, more elementary, than perceptions arising externally and they can come about even when consciousness is clouded. I have elsewhere[5] expressed my views about their greater economic significance and the metapsychological reasons for this. These sensations are multilocular, like external perceptions; they may come from different places simultaneously and may thus have different or even opposite qualities.

Sensations of a pleasurable nature have not anything inherently impelling about them, whereas unpleasurable ones have it in the highest degree. The latter impel towards change, towards discharge, and that is why we interpret unpleasure as implying a heightening and pleasure a lowering of energic cathexis.[6] Let us call what becomes conscious as pleasure and unpleasure a quantitative and qualitative 'something' in the course of mental events; the question then is whether this 'something' can become conscious in the place where it is, or whether it must first be transmitted to the system *Pcpt.*

Clinical experience decides for the latter. It shows us that this 'something' behaves like a repressed impulse. It can exert driving force without the ego noticing the compulsion. Not until there is resistance to the compulsion, a hold-up in the discharge-reaction, does the 'something' at once become conscious as unpleasure. In the same way that tensions arising from physical needs can remain unconscious, so also can pain – a thing intermediate between external and internal perception, which behaves like an internal perception even when its source is in the external world. It remains true, therefore, that sensations and feelings, too, only become conscious through reaching the system *Pcpt.*; if the way forward is barred, they do not come into being as sensations, although the 'something' that corresponds to them in the course of excitation is the same as if they did. We then come to speak, in a condensed and not entirely correct manner, of 'unconscious feelings,' keeping up an analogy with unconscious ideas which is not altogether justifiable. Actually the difference is that, whereas with *Ucs.* ideas connecting links must be created before they can be brought into the *Cs.*, with *feelings*, which are themselves transmitted directly, this does not occur. In other words: the distinction between *Cs.* and *Pcs.* has no meaning where feelings are concerned; the *Pcs.* here drops out – and feelings are either conscious or unconscious. Even when they are attached to word-presentations, their becoming conscious is not due to that circumstance, but they become so directly.

The part played by word-presentations now becomes perfectly clear. By their interposition internal thought-processes are made into perceptions. It is like a demonstration of the theorem that all knowledge has its origin in external perception. When a hypercathexis of the process of thinking takes place, thoughts are *actually* perceived – as if they came from without – and are consequently held to be true.

After this clarifying of the relations between external and internal perception and the superficial system *Pcpt.-Cs.*, we can go on to work out our idea of the ego. It starts out, as we see, from the system *Pcpt.*, which is its nucleus, and begins by embracing the *Pcs.*, which is adjacent to the mnemic residues. But, as we have learnt, the ego is also unconscious.

Now I think we shall gain a great deal by following the suggestion of a writer who, from personal motives, vainly asserts that he has nothing to do with the rigours of pure science. I am speaking of Georg Groddeck, who is never tired of insisting that what we call our ego behaves essentially passively in life, and that, as he expressed it, we are 'lived' by unknown and uncontrollable forces.[7] We have all had impressions of the same kind, even though they may not have overwhelmed us to the exclusion of all others, and we need feel no hesitation in finding a place for Groddeck's discovery in the structure of science. I propose to take it into account by calling the entity which starts out from the system *Pcpt.* and begins by being *Pcs.* the 'ego,' and by following Groddeck in calling the other part of the mind, into which this entity extends and which behaves as though it were *Ucs.*, the 'id.'

We shall soon see whether we can derive any advantage from this view for purposes either of description or of understanding. We shall now look upon an individual as a psychical id, unknown and unconscious, upon whose surface rests the ego, developed from its nucleus the *Pcpt.* system. If we make an effort to represent this pictorially, we may add that the ego does not completely envelop the id, but only does so to the extent to which the system *Pcpt.* forms its [the ego's] surface, more or less as the germinal disc rests upon the ovum. The ego is not sharply separated from the id; its lower portion merges into it.

But the repressed merges into the id as well, and is merely a part of it. The repressed is only cut off sharply from the ego by the resistances of repression; it can communicate with the ego through the id. We at once realize that almost all the lines of demarcation we have drawn at the instigation of pathology relate only to the superficial strata of the mental apparatus – the only ones known to us. The state of things which we have been describing can be represented diagrammatically (Fig. 1); though it must be remarked that the form chosen has no pretensions to any special applicability, but is merely intended to serve for purposes of exposition.

We might add, perhaps, that the ego wears a 'cap of hearing' – on one side only, as we learn from cerebral anatomy. It might be said to wear it awry.

It is easy to see that the ego is that part of the id which has been modified by the direct influence of the external world through the medium of the *Pcpt.-Cs.*; in a sense it is an extension of the surface-differentiation. Moreover, the ego seeks to bring the influence of the external world to bear upon the id and its tendencies, and endeavours to substitute the reality principle for the pleasure principle which reigns unrestrictedly in the id. For the ego, perception plays the part which in the id falls to instinct. The ego represents what may be called reason and common sense, in contrast to the id, which contains the passions. All this falls into line with popular distinctions which we are all familiar with; at the same time, however, it is only to be regarded as holding good on the average or 'ideally.'

The functional importance of the ego is manifested in the fact that normally control over the approaches to motility devolves upon it. Thus in its relation to the id it is like

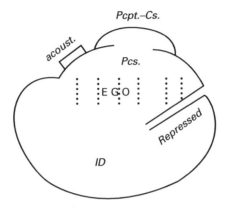

Fig. 1.

a man on horseback, who has to hold in check the superior strength of the horse; with this difference, that the rider tries to do so with his own strength while the ego uses borrowed forces. The analogy may be carried a little further. Often a rider, if he is not to be parted from his horse, is obliged to guide it where it wants to go; so in the same way the ego is in the habit of transforming the id's will into action as if it were its own.

Another factor, besides the influence of the system *Pcpt.*, seems to have played a part in bringing about the formation of the ego and its differentiation from the id. A person's own body, and above all its surface, is a place from which both external and internal perceptions may spring. It is *seen* like any other object, but to the *touch* it yields two kinds of sensations, one of which may be equivalent to an internal perception. Psycho-physiology has fully discussed the manner in which a person's own body attains its special position among other objects in the world of perception. Pain, too, seems to play a part in the process, and the way in which we gain new knowledge of our organs during painful illnesses in perhaps a model of the way by which in general we arrive at the idea of our body.

The ego is first and foremost a bodily ego; it is not merely a surface entity, but is itself the projection of a surface. If we wish to find an anatomical analogy for it we can best identify it with the 'cortical homunculus' of the anatomists, which stands on its head in the cortex, sticks up its heels, faces backwards and, as we know, has its speech-area on the left-hand side.

The relation of the ego to consciousness has been entered into repeatedly; yet there are some important facts in this connection which remain to be described here. Accus-tomed as we are to taking our social or ethical scale of values along with us wherever we go, we feel no surprise at hearing that the scene of the activities of the lower pas-sions is in the unconscious; we expect, moreover, that the higher any mental function ranks in our scale of values the more easily it will find access to consciousness assured to it. Here, however, psychoanalytic experience disappoints us. On the one hand, we have evidence that even subtle and difficult intellectual operations which ordinarily require strenuous reflection can equally be carried out preconsciously and without coming into consciousness. Instances of this are quite incontestable; they may occur, for example, during the state of sleep, as is shown when someone finds, immediately after waking, that he knows the solution to a difficult mathematical or other problem with which he had been wrestling in vain the day before.

There is another phenomenon, however, which is far stranger. In our analyses we discover that there are people in whom the faculties of self-criticism and conscience – mental activities, that is, that rank as extremely high ones – are unconscious and unconsciously produce effects of the greatest importance; the example of resistance remaining unconscious during analysis is therefore by no means unique. But this new discovery, which compels us, in spite of our better critical judgement, to speak of an 'unconscious sense of guilt', bewilders us far more than the other and sets us fresh problems, especially when we gradually come to see that in a great number of neuroses an unconscious sense of guilt of this kind plays a decisive economic part and puts the most powerful obstacles in the way of recovery. If we come back once more to our scale of values, we shall have to say that not only what is lowest but also what is highest in the ego can be unconscious. It is as if we were thus supplied with a proof of what we have just asserted of the conscious ego: that it is first and foremost a body-ego.

Notes

1 'Beyond the Pleasure Principle,' *On Metapsychology*, p. 297.
2 'The Unconscious', *On Metapsychology*, pp. 206 ff.
3 Freud distinguishes the unconscious (*Ucs.*) and conscious (*Cs.*) as follows (*On Metapsychology*, pp. 50–1):

> let us call 'conscious' the conception which is present to our consciousness and of which we are aware, and let this be the only meaning of the term 'conscious.' As for latent conceptions, if we have any reason to suppose that they exist in the mind – as we had in the case of memory – let them be denoted by the term 'unconscious.'

The preconscious (*Pcs.*) refers to psychical activity that is not yet conscious but is capable of becoming conscious, that 'can now, given certain conditions, become an object of consciousness without any special resistance' (p. 175). *Pcpt-Cs.* refers to the function of consciousness (*Cs.*) in registering perceptions, whether of internal or external origin. All perceptions, says Freud, are conscious from the start (p. 357). [KA]

4 [Cf. J. Varendonck, *The Psychology of Day-Dreams* (1921), a book to which Freud contributed an introduction.]
5 'Beyond the Pleasure Principle', *On Metapsychology*, p. 300.
6 Ibid, p. 276.
7 Georg Groddeck, *The Book of the It* (1923).

16

COMMENTARY ON FOUCAULT

Michel Foucault (1926–1984) was born in Poitiers, France. He studied at the École Normale Supérieure in Paris during the 1940s when existential phenomenology was in its prime. He is one of the foremost representatives of post-structuralism, whose work emphasizes the fragmentary, composite, and multiple nature of subjectivity constructed discursively through language and social practices. Foucault was also known for his political activities, speaking out for various marginalized groups.

Foucault considered himself a Nietzschean, adopting Nietzsche's genealogical method, his organic conception of power, and the view that ethical life is concerned with an aesthetic of the self. Foucault was also strongly influenced by French philosopher of science, Georges Canguilhem, who imparted to Foucault an outlook that stressed the organizing force of reason in forms of human life.[1] Foucault's other great influences were the structuralists Ferdinand de Saussure and Jacques Lacan, as well as Karl Marx and Louis Althusser.

Foucault's work can be described as a history of thought. His method has been to excavate the more or less hidden history that attaches to all practices and bodies of knowledge in the human sciences in order to illuminate the context and contingency of claims to truth. In doing so, Foucault endeavors to identify the various ways in which claims of truth intersect with structures of power to articulate forms of human subjectivity. Foucault's work in the social construction of subjectivity has been an important contribution to feminist and political philosophy by providing a conceptual framework in which to understand the intersection of moral agency and coercive ideology.[2]

Foucault characterizes his early work as historical, in contrast to his later work, which he calls genealogical. Of the historical method, he reports being unhappy with the alternatives of, on the one hand philosophical anthropology, which dealt with the realm of persons and experience, and on the other hand social history, which dealt with categories of economics and demographics.[3] In taking a genealogical approach, Foucault set out to establish a history of thought itself that would cut across these alternatives. Foucault defines thought as:

what establishes, in a variety of possible forms, the play of true and false, and which as a consequence constitutes the human being as a subject of learning (*connaissance*); in other words it is a basis for accepting or refusing rules, and constitutes human beings as social and juridical subjects; it is what establishes the relation with oneself and with others, and constitutes the self as an ethical subject.[4]

In *The Archaeology of Knowledge*, Foucault identifies the specific conditions that have enabled systems of thought to produce truths and falsities through discourse. By "discourse" Foucault means practices that systematically interweave linguistic propositional structures and the subject–positions they presuppose with nonlinguistic procedures (the physical activities that the propositions are about). This gives rise to a discursive formation, a complex "doing" organized around conceptual rules that together define what counts as true or false and articulate a certain subject-position.[5] Because practices are structured around rules for truth and falsity, Foucault regards them as discourses of power: the rules determine norms of behavior and subject-positions that are privileged, deviant, or excluded. By determining behavior, discourse is said to "inscribe" social norms on the bodies of individuals.

Foucault considers power to be both productive and destructive. Like the Nietzschean will to power, power for Foucault is an articulating quasi-organic force manifest in the practical capacity of the body to act. As such, power is not tied to any particular normative model, nor is it tied to evaluation. Although his conception of power is nonevaluative, Foucault is concerned with power in terms of domination and discipline. In *Madness and Civilisation* and *Discipline and Punish* he describes the ways in which practices across the whole of modern society have been permeated by techniques for normalizing behavior considered deviant through the application of means involving observation, examination, and normalizing judgment. He calls these "normalizing practices" or "disciplinary practices" in contrast to constructive power expressed in some aesthetic and erotic experiences.[6] These practices give rise to what Foucault calls "docile bodies" – in other words, conformist and cooperative subjects.

Although Foucault has been criticized for not providing a normative criterion for distinguishing the legitimate and illegitimate uses of power,[7] he does object to the disciplinary use of power. The basis for his objection is that disciplinary power narrows possibilities for human living, undermining one's ability to create one's own form of existence by excluding alternative discourses (such as the aesthetic and erotic), and by coercing individuals to conform to a limited range of experiences. The only response to power, says Foucault, is resistance. Resistance can be exercised by individuals in pursuing "limit experiences," and by institutions pursuing an ethical basis for justice that is premised upon the productive powers of an aesthetic model.

Foucault's genealogy shows that subjectivity has not been the same for every age, and that the idea that there can be direct unmediated apprehension and understanding of the self or subjectivity through introspection is deeply mistaken – it is in fact, a result of a certain kind of thought that came about at a certain time in history, namely, with Descartes. For Foucault, forms of subjectivity are determined by the rationality embedded in the discursive practices of the times and the subject-positions they articulate. Subjectivity is a discursive formation.

Foucault identifies four "techniques" which characterize human societies and are part of their discursive nature:

1   Techniques to transform or manipulate things (production);
2   Techniques of sign systems (signification);
3   Techniques for determining the conduct of individuals (domination);
4   Techniques of the self.

It is the fourth technique that particularly occupies Foucault's attention in his later work. Techniques of the self concern "those forms of understanding which the subject creates about himself."[8] These techniques allow individuals to effect changes to their bodies, thoughts, and conduct, and in so doing, transform themselves. Techniques of the self, then, concern agency – one's relation to oneself as the subject of one's thoughts and actions. In the Dartmouth lectures, Foucault stresses the complexity of the relationship between powers of domination and technologies of the self, urging us to pay more attention to "the points where the technologies of domination of individuals over one another have recourse to processes by which the individual acts upon himself."[9]

Foucault came to realize that the constructive and mediated nature of one's relation to oneself posed a particular peril to the individual in the modern age where interests of business and government lead them to employ a high degree of coercive discourse. The relational nature of self provides a point of entry into an individual's own thought processes (and subjectivity) through the mediation of normalizing discourse. Taking up a subject-position in a certain social discourse provides the individual with knowledge and rationale for actions with which the individual unwittingly identifies. In identifying as its subject, the individual assumes responsibility for the ideas and actions to which that discourse gives rise. So, for example, the woman who identifies as the subject of a certain normalizing discourse on female beauty believes that she freely chooses to apply make-up every day, and that it is her choice to monitor and discipline her bodily functions in such a way as to keep her weight and appearance within certain norms. The appearance of choice is served by the impersonal and invisible nature of disciplinary discourse: there is no obvious cause for this woman's behavior other than her own thoughts and actions.[10]

Foucault's concern with technologies of the self arises from his earlier work tracing the emergence of the "hermeneutic self" (a self who understands himself or herself through self-interpretation) from Christian confessional practices, which he thought offered a particularly clear view of the interplay of institutional power and subjectivity. Foucault notes that the goal of conduct of the ancient Greeks and Romans was self-mastery. By contrast, in the disciplinary discourse of the early Christians individual sinners were required to bear witness to themselves by employing various means of publicizing their inner thoughts and desires: as the penitents who announce their sins in sackcloth and ashes, or the monk who verbalizes his every thought to his superior.

In this way, Christianity gave rise to a distinct knowledge of the self (a "subjective field of data") which articulates its own subject-position, namely, that of the subject of a publicly mediated self-interpretation. Henceforth, the subjects speak the truth about themselves *to another* and then understand who they are in relation to the public/expert interpretation of their confession/narrative. This technology of the self rests upon the key Christian idea that God speaks the truth within oneself, and that bringing the truth to light brings freedom (Foucault calls this the "repressive hypothesis"). This system of thought has become so pervasive that it can be found everywhere from the psychiatrist's couch to performance management in the workplace to children's stories.

For Foucault the techniques of the self are directly concerned with ethics. This is because ethics concerns one's relation to oneself – what one is to make of oneself – and in this sense concerns one's moral agency. Like Nietzsche, Foucault regards ethics as a kind of aesthetics, which he calls *rapport à soi*, or "care of the self." He argues that the hermeneutic self adds another level of complexity to the means by which techniques of domination can permeate subjectivity, because the modern subjects now constitute themselves *as* subjects only through constituting themselves as the subject of disciplinary discourses which they regard as originating in their own thoughts, tastes, and choices. With such a close attachment to agency, the danger is that disciplinary discourses threaten to colonize the entirety of moral life.

Foucault warns that philosophy must come to grips with the fact that self is "the historical correlation of the technology built into our history"[11] if it is to find a suitable basis for ethics and politics. He sounds a clear warning about the dangers of the increasingly popular narrative conception of self. Without a critical capacity, such a model is going to succumb to the coercive discourses of modernity. However, it is not clear that Foucault's nonnormative, nonevaluative account of power can provide the necessary moment for critical reflection either. What Foucault needs is an aesthetic model with a critical capacity. This is what Paul Ricoeur tries to provide in his account of the narrative self.

Notes

1   See Georges Canguilhem, *The Normal and the Pathological*, trans. Carolyn Fawcett (New York: Zone Books, 1991), pp. 141–3.
2   See, for example, Irene Diamond and Lee Quinby (eds.), *Foucault and Feminism: Reflections on Resistance* (Boston: Northeastern University Press, 1988); Lois Macnay, *Foucault and Feminism: Power, Gender and Self* (Cambridge, UK: Polity, 1992).
3   Michel Foucault, "Preface" to *The History of Sexuality*, vol. II, reprinted in Paul Rabinow (ed.), *The Foucault Reader* (London and New York: Penguin, 1991), p. 334.
4   Rabinow (1991), p. 334.
5   For example, Luce Irigaray provides a sustained critique of the ways in which philosophical discourses presuppose a masculine subject. See *Speculum of the Other Woman*, trans. Gillian C. Gill (Ithaca, NY: Cornell University Press, 1987).
6   Hubert Dreyfus and Paul Rabinow, *Michel Foucault: Beyond Structuralism and Hermeneutics*, 2nd edn. (Chicago: University of Chicago Press, 1983), p. 173.
7   Jürgen Habermas, *The Philosophical Discourse of Modernity*, trans. Frederick Lawrence (Cambridge, UK: Polity, 1987).
8   Michel Foucault, "About the Beginning of the Hermeneutic of the Self," *Political Theory*, 21 (2), 1993, p. 203.

9   Foucault (1993), p. 203.

10 Susan Bordo, "Anorexia Nervosa: Psychopathology as the Crystallization of Culture," in Diamond and Quinby (1988), pp. 87–117.

11 Foucault (1993), p. 222.

Main Texts by Foucault

Alan Sheridan (trans.), *The Archaeology of Knowledge* (London: Tavistock, 1972).

Alan Sheridan (trans.), *The Birth of the Clinic* (London: Tavistock, 1973).

Robert Hurley (trans.), *The Care of the Self: The History of Sexuality,* vol. 3 (New York: Pantheon, 1985).

Alan Sheridan (trans.), *Discipline and Punish* (London: Allen and Unwin, 1977).

Robert Hurley (trans.), *The History of Sexuality, Volume 1: An Introduction* (London: Allen and Unwin/Penguin, 1978).

Alan Sheridan (trans.), *The Order of Things: An Archaeology of the Human Sciences* (London: Tavistock, 1970).

Robert Hurley (trans.), *The Uses of Pleasure: The History of Sexuality,* vol. 2 (New York: Pantheon 1985).

Further Reading

Bernauer, J. and D. Rassmussen (eds.), *The Final Foucault* (Cambridge, MA: MIT Press, 1992).

Dreyfus, H. and P. Rabinow, *Michel Foucault: Beyond Structuralism and Hermeneutics,* 2nd edn. (Chicago: University of Chicago Press, 1983).

Gutting, Gary (ed.), *The Cambridge Companion to Foucault* (Cambridge, UK: Cambridge University Press, 1994).

Han, Béatrice, *Foucault's Critical Project: Between the Transcendental and the Historical,* trans. Edward Pile (Stanford, CA: Stanford University Press, 2002).

Hoy, David (ed.), *Foucault: A Critical Reader* (Oxford: Blackwell, 1986).

Lois McNay, *Foucault: A Critical Introduction* (Cambridge, UK: Polity, 1994).

"ABOUT THE BEGINNINGS OF THE HERMENEUTICS OF THE SELF: TWO LECTURES AT DARTMOUTH"

Michel Foucault

Subjectivity and Truth

In a work consecrated to the moral treatment of madness and published in 1840, a French psychiatrist, Leuret, tells of the manner in which he has treated one of his patients – treated and, as you can imagine, of course, cured. One morning Dr. Leuret takes Mr. A., his patient, into a shower room. He makes him recount in detail his delirium.

"Well, all that," says the doctor, "is nothing but madness. Promise me not to believe in it anymore."

The patient hesitates, then promises.

"That's not enough," replies the doctor. "You have already made similar promises, and you haven't kept them." And the doctor turns on a cold shower above the patient's head.

"Yes, yes! I am mad!" the patient cries.

The shower is turned off, and the interrogation is resumed.

"Yes, I recognize that I am mad," the patient repeats, adding, "I recognize, because you are forcing me to do so."

Another shower. Another confession. The interrogation is taken up again.

"I assure you, however," says the patient, "that I have heard voices and seen enemies around me."

Another shower.

"Well," says Mr. A., the patient, "I admit it. I am mad; all that was madness."[1]

★ ★ ★ ★ ★

To make someone suffering from mental illness recognize that he is mad is a very ancient procedure. Everybody in the old medicine, before the middle of the nineteenth

From *Political Theory*, 21 (1993), pp. 200–4, 210–15, 223–7 (notes). Reprinted by permission of Sage Publications.

century, everybody was convinced of the incompatibility between madness and recognition of madness. And in the works, for instance, of the seventeenth and of the eighteenth centuries, one finds many examples of what one might call truth-therapies. The
mad would be cured if one managed to show them that their delirium is without any
relation to reality.

But, as you see, the technique used by Leuret is altogether different. He is not trying
to persuade his patient that his ideas are false or unreasonable. What happens in the
head of Mr. A. is a matter of indifference for the doctor. Leuret wishes to obtain a
precise act: the explicit affirmation, "I am mad." It is easy to recognize here the trans-
position within psychiatric therapy of procedures which have been used for a long time
in judicial and religious institutions. To declare aloud and intelligibly the truth about
oneself – I mean, to confess – has in the Western world been considered for a long
time either as a condition for redemption for one's sins or as an essential item in the
condemnation of the guilty. The bizarre therapy of Leuret may be read as an episode
in the progressive culpabilization of madness. But, I would wish, rather, to take it as a
point of departure for a more general reflection on this practice of confession, and on
the postulate, which is generally accepted in Western societies, that one needs for his
own salvation to know as exactly as possible who he is and also, which is something
rather different, that he needs to tell it as explicitly as possible to some other people.
The anecdote of Leuret is here only as an example of the strange and complex
relationships developed in our societies between individuality, discourse, truth, and
coercion.

In order to justify the attention I am giving to what is seemingly so specialized a
subject, let me take a step back for a moment. All that, after all is only for me a means
that I will use to take on a much more general theme – that is, the genealogy of the
modern subject.

In the years that preceded the second war, and even more so after the second war,
philosophy in France and, I think, in all continental Europe, was dominated by the philosophy of the subject. I mean that philosophy set as its task *par excellence* the foundation of all knowledge and the principle of all signification as stemming from the
meaningful subject. The importance given to this question of the meaningful subject
was of course due to the impact of Husserl – only his *Cartesian Meditations* and the
Crisis were generally known in France[2] – but the centrality of the subject was also tied
to an institutional context. For the French university, since philosophy began with
Descartes, it could only advance in a Cartesian manner. But we must also take into
account the political conjuncture. Given the absurdity of wars, slaughters, and despot-
ism, it seemed then to be up to the individual subject to give meaning to his existential choices.

With the leisure and distance that came after the war, this emphasis on the philosophical subject no longer seemed so self-evident. Two hitherto-hidden theoretical
paradoxes could no longer be avoided. The first one was that the philosophy of
consciousness had failed to found a philosophy of knowledge, and especially scientific
knowledge, and the second was that this philosophy of meaning paradoxically had failed
to take into account the formative mechanisms of signification and the structure of
systems of meaning. I am aware that another form of thought claimed then to have
gone beyond the philosophy of the subject – this, of course, was Marxism. It goes

without saying – and it goes indeed better if we say it – that neither materialism nor the theory of ideologies successfully constituted a theory of objectivity or of signification. Marxism put itself forward as a humanistic discourse that could replace the abstract subject with an appeal to the real man, to the concrete man. It should have been clear at the time that Marxism carried with it a fundamental theoretical and practical weakness: the humanistic discourse hid the political reality that the Marxists of this period nonetheless supported.

With the all-too-easy clarity of hindsight – what you call, I think, the "Monday morning quarterback" – let me say that there were two possible paths that led beyond this philosophy of the subject. First, the theory of objective knowledge and, two, an analysis of systems of meaning, or semiology. The first of these was the path of logical positivism. The second was that of a certain school of linguistics, psychoanalysis, and anthropology, all generally grouped under the rubric of structuralism.

These were not the directions I took. Let me announce once and for all that I am not a structuralist, and I confess with the appropriate chagrin that I am not an analytic philosopher – nobody is perfect. I have tried to explore another direction. I have tried to get out from the philosophy of the subject through a genealogy of this subject, by studying the constitution of the subject across history which has led us up to the modern concept of the self. This has not always been an easy task, since most historians prefer a history of social processes, and most philosophers prefer a subject without history. This has neither prevented me from using the same material that certain social historians have used, nor from recognizing my theoretical debt to those philosophers who, like Nietzsche, have posed the question of the historicity of the subject.

Up to the present I have proceeded with this general project in two ways. I have dealt with the modern theoretical constitutions that were concerned with the subject in general. I have tried to analyze in a previous book theories of the subject as a speaking, living, working being.[3] I have also dealt with the more practical understanding formed in those institutions like hospitals, asylums, and prisons, where certain subjects became objects of knowledge and at the same time objects of domination.[4] And now, I wish to study those forms of understanding which the subject creates about himself. Those forms of self-understanding are important I think to analyze the modern experience of sexuality.[5]

But since I have started with this last type of project I have been obliged to change my mind on several important points. Let me introduce a kind of autocritique. It seems, according to some suggestions by Habermas, that one can distinguish three major types of techniques in human societies: the techniques which permit one to produce, to transform, to manipulate things; the techniques which permit one to use sign systems; and the techniques which permit one to determine the conduct of individuals, to impose certain wills on them, and to submit them to certain ends or objectives. That is to say, there are techniques of production, techniques of signification, and techniques of domination.[6]

Of course, if one wants to study the history of natural sciences, it is useful if not necessary to take into account techniques of production and semiotic techniques. But since my project was concerned with the knowledge of the subject, I thought that the techniques of domination were the most important, without any exclusion of the rest. But, analyzing the experience of sexuality, I became more and more aware that there is in all societies, I think, in all societies whatever they are, another type of techniques: techniques which permit individuals to effect, by their own means, a certain number of operations on their own bodies, on their own souls, on their own thoughts, on their own conduct, and this in a manner so as to transform themselves, modify themselves, and to attain a certain state of perfection, of happiness, of purity, of supernatural power, and so on. Let's call this kind of techniques a techniques or technology of the self.[7]

I think that if one wants to analyze the genealogy of the subject in Western civilization, he has to take into account not only techniques of domination but also techniques of the self. Let's say: he has to take into account the interaction between those two types of techniques – techniques of domination and techniques of the self. He has to take into account the points where the technologies of domination of individuals over one another have recourse to processes by which the individual acts upon himself. And conversely, he has to take into account the points where the techniques of the self are integrated into structures of coercion or domination. The contact point, where the individuals are driven by others is tied to the way they conduct themselves, is what we can call, I think, government.[8] Governing people, in the broad meaning of the word, governing people is not a way to force people to do what the governor wants; it is always a versatile equilibrium, with complementarity and conflicts between techniques which assure coercion and processes through which the self is constructed or modified by himself.

When I was studying asylums, prisons, and so on, I insisted, I think, too much on the techniques of domination. What we can call discipline is something really important in these kinds of institutions, but it is only one aspect of the art of governing people in our society. We must not understand the exercise of power as pure violence or strict coercion. Power consists in complex relations: these relations involve a set of rational techniques, and the efficiency of those techniques is due to a subtle integration of coercion-technologies and self-technologies. I think that we have to get rid of the more or less Freudian schema – you know it – the schema of interiorization of the law by the self. Fortunately, from a theoretical point of view, and maybe unfortunately from a practical point of view, things are much more complicated than that. In short, having studied the field of government by taking as my point of departure techniques of domination, I would like in years to come to study government – especially in the field of sexuality – starting from the techniques of the self.[9]

Among those techniques of the self in this field of the self-technology, I think that the techniques oriented toward the discovery and the formulation of the truth concerning oneself are extremely important; and, if for the government of people in our societies everyone had not only to obey but also to produce and publish the truth about oneself, then examination of conscience and confession are among the most important of those procedures. Of course, there is a very long and very complex history, from the Delphic precept, *gnothi seauton* ("know yourself") to the strange therapeutics promoted by Leuret, about which I was speaking in the beginning of this lecture. There is a very long way from one to the other, and I don't want, of course, to give you even a survey this evening. I'd like only to underline a transformation of those practices, a transformation which took place at the beginning of the Christian era, of the Christian period, when the ancient obligation of knowing oneself became the monastic precept "confess, to your spiritual guide, each of your thoughts." This transformation is, I think, of some importance in the genealogy of modern subjectivity. With this transformation starts what we would call the hermeneutics of the self.

[. . .]

Christianity and Confession

The theme of this lecture is the same as the theme of last week's lecture. The theme is: how was formed in our societies what I would like to call the interpretive analysis of the self; or, how was formed the hermeneutics of the self in the modern, or at least in the Christian and the modern, societies? In spite of the fact that we can find very early in the Greek, in the Hellenistic, in the Latin cultures, techniques such as self-examination and confession, I think that there are very large differences between the Latin and Greek – the Classical – techniques of the self and the techniques developed in Christianity. And I'll try to show this evening that the modern hermeneutics of the self is rooted much more in those Christian techniques than in the Classical ones. The *gnothi seauton* is, I think, much less influential in our societies, in our culture, than is supposed to be.

As everybody knows, Christianity is a confession. That means that Christianity belongs to a very special type of religion, the religions which impose on those who practice them obligation of truth. Such obligations in Christianity are numerous; for instance, a Christian has the obligation to hold as true a set of propositions which con-stitutes a dogma; or, he has the obligation to hold certain books as a permanent source of truth; or, he has the obligation to accept the decisions of certain authorities in matters of truth.

But Christianity requires another form of truth obligation quite different from those I just mentioned. Everyone, every Christian, has the duty to know who he is, what is happening in him. He has to know the faults he may have committed: he has to know the temptations to which he is exposed. And, moreover, everyone in Christianity is obliged to say these things to other people, to tell these things to other people, and hence, to bear witness against himself.

A few remarks. These two ensembles of obligations, those regarding the faith, the book, the dogma, and the obligations regarding the self, the soul, the heart, are linked together. A Christian is always supposed to be supported by the light of faith if he wants to explore himself, and, conversely, access to the truth of the faith cannot be conceived of without the purification of the soul. As Augustine said, in a Latin formula I'm sure you'll understand, *qui facit veritatem venit ad lucem.* That means: *facite veritatem*, "to make truth inside oneself," and *venire ad lucem*, "to get access to the light." Well, to make truth inside of oneself, and to get access to the light of God, and so on, those two processes are strongly connected in the Christian experience. But those two relationships to truth, you can find them equally connected, as you know, in Buddhism, and they were also connected in all the Gnostic movements of the first centuries. But there, either in Buddhism or in the Gnostic movements, those two relationships to truth were connected in such a way that they were almost identified. To discover the truth inside oneself, to decipher the real nature and the authentic origin of the soul, was consid-ered by the Gnosticists as one thing with coming through to the light.

On the contrary, one of the main characteristics of orthodox Christianity, one of the main differences between Christianity and Buddhism, or between Christianity and Gnosticism, one of the main reasons for the mistrust of Christianity toward mystics, and one of the most constant historical features of Christianity, is that those two systems of obligation, of truth obligation – the one concerned with access to light and the one concerned with the making of truth, the discovering of truth inside oneself – those two systems of obligation have always maintained a relative autonomy. Even after Luther, even in Protestantism, the secrets of the soul and the mysteries of the faith, the self and the book, are not in Christianity enlightened by exactly the same type of light. They demand different methods and put into operation particular techniques.

★ ★ ★ ★ ★

Well, let's put aside the long history of their complex and often conflictual relations before and after the Reformation. I'd like this evening to focus attention on the second of those two systems of obligation. I'd like to focus on the obligation imposed on every Christian to manifest the truth about himself. When one speaks of confession and self-examination in Christianity, one of course has in mind the sacrament of penance and the canonic confession of sins. But these are rather late innovations in Christianity. Christians of the first centuries knew completely different forms for the showing forth of the truth about themselves, and you'll find these obligations of manifesting the truth about oneself in two different institutions – in penitential rites and monastic life. And I would like first to examine the penitential rites and the obligations of truth, the truth obligations which are related, which are connected with those penitential rites. I will not enter, of course, into the discussions which have taken place and which continue until now as to the progressive development of these rites. I would like only to under-line one fundamental fact: in the first centuries of Christianity, penance was not an act. Penance, in the first centuries of Christianity, penance is a status, which presents several characteristics. The function of this status is to avoid the definitive expulsion from the church of a Christian who has committed one or several serious sins. As penitent, this Christian is excluded from many of the ceremonies and collective rites, but he does not cease to be a Christian, and by means of this status he can obtain his reintegration. And this status is therefore a long-term affair. This status affects most aspects of his life – fasting obligations, rules about clothing, interdictions on sexual relations – and the individual is marked to such an extent by this status that even after his reconciliation, after his reintegration in the community, he will still suffer from a certain number of prohibitions (for instance, he will not be able to become a priest). So penance is not an act corresponding to a sin; it is a status, a general status in the existence.

Now, amongst the elements of this status, the obligation to manifest the truth is fun-damental. I don't say that enunciation of sins is fundamental; I employ a much more imprecise and obscure expression. I say that manifestation of the truth is necessary and is deeply connected with this status of penance. In fact, to designate the truth games or the truth obligations inherent to penitents, the Greek fathers used a word, a very specific word (and very enigmatic also); the word *exomologesis*. This word was so spe-cific that even Latin writers, Latin fathers, often used the Greek word without even translating it.[10]

What does this term *exomologesis* mean? In a very general sense, the word refers to the recognition of an act, but more precisely, in the penitential rite, what was the *exomologesis?* Well, at the end of the penitential procedure, at the end and not at the beginning, at the end of the penitential procedure, when the moment of the reintegration came, an episode took place which the texts regularly call *exomologesis*. Some descriptions are very early and some very late, but they are quite identical. Tertullian, for instance, at the end of the second century, describes the ceremony in the following manner. He wrote, "The penitent wears a hair shirt and ashes. He is wretchedly dressed. He is taken by the hand and led into the church. He prostrates himself before the widows and the priest. He hangs on the skirts of their garments. He kisses their knees."[11] And much later after this, in the beginning of the fifth century, Jerome described in the same way the penitence of Fabiola. Fabiola was a woman, a well-known Roman noblewoman, who had married a second time before the death of her first husband, which was something quite bad, and she then was obliged to do penance. And Jerome describes thus this penance: "During the days which preceded Easter," which was the moment of the reconciliation,

> during the days which preceded Easter, Fabiola was to be found among the ranks of the penitents. The bishop, the priests, and the people wept with her. Her hair disheveled, her face pale, her hands dirty, her head covered in ashes, she chastened her naked breast and the face with which she had seduced her second husband. She revealed to all her wound, and Rome, in tears, contemplated the scars on her emaciated body.[12]

No doubt Jerome and Tertullian were liable to be rather carried away by such things; however, in Ambrose and in others one finds indications which show clearly the existence of an episode of dramatic self-revelation at the moment of the reconciliation of the penitent. That was, specifically, the *exomologesis*.

But the term of *exomologesis* does not apply only to this final episode. Frequently the word *exomologesis* is used to designate everything that the penitent does to obtain his reconciliation during the time in which he retains the status of penitent. The acts by which he punishes himself must be indissociable from the acts by which he reveals himself. The punishment of oneself and the voluntary expression of oneself are bound together.

A correspondent of Cyprian in the middle of the third century writes, for instance, that those who wish to do penance must, I quote, "prove their suffering, show their shame, make visible their humility, and exhibit their modesty."[13] And, in the *Paraenesis*, Pacian says that the true penance is accomplished not in a nominal fashion but finds its instruments in sackcloth, ashes, fasting, affliction, and the participation of a great number of people in prayers. In a few words, penance in the first Christian centuries is a way of life acted out at all times out of an obligation to show oneself. And that is, exactly, *exomologesis*.

As you see, this *exomologesis* did not obey a judicial principle of correlation, of exact correlation, adjusting the punishment to the crime. *Exomologesis* obeyed a law of dramatic emphasis and of maximum theatricality. And, neither did this *exomologesis* obey a truth principle of correspondence between verbal enunciation and reality. As you see, no description in this *exomologesis* is of a penance; no confession, no verbal enumeration of sins, no analysis of the sins, but somatic expressions and symbolic expressions.

Fabiola did not confess her fault, telling to somebody what she has done, but she put under everybody's eyes the flesh, the body, which has committed the sin. And, paradoxically, the *exomologesis* is this time to rub out the sin, restitute the previous purity acquired by baptism, and this by showing the sinner as he is in his reality – dirty, defiled, sullied.

Tertullian has a word to translate the Greek word *exomologesis*; he said it was *publicatio sui*, the Christian had to publish himself.[14] Publish oneself, that means that he has two things to do. One has to show oneself as a sinner; that means, as somebody who, choosing the path of the sin, preferred filthiness to purity, earth and dust to heaven, spiritual poverty to the treasures of faith. In a word, he has to show himself as somebody who preferred spiritual death to earthen life. And that was the reason why *exomologesis* was a kind of representation of death. It was the theatrical representation of the sinner as dead or as dying. But this *exomologesis* was also a way for the sinner to express his will to get free from this world, to get rid of his own body, to destroy his own flesh, and get access to a new spiritual life. It is the theatrical representation of the sinner as willing his own death as a sinner. It is the dramatic manifestation of the renunciation to oneself.

To justify this *exomologesis* and this renunciation to oneself in manifesting the truth about oneself, Christian fathers had recourse to several models. The well-known medical model was very often used in pagan philosophy: one has to show his wounds to the physicians if he wants to be healed. They also used the judicial model: one always appeases the court when spontaneously confessing the faults. But the most important model to justify the necessity of *exomologesis* is the model of martyrdom. The martyr is he who prefers to face death rather than to abandon his faith. The sinner abandons the faith in order to keep the life of here below; he will be reinstated only if in his turn he exposes himself voluntarily to a sort of martyrdom to which all will be witnesses, and which is penance, or penance as *exomologesis*. Such a demonstration does not therefore have as its function the establishment of the personal identity. Rather, such a demonstration serves to mark this dramatic demonstration of what one is: the refusal of the self, the breaking off from one's self. One recalls what was the objective of Stoic technology: it was to superimpose, as I tried to explain to you last week, the subject of knowledge and the subject of will by means of the perpetual rememorizing of the rules. The formula which is at the heart of *exomologesis* is, in contrary, *ego non sum ego*. The *exomologesis* seeks, in opposition to the Stoic techniques, to superimpose by an act of violent rupture the truth about oneself and the renunciation of oneself. In the ostentatious gestures of maceration, self-revelation in *exomologesis* is, at the same time, self-destruction.

Notes

1   See François Leuret, *Du traitement morale de la folie* (Paris: J. B. Bailliere, 1840), and Foucault, *Maladie mentale et psychologie*, 3rd edn (Paris: PUF, 1966), pp. 85–6; *Mental Illness and Psychology*, translated by Alan Sheridan (New York: Harper & Row, 1976), p. 72.
2   Edmund Husserl, *Méditations Cartésiennes*, translated by Gabrielle Peiffer and Emmanuel Lewis (Paris: Arman Colin, 1931); *Cartesian Meditations: An Introduction to Phenomenology*, translated by Dorian Cairns (The Hague: Martinus Nijhoff, 1973).

3   *Les Mots et les choses* (Paris: Gallimard, 1966); *The Order of Things*, translated by Alan Sheridan (New York: Pantheon, 1970).

4   *Naissance de la clinique* (Paris: Presses Universitaires de France, 1963, 1972); *The Birth of the Clinic*, translated by Alan Sheridan (New York: Pantheon, 1973) and *Surveiller et punir* (Paris: Gallimard, 1975); *Discipline and Punish*, translated by Alan Sheridan (New York: Pantheon, 1977).

5   *La Volonté de savoir* (Paris: Gallimard, 1976); *The History of Sexuality, vol. I: An Introduction*, translated by Robert Hurley (New York: Pantheon, 1978); *L' Usage des plaisirs* (Paris: Gallimard, 1984); *The Use of Pleasure*, translated by Robert Hurley (New York: Pantheon, 1985); *Le Souci de soi* (Paris: Gallimard, 1984); *The Care of the Self*, translated by Robert Hurley (New York: Pantheon, 1986).

6   Jürgen Habermas, *Erkenntnis und Interesse* (Frankfurt am Main: Suhrkamp Verlag, 1968) and appendix in *Technik und Wissenschaft als "Ideologie"* (Frankfurt am Main: Suhrkamp Verlag, 1968); *Knowledge and Human Interests*, translated by Jeremy Shapiro (Boston: Beacon, 1971), esp. "Appendix: Knowledge and Human Interests, A General Perspective," p. 313.

7   *Technologies of the Self: A Seminar with Michel Foucault*, edited by Luther H. Martin, Huck Gutman, and Patrick H. Hutton (Amherst: University of Massachusetts Press, 1988).

8   *The Foucault Effect: Studies in Governmentality*, edited by Graham Burchell et al. (Chicago: University of Chicago Press, 1991).

9   *Resumé de cours, 1970–1982* (Paris: Julliard, 1989), pp. 133–66; "Sexuality and Solitude," *London Review of Books*, 3, no. 9 (May 21–June 3, 1981), pp. 3, 5–6.

10 *Technologies of the Self*, pp. 39–43.

11 Tertullian, "On Repentance," in *The Ante-Nicene Fathers*, edited by A. Roberts and J. Donaldson (Grand Rapids, MI: Eerdmans, n.d., repr. 1979), pp. 657–68, esp. "Exomologesis," chaps. 9–12, 664–6.

12 Jerome, "Letter LXXVII, to Oceanus," in *The Principal Works of St. Jerome*, translated by W. H. Freemantle, vol. 6 in *A Select Library of Nicene and Post-Nicene Fathers* (New York: Christian Literature Co., 1893), pp. 157–62, esp. 159–60.

13 Cyprian, "Letter XXXVI, from the Priests and Deacons Abiding in Rome to Pope Cyprian," in *Saint Cyprian: Letters (1–81)*, 90–94 at 93, translated by Sister Rose Bernard Donna, C. S. J., vol. 51 in *The Fathers of the Church* (Washington, DC: Catholic University of America Press, 1964).

14 "On Repentance," chap. 10.

17

COMMENTARY ON RICOEUR

French philosopher Paul Ricoeur (born 1913) is Emeritus Professor of Philosophy at the Universities of Chicago and Paris. His work is distinctive in its breadth and depth of scholarship and innovative style, which brings together the methods of philosophy of language with the textual strategies of post-structuralism in the context of a practical ontology. Writing within the phenomenological tradition, Ricoeur's main focus has been a hermeneutics of the self, from which he has developed his narrative theory. He argues that our self-understandings are "fictive," that is, subject to the productive effects of the imagination through interpretative processes which take a narrative form. It is Ricoeur's contention that narrative alone can respond appropriately to the exigencies of the human, embodied situation.

Ricoeur argues that human embodiment endows us with a "double allegiance": on one hand, we are bound by the laws of the natural world in virtue of our bodily existence, and on the other to the phenomenal world of freedom by which we break away from those laws through action.[1] Significantly, this means that we can, to some extent, act upon and change ourselves through our own efforts. This double nature structures human existence with a series of dialectically related dualities, for example, activity and passivity, subjectivity and objectivity, identity and diversity, particularity and multiplicity. Significant among these dual structures are two orders of time: the time of the natural world (cosmological or objective time), and the time of consciousness (phenomenological time). We belong to cosmological time insofar as we are born, grow, and die. In that sense the beginnings, middles, and ends of life are given and immutable. However, we employ another, phenomenological, sense of "beginning," "middle," and "end," which refers to the stages of actions. On Ricoeur's view, the continuity and coherence of a person's life turns on the integration of these two orders of time. Ricoeur argues that the resources for this kind of integration are found, not in philosophy, but in literature, in the textual strategies of narrative.

The twin experience of time gives rise to specific problems when it comes to personal identity, because identity concerns sameness over time. In this excerpt from *Oneself as Another*, Ricoeur turns his attention to the question of a conception of sameness that would be appropriate to the temporality of human being. He notes that "sameness" conveys several senses: numerical identity (being one and the same); qualitative identity (extreme resemblance) and uninterrupted continuity (being the same living thing) – all of which pertain to the complex phenomenon of personal identity. The difficulty for an account of personal identity is to find a model of permanence in time that can express each of the different temporal senses of "same."

The traditional philosophical approach has endeavored to explain *what* it is that makes a person the same at different times. However, Ricoeur argues that any account of personal identity must acknowledge our double allegiance by regarding a person as both a material object (a "what") and as an agent of his or her actions (a "who"). The two corresponding conceptions of identity here are what Ricoeur calls *idem* identity and *ipse* identity (or ipseity). *Idem* identity refers to the sameness of objects and is expressed in objective terms (in the third person). *Ipse* identity refers to the sameness of self and is expressed only in the first person. What Ricoeur is looking for is a model which can express and relate these two aspects of selfhood.

Ricoeur nominates two candidates for this role: character and keeping one's word, each of which are said to represent a pole in "a single existential of selfhood" – a structure that, ultimately, will be mediated through the resources of narrative. Ricoeur's theoretical guides in this respect are Kant and the spontaneity of the productive imagination, Heidegger's concept of Dasein, and Merleau-Ponty's account of the schematizing role of one's own body.

Ricoeur describes the permanence of character as "the set of lasting dispositions by which a person is recognized."[2] The dispositional nature of character lends it an air of fixity which grants its status as the "what" of identity. However, the stability of character conceals an essentially dynamic process whereby character traits are laid down through "innovation" and "sedimentation." It is the sedimentation of actively acquired attributes into bodily dispositions that produces the objective "what" by which we understand a person's character. This occurs when a novel experience (innovation) gives rise to ideas and emotions that are then taken on as attributes of one's consciousness and personality. Importantly, for Ricoeur, innovative attribution is not a passive process, but an active process of integration into the conceptual and practical system that is the embodied subject. Sedimentation, on the other hand, is the settled and habitual ways of perceiving and thinking through attributes laid down in innovation. In this way, sedimentation gives rise to character traits – states of affairs – that conform to *idem* identity, the "what" of identity.

Ricoeur turns his attention to the "who" of identity. He notes that the formation of character and personal identity involves a form of "fidelity to self," or self-appropriation. This is demonstrated, he claims, in those cases of "acquired identifications" where one actively identifies with certain *given* norms and ideals and in doing so, recognizes oneself through those identifications.[3] This, he says, forms the second model of permanence in time – ipseity or self-constancy. Ipseity brings to the processes by which the permanence of character is instituted an inner, first-person self-referential activity in which one takes one's attributes *as* one's own and in doing so, carries those attributes forward in time, constituting the continuity (permanence in time) of *who* one is.

Ricoeur develops his account of self-constancy from Heidegger's conception of Dasein. Recall that on this view, it is of the essence of selfhood that one take one's existence as an issue for oneself; a self is given to oneself as a question. For Ricoeur and Heidegger, the question "who?" pertains uniquely to the kind of being which is characterized by the capacity to question itself and relate itself to its own being. Having the existential structure of a question, selfhood has a temporal gap at its heart, a fundamental indeterminacy and openness that drives the need for meaning. Because the self is ontologically "at a distance" from itself, so to speak, it has to fill that gap itself, since the gap is nothing other than the question of its own meaning *for itself*. Selfhood, by its very nature then, demands that the self constitute its own continuity. The permanence in time appropriate here is exemplified in the case of keeping one's word. In keeping one's word, one projects who one is now forward to a future time, and at that future time remains faithful to one's earlier professions concerning who one is. In this way one effects self-constancy and one's permanence in time.

The coordination of these two kind of permanence in time (*idem* and ipseity) requires complex conceptual and temporal strategies. For Ricoeur, those strategies are to be found in narrative. Ricoeur's arguments here are complex and are set out in detail in the three volumes of *Time and Narrative*. Briefly, narrative is said to provide the means for creating a temporally continuous conceptual whole out of the heterogeneous elements of a life by bringing those elements into relations of emplotment. Narrative has this particular capacity because it is, to cite Aristotle, "the imitation of an action," and the human world is a world of action. Narrative and action, says Ricoeur, share a semantic network which systematically connects its heterogeneous elements – the who, what, where, how, why, with whom, under what circumstances, with what object, and so forth – to comprise the intelligibility of "doing something." Ricoeur claims that it is these synthetic powers of narrative that provide the strategies that make our double-natured (that is, heterogeneous) lives coherent and meaningful. The narrative coherence and intelligibility of one's life turns on the integration of one's beliefs, experiences, emotions, desires, actions, bodily and rational capacities, which follows a process that Ricoeur likens to the role of the schematizing productive imagination in Kant's epistemology (an argument he presents in his account of the productive powers of metaphor, in *The Rule of Metaphor*).

Importantly, on Ricoeur's account, narrative deploys a moral, critical capacity – the capacity to reflect upon and evaluate one's character or one's actions, or one's life as a whole. Ricoeur describes ethics as the "the plane of action and evaluation." Because we act, we necessarily evaluate our actions. Actions necessitate evaluation because they aim at something, and so can be judged with respect to whether or how that aim is achieved. Ricoeur argues that the teleological structure of action extends over a whole life because, understood narratively, a life just is a complex of interrelated actions. He maintains that life thus understood has a *telos*, namely the good life.[4] The ethical aim of the "good life" is a broad evaluation of the complex of actions that constitute one's whole life. Importantly, this kind of evaluation is possible only if one takes a narrative view of one's life. In evaluating one's actions or life, Ricoeur argues that one is not free to construct any narrative at all, but is constrained by the intersubjective and objective factors in one's existence. On Ricoeur's view, the justification for a narrative is forensic and made by appeal to evidence, similar to the processes followed in courts of law.[5] A narrative is preferred to another when it is more explanatory, has a higher degree of integration of its various elements, and therefore provides more compelling reasons for the claims it makes.

The narrative view is, relatively speaking, in its philosophical infancy, but its synthetic and imaginative strategies offer an innovative and complex response to the challenges posed by the decentering and fragmenting of subjectivity within postmodern philosophies influenced by Nietzsche and Freud; the impersonality of reductionist philosophies of mind; as well as the threat of relativism within a multicultural, global, moral community.

Notes

1 See Paul Ricoeur, "Explanation and Understanding," in Charles Reagan and David Stewart (eds.), *The Philosophy of Paul Ricoeur: An Anthology of his Work* (Boston: Beacon Press, 1978), pp. 149–66.

2 Paul Ricoeur, *Oneself As Another*, trans. Kathleen Blamey (Chicago: University of Chicago Press, 1992), p. 121.

3 Ibid.

4 Ibid, Study 7, "The Self and The Ethical Aim."

5 *Time and Narrative*, vol. 1, trans. Kathleen McLaughlin and David Pellauer (Chicago: University of Chicago Press, 1984), pp. 74–5.

Main Texts by Ricoeur

Don Ihde (ed.), Willis Domingo et al. (trans.), *The Conflict of Interpretations: Essays in Hermeneutics* (Evanston, IL: Northwestern University Press, 1974).

Kathleen Blamey (trans.), *Critique and Conviction* (New York: Columbia University Press, 1998).

Walter J. Lowe (trans. and introduction), *Fallible Man* (New York: Fordham University Press, 1986).

Denis Savage (trans.), *Freud and Philosophy: An Essay on Interpretation* (New Haven, CT: Yale University Press, 1970).

John B. Thompson (ed. and trans.), *Hermeneutics and the Human Sciences: Essays on Language, Action and Interpretation* (Cambridge, UK: Cambridge University Press, 1981).

Kathleen Blamey (trans.), *Oneself as Another* (Chicago: University of Chicago Press, 1992).

Robert Czerny with Kathleen McLaughlin and John Costello (trans.), *The Rule of Metaphor: Multi-Disciplinary Studies in the Creation of Meaning in Language* (London: Routledge and Kegan Paul, 1978).

Emerson Buchanan (trans.), *The Symbolism of Evil* (New York: Harper and Row, 1967).

Kathleen McLaughlin and David Pellauer (trans.), *Time and Narrative*, 3 vols. (Chicago: University of Chicago Press, 1984, 1985, 1988).

M. B. DeBevoise (trans.), *What Makes Us Think? A Neuroscientist and a Philosopher Argue About Ethics, Human Nature and the Brain*, with Jean-Pierre Changeux (Princeton, NJ and Oxford: Princeton University Press, 2000).

Further Reading

Clark, S. H., *Paul Ricoeur* (London and New York: Routledge, 1990).

Hahn, Lewis E. (ed.), *The Philosophy of Paul Ricoeur* (Chicago and La Salle, IL: Open Court, 1995).

Ihde, Don, *Hermeneutic Phenomenology: The Philosophy of Paul Ricoeur* (Evanston, IL: Northwestern University Press, 1971).

Kemp, T. P. and D. Rasmussen (eds.), *The Narrative Path: The Later Works of Paul Ricoeur* (Cambridge, MA: MIT Press, 1989).

Klemm, David E. and William Schweiker (eds.), *Meaning in Texts and Action: Questioning Paul Ricoeur* (Charlottesville: University Press of Virginia, 1993).

MacIntyre, Alasdair, *After Virtue* (London: Duckworth, 1981).

Reagan, Charles E. and David Stewart (eds.), *The Philosophy of Paul Ricoeur: An Anthology of his Work* (Boston: Beacon Press, 1978).

Wall, William and W. David Hall (eds.), *Paul Ricoeur and Contemporary Moral Thought* (New York and London: Routledge, 2002).

Wood, David (ed.), *On Paul Ricoeur* (London and New York: Routledge, 1991).

"PERSONAL IDENTITY AND NARRATIVE IDENTITY"

Paul Ricoeur

The Problem of Personal Identity

The problem of personal identity constitutes, in my opinion, a privileged place of confrontation between the two major uses of the concept of identity, which I have evoked many times without ever actually thematizing them. Let me recall the terms of the confrontation: on one side, identity as *sameness* (Latin *idem*, German *Gleichheit*, French *mêmeté*); on the other, identity as *selfhood* (Latin *ipse*, German *Selbstheit*, French *ipséité*). Selfhood, I have repeatedly affirmed, is not sameness. Because the major distinction between them is not recognized . . . the solutions offered to the problem of personal identity which do not consider the narrative dimension fail. If this difference is so essential, one might ask, why was it not treated in a thematic manner earlier, since its ghost has continually haunted the preceding analyses? The reason is that it is raised to the level of a problem only after the temporal implications have themselves moved to the forefront. Indeed, it is with the question of *permanence in time* that the confrontation between our two versions of identity becomes a genuine problem for the first time.

At first sight, in fact, the question of permanence in time is connected exclusively to *idem*-identity, which in a certain sense it crowns. It is indeed under this heading alone that the analytic theories that we will examine later approach the question of personal identity and the paradoxes related to it. Let us recall rapidly the conceptual articulation of sameness in order to indicate the eminent place that permanence in time holds there.

Sameness is a concept of relation and a relation of relations. First comes *numerical* identity: thus, we say of two occurrences of a thing, designated by an invariable noun in ordinary language, that they do not form two different things but "one and the same" thing. Here, identity denotes oneness: the contrary is plurality (not one but two or

From *Oneself As Another*, translated by Kathleen Blamey (Chicago and London: University of Chicago Press, 1992), pp. 115–18, 129–39. Reprinted by permission of the University of Chicago Press and Paul Ricoeur.

several). To this first component of the notion of identity corresponds the notion of identification, understood in the sense of the reidentification of the same, which makes cognition recognition: the same thing twice, *n* times.

In second place we find *qualitative* identity, in other words, extreme resemblance: we say that *x* and *y* are wearing the same suit – that is, clothes that are so similar that they are interchangeable with no noticeable difference. To this second component corresponds the operation of substitution without semantic loss, *salva veritate*.

These two components of identity are irreducible to one another, as are in Kant the categories of quantity and quality. But they are not thereby foreign to one another; it is precisely to the extent that time is implied in the series of occurrences of the same thing that the reidentification of the same can provoke hesitation, doubt, or contestation; the extreme resemblance between two or more occurrences can then be invoked as an indirect criterion to reinforce the presumption of numerical identity. This is what happens when we speak of the physical identity of a person. We have no trouble recognizing someone who simply enters and leaves, appears, disappears and reappears. Yet doubt is not far away when we compare a present perception with a recent memory. The identification of an aggressor by a victim from among a series of suspects who are presented affords an initial opportunity to introduce doubt; and with the distance of time, it grows. Hence a defendant appearing in court may object that he is not the same as the one who was incriminated. What happens then? One compares the individual present to the material marks held to be the irrecusable traces of his earlier presence in the very places at issue. It happens that this comparison is extended to eyewitness accounts, which, with a much greater margin of uncertainty, are held to be equivalent to the past presentation of the individual examined. The question of knowing whether the person here present in court and the presumed author of an earlier crime are one and the same individual may then remain without any sure answer. The trials of war criminals have occasioned just such confrontations along with, as we know, the ensuing risks and uncertainties.

The weakness of this criterion of similitude, in the case of a great distance in time, suggests that we appeal to another criterion, one which belongs to the third component of the notion of identity, namely the *uninterrupted continuity* between the first and the last stage in the development of what we consider to be the same individual. This criterion is predominant whenever growth or aging operate as factors of dissemblance and, by implication, of numerical diversity. Thus, we say of an oak tree that it is the same from the acorn to the fully developed tree; in the same way, we speak of one animal, from birth to death; so, too, we speak of a man or of a woman – I am not saying of a person – as a simple token of a species. The demonstration of this continuity functions as a supplementary or a substitutive criterion to similitude; the demonstration rests upon the ordered series of small changes which, taken one by one, threaten resemblance without destroying it. This is how we see photos of ourselves at successive ages of our life. As we see, time is here a factor of dissemblance, of divergence, of difference.

This is why the threat it represents for identity is not entirely dissipated unless we can posit, at the base of similitude and of the uninterrupted continuity, a principle of *permanence in time*. This will be, for example, the invariable structure of a tool, all of whose parts will gradually have been replaced. This is also the case, of supreme interest to us, of the permanence of the genetic code of a biologic individual; what remains here is the organization of a combinatory system. The idea of structure, opposed to that of event, replies to this criterion of identity, the strongest one that can be applied. It confirms the relational character of identity, which does not appear in the ancient formulation of substance but which Kant reestablishes by classifying substance among the categories of relation, as the condition of the possibility of conceiving of change as happening to something which does not change, at least not in the moment of attributing the accident to the substance; permanence in time thus becomes the transcendental of numerical identity.[1] The entire problematic of personal identity will revolve around this search for a relational invariant, giving it the strong signification of permanence in time.

Having performed this conceptual analysis of identity as sameness, we can now return to the question that directs the present study: Does the selfhood of the self imply a form of permanence in time which is not reducible to the determination of a substratum, not even in the relational sense which Kant assigns to the category of substance; in short, is there a form of permanence in time which is not simply the schema of the category of substance? Returning to the terms of the opposition which has repeatedly appeared in the earlier studies, we ask, Is there a form of permanence in time which can be connected to the question "who?" inasmuch as it is irreducible to any question of "what?"? Is there a form of permanence in time that is a reply to the question "Who am I?"?

[. . .]

[R]ather than entering into a discussion of the criteria of personal identity, I have deliberately chosen to wrestle with a major work which, transcending the debate on the respective merits of the psychological criterion and the corporeal criterion, addresses itself directly to the *beliefs* that we ordinarily attach to the claim of personal identity. This outstanding work is Derek Parfit's *Reasons and Persons*. I have found in it the most formidable adversary (not an enemy – far from it!) to my thesis of narrative identity, in that these analyses are situated on a plane where identity can signify only sameness, to the express exclusion of any distinction between sameness and selfhood, and hence of any dialectic – narrative or other – between sameness and selfhood. The work recalls that of Locke – due less to the place occupied by memory in it than to its recourse to puzzling cases – and that of Hume, in its skeptical conclusion. The famous puzzling cases which serve as truth tests throughout Parfit's book do indeed lead us to think that the very question of identity can prove to be meaningless, to the extent that, in the paradoxical cases at least, the answer is undetermined. The question for us will be whether, as in the case of Hume, Parfit was not looking for something he could not find, namely a firm status for personal identity defined in terms of sameness, and whether he does not presuppose the self he was not seeking, principally when he develops, with uncommonly vigorous thinking, the moral implications of his thesis and then writes of it: "Personal identity is not what matters."[2]

Parfit attacks the basic beliefs underlying our use of identity criteria. For didactic purposes, our ordinary beliefs regarding personal identity can be arranged in three series of assertions. The first concerns what we are to understand by identity, namely the separate existence of a core of permanence; the second consists in the conviction that a determined response can always be given concerning the existence of such permanence; and the third states that the question posed is important if the person is to claim the status of a moral subject. Parfit's strategy consists in the successive dismantling of these three series of assertions, which are less juxtaposed than superimposed on one another, from the most obvious to the most deeply concealed.

Parfit's first thesis is that common belief has to be reformulated in terms that are not its own, namely in terms of the inverse thesis, which he holds to be the only true one and which he calls the reductionist thesis. The adverse thesis will therefore be called the nonreductionist thesis. According to the reductionist thesis, identity through time amounts, without remainder, to the fact of a certain connectedness between events, whether these be of a physical or mental nature. The two terms employed here must be properly understood: by "event," we are to understand any occurrence capable of being described *without* it being explicitly affirmed that the experiences that make up a personal life are the possession of that person, without it being affirmed that this person exists. It is under the condition of an impersonal description such as this that any search for connections can be undertaken, whether this be on the physical or corporeal level or on the mental or psychic level.

The reductionist thesis therefore reintroduces into the debate the neutral notion of *event* which we first confronted within the framework of the theory of action when we considered Donald Davidson's theses concerning the relation between action and events.[3] As in Davidson, the category of event appears to be primitive, that is, not dependent on the category of substantial entity, unlike the notion of state, which, it seems, has to be the state of some entity. Once the notion of event is taken in this broad sense, including mental events and physical events, the reductionist thesis can then be formulated: "A person's existence just consists in the existence of a brain and body, and the occurrence of a series of interrelated physical and mental events."[4]

What does the reductionist thesis exclude? Precisely: "that we are separately existing entities" (p. 210). In relation to simple mental or psychological continuity, the person constitutes "a separate further fact." Separate, in what sense? In the sense that the person is distinct from his brain and his experiences. For Parfit, the notion of spiritual substance, with which he identifies the pure Cartesian ego, is doubtless only one of the versions of the nonreductionist thesis, but it is the best-known one, even if a materialist version is equally conceivable. Essential to it is the idea that identity consists in an additional fact in relation to physical and/or mental continuity: "I call this the *Further Fact View*" (ibid.).

Before proceeding any further, it is important to underscore the point that it is the reductionist thesis which establishes the terms of reference in which the adverse thesis is then formulated, namely the vocabulary of events, of facts, described in an impersonal manner; in relation to this basic vocabulary, the adverse thesis is defined both by what it denies (reductionism) and by what it adds (the further fact). In this way, the central phenomenon which the theory reduces is, in my opinion, eluded, namely that someone possesses her body and her experience. The choice of the event as the term of reference expresses (better, accomplishes) this evasion (better, this elision) of mineness. And it is in the vocabulary of the event, resulting from just such an elision, that the existence of the person appears as a further fact. The thesis to be nonreductionist is thus made parasitic on the reductionist thesis, set up as the basic unit. Now, the entire question is to know whether mineness belongs to the range of facts, to the epistemology of observable entities, and, finally, to the ontology of events. We are thus carried back once again to the distinction between problematics of identity, that of *ipse* and that of *idem*. It is because he neglects this possible dichotomy that Parfit has no other recourse than to consider as superfluous, in the precise sense of the word, the phenomenon of mineness in relation to the factual character of the event.

The failure to recognize this produces as its corollary the false appearance that the thesis called nonreductionist finds its most remarkable illustration in the spiritual dualism to which Cartesianism is itself all too rapidly assimilated. As far as I am concerned, what the reductionist thesis reduces is not only, nor even primarily, the mineness of experience but, more fundamentally, that of my own body. The impersonal character of the event marks above all the neutralization of one's own body. Thereafter, the true difference between the nonreductionist thesis and the reductionist thesis in no way coincides with the so-called dualism between spiritual substance and corporeal substance, but between my own possession and impersonal description. To the extent that the body as my own constitutes one of the components of mineness, the most radical confrontation must place face-to-face two perspectives on the body – the body as mine, and the body as one body among others. The reductionist thesis in this sense marks the reduction of one's own body to the body as impersonal body. This neutralization, in all the thought experiments that will now appear, will facilitate focusing on the brain the entire discourse on the body. The *brain*, indeed, differs from many other parts of the body, and from the body as a whole in terms of an integral experience, inasmuch as it is stripped of any phenomenological status and thus of the trait of belonging to me, of being my possession. I have the experience of my relation to my members as organs of movement (my hands), of perception (my eyes), of emotion (the heart), or of expression (my voice). I have no such experience of my brain. In truth, the expression "my brain" has no meaning, at least not directly: absolutely speaking, there is a brain in my skull, but I do not feel it. It is only through the global detour by way of my body, inasmuch as my body is also a body and as the brain is contained in this body, that I can say: "my brain." The unsettling nature of this expression is reinforced by the fact that the brain does not fall under the category of objects perceived at a distance from one's own body. Its proximity in my head gives it the strange character of non-experienced interiority.

Mental phenomena pose a comparable problem. In this respect, the most critical moment in the entire enterprise can be held to occur in the attempt to dissociate the psychological criterion from the trait of belonging to me (*appartenance mienne*). If, Parfit judges, the Cartesian cogito obviously cannot be stripped of the trait of being in the first person, the same thing is not true of identity defined by mental or physical continuity. One must therefore be able to define *mnemonic* continuity without any reference to mine, yours, his, or hers. If one could, one would genuinely be rid of the trait of belonging to me – in short, of "one's own." One could do this if one were able to create a replica of the memory of someone in the brain of someone else. (This, of course, involves manipulations of the brain, but later we will see the place that such manipulations and other similar operations hold in the imaginary experiences constructed by Parfit.) Memory can then be held to be equivalent to a cerebral trace. We will speak in this sense of memory traces. There is then nothing in the way of building a replica of these traces. On this basis, we can define a broad concept of *quasi memory*, of which ordinary memory would be a subclass, namely that of the quasi memories of our own past experiences (p. 220). But can what is one's own be a particular case of the impersonal? In fact, all of this was granted when we agreed to substitute for one's own memory the notion of mnemonic trace, which indeed belongs to the problematic of neutral events. This initial slippage authorizes treating the specific connection between past experience and present experience in terms of causal dependence.

The case of memory is only the most striking case in the order of psychic continuity. What is at issue is the ascription of thought to a thinker. Can one substitute, without any semantic loss, "the thinking is that . . ." (or "thought is occurring") for "I think"? Self-ascription and other-ascription, to return to Strawson's vocabulary, seem untranslatable into the terms of impersonal description.

The second belief Parfit attacks is the belief that the question of identity is always determinable, hence that all apparent cases of indeterminacy can be decided by yes or by no. In truth, this belief is found to underlie the preceding one: it is because we take aberrant cases to be determinable that we seek the stable formula of identity. In this respect, the invention of puzzling cases with the help of science fiction, where the indecidability of the question of identity is attested to, exercises such a decisive strategic function that Parfit begins the third part of his book, which deals with personal identity, by presenting the most troubling of these puzzling cases. Thus from the very beginning, the author insinuates the vacuity of a question which would give rise to such indetermination in the response. I have nevertheless preferred to begin by presenting the reductionist thesis because it does, in fact, govern the construction and selection of the puzzling cases.

In a sense, the question of identity has always stimulated an interest in paradoxical cases. Religious and theological beliefs about the transmigration of souls, immortality, and the resurrection of the flesh have not failed to intrigue the most speculative of minds (we find testimony to this in Saint Paul's response to the Corinthians in 1 Cor. 15:35ff.). We saw above in what way Locke makes use of a troubling imaginary case, not, to be sure, to undermine belief, but in order to put to the test of paradox his own thesis on the equation between personal identity and memory. It was his successors who transformed Locke's paradox into a puzzling case. The literature of personal identity is full of inventions of this sort: transplanting, bisecting brains, duplicating the cerebral hemispheres, and so on, to say nothing of the cases offered by clinical observations of split personalities, cases familiar to the general public. I too will be led to assign a considerable place to the equivalent of Parfit's puzzling cases within the framework of a narrative conception of personal identity. The confrontation between the two sorts of puzzling cases will even be one of the strong points of the argument on behalf of my own thesis. Let us confine ourselves for the moment to the following observation: this striking continuity in the recourse of imagination to cases capable of paralyzing reflection allows us to see that the question of identity constitutes a privileged place of aporias. Perhaps we must conclude, not that the question is an empty one, but that it can remain a question without an answer: this is precisely what is at stake in this singular strategy.

It is important to underscore vigorously that Parfit's selection of puzzling cases is governed by the reductionist hypothesis that has just been discussed. Take, for instance, the fictional experience of teletransportation which opens the third section of *Reasons and Persons* in grand style. The author proposes two versions of it; in both cases, an exact copy is made of my brain. This copy is transmitted by radio to a receiver placed on another planet, where a replicator reconstitutes an exact replica of me on the basis of this information, identical in the sense of exactly similar as to the organization and sequence of states of affairs and events. In the first case, my brain and my body are destroyed during my space voyage. The question is whether I survived in my replica or whether I died. The case is undecidable: with respect to numerical identity, my replica is other than I; with respect to qualitative identity, it is indistinguishable from me, hence substitutable. In the second case, my brain and my body are not destroyed, but my heart is damaged; I encounter my replica on Mars, I coexist with it; it knows that I am going to die before it does and attempts to console me by promising that it will take my place. What can I expect from the future? Am I going to die or survive in my replica?

What presupposition grounds the construction of this puzzling case and a good many others, each more ingenious than the next? First of all, these are imaginary cases which remain conceivable, even when they may not be technically realizable. It is enough that they be neither logically nor physically impossible. The question will be whether they do not violate a constraint of another order, concerning human rootedness on this earth. We will return to this later when the science fiction scenarios will be compared with literary fictions of a narrative sort. In addition, these are highly technological manipulations performed on the brain, taken as equivalent to the person. It is here that the reductionist thesis exercises its control; in an ontology of events and an epistemology of the impersonal description of identity-bearing sequences, the privileged place of occurrences in which the person is mentioned, without any distinct existence being explicitly claimed, is the brain. It is clear that Parfit's fictions, unlike the literary fictions of which we will speak later, concern entities of a manipulable nature from which the question of selfhood has been eliminated as a matter of principle.

The conclusion Parfit draws from the indecidability of his puzzling cases is that the question posed was itself empty. If one holds that identity means sameness, this conclusion is irresistible; in fact, in the most troublesome cases none of the three solutions envisaged is plausible. They are:

1   no person exists who is the *same* as me;
2   I am the *same* as one of the two individuals resulting from the experiment;
3   I am the *same* as both individuals.

The paradox is indeed a paradox of sameness: it was necessary to maintain as equivalent the question Am I going to survive? and the question Will there be a person who will be the *same* person as I? In this predetermined framework, resolving the paradox is dissolving the question – in short, considering it to be empty. If, through a sort of debatable extrapolation, Parfit grants the puzzling cases such a major role, it is because they dissociate the components that in everyday life we take as indissociable and whose connectedness we even take to be noncontingent, namely the overlapping between psychological (and possibly corporeal) connectedness, which can, if need be, involve an impersonal description, and the feeling of belonging – of memories, in particular – to someone capable of designating himself or herself as their owner. It will be one of the functions of the subsequent comparison between science fiction and literary fiction to place back on the drawing board the question of the presumed contingency of the most fundamental traits of the human condition. Among these, there is at least one which, in the imaginary experiences of teletransportation, seems irrefutable, namely the *temporal-*

ity, not of the voyage, but of the teletransported voyager. As long as we consider only the adequation of the replica of the brain, the only thing that counts is the structural identity, comparable to that of the genetic code, preserved throughout experience.[5] As for me, the one who is teletransported, something is always happening to me; I am afraid, I believe, I doubt, I wonder if I am going to die or survive – in short, I am worried about myself. In this respect, the shift in the discussion from problems of *memory* to problems of *survival* marks the appearance on the stage of a dimension of historicality which, it would seem, is quite difficult to describe in impersonal terms.[6]

The third belief that Parfit submits to his virulent critique concerns the judgment of importance which we attach to the question of identity. I have already quoted his remarkable expression: "Identity is not what matters." The tie between the belief attacked here and the preceding belief is this: if indecidability seems unacceptable to us, it is because it troubles us. This is clear in all the bizarre cases in which survival is at issue: What is going to happen to me? I ask. Now if we are troubled, it is because the judgment of identity seems important to us. If we give up this judgment of importance, we cease to be troubled. Presented with the options opened by the puzzling cases, we are ready to concede that we know all there is to know about the case in question and to stop the investigation there: "Even when we have no answer to a question about personal identity, we can know everything about what happens" (p. 266).

This attack on what matters occupies, in fact, a central strategic position in Parfit's entire work. I have neglected to state that the problem of identity discussed in the third part of the book is destined to resolve a moral problem posed in the two preceding parts, namely the problem of the *rationality* of the ethical choice posed by the utilitarian ethics which predominates in the English-language world. Parfit attacks the most egotistic version of it, which he terms the "self-interest theory."[7] What is at stake here is indeed the self in its ethical dimension. Parfit's thesis is that the argument between egoism and altruism cannot be decided on the level where it unfolds if one has not first taken a position on the question of what sort of entities persons are (whence the title of the work *Reasons and Persons*). The valid reasons for ethical choices pass by way of the dissolution of false beliefs concerning the ontological status of persons. So, at the end of the third part of the work we return to the question raised in the first part. And now the entire weight of the ethical questions falls back upon the question of identity. The latter then becomes a genuinely axiological issue. The judgment of what matters is a judgment that ranks in the hierarchy of evaluations. But which identity – identity in what sense of the term – are we asked to renounce? Is it the sameness that Hume held impossible to find and little worthy of our interest? Or mineness, which, in my opinion, constitutes the core of the nonreductionist thesis? Actually, everything leads me to think that Parfit, by reason of not distinguishing between selfhood and sameness, aims at the former through the latter. This is far from uninteresting, for the sort of Buddhism insinuated by Parfit's ethical thesis consists precisely in not making any difference between sameness and mineness. In doing this, does he not risk throwing out the baby with the bathwater? For, as much as I am willing to admit that imaginative variations on personal identity lead to a crisis of selfhood as such – and problem cases in the narrative order which we shall consider later will certainly confirm this – I still do not see how the question "who?" can disappear in the extreme cases in which it remains without an answer. For really, how can we ask ourselves about *what* matters if we could not ask *to whom* the thing mattered or not? Does not the questioning about what matters or not depend upon self-concern, which indeed seems to be constitutive of selfhood? And when we move from the third level to the second, and then to the first level of beliefs sifted out by the critique, do we not continue to move within the element of belief, of the belief concerning what *we* are? The tenacity of personal pronouns, even in the statement of the reductionist thesis from which we started, reveals something more profound than the rhetoric of argumentation: it marks the resistance of the question "who?" to its elimination in an impersonal description.[8]

In the last analysis, it is a matter of changing the conception we have about "ourselves, and about our actual lives" (p. 217). It is "our view" of life that is at issue.

It will be objected here to my plea on behalf of the irreducibility of the trait of mineness and, by implication, of the very question of selfhood that Parfit's quasi Buddhism does not leave even the assertion of selfhood intact. What Parfit asks is that we concern ourselves less with ourselves, with our aging and our death among other things, that we attach less importance to the question of "whether experiences come within the same or different lives" (p. 341); hence, that we take an interest in the "experiences" themselves rather than in "the person, the subject of experiences" (ibid.); that we place less emphasis on differences between ourselves at different periods and others who have had experiences similar to our own; that we ignore as much as possible the boundaries between lives by giving less importance to unity of each life; that we make the very unity of our life more a work of art than a claim to independence. Is it not to the very neutralization of the question of selfhood, beyond the impersonal observation of the connectedness of a life, that Parfit, the moralist, invites us? Does not Parfit oppose *care-freeness* (which, after all, was also preached by Jesus in his Sermon on the Mount) to *care*? I well understand the objection. But I think that it can be incorporated into the defense of selfhood in its confrontation with sameness. What Parfit's moral reflection provokes is, finally, a crisis *within* selfhood. The crisis consists in the fact that the very notion that my experiences belong to me has an ambiguous sense; there are different types of ownership (what I have and who I am). What Parfit is aiming at is precisely the egotism that nourishes the thesis of self-interest, against which his work is directed. But is not a moment of self-dispossession essential to authentic selfhood? And must one not, in order to make oneself open, available, belong to oneself in a certain sense? We have already asked: Would the question of what matters arise if there were no one to whom the question of identity mattered? Let us now add: if my identity were to lose all importance in every respect, would not the question of others also cease to matter?[9]

We will encounter these same questions at the end of our plea on behalf of a narrative interpretation of identity; the latter, we shall see, also has its bizarre cases which reshape the assertion of identity in the form of a question – and at times of a question without an answer: Who am I, actually? It is here that narrative theory, called upon to wrestle with Parfit's questions, will be invited, in its turn, to explore its common boundary with ethical theory.

Notes

1   In Kant, the shift of the idea of substance from the ontological to the transcendental domain is marked by the simple correspondence between the category, its schema, and the principle (or first judgment). To substance, the first category of relation, corresponds the schema,

which expresses its temporal constitution, namely: "permanence [*Beharrlichkeit*] of the real in time, that is, the representation of the real as a substrate of empirical determination of time in general, and so as abiding while all else changes" (*Critique of Pure Reason*, A143, B183, p. 184). To the schema of substance corresponds the principle expressing its relational constitution, namely ("The First Analogy of Experience"): "All appearances contain the permanent [*das Beharrliche*] (substance) as the object itself, and the transitory as its mere determination" (A182, p. 212). And in the second edition: "In all change of appearances substance is permanent [*beharrt*]; its quantum in nature is neither increased nor diminished" (B224, p. 212).

2   Derek Parfit, *Reasons and Persons* (Oxford: Oxford University Press, 1986), p. 255 and passim. One will note that Parfit sometimes writes: "Our identity is not what matters" (p. 245 and passim), an expression that will not fail to reintroduce the question of ownership.

3   See *Oneself as Another*, third study, sec. 4. Davidson, *Essays on Actions and Events* (Oxford: Clarendon Press, 1980).

4   Parfit, *Reasons and Persons*, p. 211. Parfit does admit two versions of the reductionist thesis: according to the first, a person is simply what has just been stated; according to the second, a person could be considered a distinct entity without that entity having a separate existence. The latter version credits the analogy proposed by Hume between the person and a republic or commonwealth; in this way, one says that France exists but not Ruritania, although the former does not exist separately apart from its citizens and its territory. It is the second version that Parfit adopts for his notion of person. In his eyes, it does not violate the reductionist thesis. In the second version, the person can be mentioned without involving any claim of existence.

5   One may well, however, object to the very construction of the imaginary case that, if the replica of my brain were a complete replica, it would have to contain, in addition to the traces of my past history, the mark of my history to come woven out of chance encounters. But this condition would indeed appear to violate the rules of what is conceivable: from the time of the separation of myself and my replica, our histories distinguish us and make us unsubstitutable. The very notion of replica is in danger of losing all meaning.

6   Concerning the problem of survival, in the sense of persisting into the future after an experience of radical alteration of personal identity, cf. in John Perry, ed., *Personal Identity* (Berkeley: University of California Press, 1975), sec. 5, "Personal Identity and Survival" (articles by Bernard Williams and Derek Parfit), pp. 179–223; in Amelie Oskenberg Rorty, ed., *Identity of Persons* (Berkeley: University of California Press, 1976), articles by David Lewis, "Survival and Identity," pp. 18–40, and Georges Rey, "Survival," pp. 41–66.

7   Parfit sums it up in the following terms: The Self-interest theory "*S* gives to each person this aim: the outcomes that would be best for himself, and that would make his life go, for him, as well as possible" (*Reasons and Persons*, p. 3).

8   One would have to cite here in their entirety the provisional conclusions reached in ibid., pp. 216 and 217, where what is in question are "our brains," "our thoughts and our actions," "our identity." The substitution of deictic forms other than personal pronouns and adjectives ("this person's brain," "these experiences") changes nothing here, considering the constitution of the deictic forms themselves. In this regard, the most astonishing expression is the one that sums up the claim as a whole: "My claim [is] that we could describe our lives in an *impersonal* way" (p. 217).

9   Concerning the kinship between Parfit's theses and Buddhism, see ibid., p. 280; Matthew Kapstein, "Collins, Parfit, and the Problem of Personal Identity in Two Philosophical Traditions – A Review of Selfless Persons," *Feature Book Review*, offprint.

PART VI

FEMINIST PHILOSOPHY

18

COMMENTARY ON DE BEAUVOIR

Simone de Beauvoir (1908–86) was one of the most famous female intellectuals of her time, and her work has been central to the feminist movement the world over. Her work is heavily influenced by Hegel and Heidegger and developed in close collaboration with her lifelong intimate, Sartre. It has been suggested that the similarities between the work of Beauvoir and her friend Merleau-Ponty is not so well known because of Beauvoir's own silence on this point – an attitude that Monika Langer attributes to Beauvoir's personal commitment to Sartre.[1]

In the Introduction to *The Second Sex*, Beauvoir provides a lively description of the situation of women and the unequal relations between men and women. She goes on to explain this oppressive relation by reference to two features of women's lives: the mediating role of political structures and social institutions in the formation of subjectivity, and the lived experience of female embodiment. Like Sartre, Beauvoir sets out with a Hegelian model of consciousness and a conception of freedom as transcendence, but she develops these accounts considerably by drawing out the implications of the inherent ambiguities of human existence. In doing so, she lays the ground for a theoretical framework in which to understand the invisible psychological dimensions of oppression that will later become important to feminist moral and political philosophy and to Michel Foucault's work on discourse and power.

Beauvoir begins by asking what may seem like an odd question: "What is a woman?" Stranger still, she asks whether women still exist. These are metaphysical questions, asked with a certain irony. Beauvoir's point is that it is widely and mistakenly believed that there is some positive content, some essence, that the concept of "woman" expresses. The irony is that this purported "essence" is conceived as something inessential. On Beauvoir's view, there is no positive philosophical account of "Woman"; "Woman" is constructed only as man's Other, and as such, operates to deny a positive value to women's lives. Beauvoir believes that by understanding the situation of women we will realize that the sexual inequality (and, in fact, any social inequality) that pervades society can be redressed only by a total reorganization of society's political structures. The necessity for reorganization comes about because subjectivity (and freedom) is not a radically uncaused power of the individual as Sartre thought, but an effect of one's *situation*, which is itself largely the effect of collective projects and social institutions. According to Beauvoir, "Woman" describes a *situation* that is imposed upon females to systematically limit their capacity to regard themselves as agents in their own lives. In short, women's subjectivity is different to men's because their situations are different.

Beauvoir notes that what men do in the name of man has automatic legitimacy, but what woman does must always be legitimated by men. Woman is defined only by her relation to man, whereas man is defined in himself; he is essential subjectivity, she is inessential; he is subject, she is Other; he is agent, she is object; he is complete, she is lack. Beauvoir argues that man earns his metaphysical status as "the One" (something) insofar as woman is nothing. In response to the valorizing of the male/self within the self–other relation, Beauvoir claims that the dyadic structure of self–other is not originally sex-specific, but rather seems to be a general structure of existence. Through a kind of Hegelian analysis, she concludes that the category of "other" is just as basic as the category of "self": a self is established and subjectivity attained only in relation to an Other. This leads Beauvoir to ask: why is woman's situation such that her subjectivity is *given* as inferior to man's? There are two prongs to Beauvoir's response to this question. The first involves an explication of the nature of freedom and the nature of situation. The second concerns the relation between women's situation and female embodiment.

The Nature of Freedom and the Nature of Situation

Beauvoir had set out her views on freedom in an earlier publication, *The Ethics of Ambiguity*. Like Merleau-Ponty, she thought that human existence was not simply a duality of for-itself and in-itself, but their ambiguous simultaneity. Human existence involves both an uncaused, subjective capacity to transcend one's given conditions and the weight of an objective causal world that functions with complete indifference to one's plans and projects. These form two reciprocal "poles" which structure our existence. Ambiguity also extends to our relations with other people. Others are both subjects and objects for me, and just as I am both subject and object for myself, so am I also subject and object for others. For example, my experience of myself as an object *for myself* is mediated through my sense of others' perception of me as an object, and so on. This is the kind of effect described by Sartre in "The Look." For Beauvoir, one's situation is structured by relations of reciprocity with the material world, the social world, and one's own body. For this reason she claims that every personal project is formed against a background of projects of others. In contrast to the violence of Sartrean interpersonal relations, she believes that others enrich one's world through the involvement of their projects in one's own. Nevertheless, this means that one's freedom (and subjectivity) is vulnerable to the interpersonal relations and social institutions that form part of one's situation.

Beauvoir argues that oppression is a specific violence directed at specific groups, which aims at systematically modifying the situation of a group of people in such a way as to prevent them from developing certain freedoms which are considered to be in competition with their oppressor's freedom.[2] Beauvoir charts a spectrum of responses of women to their oppression, ranging from conscious complicity, through varying degrees of bad faith,[3] to genuine belief that a woman's situation is natural. Against Sartre, Beauvoir argues that some situations cannot be transcended because they are structured so as to inhibit a person's acting or willing otherwise. This occurs in the situation where persons believe that the limits of their situation are natural and therefore insurmountable, after all, "one cannot revolt against nature."[4] Being ignorant of the possibility of freedom, the oppressed are preventing from rebelling against their oppressors. In these cases, women live as inferiors because it is *given* in their situation. Beauvoir's insight into the psychological nature of oppression through the "naturalization" of woman's situation is the key to her understanding of the ontological origins of sexual inequality.

Throughout *The Second Sex* Beauvoir describes the various processes that a female undergoes during her life that have the effect of creating her subjectivity as Other to man. These are processes that erode the development of autonomy by making girls feel that they are neither agents nor capable of becoming agents. Instrumental in these processes are social institutions which are said to function analogously to nature by causing women to feel that the capacities (and deficiencies) they find themselves with, or which are expected of them, are as natural and immutable as the laws of physics. As a result, social institutions, especially marriage and its associated practices, determine in advance that males and females encounter each other as unequals. These institutions are themselves premised upon sexual inequality and so determine the meaning of the situations into which girls are born and grow up and in which they encounter men. Even in the best case, argues Beauvoir, the woman who pursues an independent life takes to a road of ceaseless conflict between her inner freedom and her socially constructed feminine destiny.[5]

Woman's Situation and Female Embodiment

Beauvoir has argued that society both gives rise to and is premised upon sexual inequality. This partly explains how woman's situation is given as inferior. However, a further explanation is needed to account for how sexual inequality can be *ontological*. Beauvoir's explanation is grounded in the ambiguities of the female body.

According to Beauvoir, morality is needed only by mortal creatures because immortals are not impelled to *become* anything. Freedom, understood as transcendence, however, requires a future of inexhaustible possibilities. This means that freedom is an essentially temporal idea: it supposes future and successive generations. Beauvoir regards the temporality of freedom as an ontological demand for the perpetuation of the species. In other words, she thinks that built into the very notion of human freedom as "becoming" is the necessity of the species to reproduce itself. Again, the ambiguity of human existence comes to the fore: transcendence turns on biology. This gives a woman's existence and her situation a specific character and predisposition. Woman's particular reproductive capacity, more so than man's, places her "in the iron grasp of the species."[6] For Beauvoir, woman's body is "one of the essential elements in her situation in the world"[7] because it necessitates that she spend large amounts of time and energy in natural functions associated with her reproductive capacity: menstruation, pregnancy, lactation, and so forth.

Beauvoir believed that the situation of women meant that they experienced a conflict that men did not, namely the conflict between species and individual.[8] She thought
that women were torn between the personal freedom they desire and deserve, and
the perpetuation of the species that such freedom entails but which also threatens it.
Female embodiment makes the achievement of subjectivity more difficult because the
strength of woman's involvement in the natural world makes her liable to succumb to
a "physiological destiny."[9] According to Beauvoir, all of this gives man an exploitative
advantage by making woman vulnerable to domestic incarceration, leaving men free to
pursue authentic, self-affirming activities.

Beauvoir has attracted criticism for underplaying the value of types of freedom made
possible through motherhood.[10] Feminists such as Luce Irigaray have accused Beauvoir
of reproducing the valorization attached to the male perspective by failing to appreciate the significance of sexual difference. This may be partly a result of Beauvoir's attachment to the notion of transcendence, which other theorists have argued is a gendered
concept that presupposes a conception of self that relies upon forms of social life and
conceptions of worthy action premised upon the containment of women in the domestic sphere.[11] Nevertheless Beauvoir's idea that the key to understanding the mechanisms
of sexual oppression lies in understanding the social situation of the female body remains
central to much contemporary feminist scholarship.

Notes

1   Monika Langer, "Beauvoir and Merleau-Ponty on Ambiguity," in *The Cambridge Compan-
    ion to Simone de Beauvoir*, ed. Claudia Card (Cambridge, UK: Cambridge University Press,
    2003), pp. 87–106.
2   Sonia Kruks, *Situation and Human Existence: Freedom, Subjectivity and Society* (London: Unwin
    Hyman, 1990), p. 96.
3   Simone de Beauvoir, *The Second Sex*, trans. H. M. Parshley (Harmondsworth, UK: Penguin,
    1988), p. 665 fn 9; hereafter *TSS*.
4   Simone de Beauvoir, *Ethics of Ambiguity*, trans. Bernard Frechtman (New York: Citadel Press,
    1967), p. 83.
5   *TSS*, p. 691.
6   *TSS*, p. 63.
7   *TSS*, p. 69.
8   See discussion in *TSS*, pp. 54–6. Beauvoir argues that in virtue of the female's (that is,
    human and nonhuman females) role in reproduction the female renounces her individual-
    ity "for the benefit of the species, which demands this abdication" (p. 55). Furthermore, she
    suggests that this fundamental difference from the male's situation is reflected in Hegel's
    idea that "Subjectivity and separateness immediately signify conflict" (p. 56). Woman's sub-
    jectivity is different because her situation is more complex, more ambiguous, and involves
    demands that engage her bodily in quite different ways than does man's situation.
9   *TSS*, p. 587.
10 See Mary Evans, *Simone de Beauvoir: A Feminist Mandarin* (London: Tavistock, 1985).
11 See Genevieve Lloyd, *The Man of Reason: "Male" and "Female" in Western Philosophy* (London:
    Methuen, 1984).

Main Texts by Beauvoir

Patrick O'Brian (trans.), *Adieux: A Farewell to Sartre* (New York: Pantheon Books, 1984).
Yvonne Moyse and Roger Senhouse (trans.), *The Ethics of Ambiguity* (London: Flamingo, 1984).
Quintin Hoare (trans.), *Letters to Sartre* (London: Radius, 1991).
James Kirkup (trans.), *Memoirs of a Dutiful Daughter* (Harmondsworth, UK: Penguin, 1963).
H. M. Parshley (trans.), *The Second Sex* (Harmondsworth, UK: Penguin, 1988).

Further Reading

Bair, Deidre, *Simone de Beauvoir: A Biography* (London: Jonathan Cape, 1990).
Barnes, Hazel, *The Literature of Possibility: A Study in Humanistic Existentialism* (London: Tavistock, 1959).
Card, Claudia (ed.), *The Cambridge Companion to Simone de Beauvoir* (Cambridge, UK: Cambridge University Press, 2003).
Fullbrook, Kate and Edward Fullbrook, *Beauvoir: A Critical Introduction* (Cambridge, UK: Polity, 1997).
Gatens, Moira, *Imaginary Bodies: Ethics. Power and Corporeality* (New York: Routledge, 1996).
Moi, Toril, *Simone de Beauvoir: The Making of an Intellectual Woman* (Oxford: Blackwell, 1994).
Sartre, Jean-Paul, *Witness to my Life: The Letters of Jean-Paul Sartre to Simone de Beauvoir, 1926–1939*, ed. Simone de Beauvoir, trans. Lee Fahnestock and Norman MacAfee (New York: Charles Scribner's Sons, 1992).

"INTRODUCTION" TO
THE SECOND SEX

Simone de Beauvoir

For a long time I have hesitated to write a book on woman. The subject is irritating, especially to women; and it is not new. Enough ink has been spilled in quarrelling over feminism, and perhaps we should say no more about it. It is still talked about, however, for the voluminous nonsense uttered during the last century seems to have done little to illuminate the problem. After all, is there a problem? And if so, what is it? Are there women, really? Most assuredly the theory of the eternal feminine still has its adherents who will whisper in your ear: 'Even in Russia women still are *women*'; and other erudite persons – sometimes the very same – say with a sigh: 'Woman is losing her way, woman is lost.' One wonders if women still exist, if they will always exist, whether or not it is desirable that they should, what place they occupy in this world, what their place should be. 'What has become of women?' was asked recently in an ephemeral magazine.

But first we must ask: what is a woman? '*Tota mulier in utero*', says one, 'woman is a womb'. But in speaking of certain women, connoisseurs declare that they are not women, although they are equipped with a uterus like the rest. All agree in recognizing the fact that females exist in the human species; today as always they make up about one half of humanity. And yet we are told that femininity is in danger; we are exhorted to be women, remain women, become women. It would appear, then, that every female human being is not necessarily a woman; to be so considered she must share in that mysterious and threatened reality known as femininity. Is this attribute something secreted by the ovaries? Or is it a Platonic essence, a product of the philosophic imagination? Is a rustling petticoat enough to bring it down to earth? Although some women try zealously to incarnate this essence, it is hardly patentable. It is frequently described in vague and dazzling terms that seem to have been borrowed from the vocabulary of the seers, and indeed in the times of St Thomas it was considered an essence as certainly defined as the somniferous virtue of the poppy.

But conceptualism has lost ground. The biological and social sciences no longer admit the existence of unchangeably fixed entities that determine given characteristics, such as those ascribed to woman, the Jew, or the Negro. Science regards any characteristic as a reaction dependent in part upon a *situation*. If today femininity no longer exists, then it never existed. But does the word *woman*, then, have no specific content? This is stoutly affirmed by those who hold to the philosophy of the enlightenment, of rationalism, of nominalism; women, to them, are merely the human beings arbitrarily designated by the word *woman*. Many American women particularly are prepared to think that there is no longer any place for woman as such; if a backward individual still takes herself for a woman, her friends advise her to be psychoanalysed and thus get rid of this obsession. In regard to a work, *Modern Woman: The Lost Sex*, which in other respects has its irritating features, Dorothy Parker has written: 'I cannot be just to books which treat of woman as woman . . . My idea is that all of us, men as well as women, should be regarded as human beings.' But nominalism is a rather inadequate doctrine, and the anti-feminists have had no trouble in showing that women simply *are not* men. Surely woman is, like man, a human being; but such a declaration is abstract. The fact is that every concrete human being is always a singular, separate individual. To decline to accept such notions as the eternal feminine, the black soul, the Jewish character, is not to deny that Jews, Negroes, women exist today – this denial does not represent a liberation for those concerned, but rather a flight from reality. Some years ago a well-known woman writer refused to permit her portrait to appear in a series of photographs especially devoted to women writers; she wished to be counted among the men. But in order to gain this privilege she made use of her husband's influence! Women who assert that they are men lay claim none the less to masculine consideration and respect. I recall also a young Trotskyite standing on a platform at a boisterous meeting and getting ready to use her fists, in spite of her evident fragility. She was denying her feminine weakness; but it was for love of a militant male whose equal she wished to be. The attitude of defiance of many American women proves that they are haunted by a sense of their femininity. In truth, to go for a walk with one's eyes open is enough to demonstrate that humanity is divided into two classes of individuals whose clothes, faces, bodies, smiles, gaits, interests, and occupations are manifestly different. Perhaps these differences are superficial, perhaps they are destined to disappear. What is certain is that they do most obviously exist.

If her functioning as a female is not enough to define woman, if we decline also to explain her through 'the eternal feminine', and if nevertheless we admit, provisionally, that women do exist, then we must face the question: what is a woman?

To state the question is, to me, to suggest, at once, a preliminary answer. The fact that I ask it is in itself significant. A man would never set out to write a book on the peculiar situation of the human male. But if I wish to define myself, I must first of all say: 'I am a woman'; on this truth must be based all further discussion. A man never begins by presenting himself as an individual of a certain sex; it goes without saying that he is a man. The terms *masculine* and *feminine* are used symmetrically only as a matter of form, as on legal papers. In actuality the relation of the two sexes is not quite like that of two electrical poles, for man represents both the positive and the neutral, as is indicated by the common use of *man* to designate human beings in general; whereas woman represents only the negative, defined by limiting criteria, without reciprocity. In the midst of an abstract discussion it is vexing to hear a man say: 'You think thus and so because you are a woman'; but I know that my only defence is to reply: 'I think thus and so because it is true,' thereby removing my subjective self from the argument. It would be out of the question to reply: 'And you think the contrary because you are a man', for it is understood that the fact of being a man is no peculiarity. A man is in the right in being a man; it is the woman who is in the wrong. It amounts to this: just as for the ancients there was an absolute vertical with reference to which the oblique was defined, so there is an absolute human type, the masculine. Woman has ovaries, a uterus: these peculiarities imprison her in her subjectivity, circumscribe her within the limits of her own nature. It is often said that she thinks with her glands. Man superbly ignores the fact that his anatomy also includes glands, such as the testicles, and that they secrete hormones. He thinks of his body as a direct and normal connection with the world, which he believes he apprehends objectively, whereas he regards the body of woman as a hindrance, a prison, weighed down by everything peculiar to it. 'The female is a female by virtue of a certain *lack* of qualities,' said Aristotle; 'we should regard the female nature as afflicted with a natural defectiveness.' And St Thomas for his part pronounced woman to be an 'imperfect man', an 'incidental' being. This is symbolized in Genesis where Eve is depicted as made from what Bossuet called 'a supernumerary bone' of Adam.

Thus humanity is male and man defines woman not in herself but as relative to him; she is not regarded as an autonomous being. Michelet writes: 'Woman, the relative being . . .' And Benda is most positive in his *Rapport d'Uriel*: 'The body of man makes sense in itself quite apart from that of woman, whereas the latter seems wanting in significance by itself . . . Man can think of himself without woman. She cannot think of herself without man.' And she is simply what man decrees; thus she is called 'the sex', by which is meant that she appears essentially to the male as a sexual being. For him she is sex – absolute sex, no less. She is defined and differentiated with reference to man and not he with reference to her; she is the incidental, the inessential as opposed to the essential. He is the Subject, he is the Absolute – she is the Other.[1]

The category of the *Other* is as primordial as consciousness itself. In the most primitive societies, in the most ancient mythologies, one finds the expression of a duality – that of the Self and the Other. This duality was not originally attached to the division of the sexes; it was not dependent upon any empirical facts. It is revealed in such works as that of Granet on Chinese thought and those of Dumézil on the East Indies and Rome. The feminine element was at first no more involved in such pairs as Varuna-Mitra, Uranus-Zeus, Sun-Moon, and Day-Night than it was in the contrasts between Good and Evil, lucky and unlucky auspices, right and left, God and Lucifer. Otherness is a fundamental category of human thought.

Thus it is that no group ever sets itself up as the One without at once setting up the Other over against itself. If three travellers chance to occupy the same compartment, that is enough to make vaguely hostile 'others' out of all the rest of the passengers on the train. In small-town eyes all persons not belonging to the village are 'strangers' and suspect; to the native of a country all who inhabit other countries are 'foreigners'; Jews are 'different' for the anti-Semite, Negroes are 'inferior' for

American racists, aborigines are 'natives' for colonists, proletarians are the 'lower class' for the privileged.

Lévi-Strauss, at the end of a profound work on the various forms of primitive societies, reaches the following conclusion: 'Passage from the state of Nature to the state of Culture is marked by man's ability to view biological relations as a series of contrasts; duality, alternation, opposition, and symmetry, whether under definite or vague forms, constitute not so much phenomena to be explained as fundamental and immediately given data of social reality.'[2] These phenomena would be incomprehensible if in fact human society were simply a *Mitsein* or fellowship based on solidarity and friendliness. Things become clear, on the contrary, if, following Hegel, we find in consciousness itself a fundamental hostility towards every other consciousness; the subject can be posed only in being opposed – he sets himself up as the essential, as opposed to the other, the inessential, the object.

But the other consciousness, the other ego, sets up a reciprocal claim. The native travelling abroad is shocked to find himself in turn regarded as a 'stranger' by the natives of neighbouring countries. As a matter of fact, wars, festivals, trading, treaties, and contests among tribes, nations, and classes tend to deprive the concept *Other* of its absolute sense and to make manifest its relativity; willy-nilly, individuals and groups are forced to realize the reciprocity of their relations. How is it, then, that this reciprocity has not been recognized between the sexes, that one of the contrasting terms is set up as the sole essential, denying any relativity in regard to its correlative and defining the latter as pure otherness? Why is it that women do not dispute male sovereignty? No subject will readily volunteer to become the object, the inessential; it is not the Other who, in defining himself as the Other, establishes the One. The Other is posed as such by the One in defining himself as the One. But is the Other is not to regain the status of being the One, he must be submissive enough to accept this alien point of view. Whence comes this submission in the case of woman?

There are, to be sure, other cases in which a certain category has been able to dominate another completely for a time. Very often this privilege depends upon inequality of numbers – the majority imposes its rule upon the minority or persecutes it. But women are not a minority, like the American Negroes or the Jews; there are as many women as men on earth. Again, the two groups concerned have often been originally independent; they may have been formerly unaware of each other's existence, or perhaps they recognized each other's autonomy. But a historical event has resulted in the subjugation of the weaker by the stronger. The scattering of the Jews, the introduction of slavery into America, the conquests of imperialism are examples in point. In these cases the oppressed retained at least the memory of former days; they possessed in common a past, a tradition, sometimes a religion or a culture.

The parallel drawn by Bebel between women and the proletariat is valid in that neither ever formed a minority or a separate collective unit of mankind. And instead of a single historical event it is in both cases a historical development that explains their status as a class and accounts for the membership of *particular individuals* in that class. But proletarians have not always existed, whereas there have always been women. They are women in virtue of their anatomy and physiology. Throughout history they have always been subordinated to men,[3] and hence their dependency is not the result of a historical event or a social change – it was not something that *occurred*. The reason why otherness in this case seems to be an absolute is in part that it lacks the contingent or incidental nature of historical facts. A condition brought about at a certain time can be abolished at some other times, as the Negroes of Haiti and others have proved; but it might seem that a natural condition is beyond the possibility of change. In truth, however, the nature of things is no more immutably given, once for all, than is historical reality. If woman seems to be the inessential which never becomes the essential, it is because she herself fails to bring about this change. Proletarians say 'We'; Negroes also. Regarding themselves as subjects, they transform the bourgeois, the whites, into 'others'. But women do not say 'We', except at some congress of feminists or similar formal demonstration; men say 'women', and women use the same word in referring to themselves. They do not authentically assume a subjective attitude. The proletarians have accomplished the revolution in Russia, the Negroes in Haiti, the Indo-Chinese are battling for it in Indo-China; but the women's effort has never been anything more than a symbolic agitation. They have gained only what men have been willing to grant; they have taken nothing, they have only received.[4]

The reason for this is that women lack concrete means for organizing themselves into a unit which can stand face to face with the correlative unit. They have no past, no history, no religion of their own; and they have no such solidarity of work and interest as that of the proletariat. They are not even promiscuously herded together in the way that creates community feeling among the American Negroes, the ghetto Jews, the workers of Saint-Denis, or the factory hands of Renault. They live dispersed among the males, attached through residence, housework, economic condition, and social standing to certain men – fathers or husbands – more firmly than they are to other women. If they belong to the bourgeoisie, they feel solidarity with men of that class, not with proletarian women; if they are white, their allegiance is to white men, not to Negro women. The proletariat can propose to massacre the ruling class, and a sufficiently fanatical Jew or Negro might dream of getting sole possession of the atomic bomb and making humanity wholly Jewish or black; but woman cannot even dream of exterminating the males. The bond that unites her to her oppressors is not comparable to any other. The division of the sexes is a biological fact, not an event in human history. Male and female stand opposed within a primordial *Mitsein*, and woman has not broken it. The couple is a fundamental unity with its two halves riveted together, and the cleavage of society along the line of sex is impossible. Here is to be found the basic trait of woman: she is the Other in a totality of which the two components are necessary to one another.

One could suppose that this reciprocity might have facilitated the liberation of woman. When Hercules sat at the feet of Omphale and helped with her spinning, his desire for her held him captive; but why did she fail to gain a lasting power? To revenge herself on Jason, Medea killed their children; and this grim legend would seem to suggest that she might have obtained a formidable influence over him through his love for his offspring. In *Lysistrata* Aristophanes gaily depicts a band of women who joined forces to gain social ends through the sexual needs of their men; but this is only a play. In the legend of the Sabine women, the latter soon abandoned their plan of remaining sterile to punish their ravishers. In truth woman has not been socially emancipated through man's need – sexual desire and the desire for offspring – which makes the male dependent for satisfaction upon the female.

Master and slave, also, are united by a reciprocal need, in this case economic, which does not liberate the slave. In the relation of master to slave the master does not make a point of the need that he has for the other; he has in his grasp the power of satisfying this need through his own action; whereas the slave, in his dependent condition, his hope and fear, is quite conscious of the need he has for his master. Even if the need is at bottom equally urgent for both, it always works in favour of the oppressor and against the oppressed. That is why the liberation of the working class, for example, has been slow.

Now, woman has always been man's dependant, if not his slave; the two sexes have never shared the world in equality. And even today woman is heavily handicapped, though her situation is beginning to change. Almost nowhere is her legal status the same as man's, and frequently it is much to her disadvantage. Even when her rights are legally recognized in the abstract, long-standing custom prevents their full expression in the mores. In the economic sphere men and women can almost be said to make up two castes; other things being equal, the former hold the better jobs, get higher wages, and have more opportunity for success than their new competitors. In industry and politics men have a great many more positions and they monopolize the most important posts. In addition to all this, they enjoy a traditional prestige that the education of children tends in every way to support, for the present enshrines the past – and in the past all history has been made by men. At the present time, when women are beginning to take part in the affairs of the world, it is still a world that belongs to men – they have no doubt of it at all and women have scarcely any. To decline to be the Other, to refuse to be a party to the deal – this would be for women to renounce all the advantages conferred upon them by their alliance with the superior caste. Man-the-sovereign will provide woman-the-liege with material protection and will undertake the moral justification of her existence; thus she can evade at once both economic risk and the metaphysical risk of a liberty in which ends and aims must be contrived without assistance. Indeed, along with the ethical urge of each individual to affirm his subjective existence, there is also the temptation to forgo liberty and become a thing. This is an inauspicious road, for he who takes it – passive, lost, ruined – becomes henceforth the creature of another's will, frustrated in his transcendence and deprived of every value. But it is an easy road; on it one avoids the strain involved in undertaking an authentic existence. When man makes of woman the *Other*, he may, then, expect to manifest deep-seated tendencies towards complicity. Thus, woman may fail to lay claim to the status of subject because she lacks definite resources, because she feels the necessary bond that ties her to man regardless of reciprocity, and because she is often very well pleased with her role as the *Other*.

But it will be asked at once: how did all this begin? It is easy to see that the duality of the sexes, like any duality, gives rise to conflict. And doubtless the winner will assume the status of absolute. But why should man have won from the start? It seems possible that women could have won the victory; or that the outcome of the conflict might never have been decided. How is it that this world has always belonged to the men and that things have begun to change only recently? Is this change a good thing? Will it bring about an equal sharing of the world between men and women?

These questions are not new, and they have often been answered. But the very fact that woman *is the Other* tends to cast suspicion upon all the justifications that men have ever been able to provide for it. These have all too evidently been dictated by men's interest. A little-known feminist of the seventeenth century, Poulain de la Barre, put it this way: 'All that has been written about women by men should be suspect, for the men are at once judge and party to the lawsuit.' Everywhere, at all times, the males have displayed their satisfaction in feeling that they are the lords of creation. 'Blessed be God . . . that He did not make me a woman,' say the Jews in their morning prayers, while their wives pray on a note of resignation: 'Blessed be the Lord, who created me according to His will.' The first among the blessings for which Plato thanked the gods was that he had been created free, not enslaved; the second, a man, not a woman. But the males could not enjoy this privilege fully unless they believed it to be founded on the absolute and the eternal; they sought to make the fact of their supremacy into a right. 'Being men, those who have made and compiled the laws have favoured their own sex, and jurists have elevated these laws into principles', to quote Poulain de la Barre once more.

Legislators, priests, philosophers, writers, and scientists have striven to show that the subordinate position of woman is willed in heaven and advantageous on earth. The religions invented by men reflect this wish for domination. In the legends of Eve and Pandora men have taken up arms against women. They have made use of philosophy and theology, as the quotations from Aristotle and St Thomas have shown. Since ancient times satirists and moralists have delighted in showing up the weaknesses of women. We are familiar with the savage indictments hurled against women throughout French literature. Montherlant, for example, follows the tradition of Jean de Meung, though with less gusto. This hostility may at times be well founded, often it is gratuitous; but in truth it more or less successfully conceals a desire for self-justification. As Montaigne says, 'It is easier to accuse one sex than to excuse the other'. Sometimes what is going on is clear enough. For instance, the Roman law limiting the rights of woman cited 'the imbecility, the instability of the sex' just when the weakening of family ties seemed to threaten the interests of male heirs. And in the effort to keep the married woman under guardianship, appeal was made in the sixteenth century to the authority of St Augustine, who declared that 'woman is a creature neither decisive nor constant', at a time when the single woman was thought capable of managing her property. Montaigne understood clearly how arbitrary and unjust was woman's appointed lot: 'Women are not in the wrong when they decline to accept the rules laid down for them, since the men make these rules without consulting them. No wonder intrigue and strife abound.' But he did not go so far as to champion their cause.

It was only later, in the eighteenth century, that genuinely democratic men began to view the matter objectively. Diderot, among others, strove to show that woman is, like man, a human being. Later John Stuart Mill came fervently to her defence. But these philosophers displayed unusual impartiality. In the nineteenth century the feminist quarrel became again a quarrel of partisans. One of the consequences of the industrial revolution was the entrance of women into productive labour, and it was just here that the claims of the feminists emerged from the realm of theory and acquired an economic basis, while their opponents became the more aggressive. Although landed property lost power to some extent, the bourgeoisie clung to the old morality that found the guarantee of private property in the solidity of the family. Woman was ordered back into the home the more harshly as her emancipation became a real menace. Even within the working class the men endeavoured to restrain woman's liberation, because they began to see the women as dangerous competitors – the more so because they were accustomed to work for lower wages.[5]

In proving woman's inferiority, the anti-feminists then began to draw not only upon religion, philosophy, and theology, as before, but also upon science – biology, experimental psychology, etc. At most they were willing to grant 'equality in difference' to the *other* sex. That profitable formula is most significant; it is precisely like the 'equal but separate' formula of the Jim Crow laws aimed at the North American Negroes. As is well known, this so-called equalitarian segregation has resulted only in the most extreme discrimination. The similarity just noted is in no way due to chance, for whether it is a race, a caste, a class, or a sex that is reduced to a position of inferiority, the methods of justification are the same. 'The eternal feminine' corresponds to 'the black soul' and to 'the Jewish character'. True, the Jewish problem is on the whole very different from the other two – to the anti-Semite the Jew is not so much an inferior as he is an enemy for whom there is to be granted no place on earth, for whom annihilation is the fate desired. But there are deep similarities between the situation of woman and that of the Negro. Both are being emancipated today from a like paternalism, and the former master class wishes to 'keep them in their place' – that is, the place chosen for them. In both cases the former masters lavish more or less sincere eulogies, either on the virtues of 'the good Negro' with his dormant, childish, merry soul – the submissive Negro – or on the merits of the woman who is 'truly feminine' – that is, frivolous, infantile, irresponsible – the submissive woman. In both cases the dominant class bases its argument on a state of affairs that it has itself created. As George Bernard Shaw puts it, in substance, 'The American white relegates the black to the rank of shoeshine boy; and he concludes from this that the black is good for nothing but shining shoes.' This vicious circle is met with in all analogous circumstances; when an individual (or a group of individuals) is kept in a situation of inferiority, the fact is that he *is* inferior. But the significance of the verb to *be* must be rightly understood here; it is in bad faith to give it a static value when it really has the dynamic Hegelian sense of 'to have become'. Yes, women on the whole *are* today inferior to men; that is, their situation affords them fewer possibilities. The question is: should that state of affairs continue?

Many men hope that it will continue; not all have given up the battle. The conservative bourgeoisie still see in the emancipation of women a menace to their morality and their interests. Some men dread feminine competition. Recently a male student wrote in the *Hebdo-Latin*: 'Every woman student who goes into medicine or law robs us of a job.' He never questioned his rights in this world. And economic interests are not the only ones concerned. One of the benefits that oppression confers upon the oppressors is that the most humble among them is made to *feel* superior; thus, a 'poor white' in the South can console himself with the thought that he is not a 'dirty nigger' – and the more prosperous whites cleverly exploit this pride.

Similarly, the most mediocre of males feels himself a demigod as compared with women. It was much easier for M. de Montherlant to think himself a hero when he faced women (and women chosen for his purpose) than when he was obliged to act the man among men – something many women have done better than he, for that matter. And in September 1948, in one of his articles in the *Figaro littéraire*, Claude

Mauriac – whose great originality is admired by all – could[6] write regarding woman: 'We listen on a tone [*sic!*] of polite indifference . . . to the most brilliant among them, well knowing that her wit reflects more or less luminously ideas that come from *us*.' Evidently the speaker referred to is not reflecting the ideas of Mauriac himself, for no one knows of his having any. It may be that she reflects ideas originating with men, but then, even among men there are those who have been known to appropriate ideas not their own; and one can well ask whether Claude Mauriac might not find more interesting a conversation reflecting Descartes, Marx, or Gide rather than himself. What is really remarkable is that by using the questionable *we* he identifies himself with St Paul, Hegel, Lenin, and Nietzsche, and from the lofty eminence of their grandeur looks down disdainfully upon the bevy of women who make bold to converse with him on a footing of equality. In truth, I know of more than one woman who would refuse to suffer with patience Mauriac's 'tone of polite indifference'.

I have lingered on this example because the masculine attitude is here displayed with disarming ingenuousness. But men profit in many more subtle ways from the otherness, the alterity of woman. Here is a miraculous balm for those afflicted with an inferiority complex, and indeed no one is more arrogant towards women, more aggressive or scornful, than the man who is anxious about his virility. Those who are not fear-ridden in the presence of their fellow men are much more disposed to recognize a fellow creature in woman; but even to these the myth of Woman, the Other, is precious for many reasons.[7] They cannot be blamed for not cheerfully relinquishing all the benefits they derive from the myth, for they realize what they would lose in relinquishing woman as they fancy her to be, while they fail to realize what they have to gain from the woman of tomorrow. Refusal to pose oneself as the Subject, unique and absolute, requires great self-denial. Furthermore, the vast majority of men make no such claim explicitly. They do not *postulate* woman as inferior, for today they are too thoroughly imbued with the ideal of democracy not to recognize all human beings as equals.

Notes

1   E. Lévinas expresses this idea most explicitly in his essay *Temps et l'Autre*. 'Is there not a case in which otherness, alterity [*altérité*], unquestionably marks the nature of a being, as its essence, an instance of otherness not consisting purely and simply in the opposition of two species of the same genus? I think that the feminine represents the contrary in its absolute sense, this contrariness being in no wise affected by any relation between it and its correlative and thus remaining absolutely other. Sex is not a certain specific difference . . . no more is the sexual difference a mere contradiction . . . Nor does this difference lie in the duality of two complementary terms, for two complementary terms imply a pre-existing whole . . . Otherness reaches its full flowering in the feminine, a term of the same rank as consciousness but of opposite meaning.'

I suppose that Lévinas does not forget that woman, too, is aware of her own consciousness, or ego. But it is striking that he deliberately takes a man's point of view, disregarding the reciprocity of subject and object. When he writes that woman is mystery, he implies that she is mystery for man. Thus his description, which is intended to be objective, is in fact an assertion of masculine privilege.

2   See C. Lévi-Strauss, *Les Structures élémentaires de la parenté*.

3   With rare exceptions, perhaps, like certain matriarchal rulers, queens, and the like. [H.M.P.]

4   See *The Second Sex*, Part II, chap. 5.

5   See *The Second Sex*, Part II, pp. 145–8.

6   Or at least he thought he could.

7   A significant article on this theme by Michel Carrouges appeared in No. 292 of the *Cahiers du Sud*. He writes indignantly: 'Would that there were no woman–myth at all but only a cohort of cooks, matrons, prostitutes, and blue–stockings serving functions of pleasure or use-fulness!' That is to say, in his view woman has no existence in and for herself; he thinks only of her *function* in the male world. Her reason for existence lies in man. But then, in fact, her poetic 'function' as a myth might be more valued than any other. The real problem is pre-cisely to find out why woman should be defined with relation to man.

19

COMMENTARY ON BUTLER

Judith Butler (born 1956) is Professor of Comparative Literature and Rhetoric at the University of California, Berkeley. She is best known for her work on gender identity, sexuality, and power, and is a key figure in post-structuralist and postmodern feminist philosophy and queer theory. Butler's work is heavily influenced by Hegel, Nietzsche, Merleau-Ponty, Beauvoir, and Lacan, but most significantly by Foucault. In her hugely popular book, *Gender Trouble*, she argues that norms of gender identity are constructed and stabilized within a cultural hegemony which chains gender to sex according to an imperative of heterosexual reproductive biology.

Butler's account of gender identity continues Foucault's Nietzschean critique of subjectivity, in which subjectivity is understood as the effect of the subject-positions articulated in discourse. However, she goes further than Foucault in her account of identity as "performative." This concept describes the mechanisms by which particular subjectivities are formed through the submission of bodies to discursive practices. Through her concept of performativity, Butler brings to light the repetition involved in the ways in which disciplinary power is lived by and habituated into the individual's life. By identifying the repetitive and reiterative processes of inscription of social norms in the body, Butler emphasizes the discontinuous nature of identity. This allows her to locate the possibility of resistance within the process of reiteration itself.

Butler takes up the issue of gender identity as part of her commitment to understanding and redressing sexual oppression. In the opening pages of *Gender Trouble*, she points out that feminist theory has assumed that "there is an existing identity, understood through the category of women" and that it is this identifiable female subject whose interests feminism has attempted to further through political representation. On the basis of a Foucauldian understanding of politics and representation, Butler believes that the attempt to represent woman (politically or otherwise) inevitably involves employing the very means by which her oppression is effected. This is because Butler regards language as a practice structured by rules of binary oppositional logic that determines its truths and falsities. She argues that this oppositional logic determines in advance that the subject is necessarily masculine, and so functions in such a way as to marginalize the feminine.[1] For this reason Butler argues that unless feminist theorists first address the operations of representation itself the effort to gain political representation can only reproduce the sexual biases built into language.[2] Feminists must first theorize the mechanism by which the symbolic structures of language organize the meaning of one's lived body to effect discipline and produce bodies gendered normatively. This is the challenge that Butler set out to meet in *Gender Trouble*.

The Critique of Substantive Identity

For Butler, one of the most salient aspects in this regard concerns the metaphysical assumptions underlying philosophical conceptions of identity and sex. In this excerpt from *Gender Trouble* Butler exposes the assumption of substance metaphysics which has been crucial to the "heterosexual hegemony" that continues to determine norms of gender identity and to underpin gender inequality.

Butler frames her enquiry with the question of the connection between personal identity and gender identity. Like personal identity, gender identity concerns continuity and coherence in one's sense of who one is. However, she claims that gender identity precedes personal identity "for the simple reason that 'persons' only become intelligible through becoming gendered in conformity with recognizable standards of gender intelligibility."[3] The idea that gender is only incidental to being a "person" is premised upon a traditional view that conceives of gender as the straightforward expression of a body's sex. On this view, sexual identity is a function of the physical substance of the body: a male sexed body is identical with a man, and a female sexed body is identical with a woman.

Butler embarks upon a Nietzschean-style critique, taking up Nietzsche's point that it is simply the subject–predicate structure of language that leads us to mistakenly believe in the existence of a "self" with agency, whereas there is only the dominant set of urges of the body expressed through will to power. Similarly, the "ego" is nothing more than a psychological category produced through a faulty grammar that leads us to take the will to be the "cause" of one's thoughts.[4] On the Nietzschean (and later Foucauldian) view, the subject is actually produced through the symbolic resources of language.

Using Monique Wittig's analysis of French and English languages, Butler argues that gender and subjectivity are articulated together grammatically along the subject–predicate axis: man is subject (Self), woman is predicate, or property (Other). Furthermore, the symbolic structures that organize meaning in language also organize the meaning of the complex of discourses that connect biology, sex, desire, gender, and sense of self. Gendered identity, then, is a coherence of discourses that are unified around the concept of sex. For Butler, gender is a "fictive construction produced through the compulsory ordering of attributes into coherent gender sequences"[5] such that one's gender appears as a given, natural, and immutable state of one's sex as woman or man.

The substantive conception of identity assumes that identity has a seamless continuity and coherence. Against this, Butler argues that the coherence and continuity in our experiences of our gender identities is the effect of sedimented regulatory practices premised upon a normative ideal of what human bodies should be like. The artificial nature of these practices becomes apparent in the case of persons who fail to conform to cultural norms of gender identity (what she calls discontinuous genders), for example, transsexuals, hermaphrodites, and homosexuals. Butler argues that an analysis of the range of genders reveals that the purportedly normal structure of gender identity is a compulsory heterosexuality, a "cultural matrix" that employs a certain logic which ensures that certain things follow from (that is, are politically entailed by) others and so ensures the continuity and coherence of normalized gender identities. As a result, the political nature of gender identity is given all of the appearance of a "natural" causal necessity.

Gender as Performative

Against the fiction of substantive identity Butler argues that gender identity is to be understood as a verb – as a performative. Identity is a verb because it is realized through repeated acts – reiterations – of cultural norms that function as signifiers of gender. Gender is constituted as real only in being continually reenacted or "performed" – in other words, resignified – in the bodies of individuals. In explaining this notion of performativity Butler draws upon Merleau-Ponty's account of bodily ambiguity. For Merleau-Ponty, meaning is constructed through the manner in which a situation is lived; it is partly given in a situation (and in this respect the body is passive), and partly created by one's active engagement in the situation. The meaning of an experience is not predetermined by the nature of things-in-themselves but by circumstances that provide the opportunity for a specific set of historical possibilities to find expression in the body. The lived body is both simultaneously active and passive in the production of meaning: "the body is not merely matter but a continual and incessant *materializing* of possibilities."[6] The embodied subject constitutes meaning by the "taking up and rendering specific of a set of possibilities."[7]

Butler describes the constitution of the meaning of the lived body as "dramatic" in the theatrical sense because in the realization of a possibility the body has an active and a passive role: a meaning is never simply imposed upon the body but must be actively incorporated into an individual's bodily repertoire of behaviors and thoughts through the body's own agency. Butler argues that in the process of the body's "materializing" or making real a meaning, social constraints are reproduced. However, they are also partly transcended because those social meanings are recontextualized within the particular individual's situation. There is a dialectical relation between the body-agent and the historically and socially constituted meanings that inform the individual's lived situation. This dialectic is effected through the medium of the ambiguous body, and so enables both discipline and transgression.

For Butler, the enactment of gender identity is a "forced reiteration of norms,"[8] an expression of social relations that compels bodies to conform to certain historical ideas in order to perpetuate heterosexual culture. The notion of forced reiteration is both active and passive because it involves force, but also the *act* of reiteration. For this reason Butler describes gender as an act of being embodied that precedes and exceeds voluntary action: "Surely, there are nuanced and individual ways of *doing* one's gender, but *that* one does it, and that one does it *in accord with* certain sanctions and proscriptions is clearly not an individual matter."[9] Understood as a kind of nonvoluntary act, performative gender has a distinct temporal quality; it is a series of temporally separated acts of reiteration. The discontinuity of acts means that between reiterations there are moments of indeterminacy. This allows identity to be interrupted and disrupted at any moment. It is in this indeterminacy that Butler locates the possibility of agency as resistance. Resistance can occur by subverting the resignification of the norm in its repetition, for example, when an individual parodies the norm, such as in the case of drag. Butler's Nietzschean message is to use moments of indeterminacy to actively subvert and transgress cultural norms – to create "gender trouble" – in order to create novel and diverse forms of living.

For Foucault, the sheer pervasiveness of discursive power leaves little conceptual room for agency, which his theory nevertheless employs. By connecting discourse to the structure of embodiment through the concept of iteration, Butler has attempted to describe a mechanism by which disciplined bodies nevertheless exceed their imposed passivity. However, Butler refuses to give content to the distinction between enabling and regressive practices on the grounds that to do so would simply create another norm that would foreclose the results of conflict and so constrain the subject.[10] The danger here is that without specifying normative content concrete conflicts cannot be resolved because the grounds of *disagreement* could never be fixed, let alone agreement. Here, the essentially conflictual nature of the Nietzschean worldview informing Butler's account comes to the fore.

Connected to this problem is the theoretical problem of ensuring the inherently resistant nature of action.[11] Unless there is some way of distinguishing acts of resistance from acts of power, then Butler will not be able to attach to the notion of resistance the critical and moral force required to underpin opposition to oppression. Recent work in feminist theories of autonomy and moral deliberation, such as Catriona Mackenzie's (discussed in the final chapter), is relevant here.[12]

Notes

1 Judith Butler, *Gender Trouble: Feminism and the Subversion of Identity* (New York: Routledge, 1990), pp. 18–20.
2 Ibid, p. 2.
3 Ibid, p. 16.
4 Ibid, pp. 20–1.
5 Ibid, p. 24.
6 Judith Butler, "Performative Acts and Gender Constitution: An Essay in Phenomenology and Feminist Theory," in Sue-Ellen Case (ed.), *Performing Feminisms: Feminist Critical Theory and Theatre* (London: Johns Hopkins Press, 1990), p. 272.
7 Ibid.
8 Lois McNay, *Gender and Agency* (Cambridge and Oxford: Polity, 2000), p. 33.
9 Butler, *Performing Feminisms*, p. 276.
10 Peter Osbourne and Lynne Segal, "Gender as Performance: An Interview with Judith Butler," *Radical Philosophy*, 67, Summer 1994, p. 39.
11 McNay (2000), p. 62.
12 For example, Catriona Mackenzie and Natalie Stoljar (eds.), *Relational Autonomy: Feminist Perspectives on Autonomy, Agency, and the Social Self* (New York and Oxford: Oxford University Press, 2000).

Main Texts by Butler

Bodies That Matter: On the Discursive Limits of "Sex" (New York: Routledge, 1993).

Contingency, Hegemony, Universality: Contemporary Dialogues on the Left, with Ernesto Laclau and Slavoj Zizek (London: Verso, 2000).

Gender Trouble: Feminism and the Subversion of Identity (New York: Routledge, 1990).

"Performative Acts and Gender Constitution: An Essay in Phenomenology and Feminist Theory," in Sue-Ellen Case (ed.), *Performing Feminisms: Feminist Critical Theory and Theatre* (Baltimore: Johns Hopkins Press, 1990), pp. 270–82.

Subjects of Desire: Hegelian Reflections in Twentieth-century France (New York: Columbia University Press, 1999).

Further Reading

Bell, Vikki (ed.), *Performativity and Belonging* (London and Thousand Oaks, CA: Sage Publications, 1999).

Hawley, John C. (ed.), *Postcolonial and Queer Theories: Intersections and Essays* (Westport, CT and London: Greenwood Press, 2001).

McNay, Lois, *Gender and Agency* (Cambridge and Oxford: Polity, 2000).

Osbourne, Peter and Lynne Segal, "Gender as Performance: An Interview with Judith Butler," *Radical Philosophy*, 67, Summer 1994, pp. 32–9.

Salih, Sara, *Judith Butler* (London and New York: Routledge, 2002).

Welton, Donn (ed.), *Body and Flesh: A Philosophical Reader* (Malden, MA and Oxford: Blackwell, 1998).

"GENDER TROUBLE: FEMINISM AND THE SUBVERSION OF IDENTITY"

Judith Butler

Identity, Sex, and the Metaphysics of Substance

What can be meant by "identity," then, and what grounds the presumption that identities are self-identical, persisting through time as the same, unified and internally coherent? More importantly, how do these assumptions inform the discourses on "gender
identity"? It would be wrong to think that the discussion of "identity" ought to proceed
prior to a discussion of gender identity for the simple reason that "persons" only become
intelligible through becoming gendered in conformity with recognizable standards of
gender intelligibility. Sociological discussions have conventionally sought to understand
the notion of the person in terms of an agency that claims ontological priority to the
various roles and functions through which it assumes social visibility and meaning.
Within philosophical discourse itself, the notion of "the person" has received analytic
elaboration on the assumption that whatever social context the person is "in" remains
somehow externally related to the definitional structure of personhood, be that consciousness, the capacity for language, or moral deliberation. Although that literature is
not examined here, one premise of such inquiries is the focus of critical exploration and
inversion. Whereas the question of what constitutes "personal identity" within philosophical accounts almost always centers on the question of what internal feature of the
person establishes the continuity or self-identity of the person through time, the question here will be: To what extent do *regulatory practices* of gender formation and division
constitute identity, the internal coherence of the subject, indeed, the self-identical status
of the person? To what extent is "identity" a normative ideal rather than a descriptive
feature of experience? And how do the regulatory practices that govern gender also
govern culturally intelligible notions of identity? In other words, the "coherence" and
"continuity" of "the person" are not logical or analytic features of personhood, but,
rather, socially instituted and maintained norms of intelligibility. Inasmuch as "identity"
is assured through the stabilizing concepts of sex, gender, and sexuality, the very notion

From *Gender Trouble: Feminism and the Subversion of Identity* (New York: Routledge, 1990), pp. 16–25. © 1990
by Judith Butler. Reproduced by permission of Routledge and Taylor & Francis Books, Inc.

of "the person" is called into question by the cultural emergence of those "incoherent" or "discontinuous" gendered beings who appear to be persons but who fail to conform to the gendered norms of cultural intelligibility by which persons are defined.

"Intelligible" genders are those which in some sense institute and maintain relations of coherence and continuity among sex, gender, sexual practice, and desire. In other words, the spectres of discontinuity and incoherence, themselves thinkable only in relation to existing norms of continuity and coherence, are constantly prohibited and produced by the very laws that seek to establish causal or expressive lines of connection among biological sex, culturally constituted genders, and the "expression" or "effect" of both in the manifestation of sexual desire through sexual practice.

The notion that there might be a "truth" of sex, as Foucault ironically terms it, is produced precisely through the regulatory practices that generate coherent identities through the matrix of coherent gender norms. The heterosexualization of desire requires and institutes the production of discrete and asymmetrical oppositions between "feminine" and "masculine," where these are understood as expressive attributes of "male" and "female." The cultural matrix through which gender identity has become intelligible requires that certain kinds of "identities" cannot "exist" – that is, those in which gender does not follow from sex and those in which the practices of desire do not "follow" from either sex or gender. "Follow" in this context is a political relation of entailment instituted by the cultural laws that establish and regulate the shape and meaning of sexuality. Indeed, precisely because certain kinds of "gender identities" fail to conform to those norms of cultural intelligibility, they appear only as developmental failures or logical impossibilities from within that domain. Their persistence and proliferation, however, provide critical opportunities to expose the limits and regulatory aims of that domain of intelligibility and, hence, to open up within the very terms of that matrix of intelligibility rival and subversive matrices of gender disorder.

Before such disordering practices are considered, however, it seems crucial to understand the "matrix of intelligibility." Is it singular? Of what is it composed? What is the peculiar alliance presumed to exist between a system of compulsory heterosexuality and the discursive categories that establish the identity concepts of sex? If "identity" is an *effect* of discursive practices, to what extent is gender identity, construed as a relationship among sex, gender, sexual practice, and desire, the effect of a regulatory practice that can be identified as compulsory heterosexuality? Would that explanation return us to yet another totalizing frame in which compulsory heterosexuality merely takes the place of phallogocentrism as the monolithic cause of gender oppression?

Within the spectrum of French feminist and poststructuralist theory, very different regimes of power are understood to produce the identity concepts of sex. Consider the divergence between those positions, such as Irigaray's, that claim there is only one sex, the masculine, that elaborates itself in and through the production of the "Other," and those positions, Foucault's, for instance, that assume that the category of sex, whether masculine or feminine, is a production of a diffuse regulatory economy of sexuality. Consider also Wittig's argument that the category of sex is, under the conditions of compulsory heterosexuality, always feminine (the masculine remaining unmarked and, hence, synonymous with the "universal"). Wittig concurs, however paradoxically, with Foucault in claiming that the category of sex would itself disappear and, indeed, *dissipate* through the disruption and displacement of heterosexual hegemony.

The various explanatory models offered here suggest the very different ways in which the category of sex is understood depending on how the field of power is articulated. Is it possible to maintain the complexity of these fields of power and think through their productive capacities together? On the one hand, Irigaray's theory of sexual difference suggests that women can never be understood on the model of a "subject" within the conventional representational systems of Western culture precisely because they constitute the fetish of representation and, hence, the unrepresentable as such. Women can never "be," according to this ontology of substances, precisely because they are the relation of difference, the excluded, by which that domain marks itself off. Women are also a "difference" that cannot be understood as the simple negation or "Other" of the always-already-masculine subject. As discussed earlier, they are neither the subject nor its Other, but a difference from the economy of binary opposition, itself a ruse for a monologic elaboration of the masculine.

Central to each of these views, however, is the notion that sex appears within hegemonic language as a *substance*, as, metaphysically speaking, a self-identical being. This appearance is achieved through a performative twist of language and/or discourse that conceals the fact that "being" a sex or a gender is fundamentally impossible. For Irigaray, grammar can never be a true index of gender relations precisely because it supports the substantial model of gender as a binary relation between two positive and representable terms.[1] In Irigaray's view, the substantive grammar of gender, which assumes men and women as well as their attributes of masculine and feminine, is an example of a binary that effectively masks the univocal and hegemonic discourse of the masculine, phallogocentrism, silencing the feminine as a site of subversive multiplicity. For Foucault, the substantive grammar of sex imposes an artificial binary relation between the sexes, as well as an artificial internal coherence within each term of that binary. The binary regulation of sexuality suppresses the subversive multiplicity of a sexuality that disrupts heterosexual, reproductive, and medicojuridical hegemonies.

For Wittig, the binary restriction on sex serves the reproductive aims of a system of compulsory heterosexuality; occasionally, she claims that the overthrow of compulsory heterosexuality will inaugurate a true humanism of "the person" freed from the shackles of sex. In other contexts, she suggests that the profusion and diffusion of a non-phallocentric erotic economy will dispel the illusions of sex, gender, and identity. At yet other textual moments it seems that "the lesbian" emerges as a third gender that promises to transcend the binary restriction on sex imposed by the system of compulsory heterosexuality. In her defense of the "cognitive subject," Wittig appears to have no metaphysical quarrel with hegemonic modes of signification or representation; indeed, the subject, with its attribute of self-determination, appears to be the rehabilitation of the agent of existential choice under the name of the lesbian: "the advent of individual subjects demands first destroying the categories of sex. . . . the lesbian is the only concept I know of which is beyond the categories of sex."[2] She does not criticize "the subject" as invariably masculine according to the rules of an inevitably patriarchal Symbolic, but proposes in its place the equivalent of a lesbian subject as language-user.[3]

The identification of women with "sex," for Beauvoir as for Wittig, is a conflation of the category of women with the ostensibly sexualized features of their bodies and, hence, a refusal to grant freedom and autonomy to women as it is purportedly enjoyed by men. Thus, the destruction of the category of sex would be the destruction of an *attribute*, sex, that has, through a misogynist gesture of synecdoche, come to take the place of the person, the self-determining *cogito*. In other words, only men are "persons," and there is no gender but the feminine:

> Gender is the linguistic index of the political opposition between the sexes. Gender is used here in the singular because indeed there are not two genders. There is only one: the feminine, the "masculine" not being a gender. For the masculine is not the masculine, but the general.[4]

Hence, Wittig calls for the destruction of "sex" so that women can assume the status of a universal subject. On the way toward that destruction, "women" must assume both a particular and a universal point of view.[5] As a subject who can realize concrete universality through freedom, Wittig's lesbian confirms rather than contests the normative promise of humanist ideals premised on the metaphysics of substance. In this respect, Wittig is distinguished from Irigaray, not only in terms of the now familiar oppositions between essentialism and materialism,[6] but in terms of the adherence to a metaphysics of substance that confirms the normative model of humanism as the framework for feminism. Where it seems that Wittig has subscribed to a radical project of lesbian emancipation and enforced a distinction between "lesbian" and "woman," she does this through the defense of the pregendered "person," characterized as freedom. This move not only confirms the presocial status of human freedom, but subscribes to that metaphysics of substance that is responsible for the production and naturalization of the category of sex itself.

The metaphysics of substance is a phrase that is associated with Nietzsche within the contemporary criticism of philosophical discourse. In a commentary on Nietzsche, Michel Haar argues that a number of philosophical ontologies have been trapped within certain illusions of "Being" and "Substance" that are fostered by the belief that the grammatical formulation of subject and predicate reflects the prior ontological reality of substance and attribute. These constructs, argues Haar, constitute the artificial philosophical means by which simplicity, order, and identity are effectively instituted. In no sense, however, do they reveal or represent some true order of things. For our purposes, this Nietzschean criticism becomes instructive when it is applied to the psychological categories that govern much popular and theoretical thinking about gender identity. According to Haar, the critique of the metaphysics of substance implies a critique of the very notion of the psychological person as a substantive thing:

> The destruction of logic by means of its genealogy brings with it as well the ruin of the psychological categories founded upon this logic. All psychological categories (the ego, the individual, the person) derive from the illusion of substantial identity. But this illusion goes back basically to a superstition that deceives not only common sense but also philosophers — namely, the belief in language and, more precisely, in the truth of grammatical categories. It was grammar (the structure of subject and predicate) that inspired Descartes' certainty that "I" is the subject of "think," whereas it is rather the thoughts that come to "me": at bottom, faith in grammar simply conveys the will to be the "cause" of one's thoughts. The subject, the self, the individual, are just so many false concepts, since they transform into substances fictitious unities having at the start only a linguistic reality.[7]

Wittig provides an alternative critique by showing that persons cannot be signified within language without the mark of gender. She provides a political analysis of the grammar of gender in French. According to Wittig, gender not only designates persons, "qualifies" them, as it were, but constitutes a conceptual episteme by which binary gender is universalized. Although French gives gender to all sorts of nouns other than persons, Wittig argues that her analysis has consequences for English as well. At the outset of "The Mark of Gender" (1984), she writes:

> The mark of gender, according to grammarians, concerns substantives. They talk about it in terms of function. If they question its meaning, they may joke about it, calling gender a "fictive sex." . . . as far as the categories of the person are concerned, both [English and French] are bearers of gender to the same extent. Both indeed give way to a primitive ontological concept that enforces in language a division of beings into sexes. . . . As an ontological concept that deals with the nature of Being, along with a whole nebula of other primitive concepts belonging to the same line of thought, gender seems to belong primarily to philosophy.[8]

For gender to "belong to philosophy" is, for Wittig, to belong to "that body of self-evident concepts without which philosophers believe they cannot develop a line of reasoning and which for them go without saying, for they exist prior to any thought, any social order, in nature."[9] Wittig's view is corroborated by that popular discourse on gender identity that uncritically employs the inflectional attribution of "being" to genders and to "sexualities." The unproblematic claim to "be" a woman and "be" heterosexual would be symptomatic of that metaphysics of gender substances. In the case of both "men" and "women," this claim tends to subordinate the notion of gender under that of identity and to lead to the conclusion that a person *is* a gender and *is* one in virtue of his or her sex, psychic sense of self, and various expressions of that psychic self, the most salient being that of sexual desire. In such a prefeminist context, gender, naively (rather than critically) confused with sex, serves as a unifying principle of the embodied self and maintains that unity over and against an "opposite sex" whose structure is presumed to maintain a parallel but oppositional internal coherence among sex, gender, and desire. The articulation "I feel like a woman" by a female or "I feel like a man" by a male presupposes that in neither case is the claim meaninglessly redundant. Although it might appear unproblematic *to be* a given anatomy (although we shall later consider the way in which that project is also fraught with difficulty), the experience of a gendered psychic disposition or cultural identity is considered an achievement. Thus, "I feel like a woman" is true to the extent that Aretha Franklin's invocation of the defining Other is assumed: "You make me feel like a natural woman."[10] This achievement requires a differentiation from the opposite gender. Hence, one is one's gender to the extent that one is not the other gender, a formulation that presupposes and enforces the restriction of gender within that binary pair.

Gender can denote a *unity* of experience, of sex, gender, and desire, only when sex can be understood in some sense to necessitate gender – where gender is a psychic and/or cultural designation of the self – and desire – where desire is heterosexual and therefore differentiates itself through an oppositional relation to that other gender it desires. The internal coherence or unity of either gender, man or woman, thereby requires both a stable and oppositional heterosexuality. That institutional

heterosexuality both requires and produces the univocity of each of the gendered terms
that constitute the limit of gendered possibilities within an oppositional, binary gender
system. This conception of gender presupposes not only a causal relation among sex,
gender, and desire, but suggests as well that desire reflects or expresses gender and that
gender reflects or expresses desire. The metaphysical unity of the three is assumed to
be truly known and expressed in a differentiating desire for an oppositional gender –
that is, in a form of oppositional heterosexuality. Whether as a naturalistic paradigm
which establishes a causal continuity among sex, gender, and desire, or as an authentic-
expressive paradigm in which some true self is said to be revealed simultaneously or
successively in sex, gender, and desire, here "the old dream of symmetry," as Irigaray has
called it, is presupposed, reified, and rationalized.

   This rough sketch of gender gives us a clue to understanding the political reasons
for the substantializing view of gender. The institution of a compulsory and naturalized heterosexuality requires and regulates gender as a binary relation in which the
masculine term is differentiated from a feminine term, and this differentiation is accomplished through the practices of heterosexual desire. The act of differentiating the
two oppositional moments of the binary results in a consolidation of each term, the
respective internal coherence of sex, gender, and desire.

   The strategic displacement of that binary relation and the metaphysics of substance
on which it relies presuppose that the categories of female and male, woman and man,
are similarly produced within the binary frame. Foucault implicitly subscribes to such
an explanation. In the closing chapter of the first volume of *The History of Sexuality*
and in his brief but significant introduction to *Herculine Barbin, Being the Recently Discovered Journals of a Nineteenth-Century Hermaphrodite*,[11] Foucault suggests that the category of sex, prior to any categorization of sexual difference, is itself constructed through
a historically specific mode of *sexuality*. The tactical production of the discrete and
binary categorization of sex conceals the strategic aims of that very apparatus of production by postulating "sex" as "a cause" of sexual experience, behavior, and desire.
Foucault's genealogical inquiry exposes this ostensible "cause" as "an effect," the
production of a given regime of sexuality that seeks to regulate sexual experience by
instating the discrete categories of sex as foundational and causal functions within
any discursive account of sexuality.

   Foucault's introduction to the journals of the hermaphrodite, Herculine Barbin, suggests that the genealogical critique of these reified categories of sex is the inadvertent
consequence of sexual practices that cannot be accounted for within the medicolegal
discourse of a naturalized heterosexuality. Herculine is not an "identity," but the sexual
impossibility of an identity. Although male and female anatomical elements are jointly
distributed in and on this body, that is not the true source of scandal. The linguistic
conventions that produce intelligible gendered selves find their limit in Herculine precisely because she/he occasions a convergence and disorganization of the rules that
govern sex/gender/desire. Herculine deploys and redistributes the terms of a binary
system, but that very redistribution disrupts and proliferates those terms outside the
binary itself. According to Foucault, Herculine is not categorizable within the gender
binary as it stands; the disconcerting convergence of heterosexuality and homosexual-
ity in her/his person are only occasioned, but never caused, by his/her anatomical discontinuity. Foucault's appropriation of Herculine is suspect,[12] but his analysis implies

the interesting belief that sexual heterogeneity (paradoxically foreclosed by a naturalized "hetero"-sexuality) implies a critique of the metaphysics of substance as it informs the identitarian categories of sex. Foucault imagines Herculine's experience as "a world of pleasures in which grins hang about without the cat."[13] Smiles, happinesses, pleasures, and desires are figured here as qualities without an abiding substance to which they are said to adhere. As free-floating attributes, they suggest the possibility of a gendered experience that cannot be grasped through the substantializing and hierarchizing grammar of nouns (*res extensa*) and adjectives (attributes, essential and accidental). Through his cursory reading of Herculine, Foucault proposes an ontology of accidental attributes that exposes the postulation of identity as a culturally restricted principle of order and hierarchy, a regulatory fiction.

If it is possible to speak of a "man" with a masculine attribute and to understand that attribute as a happy but accidental feature of that man, then it is also possible to speak of a "man" with a feminine attribute, whatever that is, but still to maintain the integrity of the gender. But once we dispense with the priority of "man" and "woman" as abiding substances, then it is no longer possible to subordinate dissonant gendered features as so many secondary and accidental characteristics of a gender ontology that is fundamentally intact. If the notion of an abiding substance is a fictive construction produced through the compulsory ordering of attributes into coherent gender sequences, then it seems that gender as substance, the viability of *man* and *woman* as nouns, is called into question by the dissonant play of attributes that fail to conform to sequential or causal models of intelligibility.

The appearance of an abiding substance or gendered self, what the psychiatrist Robert Stoller refers to as a "gender core,"[14] is thus produced by the regulation of attributes along culturally established lines of coherence. As a result, the exposure of this fictive production is conditioned by the deregulated play of attributes that resist assimilation into the ready made framework of primary nouns and subordinate adjectives. It is of course always possible to argue that dissonant adjectives work retroactively to redefine the substantive identities they are said to modify and, hence, to expand the substantive categories of gender to include possibilities that they previously excluded. But if these substances are nothing other than the coherences contingently created through the regulation of attributes, it would seem that the ontology of substances itself is not only an artificial effect, but essentially superfluous.

In this sense, *gender* is not a noun, but neither is it a set of free-floating attributes, for we have seen that the substantive effect of gender is performatively produced and compelled by the regulatory practices of gender coherence. Hence, within the inherited discourse of the metaphysics of substance, gender proves to be performative – that is, constituting the identity it is purported to be. In this sense, gender is always a doing, though not a doing by a subject who might be said to preexist the deed. The challenge for rethinking gender categories outside of the metaphysics of substance will have to consider the relevance of Nietzsche's claim in *On the Genealogy of Morals* that "there is no 'being' behind doing, effecting, becoming; 'the doer' is merely a fiction added to the deed – the deed is everything."[15] In an application that Nietzsche himself would not have anticipated or condoned, we might state as a corollary: There is no gender identity behind the expressions of gender; that identity is performatively constituted by the very "expressions" that are said to be its results.

Notes

1   For a fuller elaboration of the unrepresentability of women in phallogocentric discourse, see Luce Irigaray, "Any Theory of the 'Subject' Has Always Been Appropriated by the Masculine," in *Speculum of the Other Woman*, trans. Gillian C. Gill (Ithaca: Cornell University Press, 1985). Irigaray appears to revise this argument in her discussion of "the feminine gender" in *Sexes et parentés*.

2   Monique Wittig, "One is Not Born a Woman," *Feminist Issues*, 1 (2), Winter 1981, p. 53.

3   The notion of the "Symbolic" [. . .] is to be understood as an ideal and universal set of cultural laws that govern kinship and signification and, within the terms of psychoanalytic structuralism, govern the production of sexual difference. Based on the notion of an idealized "paternal law," the Symbolic is reformulated by Irigaray as a dominant and hegemonic discourse of phallogocentrism. Some French feminists propose an alternative language to one governed by the Phallus or the paternal law, and so wage a critique against the Symbolic. Kristeva proposes the "semiotic" as a specifically maternal dimension of language, and both Irigaray and Hélène Cixous have been associated with *écriture feminine*. Wittig, however, has always resisted that movement, claiming that language in its structure is neither misogynist nor feminist, but an *instrument* to be deployed for developed political purposes. Clearly her belief in a "cognitive subject" that exits prior to language facilitates her understanding of language as an instrument, rather than as a field of significations that preexist and structure subject-formation itself.

4   Monique Wittig, "The Point of View: Universal or Particular?" (*Feminist Issues*, 3 (2), Fall 1983, p. 64.

5   "One must assume both a particular *and* a universal point of view, at least to be part of literature," Monique Wittig, "The Trojan Horse," *Feminist Issues*, 4 (2), Fall 1984, p. 68.

6   The journal, *Questions Feministes*, available in English translation as *Feminist Issues*, generally defended a "materialist" point of view which took practices, institution, and the constructed status of language to be the "material grounds" of the oppression of women. Wittig was part of the original editorial staff. Along with Monique Plaza, Wittig argued that sexual difference was essentialist in that it derived the meaning of women's social function from their biological facticity, but also because it subscribed to the primary signification of women's bodies as maternal and, hence, gave ideological strength to the hegemony of reproductive sexuality.

7   Michel Haar, "Nietzsche and Metaphysical Language," *The New Nietzsche: Contemporary Styles of Interpretation*, ed. David Allison (New York: Delta, 1977), pp. 17–18.

8   Monique Wittig, "The Mark of Gender," *Feminist Issues*, 5 (2), Fall 1985, p. 4.

9   Ibid., p. 3.

10 Aretha's song, originally written by Carole King, also contests the naturalization of gender. "Like a natural woman" is a phrase that suggests that "naturalness" is only accomplished through analogy or metaphor. In other words, "You make me feel like a metaphor of the natural," and without "you," some denaturalized ground would be revealed. For a further discussion of Aretha's claim in light of Simone de Beauvoir's contention that "one is not born, but rather becomes a woman," see my "Beauvoir's Philosophical Contribution," in eds. Ann Garry and Marjorie Pearsall, *Women, Knowledge, and Reality* (Rowman and Allenheld, 1989), pp. 253–62.

11 Michel Foucault, ed., *Herculine Barbin, Being the Recently Discovered Memoirs of a Nineteenth-Century Hermaphrodite*, trans. Richard McDougall (New York: Colophon, 1980), originally published as *Herculine Barbin, dite Alexina B. presenté par Michel Foucault* (Paris: Gallimard,

1978). The French version lacks the introduction supplied by Foucault with the English translation.

12 See chapter 2, section ii.

13 Foucault, ed., *Herculine Barbin*, p. x.

14 Robert Stoller, *Presentations of Gender* (New Haven: Yale University Press, 1985), pp. 11–14.

15 Friedrich Nietzsche, *On the Genealogy of Morals*, trans. Walter Kaufmann (New York: Vintage, 1969), p. 45.

20

COMMENTARY ON IRIGARAY

Luce Irigaray was born in Belgium in 1930 or 1932 and holds doctoral degrees in philosophy and linguistics. She also trained in psychoanalysis at the École Freudienne de Paris (Freudian School of Paris), which was founded by Jacques Lacan. Her work can be broadly described as post-structuralist feminist philosophy, primarily concerned with the way in which female subjectivity is directed and distorted by political and intellectual forces. More recently she has been concerned with issues of political justice and community.

Irigaray's writing is often poetic, employing metaphors, puns, double entendres, and colloquialisms to deliberately disrupt the reading of her texts and those she discusses. This strategy is integral to her argument that traditional philosophical texts – and traditional readings of those texts – systematically marginalize women's situations and experiences. In this way, politically dominant intellectual discourses operate to constrain how women can regard themselves and express their subjectivity. Moreover, she argues that philosophical discourse not merely omits the feminine, but *disavows* it. In short, Irigaray claims that philosophy contains an inherent bias that suppresses sexual difference and, in doing so, severely constrains female subjectivity. In response, she endeavors to expose the bias and contradictions of philosophy, exploiting the meanings suppressed in texts through the specific textual strategy of deconstruction.

Deconstruction is a form of textual analysis made famous by French philosopher Jacques Derrida, and works on the principle that meaning is always overdetermined.[1] On this view, every linguistic term draws its meaning from its connections to a network of other terms that form its unnoticed background. The positive value of a term is actually a function of its difference from all other possible terms – terms to which it implicitly refers.[2] Deconstruction unmasks claims to truth by exposing meaning as a function of discourse, and unseats the claim that a meaning refers to a definite and inherently stable state of affairs. Deconstruction has been used, for example, to show how a concept produces meaning (its purported truth), by suppressing an opposite concept that it presupposes. To illustrate, on this view the privilege attached to the concept of reason in philosophical theories has been effected by the suppression of its logical relation to concepts of desire and emotion. Instead of regarding reason as being integrally tied to desire and emotion, reason has been presented as their opposite or negation.

In exposing a text's hidden debts, deconstruction aims to put a text to work against itself to destabilize its ostensible meanings. Deconstruction challenges the idea that a text has a single meaning, or represents a single, true state of affairs, and instead emphasizes the text's ambiguity, polysemy, and surplus meaning. A similar principle was noted by Freud when he identified the overdetermination of meaning in dreams and symptoms, which, he argued, was effected by the efforts of the unconscious to bypass mechanisms of repression. Irigaray uses these insights of philosophy and psychoanalysis against those same theories to argue that each is overdetermined and haunted by its own suppressed background or "unconscious" equivalent, namely woman.[3]

Common to feminism and deconstruction is the idea that oppression is effected through discourses that employ a binary, oppositional logic. A binary logical structure is a dichotomous system in which two terms are presented as contradictory, thus mutually exclusive. These two binary terms are also said to cover all possible situations in the field to which they refer, so there is no middle ground between them. The first of these terms has a positive value while the second is said to be a negation of the first. While the first has determinate content, the second refers to everything that is not defined positively, and refers only in terms of the privation of the values and attributes of the positive term.[4] So, for example, in the Western philosophical tradition we find a series of concepts linked to man by virtue of their positive value – reason, enlightenment, power, truth, unity, universality, autonomy, subjectivity – while another series of concepts is linked to woman in terms of a negation of man's positive qualities – emotion, carnality, irrationality, multiplicity, dependence, and otherness.[5] These two sets of meanings are also regarded as mutually exclusive and exhaustive. This system has come to be called "phallocentrism," a kind of semantic economy that turns on the principle value of the masculine (the "phallus"). Irigaray sets out to expose the phallocentrism of philosophy and its indebtedness to its oppressed Other – woman – in order to undo its pretensions to universality and truth, and to open the possibility for conceiving subjectivity in terms of sexual difference. As the title of her essay states, Irigaray claims that within philosophy, all theories of subjectivity have presupposed that subjects are male. Since the binary logic governing these theories dictates that subjectivity is a masculine domain defined by the exclusion of the feminine, the challenge is how to articulate a philosophy of feminine subjectivity.

Irigaray's aim is to provide a philosophical account of sexual difference from within philosophy itself by deconstructing its texts to reveal, as it were, the "feminine within," the excluded terms from which philosophical concepts nevertheless draw their meaning. She draws upon her psychoanalytic training to argue that the exclusion of the feminine through a binary logic is a system for protecting masculine power from acknowledging its maternal debt. Her point is not merely that men have forgotten the labors and sacrifices of their mothers, but that the very processes whereby meaning is produced through the symbolic resources of language is tied up with the corporeality of the maternal relation. On this view, meaning is not produced by a disembodied mind apprehending true reality through some kind of intellectual intuition. Instead, it is produced in a sensate body whose sense of self and world is developed only on the condition that its impulses, emotions, and feelings are integrated, disciplined, and directed through its relation with, and separation from, the mother's body. On this view, the unity of consciousness, for example, which is central to every account of subjectivity, is not an *a priori* fact about consciousness but a developmental achievement of bodily unity premised upon the child's infantile experiences of its own body in relation to its maternal carer.[6] Irigaray argues that the maternal grounds of our very capacity for symbolic representation form the "blind spot" of philosophy and its theories of subjectivity. It is these blind spots that she endeavors to render visible.

Although Irigaray regards psychoanalytic theory as an integral part of the phallocentric tradition, she thinks that psychoanalysis offers particularly useful deconstructive tools. As well as appreciating the overdetermination of representations, psychoanalysis acknowledges the importance of the infant–maternal corporeal experience, the emotions, and the role of the body in the formation of the psyche. Significantly, through the idea of repression and its role in the formation of consciousness, psychoanalysis provides a clear analogy for the kind of textual suppression – and its disruption – that interests Irigaray. While Irigaray regards psychoanalysis as a theory constructed according to binary logic, it nevertheless produces concepts that ultimately work against that logic, and which can only be maintained at the cost of contradiction. This is demonstrated powerfully in the first section of *Speculum of the Other Woman*, which focuses specifically on Freudian psychoanalytic theory.

In *The Second Sex*, Beauvoir described at length the processes by which girls are turned into women through the social organization of the female body.[7] In a similar way, Irigaray argues that the process of acquiring language and skills of signification demands that one's body be organized into a cohesive, controlled and representable unity – in other words, that it take on a certain "morphology," a socially meaningful form. Through such a process the male body comes to function as representative of the subject and subjectivity becomes a zone of exclusion of the female body. However, because body morphology is a cultural achievement and not an anatomical fact, that construction can be deconstructed. To this end Irigaray takes up the metaphor of woman as mirror.

The "speculum" in the title of Irigaray's book is loaded with meanings. It refers to a gynecological instrument used to examine the vagina, as well as to a concave mirror, a distorting reflective surface which Irigaray employs as an analytical and metaphorical tool for reversing the perspective of phallocentrism. The speculum is a mirror for reflecting the "mirror" that is woman; for turning the text back on itself in reflecting the speculative nature of "man." She employs this textual strategy to turn psychoanalysis against itself in her attack on the claim (made in the theory of the Oedipal complex), that the phallus (maleness) is the organizing element in the pleasure economy that underlies the formation of sexual identity, desire, and psychical health. On the psychoanalytic account, the female lacks the phallus and, therefore, is said to be castrated. Thus, in the economy of pleasure, woman necessarily desires the phallus (which is why she is said to suffer from "penis envy"). On this view, women's sexual health and pleasure is dependent upon procuring the phallus, and so cannot be achieved unless woman's desire conforms to the heterosexual paradigm.

Irigaray proceeds to deconstruct the Freudian framework of genital pleasure by taking it to be literally true and then reversing the perspective by substituting female genitalia (labia) for the male phallus. As a result, the plurality and ambiguity of the two lips disrupts the phallic economy. The female genital model is one in which sexual experience is both active and passive, unlike the passivity determined by the phallic model. Furthermore the ambiguity of the two lips touching allows for sexual activity and pleasure without a phallus or any of its representatives. In short, by taking the theory at its word (that is, that genital pleasure is the organizing element of sexual identity), the role of the female genitalia completely displaces the primacy given to the phallus and shows it to be little more than an exercise of power. Irigaray's point here is not that conventional heterosexual relations cannot provide women with satisfactory pleasure, but rather that conventional heterosexual practice is arbitrary, not necessary. It is only one mode of pleasure among others.

Irigaray deliberately adopts a kind of "hysterical" attitude by mimicking to excess the phallocentric conception of the feminine in order to force open the duplicities and blind spots of philosophies of the subject in the promise of articulating a form of genuinely female subjectivity, a discourse of sexual difference. The project to articulate non-phallocentric conceptions of female sexuality and gender identity finds a powerful ally in the work of theorists such as Judith Butler.

Notes

1   Jacques Derrida, *Of Grammatology*, trans. Gayatri Spivak (Baltimore and London: Johns Hopkins University Press, 1967).
2   Jacques Derrida, "Différance," in *Margins of Philosophy*, trans. Alan Bass (Brighton, UK: Harvester Press, 1982), pp. 1–28.
3   Luce Irigaray, *Speculum of the Other Woman*, trans. Gillian Gill (Ithaca: Cornell University Press, 1985), p. 141.
4   Elizabeth Grosz, *Sexual Subversions* (London and Sydney: Allen and Unwin, 1989), p. 106.
5   See Genevieve Lloyd, *The Man of Reason* (London: Methuen, 1984).
6   See, for example, Jacques Lacan, "The Mirror Stage as Formative of the I as Revealed in Psychoanalytic Experience," in *Écrits: A Selection*, trans. Alan Sheridan (New York: Norton, 1977), pp. 1–7.
7   Simone de Beauvoir, *The Second Sex*, trans. H. M. Parshley (Harmondsworth, UK: Penguin, 1988), p. 111.

Main Texts by Irigaray

Kirsteen Anderson (trans.), *Democracy Begins Between Two* (New York: Routledge, 2000).
Carolyn Burke and Gillian C. Gill (trans.), *An Ethics of Sexual Difference* (Ithaca, NY: Cornell University Press, 1993).
Alison Martin (trans.), *Je, Tu, Nous: Towards a Culture of Difference* (New York: Routledge, 1993).
Gillian C. Gill (trans.), *Marine Lover of Friedrich Nietzsche* (New York: Columbia University Press, 1991).
Gillian C. Gill (trans.), *Speculum of the Other Woman* (Ithaca, NY: Cornell University Press, 1985).
Catherine Porter and Carolyn Burke (trans.), *This Sex Which is Not One* (Ithaca, NY: Cornell University Press, 1985).

Further Reading

Chanter, Tina, *Ethics of Eros: Irigaray's Re-Writing of the Philosophers* (New York: Routledge, 1995).

Fuss, Diana, *Essentially Speaking: Feminism, Nature and Difference* (New York: Routledge, 1989).

Gatens, Moira, *Imaginary Bodies: Ethics, Power, and Corporeality* (New York: Routledge, 1996).

Grosz, Elizabeth, *Volatile Bodies: Towards a Corporeal Feminism* (Indianapolis: Indiana University Press, 1994).

Mitchell, Juliet and Jacqueline Rose (eds.), *Feminine Sexuality* (New York: W.W. Norton & Co., 1985).

Whitford, Margaret, *Luce Irigaray: Philosophy in the Feminine* (New York: Routledge, 1991).

"ANY THEORY OF THE 'SUBJECT' HAS ALWAYS BEEN APPROPRIATED BY THE 'MASCULINE'"

Luce Irigaray

We can assume that any theory of the subject has always been appropriated by the "masculine." When she submits to (such a) theory, woman fails to realize that she is renouncing the specificity of her own relationship to the imaginary. Subjecting herself to objectivization in discourse – by being "female." Re-objectivizing her own self whenever she claims to identify herself "as" a masculine subject. A "subject" that would re-search itself as lost (maternal-feminine) "object"?

Subjectivity denied to woman: indisputably this provides the financial backing for every irreducible constitution as an object: of representation, of discourse, of desire. Once imagine that woman imagines and the object loses its fixed, obsessional character. As a bench mark that is ultimately more crucial than the subject, for he can sustain himself only by bouncing back off some objectiveness, some objective. If there is no more "earth" to press down/repress, to work, to represent, but also and always to desire (for one's own), no opaque matter which in theory does not know herself, then what pedestal remains for the ex-sistence of the "subject"? If the earth turned and more especially turned upon herself, the erection of the subject might thereby be disconcerted and risk losing its elevation and penetration. For what would there be to rise up from and exercise his power over? And in?

The Copernican revolution has yet to have its final effects in the male imaginary. And by centering man outside himself, it has occasioned above all man's ex-stasis within the transcendental (subject). Rising to a perspective that would dominate the totality, to the vantage point of greatest power, he thus cuts himself off from the bedrock, from his empirical relationship with the matrix that he claims to survey. To specularize and to speculate. Exiling himself ever further (toward) where the greatest power lies, he thus becomes the "sun" if it is around him that things turn, a pole of attraction stronger than the "earth." Meanwhile, the excess in this universal fascination is that "she" also turns

upon herself, that she knows how to re-turn (upon herself) but not how to seek outside
for identity within the other: nature, sun, God . . . (woman). As things now go, man
moves away in order to preserve his stake in the value of his representation, while
woman counterbalances with the permanence of a (self)recollection which is unaware
of itself as such. And which, in the recurrence of this re-turn upon the self – and its
special economy will need to be located – can continue to support the illusion that
the object is inert. "Matter" upon which he will ever and again return to plant his foot
in order to spring farther, leap higher, although he is dealing here with a nature that is
already self-referential. Already fissured and open. And which, in her circumvolutions
upon herself, will also carry off the things confided to her for re-presentation. Whence,
no doubt, the fact that she is said to be restless and unstable. In fact it is quite rigorously true that she is never exactly the same. Always whirling closer or farther from the
sun whose rays she captures and sends curving to and fro in turn with her cycles.

Thus the "object" is not as massive, as resistant, as one might wish to believe. And
her possession by a "subject," a subject's desire to appropriate her, is yet another of his
vertiginous failures. For where he projects a something to absorb, to take, to see, to
possess . . . as well as a patch of ground to stand upon, a mirror to catch his reflection,
he is already faced by another specularization. Whose twisted character is her inability
to say what she represents. The quest for the "object" becomes a game of Chinese boxes.
Infinitely receding. The most amorphous with regard to ideas, the most obviously
"thing," if you like, the most opaque matter, opens upon a mirror all the purer in that
it knows and is known to have no reflections. Except those which man has reflected
there but which, in the movement of that concave speculum, pirouetting upon itself,
will rapidly, deceptively, fade.

And even as man seeks to rise higher and higher – in his knowledge too – so the
ground fractures more and more beneath his feet. "Nature" is forever dodging his projects of representation, of reproduction. And his grasp. That this resistance should all too
often take the form of rivalry within the hom(m)ologous, of a death struggle between
two consciousnesses, does not alter the fact that at stake here somewhere, ever more
insistent in its deathly hauteur, is the risk that the subject (as) self will crumble away.
Also at stake, therefore, the "object" and the modes of dividing the economy between
them. In particular the economy of discourse. Whereby the silent allegiance of the one
guarantees the auto-sufficiency, the auto-nomy of the other as long as no questioning
of this mutism as a symptom – of historical repression – is required. But what if the
"object" started to speak? Which also means beginning to "see," etc. What disaggrega-
tion of the subject would that entail? Not only on the level of the split between him
and his other, his variously specified alter ego, or between him and the Other, who is
always to some extent *his* Other, even if he does not recognize himself in it, even if he
is so overwhelmed by it as to bar himself out of it and into it so as to retain at the very
least the power to promote his own forms. Others who will always already have been
in the service of the same, of the presuppositions of the same logos, without changing
or prejudicing its character as discourse. Therefore not really others, even if the one,
the greatest, while holding back his reserves, perhaps contains the threat of otherness.
Which is perhaps why he stands off-stage? Why he is repressed too? But high up, in
"heaven"? Beyond, like everything else? Innocent in his exorbited empire. But once

you get suspicious of the reasons for extrapolation, and at the same time interpret the subject's need to re-duplicate himself in a thought – or maybe a "soul"? – then the function of the "other" is stripped of the veils that still shroud it.

Where will the other spring up again? Where will the risk be situated which sublates the subject's passion for remaining ever and again the same, for affirming himself ever and again the same? In the *duplicity* of his speculation? A more or less conscious duplicity? Since he is only partially and marginally where he reflects/is reflected? Where he knows (himself)? As likeness whose price can be maintained by the "night" of the unconscious? The Other, lapsed within, disquieting in its shadow and its rage, sustaining the organization of a universe eternally identical to the self. The backside of (self)representation, of the visual plane where he gazes upon himself? Therefore, resemblance proliferates all the more in a swarm of analogues. The "subject" henceforth will be multiple, plural, sometimes di-formed, but it will still postulate itself as the cause of all the mirages that can be enumerated endlessly and therefore put back together again as one. A fantastic, phantasmatic fragmentation. A destruc(tura)tion in which the "subject" is shattered, scuttled, while still claiming surreptitiously that he is the reason for it all. Is reason feigned perhaps? Certainly, it is *one*. For this race of signifiers spells out again the solipsism of him who summons them, convokes them, even if only to disperse them. The "subject" plays at multiplying himself, even deforming himself, in this process. He is father, mother, and child(ren). And the relationships between them. He is masculine and feminine and the relationships between them. What mockery of generation, parody of copulation and genealogy, drawing its *strength* from the same model, from the model of the same: the subject. In whose sight everything *outside* remains forever a condition making possible the image and the reproduction of the self. A faithful, polished mirror, empty of altering reflections. Immaculate of all autocopies. Other because wholly in the service of the same subject to whom it would present its surfaces, candid in their self-ignorance.

    [. . .]

For, when Freud reaffirms the incest taboo, he simply reannounces and puts back in place the conditions that constitute the speculative matrix of the "subject." He reinforces his positions in a fashion yet more "scientific," more imperious in their "objectivity." A demonstration he clearly needed himself if he is to "sublimate" in more universal interests his own desire for his/the mother. But as a result of using psychoanalysis (his psychoanalysis) only to scrutinize the history of his subject and his subjects, without interpreting *the historical determinants of the constitution of the "subject" as same,* he was restoring, yet again, that newly pressed down/repressed earth, upon which he stands erect, which for him, following tradition though in more explicit fashion, will be the body/sex of the mother/nature. He must challenge her for power, for productivity. He must resurface the earth with this floor of the ideal. Identify with the law-giving father, with his proper names, his desires for making capital, in every sense of the word, desires that prefer the possession of territory, which includes language, to the exercise of his pleasures, with the exception of his pleasure in trading women – fetishized objects, merchandise of whose value he stands surety – with his peers. The ban upon returning, regressing to the womb, as well as to the language and dreams shared with the mother, this is indeed the point, the line, the surface upon which the "subject" will continue to stand, to advance, to unfold his discourse, even to make it whirl. Though he has barely escaped the ring, the vault, the snare of reconciling his end and his archives, those calls, resurgent, of his beginnings. Though that he-who-is-the-cause is barely keeping his balance. But since he now knows the reason for his wobbling. . . . And, after all, the acquisition of new riches is certainly part of this? Overdetermination, deferred action, dreams, fantasies, puns. . . . Language, by adopting its/these "annexes" – also ocular, uterine, embryonic – adds to its wealth, gains "depth," consistency, diversity, and multiplication of its processes and techniques. Was language once believed threatened? Here it is dancing, playing, writing itself more than ever. It is even claimed that language is "truer" than in the past, reimpregnated with its childhood. A consciousness yet more consciously pregnant with its relationship with the mother.

Whereas "she" comes to be unable to say what her body is suffering. Stripped even of the words that are expected of her upon that stage invented to listen to her. In an admission of the wear and tear on language or of its fetishistic denial? But hysteria, or at least the hysteria that is the privileged lot of the "female," *now has nothing to say.* What she "suffers," what she "lusts for," even what she "takes pleasure in," all take place upon another stage, in relation to already codified representations. Repression of speech, interdicted in "hieroglyphic" symptoms – an already suspicious designation of something prehistoric – which will doubtless never again be lifted into current history. Unless it be by making her enter, in contempt of her sex, into "masculine" games of tropes and tropisms. By converting her to a discourse that denies the specificity of her pleasure by inscribing it as the hollow, the intaglio, the negative, even as the censured other of its phallic assertions. By hom(m)osexualizing her. By perversely travestying her for the pederastic, sodomizing satisfactions of the father/husband. She shrieks out demands too innocuous to cause alarm, that merely make people smile. Just the way one smiles at a child when he shouts aloud the mad ambitions adults keep to themselves. And which one knows he can never realize. And when she also openly displays their power fantasies, this serves as a re-creation to them in their struggle for power. By setting before them, keeping in reserve for them, in her in-fancy, what they must of course keep clear of in their pursuit of mastery, but which they yet cannot wholly renounce for fear of going off course. So she will be the Pythia who apes induced desires and suggestions foreign to her still hazy consciousness, suggestions that proclaim their credibility all the louder as they carry her ever further from her interests. By resubmitting herself to the established order, in this role of delirious double, she abandons, even denies, the prerogative histrocially granted her: unconsciousness. She prostitutes the unconscious itself to the ever present projects and projections of masculine consciousness.

For whereas the man Freud – or woman, were she to set her rights up in opposition – *might have been able* to interpret what the overdetermination of language (its effects of deferred action, its subterranean dreams and fantasies, its convulsive quakes, its paradoxes and contradictions) owed to the repression (which may yet return) of maternal power – or of the matriarchy, to adopt a still prehistorical point of reference – whereas he might have been able also to interpret the repression of the history of female sexuality, we shall in fact receive only confirmation of the discourse of the same, through comprehension and extension. With "woman" coming once more to be embedded in, enclosed in, impaled upon an architectonic more powerful than ever. And she herself is sometimes

happy to request a recognition of consciousness thereby, even an appropriation of unconsciousness that cannot be hers. Unconsciousness she is, but not for herself, not with a
subjectivity that might take cognizance of it, recognize it as her own. Close to herself,
admittedly, but in a total ignorance (of self). She is the reserve of "sensuality" for the
elevation of intelligence, she is the matter used for the imprint of forms, gage of possible regression into naive perception, the representative representing negativity (death),
dark continent of dreams and fantasies, and also eardrum faithfully duplicating the music,
though not all of it, so that the series of displacements may continue, for the "subject."
And she will serve to assure his determination only if she now seeks to reclaim his property from him: this (of his) elaborated as same out of this (of hers) foreclosed from
specula(riza)tion. The same thing will always be at stake. The profiteering will barely
have changed hands. A barter solution that she would adopt out of the void of her desire.
And always one step behind in the process, the progress of history.

But if, by exploits of her hand, woman were to reopen paths into (once again) a/one
logos that connotes her as castrated, especially as castrated of words, excluded from the
work force except as prostitute to the interests of the dominant ideology – that is of
hom(m)osexuality and its struggles with the maternal – then a certain sense, which still
constitutes the sense of history also, will undergo unparalleled interrogation, revolution.
But how is this to be done? Given that, once again, the "reasonable" words – to which
in any case she has access only though mimicry – are powerless to translate all that
pulses, clamors, and hangs hazily in the cryptic passages of hysterical suffering-latency.
Then. . . . Turn everything upside down, inside out, back to front. *Rack it with radical
convulsions*, carry back, reimport, those crises that her "body" suffers in her impotence
to say what disturbs her. Insist also and deliberately upon those *blanks* in discourse which
recall the places of her exclusion and which, by their *silent plasticity*, ensure the cohesion, the articulation, the coherent expansion of established forms. Reinscribe them
hither and thither *as divergencies*, otherwise and elsewhere than they are expected, in
ellipses and *eclipses* that deconstruct the logical grid of the reader-writer, drive him out
of his mind, trouble his vision to the point of incurable diplopia at least. *Overthrow
syntax* by suspending its eternally teleological order, by snipping the wires, cutting the
current, breaking the circuits, switching the connections, by modifying continuity, alternation, frequency, intensity. Make it impossible for a while to predict whence, whither,
when, how, why . . . something goes by or goes on: will come, will spread, will reverse,
will cease moving. Not by means of a growing complexity of the same, of course, but
by the irruption of other circuits, by the intervention at times of short-circuits that will
disperse, diffract, deflect endlessly, making energy explode sometimes, with no possibility of returning to one single origin. A force that can no longer be channeled according to a given *plan/e*: a projection from a single source, even in the secondary circuits,
with retroactive effects.

All this already applies to words, to the "lexicon" (as it is called), which is also connected up, and in the same direction. But we must go on questioning words as the
wrappings with which the "subject," modestly, clothes the "female." Stifled beneath all
those eulogistic or denigratory metaphors, she is unable to unpick the seams of her disguise and indeed takes a certain pleasure in them, even gilding the lily further at times.
Yet, ever more hemmed in, cathected by tropes, how could she articulate any sound

from beneath this cheap chivalric finery? How find a voice, make a choice strong enough, subtle enough to cut through those layers of ornamental style, that decorative sepulcher, where even her breath is lost. Stifled under all those airs. She has yet to feel the need to get free of fabric, reveal her nakedness, her destitution in language, explode in the face of them all, words too. For the imperious need for her shame, her chastity – duly fitted out with the belt of discourse –, of her decent modesty, continues to be asserted by every man. In every kind of tone, form, theory, style, with the exception of a few that in fact rouse suspicion also by their pornographically, hom(m)osexual excess. Common stock, one may assume, for their production.

The (re)productive power of the mother, the sex of the woman, are both at stake in the proliferation of systems, those houses of ill fame for the subject, of fetish-words, sign-objects whose certified truths seek to palliate the risk that values may be recast into/by the other. But no clear univocal utterance, can in fact, pay off this mortgage since all are already trapped in the same credit structure. All can be recuperated when issued by the signifying order in place. It is still better to speak only in riddles, allusions, hints, parables. Even if asked to clarify a few points. Even if people plead that they just don't understand. After all, they never have understood. So why not double the misprision to the limits of exasperation? Until the ear tunes into another music, the voice starts to sing again, the very gaze stops squinting over the signs of auto-representation, and (re)production no longer inevitably amounts to the same and returns to the same forms, with minor variations.

This disconcerting of language, though anarchic in its deeds of title, nonetheless demands patient exactitude. The symptoms, for their part, are implacably precise. And if it is indeed a question of breaking (with) a certain mode of specula(riza)tion, this does not imply renouncing all mirrors or refraining from analysis of the hold this plan/e of representation maintains, rendering female desire aphasic and more generally atonic in all but its phallomorphic disguises, masquerades, and demands. For to dodge this time of interpretation is to risk its freezing over, losing hold, cutting back. All over again. But perhaps through this specular surface which sustains discourse is found not the void of nothingness but the dazzle of multifaceted speleology. A scintillating and incandescent concavity, of language also, that threatens to set fire to fetish-objects and gilded eyes. The recasting of their truth value is already at hand. We need only press on a little further into the depths, into that so-called dark cave which serves as hidden foundation to their speculations. For there where we expect to find the opaque and silent matrix of a logos immutable in the certainty of its own light, fires and mirrors are beginning to radiate, sapping the evidence of reason at its base! Not so much by anything stored in the cave – which would still be a claim based on the notion of the closed volume – but again and yet again by their indefinitely rekindled hearths.

But which "subject" up till now has investigated the fact that a *concave mirror* concentrates the light and, specifically, that this is not wholly irrelevant to woman's sexuality? Any more than is a man's sexuality to the convex mirror? Which "subject" has taken an interest in the anamorphoses produced by the conjunction of such curvatures? What impossible reflected images, maddening reflections, parodic transformations took place at each of their articulations? When the "it is" annuls them in the truth of a copula in which "he" still forever finds the resources of his identification as same. Not one subject has done so, on pain of tumbling from his ex-sistence. And here again, here too, one will rightly suspect any perspective, however surreptitious, that centers the subject, any autonomous circuit of subjectivity, any systematicity hooked back onto itself, any closure that claims for whatever reason to be metaphysical – or familial, social, economic even –, to have rightfully taken over, fixed, and framed that concave mirror's incandescent hearth. If this mirror – which, however, makes a *hole* – sets itself up pompously as an authority in order to give shape to the imaginary orb of a "subject," it thereby defends itself phobically in/by this inner "center" from the fires of the desire of/for woman. Inhabiting a securing morphology, making of its very structure some comfortable sepulcher from whence it may, possibly, by some hypothetical survival, be able to look out. (Re)g(u)arding itself by all sorts of windows-on-wheels, optical apparatuses, glasses, and mirrors, from/in this burning glass, which enflames all that falls into its cup.

But, may come the objection, – defending again the objective and the object – the speculum is not necessarily a mirror. It may, quite simply, be an instrument to *dilate* the lips, the orifices, the walls, so that the eye can penetrate the *interior*. So that the eye can enter, to see, notably with speculative intent. Woman, having been misinterpreted, forgotten, variously frozen in show-cases, rolled up in metaphors, buried beneath carefully stylized figures, raised up in different idealities, would now become the "object" to be investigated, to be explicitly granted consideration, and thereby, by this deed of title, included in the theory. And if this center, which fixed and immobilized metaphysics in its closure, had often in the past been traced back to some divinity or other transcendence invisible as such, in the future its ultimate meaning will perhaps be discovered by tracking down what there is to be *seen* of female sexuality.

Yes, man's eye – understood as substitute for the penis – will be able to prospect woman's sexual parts, seek there new sources of profit. Which are equally theoretical. By doing so he further fetishizes (his) desire. But the desire of the mystery remains, however large a public has been recruited of late for "hysteroscopy." For even if the place of origin, the original dwelling, even if not only the woman but the mother can be unveiled to his sight, what will he make of the exploration of this mine? Except usurp even more the right to look at everything, at the whole thing, thus reinforcing the erosion of his desire in the very place where he firmly believes he is working to reduce an illusion. Even if it should be a transcendental illusion. What will he, what will they, have *seen* as a result of that dilation? And what will they get out of it? A disillusion quite as illusory, since the transcendental keeps its secret. Between empirical and transcendental *a suspense will still remain inviolate*, will escape prospection, then, now, and in the future. The space-time of the risk that fetishes will be consumed, catch fire. In this fire, in this light, in the optical failure, the impossibility of gazing on their encounters in flame, the split (schize) founding and structuring the difference between experience and transcendental (especially phallic) eminence will burn also. *Exquisite/exschizoid crisis of ontico-ontological difference.* What manner of recasting all economy will ensue? To tell the truth, no one knows. And, to stay with truth, you can only fear the worst. For you may fear a general crisis in the value system, a foundering of the values now current, the devaluation of their standard and of their regimen of monopolies.

The copulative effusion, and fusion, melts down the mint's credit with each moment of bliss. Renews and redistributes the accepted stakes: between two crises, two explosions, two incandescences of fetish mineral. And it is no easy matter to foresee whether, in that game, the one – the man? – who has recouped the biggest pile of chips will be the winner. It is equally possible to imagine that the one – the woman – who has spent her time polishing her mine will carry the day. Since the abrasion of the stores entrusted to the reflecting surface renders that surface more likely to set aflame the supplies and capitalizations of the one who, under cover and pretext of seduction, puts his riches on display.

But, will come the objection once again – in the name of some other objectality – we are not fed by fire and flames. Maybe. But then neither are we by fetishes and gazes. And when will they cease to equate woman's sexuality with her reproductive organs, to claim that her sexuality has value only insofar as it gathers the heritage of her maternity? When will man give up the need or desire to drink deep in all security from his wife/mother in order to go and show off to his brothers and buddies the fine things he formed while suckling his nurse? And/or when will he renounce (reversing roles so as better to retain them) the wish to preserve his wife/child in her inability, as he sees it, to produce for the marketplace? With "marriage" turning out to be a more or less subtle dialectization of the nurturing relationship that aims to maintain, at the very least, the mother/child, producer/consumer distinction, and thereby perpetuate this economy?

To return to the gaze, it will be able to explore all the inner cavities. Although, in the case of the most secret, it will need the help of ancillary light and mirror. Of appropriate sun and mirrors. The instrumental and technical exploitation of sun and mirror will have shown the gaze, proved to it, that those mines contained no gold. Then the gaze, aghast at such bareness, will have concluded that at any rate all brilliance was its own preserve, that it could continue to speculate without competition. That the childish, the archaic credit accorded to the all-powerful mother was nothing, was but fable. But how is one to desire without fiction? What pleasure is there in stockpiling goods without risks, without expenditures?

You will have noted, in fact, that what polarizes the light for the exploration of internal cavities is, in paradigmatic fashion, *the concave mirror*. Only when that mirror has concentrated the feeble rays of the eye, of the sun, of the sun–blinded eye, is the secret of the caves illumined. Scientific technique will have taken up the condensation properties of the "burning glass," in order to pierce the mystery of woman's sex, in a new distribution of the power of the scientific method and of "nature." A new despecularization of the maternal and the female? Scientificity of fiction that seeks to exorcise the disasters of desire, that mortifies desire by analyzing it from all visual angles, but leaves it also intact. Elsewhere. Burning still.

21

COMMENTARY ON MACKENZIE

Catriona Mackenzie (born 1960) is an Australian philosopher whose research takes in four broad areas: moral psychology, moral philosophy, feminist philosophy, and applied ethics. She is particularly concerned with issues of autonomy, agency, and practical deliberation; conceptions of selfhood and identity; philosophy of the emotions; and theories of imagination.

Mackenzie's work is part of a body of feminist scholarship endeavoring to reconceptualize autonomy away from the classical liberal conception with its abstract subject disconnected from relations of race, gender, family, class, or even body.[1] This thought is well represented, for example, in Seyla Benhabib's critique of the notion of the "generalized other" upon which much of liberal moral philosophy is premised.[2] Benhabib argues that, as a result of sociopolitical changes that accompanied the transition from a teleological medieval worldview to that of capitalism, morality shifted from a concern with the realization of human nature to a political concept pertaining to social obligation and rights within the ambit of a social contract.[3] This in turn led to what has become known as the public/private dichotomy: the idea that the public realm is the rightful sphere of men and the private realm is the appropriate sphere of women (who are thereby subject to the property rights of men).

Benhabib argues that as a result of these sociopolitical changes autonomy became premised upon a masculine notion of self that was "narcissistic," disengaged from "the most basic bond of dependence," and epitomized in Hobbes's metaphor of men as "like mushrooms, come to full maturity, without all kind of engagement to each other."[4] She argues that this conception of self has been internalized into the male ego to the extent that men had come to regard moral reasoning as a process that entailed regarding people as substitutable, generalizable, abstract agents unconnected to place, person, or culture.

Benhabib argues that not only is this view of morality sexist and oblivious to the actual conditions under which reasoning occurs, but it is also incoherent. Using Rawls's theory of justice to demonstrate the vacuity of the concept of the "generalized other," she argues that such a subject, entirely abstracted from any ties to person, place, object, beliefs, desires, or abilities, cannot be a human subject. Furthermore, she notes that when individuals are deprived of concrete characteristics, the notion of a plurality of perspectives, to which Rawls's theory is oriented, also disappears. Behind the veil of ignorance, the otherness of the "other" vanishes, and with it the notion of difference upon which relations of reversibility and obligations of reciprocity (which underpin the universality of liberalism), are premised. The corrective to this situation, says Benhabib, is to reconsider the nature of the self and autonomy in the light of our actual conditions of existence and the necessity of our relations with concrete others, paying special attention to the relations of care which frequently characterize women's moral deliberations.[5]

It is with a similar aim that recent feminist moral philosophy has seen the development of relational models of autonomy. These are models that emphasize the social situatedness of the individual and the role of personal relations in the acquisition of the skills and competencies necessary for the exercise of autonomy.[6] Against the politicization of the concept of autonomy, Mackenzie differentiates political autonomy – which involves freedoms such as the right to participate in the political process; rights to freedom of expression, assembly, and religion; and privacy – from personal autonomy, which requires the exercise of certain basic "autonomy competencies": skills in deliberation, decision making, and action, all of which depend upon a unified and valued self-conception. On Mackenzie's view, having political autonomy does not guarantee personal autonomy.

In this excerpt, Mackenzie argues for the importance of imaginative thinking in the acquisition (or failure) of personal autonomy. Drawing upon Richard Wollheim's account of a person's point of view, and emphasizing the role he gives to imaginative activities, Mackenzie argues that the affective and cognitive effects of imaginative thinking can function to either liberate or constrain one's self-conception. Furthermore, one's self-conception is mediated through the culturally available images and representations on which the imagination draws. In this way, imaginative thinking can facilitate or limit one's autonomy, depending upon the images available to it (and the emotions they arouse). Mackenzie's aim is to bring out the connection between autonomy and imagination by investigating "the role played by imaginative mental activity in self-reflection and in deliberation about the self."[7] In doing so, she provides "an integration account of the process of self-definition".[8]

Mackenzie argues that autonomy competencies depend upon an integrated self-definition formed through a dynamic process in which a person achieves a "reflective equilibrium." This equilibrium consists in a stable configuration of three constitutive aspects of one's existence: one's self-conception; one's point of view; and one's values, ideals, and commitments (the last is what Mackenzie refers to as what one "cares about"). This equilibrium is brought about through critical reflection upon, and optimal integration of, each aspect of the triadic complex. It is not characterized by the absence of tension or conflict, but rather the minimization of tensions such that one achieves and maintains a "practical unity necessary to deliberate, make decisions and choices, and act."[9]

Each element of this triad has its own complexity and provides a distinct source of motives for one's actions, thoughts, and feelings. To illustrate, our self-conceptions are made up of various emotional dispositions, beliefs, and desires. Where these elements are in conflict with each other, or where, for example, one's self-conception is in conflict with the emotions, beliefs, and desires which comprise one's point of view then one will not achieve a reflective equilibrium, nor consequently, a well-integrated sense of who one is and what matters to oneself. Where the aspects of one's existence are poorly integrated, or where there is serious conflict between them, a person cannot form the kind of practical unity fundamental to the ability to act, namely, the unity that links agency to motive, means, and object of an action. If this kind of disunity becomes severe, such a person can be said to lack agency and autonomy on the grounds that she lacks the capacity to direct her actions in accordance with self-determined and critically evaluated beliefs, values, and goals.

Mackenzie argues that fundamental to achieving reflective equilibrium is the formation of a self-conception that is guided by critical reflection upon what matters to oneself. This self-conception must be such that one evaluates oneself as genuinely worthy, because without a strong sense of self-worth, one lacks the sufficient reason (emotional and cognitive) to form goals according to self-determined and critically evaluated beliefs and values. Mackenzie describes the shaping of one's self-conception through one's reflections upon various aspects of one's point of view or values as involving "externalizing, distancing, or dissociating ourselves from certain aspects of ourselves and appropriating others."[10] We externalize (or distance or dissociate) an aspect of ourselves by singling it out and evaluating it as undesirable or unworthy. We appropriate an aspect when we single it out and evaluate it as desirable, or worthy. Mackenzie claims that by identifying and critically evaluating aspects of our character, values, or point of view, we can, by virtue of the affective and cognitive force of those evaluations, loosen (or reinforce) the motivational pull those aspects exert over our behavior. In this way we can determine the attributes we will or will not have, and thus determine our self-conceptions.

Central to the formation of a sense of self that one critically evaluates as worthy, is imaginative thinking, specifically, the capacity of imaginative activity to mobilize the affective and cognitive forces of the emotions which attach to our evaluations of various aspects of ourselves. Mackenzie argues that imagination can set in train self-reflection and self-definition by prompting an emotional response to a representation or idea and, through that response, give rise to an evaluative judgment. In this way, imaginative activity can promote self-understanding because it can pull us out of our habitual ways of thinking and "provide a window into our own emotional states, our points of view, and our self-conceptions."[11] For example, she notes that being attentive to anomalous emotions can be a trigger for reconceiving oneself – for imagining oneself otherwise – and for acquiring aspects of oneself with the aim of an integrated and expansive self-conception.

Mackenzie goes on to argue that the imaginative activities that facilitate autonomy are socially mediated. This means that a healthy self-conception and the acquisition of autonomy competencies requires social recognition. She provides two reasons for this:

1 The self-knowledge presupposed in autonomy can only be acquired through relations with other people;
2 Self-worth, necessary to the achievement of a reflective equilibrium, is bound up with social recognition.

Mackenzie argues that our personal repertoire of images and representations which shape our core values, desires, emotions, beliefs, and self-conceptions are drawn from the culturally available images in our society (the "cultural imaginary"). As she notes earlier in the essay, imagination is ambivalent; it can open up possibilities for imagining oneself or close them down, depending upon the intention behind the imaginative activity. She points out that imagining done with the intention of experiencing pleasure characteristically narrows the content of what is imagined in order to exclude elements that distract from the pleasurable object. By contrast, imagining done with the intention of increasing understanding typically broadens the representational content. This ambivalence operates at the level of the cultural imaginary as well. The pleasure afforded by social recognition of certain images operates as a powerful incentive to conform to those images and, as such, can restrict one's capacity to imagine oneself otherwise. This is, again, because of the capacity of imagination to evoke emotions that drive self-evaluation. Where a society places a low value on certain attributes, one is likely to have a negative emotional response to that attribute, and one is more likely to externalize it rather than appropriate it. Mackenzie's point is that imagination is not an abstract process but one inextricably linked to one's emotions, self-conception, and to one's sense of where and how one fits into a wider, social world. This means that women cannot be indifferent to culturally available images of women. Mackenzie concludes that the cultural imaginary interferes with autonomy at the level of the formation of beliefs, desires, patterns of emotional interaction, and self-conception. Operating at this level, a person's autonomy can be stymied by her inability to imagine herself otherwise.

The focus on the practical context of identity, self-worth, and its relation to autonomy has vast implications for issues of consent and decision making in general. This is of increasing importance in bioethics, for example, where the complexity of medical technology places it beyond the understanding of many of the people who become subject to it. Relational models of autonomy promise to broaden our descriptions of moral situations and to give voice to the perspectives of the concrete individuals who comprise them.

Notes

1   For example, Simone de Beauvoir, *The Second Sex*, trans. H. M. Parshley (Harmondsworth, UK: Penguin, 1988); Susan Moller Okin, *Justice, Gender, and the Family* (New York: Basic Books, 1989); Diana Meyers, *Self, Society, and Personal Choice* (New York: Columbia University Press, 1989).

2   Seyla Benhabib, "The Generalized and The Concrete Other: The Kohlberg–Gilligan Controversy and Moral Theory," in Eva Feder Kittay and Diana T. Meyers (eds.), *Women and Moral Theory* (Totowa, NJ: Rowman and Littlefield, 1987), pp. 154–77.

3   Ibid, p. 160.

4   Ibid, p. 161.

5   Ibid, pp. 155–8. Benhabib's target here is Lawrence Kohlberg's account of the differential development of moral judgment in men and women, and the debate with Carol Gilligan.

6   See Meyers (1989); Marilyn Friedman, "Autonomy and Social Relations: Rethinking the Feminist Critique," in Diana Tietjen Meyers (ed.), *Feminists Rethink the Self* (Boulder, CO: Westview Press, 1997), pp. 40–61.

7   Catriona Mackenzie and Natalie Stoljar (eds.), *Relational Autonomy: Feminist Perspectives on Autonomy, Agency, and the Social Self* (New York and Oxford: Oxford University Press, 2000), p. 125.

8   Ibid.
9   Ibid, p. 135.
10   Ibid, p. 134.
11   Ibid, p. 138.

Main Texts by Mackenzie

"Abortion and Embodiment," *Australasian Journal of Philosophy*, 70 (2), 1992, pp. 136–55.

"Critical Reflection, Self Knowledge and the Emotions", *Philosophical Explorations: An International Journal for the Philosophy of Mind and Action*, 5 (3), 2002, pp. 186–206.

"On Bodily Autonomy," in S. K. Toombs (ed.), *Philosophy and Medicine, Vol. 68: Handbook of Phenomenology and Medicine* (Dordrecht: Kluwer Academic Press, 2001), pp. 417–39.

Relational Autonomy, Feminist Perspectives on Autonomy, Agency, and the Social Self, with Natalie Stoljar (eds.) (New York and Oxford: Oxford University Press, 2000).

Further Reading

Christman, John (ed.), *The Inner Citadel* (New York: Oxford University Press, 1989).

Friedman, Marilyn, "Autonomy and Social Relationships," in Diana Tietjen Meyers (ed.), *Feminists Rethink the Self* (Boulder, CO: Westview Press, 1997), pp. 40–61.

Friedman, Marilyn, "Autonomy, Social Disruption, and Women," in Catriona Mackenzie and Natalie Stoljar (eds.), *Relational Autonomy: Feminist Perspectives on Autonomy, Agency, and the Social Self* (New York and Oxford: Oxford University Press, 2000), pp. 35–51.

Meyers, Diana Tietjen, *Self, Society and Personal Choice* (New York: Columbia University Press, 1989).

Meyers, Diana Tietjen (ed.), *Feminists Rethink the Self* (Boulder, CO: Westview Press, 1997).

Wollheim, Richard, *The Thread of Life* (Cambridge, UK: Cambridge University Press, 1984).

Young, Robert, *Personal Autonomy: Beyond Negative and Positive Liberty* (London: Croom Helm, 1986).

"IMAGINING ONESELF OTHERWISE"

Catriona Mackenzie

Self-Definition, Deliberation, and Imagination

Diana Meyers has argued that self-definition is one of the capacities necessary for autonomy.[1] I develop, concurrently, three interrelated suggestions concerning self-definition. The first is that the process of self-definition should be thought of as a process of negotiation among three related but distinguishable elements of the person: her point of view; her self-conception; and her values, ideals, commitments, and cares, in short, what matters to her. The aim of this process of negotiation is to achieve a kind of reflective equilibrium among these different elements of the self.[2] A reflective equilibrium is achieved when these elements are integrated in a relatively stable way, that is, when there are not serious and persistent conflicts among them. Thus, I am proposing an integration account of self-definition. I regard the kind of integration I describe as a necessary, if not a sufficient, condition for autonomy.[3] Second, I characterize the process of formation of a person's *self-conception* as a process whereby, through reflection guided by her values, ideals, commitments, and cares, a person constitutes certain elements of herself, or certain features of her point of view, as external to herself while appropriating others. Third, I argue that the various modes of imagining already described play an important but overlooked role in the formation of a person's self-conception and in the process of achieving an integration among the different elements of the self.

Integration and Self-Definition

Following Wollheim, I have characterized a person's *point of view* as a network of interrelated emotions, beliefs, desires, and mental and bodily traits and dispositions, shaped by the influence of the past and directed by self-concern for the future. A person's *self-conception* delimits that part of the network that the person regards as defining herself

From Catriona Mackenzie and Natalie Stoljar (eds.), *Relational Autonomy: Feminist Perspectives on Autonomy, Agency, and the Social Self* (New York and Oxford: Oxford University Press, 2000), pp. 133–4,146–50 (notes).

or with which she identifies. Wollheim's metaphors of the empathic internal audience and the reflective internal observer help clarify the relationship between a person's point of view and her self-conception. Recall that the difference between internal audience and internal observer is that whereas both are internal, they stand in different relations to the imaginative project. The internal audience is caught up within the imaginative project and emotionally identifies with it. The internal observer, on the other hand, stands outside the imaginative project; may react to it emotionally in a range of different ways; and reflects on and evaluates the desires, emotions, and beliefs represented or manifested in the imagining.[4]

Elaborating from these metaphors, we can identify two salient features of the relationship between a person's point of view and her self-conception. First, like internal audience and internal observer, both my point of view and my self-conception are internal to me in the sense that both are constitutive aspects of my identity. To characterize a person's identity solely in terms of one of these aspects rather than both would be mistaken because both motivate our actions and our responses. Thus, on the one hand, our actions are often motivated, in ways that we either may not be aware of or cannot change, by mental or bodily dispositions and habits, desires, character traits, and so on that do not accord with our self-conceptions.[5] On the other hand, part of what it is to be an agent is to be able, at least within certain limits, to modify oneself in line with one's self-conception.

Second, although both our points of view and our self-conceptions are constitutive of our identities, like the internal observer we shape our self-conceptions by reflecting on different aspects of our points of view. This reflective activity can be thought of as a process of externalizing, distancing, or dissociating ourselves from certain aspects of ourselves and appropriating others.[6] The activity of externalizing an element of oneself, for example, a desire, involves reconfiguring the network or structure of beliefs, emotions, dispositions, desires, and so on that constitute one's point of view in order to lessen, perhaps eventually eliminate, the motivational pull of this desire. So to externalize an element of oneself is to reject it as a motivating factor in one's actions. To appropriate an element of oneself is to acknowledge and accept it as one of the aspects of one's identity that guides one's actions. It is in this sense that we identify ourselves, or our self-conceptions, with those aspects of ourselves that we appropriate. In some cases, appropriation may involve endorsement. But appropriation may also be consistent with equivocal endorsement or in some cases just with acceptance.

The metaphor of the internal observer brings into focus two central features of externalizing and appropriating, namely, that they involve both emotional response and evaluation. In reflecting on and reacting to our own desires, habits, character traits, and so on, we respond to these affectively – with pride, shame, or embarassment, for example. These emotional responses are both guided by and shape our self-conceptions. So, for example, we might feel shame when we find ourselves acting on a desire that conflicts with our self-conception. But our emotional responses and our self-conceptions are in turn guided by our valuations and our judgments about what matters. Several philosophers have argued that our identities or self-conceptions are shaped by what matters to us. Thus Williams talks of a person's identity as being bound up with her "ground projects" and commitments;[7] Ronald Dworkin aligns the person with her critical, as opposed to experiential, interests, that is, with those interests that incorporate a person's critical or reflective judgments about what constitutes a good life, what is important, what is worth doing and valuing, what ideals she should live her life by, and so on;[8] and Frankfurt suggests that the boundaries of a person's will are defined by what she cares about.[9] For the purposes of this discussion, I ignore some of the philosophical differences among these accounts and draw on some of the intuitions that unite them in order to clarify the evaluative dimension of externalizing and appropriating.

Two central intuitions are shared by these views. The first is that our projects, cares, values, or critical interests guide the process of distinguishing our self-conceptions from our points of view. The judgment of whether we wish to appropriate or dissociate ourselves from a desire, dispositions, or characteristic is related to our assessment of whether this element of our psychology strengthens or undermines our commitment to these cares, values, or critical interests.[10] So the formation of a person's self-conception could be understood as the attempt to bring the different aspects of the self into line with what matters to her. At the same time, making judgments about whether we wish to appropriate or dissociate ourselves from certain aspects of ourselves is a process that also involves engaging in a reflective assessment of our values, ideals, cares, or in short what matters to us. In reflecting on whether a certain desire or set of desires, for example, undermines our commitment to what we care about, we are also reflecting on whether what we care about is worth caring about or worth caring about in the way or to the extent that we do.[11]

The second intuition is that what we are and what matters to us are not simple matters of choice. To say that what we are is not a simple matter of choice is to say that the network or configuration of emotions, beliefs, dispositions, and desires that constitute our points of view is, to some degree, not voluntary. Our identities are shaped in fairly determinate ways by our various characteristics, by the relations between these characteristics and our social context, and by what matters to us. To say that what matters to us is not a simple matter of choice is to say that to a certain degree, we just find certain things mattering to us. This may be because we are disposed in certain ways by the manner in which different aspects of our identities, for example, our temperament and talents, reinforce one another; what matters to us may be connected with commitments to others, for example, parents, that are not entirely of our choosing;[12] or, what matters may be the result of significant events in our particular histories or of decisions we made in the past that are now no longer a matter of choice. Thus, we cannot simply choose to abandon our cares or to give up what matters to us. Or rather, we cannot do so without forfeit or loss. Certainly what matters to a person may change, perhaps because of a decision she has made or because of an event or action that has intervened to disrupt the reflective equilibrium she had established among different aspects of herself.[13] But something that has mattered usually cannot simply cease to matter. It can only do so, or come to matter in a different way, as a result of a process of readjustment of the elements of the self.

However, although what we are and what matters to us are not under our immediate voluntary control, this should not be taken to imply that we are passive with respect to ourselves. Self-definition or self-formation is a matter of actively negotiating the relationships among one's point of view, one's self-conception, and one's values. A reflective equilibrium among the different aspects of one's self is achieved when these elements are integrated in a relatively stable way, that is, when there are not serious and persistent conflicts among them. The notion of stability does not imply that there cannot be tension or inconsistency within or among the different elements of the self, that the self is seamless. Nor does it imply that an integrated self is static. In fact the process of self-integration is an ongoing and dynamic process precisely because of inevitable tensions and inconsistencies within the self and because the different elements of the self are constantly undergoing transformation.[14] The notion of stability does imply, however, that an agent who is persistently internally divided or whose sense of self is seriously fragmented cannot achieve the kind of reflective equilibrium necessary for unified agency.[15] By unified agency I mean the kind of practical unity necessary to deliberate, make decisions and choices, and act.[16]

For the remainder of this section I want to develop the idea that imaginative mental activity plays a crucial role in self-definition, as I have characterized it, and in the deliberative processes that precede self-formative decisions. To explain this role, I want to recall two points that were made earlier in the discussion. The first is that mental imagery, because of its iconicity, has psychic force or cogency; it is able to rearouse emotions or simulate the effect of emotions. The second is that in discussing the relationship between a person's point of view and her self-conception, I likened this relationship to that between Wollheim's internal audience and internal observer. This comparison brought to the fore two central features of the kind of reflection that is involved in negotiating the relationships among our points of view, our self-conceptions, and what matters to us, namely, that reflection involves both an affective and an evaluative response.

Putting these two points together, we can begin to see the role played by the various modes of imagining in the process of self-definition. By virtue of its power to rearouse or simulate emotions, imaginative mental activity initiates self-reflection by prompting an emotional response and, through that, an evaluative judgment. The cognitive power of this process is reasonably evident in the case of experiential memory. Because experiential memories are representations of experiences we have lived through, such memories can enable us to understand and reshape ourselves by enabling us to understand the ways in which our present points of view, self-conceptions, values, ideals, and commitments have been influenced by our past. The memories rearouse the emotions associated with the original experience. But the interval between the past and the present and the way in which the web of dispositions within which the memory is embedded has been modified by the history of the person during that interval, enable the person to respond to the original emotions with a further set of emotional reactions, which I call reactive emotions. These reactive emotions then prompt evaluative judgments, which enable the person to gain some understanding of the significance of past experiences and to gain some measure of control over the psychic force of those experiences. For example, the process of sifting through and evaluating memories, externalizing some and appropriating others, is one way in which a person can come to terms with a traumatic event in her past and reestablish some kind of equilibrium among the different elements of herself.[17]

However, it might be thought that if there is some truth to the claim that iconic mental representations have cognitive power and motivational force, if it is true that they are indeed able not only to yield self-understanding but also to inaugurate a reconfiguration of the various elements of the self, that this will be true mainly of those cases

of imagining that are accompanied by belief, namely, experiential memory and previsagement. On the other hand, it might seem that because they typically manifest desire,
iconic imagining, future-directed fantasy, and counterfactual speculation are modes of
imagining that are more likely to be invoked in the service of self-deception than as an
aid to self-understanding. Although I try to show that imagining of these varieties can
contribute in a positive way to practical deliberation about the self, this objection certainly has force. The imagination can be delusional, and its role in self-understanding is
ambivalent. There are a number of ways in which imagining can block, rather than aid,
self-understanding and practical deliberation about the self. The first [. . .] is when the
imaginer intentionally restricts the repertoire invoked in the imagining, so that no beliefs,
desires, or emotions that might threaten the pleasure she seeks gain admittance to the
imaginative project. This kind of restriction of the imaginative project can, of course,
also occur when experiential memory and previsagement are invoked in the service of
desire. The second way is when a person's imaginings and the repertoire she invokes in
her imaginative projects are limited by the culturally available images and representations that provide the raw material on which we draw in our own imaginative activities. I turn to this issue later.

To understand the role that the species of imagining that includes counterfactual
speculation, future-directed fantasy, and iconic imagination can play in self-definition,
I want to focus a bit more closely on the emotional response prompted by an imagining. My emotional response to an imagining involves a number of interwoven
components, including my response to the content of the representation, my response
to the emotions that I perceive to have been aroused or simulated in me by the representation, and my response to what I perceive the representation and the emotions
it generates in me disclose about me. For example, let us say that I imagine myself being
told of the death of someone I believe I love. This imagining might arise involuntar-
ily or it might be invoked deliberately to represent to myself my own feelings for this
person. But let us say that as the imagining unfolds, I unexpectedly find myself representing myself, as the protagonist, as experiencing somewhat mixed emotions to this
event: dread, grief and sorrow, to be sure, but also relief. As internal audience, the imagining simulates in me the effect of these different emotions. As internal observer, I
respond to these different emotions with reactive emotions. My reactive emotions
include those that are in accord with the emotions simulated by the imagining, for
example, a heightening of sorrow and dread. These reactive emotions are direct
responses to the content of the representation, that is, to the representation of the loss
of the loved person, and they are also responses to the emotions simulated by the imagining. Furthermore, since I believe I love this person, these emotions concur with
and confirm my self-conception. However, in this case my reactive emotions will also
include a response to the apparently anomalous emotions simulated by the imagining,
the emotion of relief, which takes me by surprise as the imagining unfolds. My reactive emotions to this emotion may include bewilderment, shame, and anxiety. These
reactive emotions will in turn prompt self-reflection and evaluative judgment – of the
imagining and the anomalous emotions of relief represented in it, of the various
reactive emotions that arose in me in response to this simulated emotion, and of my
self-conception and my sense of what matters. The judgment I arrive at may be that
this simulated emotion is indeed anomalous and external to me, and so the judgment

confirms my self-conception. However, it may be that this imagining sets in train, or at least forms part of, a process of coming to realize that I do not love this person any more, and so of reconfiguring my self-conception and my sense of what matters.

This example shows that in imagining, we present aspects of ourselves to ourselves for reflection and evaluation, not only directly or indirectly in the content of the representation, but also because their cogency enables such representations to provide a window into our own emotional states, our points of view, and our self-conceptions. In those cases in which imagining is invoked in the service of self-knowledge, we allow as much knowledge of ourselves as we can into the representation in order to make this window as wide as possible. In those cases in which imagining is invoked in the service of desire, we narrow this window, sometimes to guarantee that the imagining will afford maximum pleasure, sometimes to ensure that we see of ourselves only what we want to see. Thus we manipulate our imaginings so that they conform to, or at least do not conflict with, our self-conceptions. However, even in these cases, we very often find ourselves unable to control the imagining to the extent that we want – beliefs, desires, and emotions that conflict with the intention of the imagining can creep in as the imagining unfolds and can provide a sometimes unwanted window into those aspects of ourselves that we would rather not see.

The example also shows that representational imagining can provide this kind of window into the self because it can abstract us from our habitual modes of understanding ourselves and our relations with others. By putting ourselves at a remove from these habitual modes of understanding, we are able to reflect on and evaluate them, and so to test our satisfaction with them. But this is not the only way in which representational imagining can aid self-understanding and self-definition. By removing us from the habitual, imagining also opens up a space within which we can try out different possibilities for ourselves – different possibilities of action, desire, emotion, and belief. This trying out of different possibilities or postures of the self is a central feature of counterfactual speculation and future-directed fantasy. In assuming different postures, say in imagining a different past for ourselves or fantasizing about the future, we hold certain elements of ourselves stable and play around with others. Thus we place in the foreground certain aspects of our identities, for example, certain ideals, characteristics, or talents, and downplay others. As internal observer, we then respond, emotionally and evaluatively, to these alternative representations of ourselves. Through this process we start distinguishing those possibilities that may be genuine possibilities for us from those possibilities that are not really thinkable for us at all. An obvious example is the kind of previsaging of different possibilities that we engage in when we are trying to make a decision between alternative courses of action – for example, choosing between two jobs in two different cities. In making decisions of this kind, much of our deliberative activity involves imaginative projection. We represent to ourselves the different kinds of life we believe we would live, given the different options, and by evaluating our responses to these representations we gradually get ourselves into a position to make a decision.

For reasons that I have already indicated, this imaginative playing around with our identities, or imagining ourselves otherwise, does not always promote adequate self-reflection or ideal deliberation. In the case of previsagement, counterfactual speculation, and future-directed fantasy, an additional problem is that these kinds of imagining can be more or less impoverished. Our ability to imagine a different past for ourselves, for example, peters out fairly quickly because we simply do not know enough about what our lives would have been like had they taken a course such as the one we imagine. Similarly, although in the kind of deliberative previsagement that precedes decisions, we build in as much knowledge of ourselves and of the different possibilities as we can to make the imagining as rich and informative as possible, in retrospect these imaginings often strike us as impoverished. Thus, after the event, we can find ourselves thinking that we might have made a different, and better, decision if only we had known ourselves better or taken into account a consideration that in retrospect seems so obvious or predicted an unforeseen outcome of our actions.

Nevertheless, bearing in mind these reservations, I contend that our ability to imagine ourselves otherwise – that is, our ability to imaginatively distance ourselves from our habitual modes of self-understanding and to envisage, in imaginative representations, alternate possibilities for ourselves – plays an important role in practical reflection and deliberation about the self, and hence in self-definition.

Imagination, Social Recognition, and the Cultural Imaginary

From the way I have been describing imaginative projection so far it may seem as though our individual lives are completely discrete and self-contained; as though our mental and bodily lives, our memories, our self-concern for our own futures, and the repertoires on which we draw in our imaginings refer only to our own experiences and points of view; and as though these exist in some kind of vacuum. But, of course, this is not so. We are social creatures who are formed and transform ourselves in our intimate and nonintimate relationships with other people.[18] We become persons and live our lives in particular social, cultural, and historical communities. Our sense of our lives as temporal, our points of view, our self-conceptions, and our values, are therefore shaped by these relationships and these communities. So, too, are our imaginative mental activities. So how can the relationship between our individual imaginative projects and the social world in which we live our lives be characterized? Or, since this is a rather large question, let me narrow it by asking how we can understand the relationship between our own imaginative representations of ourselves and cultural images and representations. In particular, how can a person's imaginative projects, and hence her capacity for self-transformation and autonomy, be stymied by the dominant cultural imaginary? These are also very large questions that cannot be explored here adequately, but I want to sketch out one possible answer. The first part of my answer involves an analysis of the role played by social recognition in self-definition and autonomous agency. The second part draws some connections between social recognition and the social imaginary.

Social Recognition and Intrapsychic Integration

Previously, I suggested that self-definition should be understood as a process of attempting to achieve a dynamic integration of the different elements of the self. Here I want to argue that social relationships more generally, and social recognition in particular, play a crucial role in achieving this kind of integration, and hence in achieving auton-omy. There are two crucial ways in which social recognition is necessary for self-definition. First, it is necessary because self-knowledge is crucial to self-definition and because we achieve self-knowledge in social relationships. Self-knowledge involves knowing which aspects of one's point of view – which desires, characteristics, traits, and so on – one identifies with; knowing what one values and cares about; and knowing how one feels and what one wants. It is precisely this kind of self-knowledge that is lacking in the case of agents whose self-conceptions are fragmented or who experi-ence persistent conflict between different aspects of themselves. Most of the time this kind of self-knowledge is tacit and taken for granted. However, in crises or when we face difficult decisions, not only does it need to become more explicit but also our knowledge of ourselves and our self-conceptions are often seriously challenged.[19] Thus an enlarged or altered self-understanding may emerge during the process of deliberat-ing and deciding – if all goes well. If all does not go well and self-knowledge only emerges after a decision has been made and actions undertaken, the result is often serious regret. Regret reveals the importance of self-knowledge to self-definition. An agent who persistently regrets her decisions is an agent whose capacity for autonomy is significantly compromised.[20] However, the affective, evaluative, and imaginative processes of reflection – by means of which we clarify what we value, distinguish our self-conceptions from our points of view, and so achieve self-knowledge – cannot be purely introspective. Our emotional responses to aspects of our identities such as our temperamental characteristics – responses, for example, of shame or pride – are shaped by and responsive to the estimations and responses of others. And these responses, at least in part, form the basis for our judgments about ourselves. Thus we come both to know and to define ourselves in our interactions with others.[21]

Second, social recognition is necessary for self-definition because a sense of self-worth is necessary to the achievement of a reflective equilibrium among the different aspects of the self and because self-worth is bound up with social recognition. In what follows I want to elaborate this second point by explaining the connections among integration, self-worth, and social recognition.[22] Having a sense of self-worth is neces-sary for integrated and self-defining agency for at least two reasons. One reason is that agents are motivated to act only if they have a conception of their actions as effective, as making a difference. This in turn requires that agents have a conception of them-selves as capable of effective action – as having the necessary capacities, talents, and attributes. Without a sense of her own worthiness as an agent and of the worthiness of her capacities, her desires, and her beliefs, an agent will not be able to conceive of herself as capable of effective action.[23] Another reason is that an agent's capacity to resolve internal conflicts is tied to whether or not she thinks that what she does or thinks or feels makes a difference. It is also tied to her sense of whether or not she thinks that it is important for her to be able to define and express herself, in other words, with whether or not she thinks that who she is matters. If an agent has little or no sense of self-worth, she will think that who she is or what she does makes no difference, and hence she will have no motivation for resolving internal conflicts, for trying to estab-lish a reflective equilibrium among the different elements of her self.

However, having a sense of self-worth is not an all-or-nothing matter. Since our identities are complex, an agent may have a reasonably strong sense of self-worth with respect to certain aspects of herself, for example, certain talents or capacities, but a rather fragile sense of self-worth with respect to other aspects of herself, for example, her physical appearance or her ability to form intimate relationships.[24] More important, self-worth is not an all-or-nothing matter because self-worth is fundamentally social. Agents live their lives in a number of overlapping but distinct social spheres, including the spheres of intimate interpersonal relationships – such as familial relationships, love relationships, and close friendships – as well as those of nonintimate social contacts and acquaintances; the sphere of work; the spheres of sport, social clubs, and artistic pursuits; the spheres of group-based ethnic or community identities and social life; the spheres of political activity and participation; and so on. These different spheres bring out different, sometimes conflicting, aspects of agents' identities and reinforce or undermine these aspects. An agent's sense of the worthiness of different aspects of her identity is bound up with the extent to which the social sphere in which those aspects are salient reinforces or undermines the relevant aspect of her sense of self-worth.

Another way of putting this point is to say that an agent's sense of self-worth is bound up with social recognition. I would suggest that there are three interconnected but distinct types of social recognition. The first, most fundamental type, which is obviously Kantian in flavor, involves recognition of the agent as a human being worthy of respect. It involves recognition of the agent as a person whose life matters to her and to others and as a being capable of feeling, thought, and self-defining agency. It is this kind of recognition that is violated by extreme forms of oppression, such as slavery or genocide, and by acts of violence committed by others, whether in their impersonal forms in warfare or in their more direct, personal forms in rape, assault, abuse, and murder. The power of this kind of violation is attested to by Susan Brison's remark that "one assailant can undo a lifetime of self-esteem."[25] The second type of social recognition involves recognition of the worth of the social group to which the agent belongs – where social groups may be defined in terms of class, racial, ethnic, gender, cultural, or religious identity or intersections of these.[26] This second dimension is clearly much more tied to sociopolitical structures and to social norms and expectations than the first. Systematic denial of social recognition of this kind tends to characterize oppressive social relations. The third type of social recognition operates at a more directly personal level and involves recognition of the worth of different aspects of an agent's identity, including her talents and capacities, mental and bodily traits and dispositions, emotions and desires, temperamental characteristics, and so on; recognition of the worth of her self-conception; recognition of her values, commitments, and ideals; and recognition of the worth of her social relationships. One of the consequences of a lack of social recognition of this kind is that it undermines an agent's sense of her own worthiness at a personal, social, and political level. I suggest below that in oppressive social contexts, this third kind of social recognition is systematically withheld from individual members of oppressed groups or is available to them only in very truncated and restricted forms.

I have argued that a sense of self-worth is necessary for integrated agency, and hence for autonomy, and that self-worth is tied to social recognition of all three kinds. However, the relationship between social recognition of the third kind and self-worth is ambivalent as far as autonomy is concerned. On the one hand, because self-worth is tied to social recognition, we emotionally invest ourselves in those aspects of our identities and self-conceptions and those social spheres that provide social recognition and that reinforce our sense of self-worth. This investment provides the kind of direction needed for autonomy. On the other hand, this kind of investment of our self-worth can be perilous and undermining of autonomy because it leaves us highly vulnerable to changes in our personal and social circumstances; witness the profound disorientation experienced by many men upon retirement, if their sense of self-worth has been overly invested in work, or by many women when their children grow up and leave home.

It is perhaps because of this ambivalence that philosophers have traditionally thought of autonomy as requiring independence from social norms, expectations, and recognition. I think this is a mistaken inference. Rather, the ambivalent relationship between self-worth and the third kind of social recognition illuminates the importance for autonomy of a robust sense of self-worth, that is, a sense of self-worth that is not overly dependent on a narrow range of forms of social recognition and that is not overly invested in a narrow range of attributes, capacities, relationships, and so on. For example, the discovery of infertility, at least in our society, is commonly extremely devastating to a woman's general sense of self-worth. But just how far-reaching and generally debilitating this feeling is depends on the extent to which a woman has invested her sense of self-worth in maternity. This in turn will depend on the importance of maternity within the central social spheres of her life, on what other social opportunities are available to her, and on whether there are other meaningful spheres of activity in her life from which she can gain social recognition.[27]

A diversity of forms of social recognition is typically absent in contexts of oppressive socialization. In such contexts, only certain aspects of the identities of agents are afforded recognition. Furthermore, their scope for self-defining agency is restricted to a limited range of social spheres. Given the connection between self-worth and social recognition, the effects are obvious. One effect is that the achievement of self-worth will be overly invested in certain aspects of the self and in certain social relationships, namely, those that conform to social norms and seriously restricted social roles, with the result that other aspects of the self are repressed or stunted. Some agents who are able to conform their self-conceptions to these restricted norms and roles may in fact be quite integrated as agents and have a reasonably strong sense of self-worth – which is why integration is a necessary, but not a sufficient, condition for autonomy.[28] More commonly, however, the effect will be some degree of internal conflict, alienation, or fragmentation of the self, as agents struggle to achieve a sense of the worthiness of their capacities in social contexts where there is restricted scope for their expression and where these are afforded little social recognition. In this kind of context it is not surprising that agents may voluntarily and apparently rationally make choices, like the choice to be a surrogate mother or to have a nose job or to undergo a sex-change operation, that promise to resolve these conflicts and provide them with greater social recognition. It should also not be surprising that the attempt to achieve integration by such means does not always succeed or enhance the agent's autonomy.

Social Recognition and the Cultural Imaginary

For the remainder of this article, I sketch an explanation of how a restricted or oppressive cultural imaginary may limit an agent's capacities for imaginative projection, and in so doing impair her capacities for self-definition, self-transformation, and autonomy.

Previously, I suggested that in imagining from someone else's point of view we assume someone else's repertoire. In imagining from our own point of view, we draw on our own repertoire – that is, on our beliefs and desires and our own experiences as these have been sedimented in memories, mental and bodily dispositions, and habits. Imagining involves elaborating from this repertoire. I have also argued that our points of view and those of others are developed in the context of particular social relationships and particular social contexts. Furthermore, our sense of self-worth and our self-conceptions are shaped by, and responsive to, social recognition. One of the most important ways in which social recognition is expressed or withheld is through cultural images, representations, symbols, and metaphors. These representations reflect, incorporate, and instantiate, often in subliminal but nevertheless powerful ways, social and cultural understandings of agents' worth, especially understandings of the significance and worth of various kinds of identities – such as gender, ethnic, racial, and religious identities.[29] Drawing these points together, I want to make three suggestions to explain the connections among the cultural imaginary, an agent's imaginative projections, and the impairment of autonomy in oppressive social contexts.

First, the repertoire on which we draw in our imaginary self-representations is mediated by the available cultural repertoire of images and representations. The social psychic force of this imagery mirrors the psychic force of mental imagery; it shapes our emotions, our desires, and our beliefs. So the medium by which the cultural imaginary informs our beliefs and shapes our desires is through our own representations; cultural imagery latches on to the individual psyche, as it were, by gripping the imagination.

Second, the ambivalent role of cultural imagery vis-à-vis our imaginations mirrors the ambivalent role of imagining in self-understanding. On the one hand, I have argued that the activity of imagining can abstract us from our habitual modes of understanding and open up a space within which to envisage new possibilities of self-definition and self-understanding. Imagining can do this because we are not restricted to representing only what we actually are or what we think is actually possible. We can represent what we might want to be, what we wish to be possible, or just what might be or might have been possible. This is what is liberating about imagining. Innovative cultural imagery plays a similarly liberating role. In representing what might be possible, it abstracts us from our habitual understandings of ourselves and others and so begins to loosen the grip of dominant imagery – which is why alternative representations of gender relations and sexual difference have been so vital to feminist efforts to restructure our social understandings. On the other hand, representations can act like compulsions to constrain the imagination, enforce habitual patterns of thought, and stymie self-understanding and self-definition. I suggested earlier that imaginative projects that are initiated in the service of desire can have this effect. The imaginer deliberately rules out beliefs, emotions, and desires that might conflict with the desire that seeks satisfaction in the imagining or that might conflict with her self-conception, and in so doing narrows the window that the imagination can open into the self. Similarly, cultural imagery enlisted, consciously or unconsciously, in the service of the desire for domination or the desire to perpetuate the status quo draws on a curtailed cultural point of view to restrict the repertoire in terms of which the culture can represent itself.[30] When these restricted cultural representations grip the imaginations of individuals, the effect is to narrow the range of the repertoires on which we can draw in our imaginative projects and so to curtail our imaginative explorations of alternative pos-sibilities of action, emotion, belief, and desire. Having a restricted repertoire is, of course, quite consistent with having a vivid imagination. There are all sorts of tediously repe-titious imaginative permutations and combinations that can be elaborated from a single theme, as Hollywood knows all too well.

Third, given the connection between an agent's sense of self-worth and social recog-nition, there is a strong incentive for agents to identify with those cultural representa-tions of their identities that seem to afford greater social recognition and to incorporate these representations into their self-conceptions and their imaginative projections. Even if these representations are oppressive, in the sense that they present agents with severely curtailed avenues for achieving social recognition, the fact that these avenues afford the main means of achieving social recognition nevertheless provides agents with a strong incentive for identifying with them. It may also provide them with a strong incentive for resisting innovative cultural imagery. Thus, whereas oppressed agents may have more or less rich fantasy lives within a restricted repertoire, their desires and capacities to *seri-ously* imagine alternative possibilities for action, emotion, and desire, that is, to *seriously* imagine alternative lives, are likely to be underdeveloped.

There are three different but interrelated levels at which socialization can impede autonomy: first, at the level of the processes of formation of our beliefs, desires, pat-terns of emotional interaction, and self-conceptions; second, at the level of the devel-opment of the skills and abilities that constitute what Diana Meyers calls autonomy competence; third, by frustrating a person's ability or freedom to act upon or realize her autonomous desires or an autonomously conceived life plan. For good reason, fem-inists have had a lot to say about how restricted social opportunities curtail autonomy at the third level, and Meyers has investigated the way in which socialization can hamper the realization of autonomy at the second level – by hampering the development of autonomy competence. Understanding the role played by imaginative representation in self-definition and understanding the relationships among our individual imaginative projects, social recognition, and the cultural imaginary are crucial parts of understand-ing how socialization can impede autonomy at the first level – at the level of the processes of formation of our beliefs, desires, patterns of emotional interaction, and self-conceptions. What it can help explain is why, in oppressive social contexts, the capac-ities of agents for autonomous action can be impaired by their own inabilities to imagine themselves otherwise.

Notes

1   Meyers, *Self, Society, and Personal Choice* (New York: Colombia University Press, 1989).
2   Amélie Rorty and Richard Wong use the notion of "reflective equilibrium" to character-ize the process whereby agents shape their self-identities. I am adopting their usage of this term. Rorty and Wong, "Aspects of Identity and Agency," in *Identity, Character, and Moral-ity: Essays in Moral Psychology*, ed. Amélie Rorty and Owen Flanagan (Cambridge, MA: MIT Press, 1990).
3   Many theorists of autonomy see some kind of intrapsychic integration as a necessary con-dition for autonomy [. . .]. I concur with this view, although I do not provide an argument

for it here. However, for reasons that are now familiar in the literature and that I discuss later, although I regard integration as I characterize it in this section as a necessary condition for autonomy, it is not a sufficient condition. My account of integration is probably closest to Marilyn Friedman's in that, like her, I resist a hierarchical account of the different elements of the self and see integration as involving a mutual process of reflection among these different elements. Friedman, "Autonomy: A Critique of the Split-Level Self," *Southern Journal of Philosophy* 24 (1986): 19–35. Where my account differs from Friedman's is in its characterization of the different elements of the self. My account also shares similarities with the accounts of Diana Meyers, who stresses the importance of conceptualizing integration within the context of a conception of the self as dynamic and capable of self-transformation. Meyers, *Self, Society, and Personal Choice*, part 2, sect. 2, and "Intersectional Identity and the Authentic Self?: Opposites Attract" in Mackenzie and Stoljar (eds.), *Relational Autonomy*. What makes the self dynamic, in my view, is first, the fact that the self is internally differentiated and not a seamless unity and, second, the fact that the self is formed and continually transformed in the context of relations with others, relations of connection and differentiation. I discuss these points more fully later.

4   It is important not to read the metaphors of the internal audience and an internal observer too literally, as implying different entities within the self. The point of the metaphors is to capture the idea that we can take up different attitudes toward ourselves and toward our own emotional states and to show that these different attitudes are characterized by different degrees of involvement.

5   Because I stress the importance of both point of view and self-conception to an agent's identity, my view is not vulnerable to the charges made against hierarchical accounts by Irving Thalberg, for example, that they give privilege to only the "higher-level" aspects of the self and so beg the question against Freudian accounts of our psychic structure. Thalberg, "Hierarchical Analyses of Unfree Action," *Canadian Journal of Philosophy* 8 (1978): 211–25. On my account, unconscious desires form part of a person's point of view.

6   My account of externalization recalls Frankfurt's notion of externality in "Identification and Externality," in *The Identities of Persons*, ed. Amélie Rorty (Berkeley: University of California Press, 1977), and "Identification and Wholeheartedness," in *Responsibility, Character and the Emotions*, ed. Ferdinand Schoeman (New York: Cambridge University Press, 1987). Both essays are reprinted in Frankfurt, *The Importance of What We Care About* (New York: Cambridge University Press, 1988).

7   See especially his critique of utilitarianism in "A Critique of Utilitarianism," in J. J. C. Smart and Bernard Williams, *Utilitarianism: For and Against* (Cambridge: Cambridge University Press, 1973).

8   Dworkin's distinction between critical and experiential interests arises in the context of his discussion of euthanasia in *Life's Dominion: An Argument about Abortion and Euthanasia* (London: Harper Collins, 1993), chap. 7.

9   See especially "Identification and Externality," "The importance of what we care about," "Identification and wholeheartedness," and "Rationality and the unthinkable," in Frankfurt, *The Importance of What We Care About*. See also "The Necessity of Ideals," in *The Moral Self*, ed. G. Noam and T. Wren (Cambridge, MA: MIT Press, 1993).

10 It is important to note the difference between dissociation and disavowal. Whereas disavowal involves denial, dissociation can involve accepting a desire or a character trait as an element of one's makeup, without endorsing it. The process of acceptance, without endorsement, can sometimes be very important to our ability to achieve a relatively stable integration among the different elements of the self since a disavowed desire is very likely to lead to serious internal conflict and self-division. A similar point is made by Jean Grimshaw, who argues for the importance of conceptualizing autonomy in such a way that it does not

require agents to disown or disavow their desires. As Grimshaw points out, in many cases acceptance of aspects of oneself that one may not particularly like or endorse is more likely to promote autonomy than disavowal. Grimshaw, "Autonomy and Identity in Feminist Thought," in *Feminist Perspectives in Philosophy*, ed. Morwenna Griffiths and Margaret Whitford (Bloomington: Indiana University Press, 1988). Susan Brison's discussion of coming to terms with traumatic memories is an example of the difference between dissociation and disavowal and highlights the importance of the former to self-formation. Brison, in "Outliving Oneself" in Diana Meyers (ed.), *Feminists Rethink the Self* (Boulder, CO: Westview, 1997), suggests that an important part of remaking herself in the aftermath of trauma involved dissociating herself from her traumatic memories. This dissociation was not a matter of denying that the remembered traumatic event happened to her and was part of her subjective history but rather a matter of dissociating her self-conception from the event and her memories of it.

11   It is because I see this process of reflection as involving a three-way process of negotiation among our points of view, self-conceptions and cares, values and ideals, with no particular element of the self given primacy, that I regard this account as non-hierarchical.

12   Anne Donchin's article in Mackenzie and Stoljar (eds.), *Relational Autonomy*, "Autonomy and Interdependence: Quandaries in Genetic Decision Making," draws attention to the nonvoluntary nature of biological and genetic ties and focuses on their implications for conceptions of autonomous decision making in genetic contexts.

13   For further discussion of the way in which the kind of fragmentation of the self that is a consequence of trauma can change a person's sense of what matters, see Brison, "Outliving Oneself," and "Surviving Sexual Violence: A Philosophical Perspective," *Journal of Social Philosophy* 24 (1993): 5–22.

14   Amy Mullin argues for a related account of integration as involving a process of negotation between diverse aspects of the self. Mullin, "Selves, Diverse and Divided: Can Feminists Have Diversity without Multiplicity?" *Hypatia* 10 (1995): 1–31.

15   The importance of this kind of intrapsychic integration to agency is made particularly clear by the effects of trauma, which is often characterized as involving loss, fragmentation, or "dismemberment" of the self, sometimes to the point of feeling that one's former self has died.

16   The notion that unified agency is a practical, not a metaphysical, matter is discussed by Korsgaard in "Personal Identity and the Unity of Agency," in *Creating the Kingdom of Ends* (Cambridge: Cambridge University Press, 1996), chap 13.

17   For a detailed discussion of this issue see Brison, "Outliving Oneself."

18   As Annette Baier points out, persons are "second persons," in a number of senses: in the sense that we only become persons after a long period of dependency on other persons from whom we learn what it is to be a person; in the sense that we can only acquire and sustain self-consciousness because we know ourselves as persons among other persons; in the sense that we each only learn to distinguish ourselves as an "I" in the context of being addressed by another as a "you" and addressing another as a "you"; and in the sense that our self-consciousness is a historical, narrative consciousness, which emerges through the "acquisition of a sense of ourselves as occupying a place in an historical and social order of persons, each of whom has a personal history interwoven with the history of a community." Baier, "Cartesian Persons," in *Postures of the Mind: Essays on Mind and Morals* (Minneapolis: University of Minnesota Press, 1985), p. 90. Baier's notion of second persons thus connects the social or relational dimensions of personhood with its historical dimensions through the notion of memory as recollection or narrative self-consciousness. These connections are also central to Genevieve Lloyd's reading of the narrative self in *Being in Time: Selves and Narrators in Literature and Philosophy* (New York: Routledge, 1993) and to

her account of the social dimensions of responsibility in "Individuals, Responsibility, and the Philosophical Imagination," in Mackenzie and Stoljar (eds.), *Relational Autonomy*.

19 Susan Brison's reflections on trauma suggest that when one's sense of self has been "dismembered," and the various elements of the self are in disequilibrium, this tacit self-knowledge is also disrupted. The survivor of trauma no longer knows who she is, what she feels, or what aspects of her former self she can continue to identify with – which is why she is unable to integrate the various aspects of her identity.

20 Diana Meyers also argues that persistent regret is a good indicator that a decision or choice was not autonomous. See *Self, Society, and Personal Choice*, part 2, sect. 1. As Bernard Williams makes clear, however, this kind of "agent-regret" may be the result nor only of failures of self-knowledge but also of bad luck. Thus, achieving an equilibrium between the different aspects of the self might be more a matter of luck than we find comfortable. Williams, "Moral Luck," in *Moral Luck* (Cambridge: Cambridge University Press, 1981).

21 This is, of course, a central theme in Hume's moral psychology, a theme emphasized in Annette Baier's interpretation of Hume. David Hume, *A Treatise of Human Nature*, ed. L. A. Selby-Bigge, rev. P. H. Nidditch (Oxford: Clarendon Press, 1978), books 2 and 3; Baier, *A Progress of Sentiments: Reflections on Hume's Treatise* (Cambridge, MA: Harvard University Press, 1991).

22 Once again, the experience of trauma illuminates the role played by social relationships and social recognition in intrapsychic integration. Trauma is characterized not only by self-alienation but also by a sense of loss of connection with intimate and nonintimate others. One symptom of this is that the agent's usual trust that others are not disposed to harm her has been shattered; another is that the agent feels that her experience of trauma puts a gulf between her and others who have not undergone the same experience. This gulf leads to the feeling, on the part of the agent, that she cannot be herself with other people. This feeling is a persistent emotion for Billy Prior, one of the central characters in Pat Barker's *The Regeneration Trilogy* (London: Viking, 1996), whose sense of alienation from civilians who have not experienced the horrors of the trenches sometimes manifests itself in an overwhelming violent hatred of them. For many of the characters in Barker's novels, including Prior, the only way to escape this sense of alienation is to go back to the trenches and to the solidarity in the face of horror that unites the soldiers there. For Brison, being able to overcome the feeling of alienation from others and to reconnect with them was one of the most important factors in regaining her sense of self, or rather remaking herself. Constructing a narrative of the experience and having others listen to it and, in doing so, acknowledge the pain she had undergone were essential to being able to reconnect with others and, through them, with her self.

23 My discussion at this point is indebted to Paul Benson's analysis of self-worth in "Free Agency and Self-Worth," *Journal of Philosophy* 91 (1994): 599–618.

24 Benson makes a similar point in "Autonomy and Oppressive Socialization," *Social Theory and Practice* 17 (1991): 385–408.

25 Brison, "Outliving Oneself," p. 30.

26 On the notion of intersectional identity, see Kimberlé Crenshaw, "Demarginalizing the Intersection of Race and Sex: A Black Feminist Critique of Antidiscrimination Doctrine, Feminist Theory, and Antiracist Politics," in *Feminist Legal Theory*, ed. Katharine T. Bartlett and Rosanne Kennedy (Boulder, CO: Westview, 1991).

27 Natalie Stoljar's discussion of autonomy and contraceptive risk taking in "Autonomy and the Feminist Intuition," in Mackenzie and Stoljar (eds.), *Relational Autonomy*, provides another example of the way in which an agent's capacities for autonomous decision may be compromised if her sense of self-worth is overly dependent on a narrow range of forms of social recognition.

28   As Benson remarks, in raising this objection against Marilyn Friedman's integration account of autonomy, "An integration view detects threats to autonomy only when the total internalization of autonomy-inhibiting socialization fails to take hold or begins to break down" ("Autonomy and Oppressive Socialization," p. 395).

29   For a recent discussion of the role played by cultural imagery in shaping identities, see Diana Meyers, *Subjection and Subjectity: Psychoanalytic Feminism and Moral Philosophy* (New York: Routledge, 1994).

30   In *Wild Swans* (London: Harper Collins, 1991), a personal and cultural autobiography of life in Mao's China, Jung Chang vividly describes how a whole country can be in the grip of such imagery.

BIBLIOGRAPHY

Allison, Henry, *Kant's Transcendental Idealism: An Interpretation and Defense* (New Haven, CT and London: Yale University Press, 1983).

Atkins, Kim, "Autonomy and the Subjective Character of Experience," *Journal of Applied Philosophy*, 17 (1), 2000, pp. 71–9.

Atkins, Kim, "Personal Identity and the Importance of One's Own Body," *International Journal of Philosophical Studies*, 8 (3), 2000, pp. 329–49.

Baggini, Julian and Jeremy Stangroom, *What Philosophers Think* (London and New York: Continuum, 2003).

Beauvoir, Simone de, *The Second Sex*, trans. H. M. Parshley (Harmondsworth, UK: Penguin, 1988).

Beauvoir, Simone de, *Ethics of Ambiguity*, trans. Bernard Frechtman (New York: Citadel Press, 1967).

Benhabib, Seyla, "The Generalized and the Concrete Other: The Kohlberg–Gilligan Controversy and Moral Theory," in Eva Kittay and Diana T. Meyers (eds.), *Women and Moral Theory* (Totowa, NJ: Rowan and Littlefield, 1987), pp. 154–77.

Benhabib, Seyla, "Autonomy, Modernity, and Communitarian and Critical Social Theory in Dialogues," in Axel Honneth, Thomas McCarthy, Claus Offe, and Albrecht Wellmer (eds.), *Cultural-Political Interventions in the Unfinished Project of Enlightenment* (Cambridge, MA: MIT Press, 1992), pp. 35–59.

Bermudez, J. L., A. Marcel, and N. Eilan (eds.), *The Body and the Self* (Cambridge, MA and London: Bradford/MIT Press, 1998).

Blattner, William, "Existence and Self-Understanding in *Being and Time*," *Philosophy and Phenomenological Research*, LVI (1), 1996, pp. 97–110.

Braddon-Mitchell, David and Frank Jackson, *The Philosophy of Mind and Cognition* (Oxford and Cambridge, MA: Blackwell, 1996).

Bricke, John, *Hume's Philosophy of Mind* (Edinburgh: Edinburgh University Press, 1980).

Brook, Andrew, *Kant and the Mind* (Cambridge, UK, New York and Melbourne: Cambridge University Press, 1994).

Butler, Judith, *Gender Trouble: Feminism and the Subversion of Identity* (New York: Routledge, 1990).

Butler, Judith, "Performative Acts and Gender Constitution: An Essay in Phenomenology and Feminist Theory," in Sue-Ellen Case (ed.), *Performing Feminisms: Feminist Critical Theory and Theatre* (London: Johns Hopkins Press, 1990), pp. 270–82.

Canguilhem, Georges, *The Normal and The Pathological*, trans. Carolyn Fawcett (New York: Zone Books, 1991).

Card, Claudia (ed.), *The Cambridge Companion to Simone de Beauvoir* (Cambridge, UK: Cambridge University Press, 2003).

Cassam, Quassim, "Kant and Reductionism," *Review of Metaphysics*, 43, September 1989, pp. 72–106.

Cassam, Quassim, "Reductionism and First Person Thinking," in D. Charles and K. Lennon (eds.), *Reductionism, Explanation and Realism* (Oxford: Clarendon Press, 1992), pp. 362–80.

Cassam, Quassim, "Parfit on Persons," *Proceedings of the Aristotelean Society*, 1993, pp. 17–37.

Cassam, Quassim, "Introspection and Bodily Self-Ascription," in J. Bermúdez, A. Marcel and N. Eilan (eds.), *The Body and the Self* (Cambridge, MA and London: Bradford/MIT Press, 1998), pp. 311–36.

Caton, Hiram, *The Origins of Subjectivity* (New Haven, CT and London: Yale University Press, 1973).

Caygill, Howard, *A Kant Dictionary* (Oxford and Cambridge, MA: Blackwell, 1995).

Carter, Richard B., *Descartes' Medical Philosophy: The Organic Solution to the Mind-Body Problem* (Baltimore and London: Johns Hopkins University Press, 1983).

Churchland Smith, Patricia, *Neurophilosophy: Toward a Unified Science of the Mind-brain* (Cambridge, MA: MIT Press, 1986).

Clark, Peter and Crispin Wright (eds.), *Mind, Psychoanalysis and Science* (Oxford: Blackwell, 1988).

Code, Lorraine, *What Can She Know? Feminist Theory and the Construction of Knowledge* (Ithaca, NY: Cornell University Press, 1991).

Cottingham, John, *Descartes*, 10th edn. (Oxford and Malden, MA: Blackwell, 1998).

Critchley, Simon and William Schroeder (eds.), *A Companion to Continental Philosophy* (Oxford and Malden, MA: Blackwell, 1998).

Delaporte, François (ed.), *A Vital Rationalist: Selected Writings from Georges Canghuilhem* (New York: Zone, 1994).

Derrida, Jacques, *Of Grammatology*, trans. Gayatri Spivak (Baltimore and London: Johns Hopkins University Press, 1967).

Derrida, Jacques, *Margins of Philosophy*, trans. Alan Bass (Brighton, UK: Harvester Press, 1982).

Descartes, René, *The Essential Descartes*, ed. Margaret D. Wilson (New York: Meridian, 1969).

Descartes, René, *The World and Other Writings*, ed. and trans. Stephen Gaukroger (Cambridge, UK and New York: Cambridge University Press, 1998).

Diamond, Irene and Lee Quinby (eds.), *Foucault and Feminism: Reflections on Resistance* (Boston: Northeastern University Press, 1988).

Dreyfus, Hubert, *Being-in-the World: A Commentary on Heidegger's Being and Time, Division I* (Cambridge, MA: MIT Press, 1991).

Dreyfus, Hubert and Paul Rabinow, *Michel Foucault: Beyond Structuralism and Hermeneutics*, 2nd edn. (Chicago: University of Chicago Press, 1983).

Elliot, Robert (ed.), *Environmental Ethics* (New York: Oxford University Press, 1995).

Evans, Mary, *Simone de Beauvoir: A Feminist Mandarin* (London: Tavistock, 1985).

Flew, Antony, "Locke and the Problem of Personal Identity," *Philosophy*, 26, 1951, pp. 53–68.

Foucault, Michel, "About the Beginning of the Hermeneutic of the Self," *Political Theory*, 21 (2), 1993, pp. 198–227.

Foucault, Michel, *The Foucault Reader*, ed. Paul Rabinow (London and New York: Penguin, 1991).

Frankfurt, Harry, "Freedom of the Will and the Concept of a Person," *The Journal of Philosophy*, LXVIII (1), 1971, pp. 5–20.

Frankfurt, Harry, *The Importance of What We Care About* (New York: Cambridge University Press, 1988).

Friedman, Marilyn, "Autonomy and Social Relations: Rethinking the Feminist Critique," in Diana Tietjen Meyers (ed.), *Feminists Rethink the Self* (Boulder, CO: Westview Press, 1997), pp. 40–61.

Freud, Sigmund, *On Metapsychology*, trans. James Strachey (London and New York: Penguin, 1991).

Freud, Sigmund, *A General Introduction to Psychoanalysis*, ed. and trans. Joan Riviere (New York: Washington Square Press, 1960).

Fuchs, Yuval "Philosophy of Methodology in Heidegger's 'Die Idee der Philosophie und Das Weltanschauungsproblem' (1919)," *Journal of the British Society for Phenomenology*, 25 (3), 1994, pp. 229–40.

Fullbrook, Kate and Edward Fullbrook, "de Beauvoir," in Simon Critchley and William Schroeder (eds.), *A Companion to Continental Philosophy* (Oxford and Malden, MA: Blackwell, 1998), pp. 269–80.

Gardner, Sebastian, *Kant and the Critique of Pure Reason* (London: Routledge, 1999).

Grene, Marjorie, *Introduction to Existentialism* (London: University of Chicago, 1959).

Grosz, Elizabeth, *Sexual Subversions* (London and Sydney: Allen and Unwin, 1989).

Gutting, Gary (ed.), *The Cambridge Companion to Foucault* (Cambridge, UK: Cambridge University Press, 1994).

Habermas, Jürgen, *The Philosophical Discourse of Modernity*, trans. Frederick Lawrence (Cambridge, UK: Polity, 1987).

Habermas, Jürgen, *Knowledge and Human Interest*, trans. J. Shapiro (Boston: Beacon Press, 1971).

Hahn, Lewis E. (ed.), *The Philosophy of Paul Ricoeur* (Chicago and La Salle, IL: Open Court, 1995).

Hayman, Ronald, *Writing Against: A Biography of Sartre* (London: George Weidenfeld and Nicolson Limited, 1986).

Heidegger, Martin, *Being and Time*, trans. John Macquarrie and Edward Robinson (New York: Harper and Row, 1962).

Heidegger, Martin, *The History of the Concept of Time*, trans. Theodore Kisiel (Bloomington: Indiana University Press, 1992).

Hegel, G. F. W., *Phenomenology of Spirit*, trans. A. V. Miller, with analysis and foreword by J. N. Findlay (Oxford: Clarendon Press, 1977).

Honneth, Axel, Thomas McCarthy, Claus Offe, and Albrecht Wellmer (eds.), *Cultural-Political Interventions in the Unfinished Project of Enlightenment* (Cambridge, MA: MIT Press, 1992).

Hume, David, *A Treatise of Human Nature*, Book One, ed. D. G. C. Macnabb (London: Fontana/Collins, 1962).

Inwood, Michael, *A Hegel Dictionary* (Oxford: Blackwell, 1992).

Irigaray, Luce, *Speculum of the Other Woman*, trans. Gillian C. Gill (Ithaca, NY: Cornell University Press, 1987).

Kant, Immanuel, *Critique of Pure Reason*, trans. Norman Kemp Smith (London: Macmillan, 1990).

Kant, Immanuel, *Groundwork of the Metaphysics of Morals*, ed. and trans. Mary Gregor (Cambridge, UK: Cambridge University Press, 1997).

Kaufman, Walter (ed.), *Existentialism from Dostoyevsky to Sartre* (New York: Meridian, 1989).

Kaufmann, Dorothy, "Simone de Beauvoir: Questions of Difference and Generation," *Yale French Studies*, 72, 1986, pp. 121–31.

Kellner, Hans, "'As Real As It Gets . . .' Ricoeur and Narrativity", *Philosophy Today*, 34 (3), 1990, pp. 229–42.

Kemp Smith, Norman, *The Philosophy of David Hume* (London: Macmillan, 1941).

Kittay, Eva Feder and Diana T. Meyers (eds.), *Women and Moral Theory* (Totowa, NJ: Rowan and Littlefield, 1987).

Korsgaard, Christine, *Creating the Kingdom of Ends* (Cambridge, UK: Cambridge University Press, 1996).

Kristeva, Julia, *Tales of Love*, trans. Leon S. Roudiez (New York: Columbia University Press, 1987).

Kruks, Sonia, *Situation and Human Existence: Freedom, Subjectivity and Society* (London: Unwin Hyman, 1990).

Levy, Oscar (ed.), *Complete Works of Nietzsche*, vol. 2 (T. N. Foulis: London and Edinburgh, 1909–1913).

Livingstone, D. and M. Martin (eds.), *Hume as Philosopher of Society, Politics, and History* (Rochester, NY: University of Rochester Press, 1991).

Lloyd, Genevieve, *The Man of Reason: 'Male' and 'Female' in Western Philosophy* (London: Methuen, 1984).

Locke, John, *An Essay Concerning Human Understanding*, ed. and foreword Peter H. Nidditch (Oxford: Oxford University Press, 1979).

Locke, John, *An Essay Concerning Human Understanding*, ed. Raymond Wilburn (London: Dent and Sons, 1948).

Mackenzie, Catriona, "Critical Reflection, Self-knowledge and the Emotions," *Philosophical Explorations*, 5 (3), 2002, pp. 186–206.

Mackenzie, Catriona, "On Bodily Autonomy," in S. K. Toombs (ed.), *Philosophy and Medicine, Vol. 68: Handbook of Phenomenology and Medicine* (Dordrecht: Kluwer Academic Press, 2001), pp. 417–39.

Mackenzie, Catriona and Natalie Stoljar (eds.), *Relational Autonomy, Feminist Perspectives on Autonomy, Agency and the Social Self* (New York & Oxford: Oxford University Press, 2000).

Mackie, J. L., *Problems From Locke* (Oxford: Clarendon Press, 1976).

Macnay, Lois, *Foucault and Feminism: Power, Gender and Self* (Cambridge, UK: Polity, 1992).

Macnay, Lois, *Gender and Agency* (Cambridge and Oxford: Polity, 2000).

Martin, Raymond, "Locke's Psychology of Personal Identity," *Journal of the History of Philosophy*, 38 (1), 2000, pp. 41–61.

Merleau-Ponty, Maurice, *The Phenomenology of Perception*, trans. Colin Smith (London: Routledge, 1992).

Meyers, Diana T., *Self, Society and Personal Choice* (New York: Columbia University Press, 1989).

Meyers, Diana T. (ed.), *Feminists Rethink the Self* (Boulder, CO: Westview Press, 1997).

Moran, V., *Introduction to Phenomenology* (London and New York: Routledge, 2000).

Morgan, George, *What Nietzsche Means* (New York and Evanston, IL: Harper and Row, 1965).

Nagel, Thomas, "Conceiving the Impossible and the Mind-Body Problem," *Philosophy*, 73, 1998, pp. 337–52.

Nagel, Thomas, *Mortal Questions* (Cambridge, UK: Cambridge University Press, 1979).

Nietzsche, Friedrich, *The Will to Power*, trans. W. Kaufman and R. Hollingdale (New York: Vintage/Random House, 1968).

Nietzsche, Friedrich, *The Genealogy of Morals*, trans. Francis Golffing (New York: Doubleday Anchor, 1956).

Nietzsche, Friedrich, *Beyond Good and Evil*, trans. R. Hollingdale (London and New York: Penguin, 1990).

O'Connor, D. J., *John Locke* (London: Penguin, 1952).

Okin, Susan Moller, *Justice, Gender, and the Family* (New York: Basic Books, 1989).

Osbourne, Peter and Lynne Segal, "Gender as Performance: An Interview with Judith Butler," *Radical Philosophy*, 67, Summer 1994, pp. 32–9.

Parfit, Derek, *Reasons and Persons* (Oxford: Clarendon Press, 1984).

Penelhum, Terence, *Hume* (London: Macmillan, 1975).

Popper, Karl, *Conjectures and Refutations: The Growth of Scientific Knowledge* (New York: Basic Books, 1962).

Poole, Ross, "Desire, Fear and the Self," *Dialectic*, 16, 1979, pp. 39–52.

Poole, Ross, "Nietzsche and the Subject of Morality," *Radical Philosophy*, 54, Spring 1990, pp. 2–9.

Rabinow, Paul (ed.), *The Foucault Reader* (London and New York: Penguin, 1991).

Reagan, Charles and David Stewart (eds.), *The Philosophy of Paul Ricoeur: An Anthology of his Work* (Boston: Beacon Press, 1978).

Redding, Paul, "Georg Wilhelm Friedrich Hegel," in Edward N. Zalta (ed.), *The Stanford Encyclopedia of Philosophy* (*Summer 2002 Edition*), <http://plato.stanford.edu/archives/sum2002/entries/hegel/>.

Ricoeur, Paul, *Freud and Philosophy: An Essay on Interpretation*, trans. Denis Savage (New Haven, CT and London: Yale University Press, 1970).

Ricoeur, Paul, "Explanation and Understanding," in Charles Reagan and David Stewart (eds.), *The Philosophy of Paul Ricoeur: An Anthology of his Work* (Boston: Beacon Press, 1978), pp. 149–66.

Ricoeur, Paul, *The Rule of Metaphor: Multi-Disciplinary Studies in the Creation of Meaning in Language*, trans. Robert Czerny with Kathleen McLaughlin and John Costello (London: Routledge and Kegan Paul, 1978).

Ricoeur, Paul, *Time and Narrative*, 3 vols., trans. Kathleen McLaughlin and David Pellauer (Chicago: University of Chicago Press, 1984, 1985, 1988).

Ricoeur, Paul, *Oneself as Another*, trans. Kathleen Blamey (Chicago: University of Chicago Press, 1992).

Rorty, Amélie Oksenberg (ed.), *The Identities of Persons* (Berkeley: University of California Press, 1976).

Sartre, Jean-Paul, *Being and Nothingness*, trans. Hazel Barnes (New York: Washington Square/Pocket Books, 1966).

Schacht, Richard, *Nietzsche* (London: Routledge and Kegan Paul, 1985).

Schechtman, Marya, *The Constitution of Selves* (Ithaca, NY: Cornell University Press, 1996).

Singer, Peter, *Hegel* (Oxford and New York: Oxford University Press, 1983).

Singer, Peter, *Practical Ethics* (Cambridge, UK: Cambridge University Press, 1993).

Shoemaker, Sydney and Richard Swinburne, *Personal Identity* (Oxford: Blackwell, 1984).

Soll, Ivan, *An Introduction to Hegel's Metaphysics* (Chicago and London: University of Chicago Press, 1976).

Solomon, Robert, *Continental Philosophy Since 1750, The Rise and Fall of the Self* (Oxford and New York: Oxford University Press, 1988).

Strawson, Peter, *Individuals: An Essay in Descriptive Metaphysics* (London: Methuen, 1977).

Tanner, Michael, *Nietzsche, A Very Short Introduction* (Oxford: Oxford University Press, 1994).

Taylor, Charles, *Sources of the Self* (Cambridge, UK: Cambridge University Press, 1989).

Tiersman, Douwe, "'Body-image' and 'Body-schema' in the Existential Phenomenology of Merleau-Ponty," *Journal of the British Society of Phenomenology*, 13 (3), 1982, pp. 246–55.

Tipton, I. C. (ed.), *Locke on Human Understanding: Selected Essays* (Oxford: Oxford University Press, 1977).

Vesey, Godfrey, *Personal Identity* (Milton Keynes, UK: Open University Press, 1973).

Warnock, V., *Imagination* (London and Boston: Faber and Faber, 1976).

Williams, Bernard, *Problems of the Self* (Cambridge, UK: Cambridge University Press, 1973).

Williams, Bernard, *Moral Luck: Philosophical Papers 1973–1980* (Cambridge, UK: Cambridge University Press, 1982).

Wolf, Susan, "Self-Interest and Interest in Selves," *Ethics*, 96, 1986, pp. 704–20.

Wollheim, Richard (ed.), *Freud, A Collection of Critical Essays* (New York: Anchor Books, 1974).

INDEX

Made in the USA
Lexington, KY
29 August 2012